THE LETTERS OF
ST. CYPRIAN OF CARTHAGE

Letters 1–27

Ancient Christian Writers

The Works of the Fathers in Translation

EDITED BY

JOHANNES QUASTEN   WALTER J. BURGHARDT

THOMAS COMERFORD LAWLER

No. 43

THE LETTERS OF ST.

CYPRIAN OF CARTHAGE

TRANSLATED AND ANNOTATED

BY

G. W. CLARKE

Professor of Classical Studies and Deputy Director,
Humanities Research Centre,
Australian
National University

Volume I
Letters 1–27

NEWMAN PRESS
New York, N.Y./Ramsey, N.J.

Library of Congress
Catalog Card Number: 83-80366

ISBN: 0-8091-0341-9

Published by Paulist Press
545 Island Road, Ramsey, N.J.

PRINTED AND BOUND IN THE UNITED STATES OF AMERICA

CONTENTS

2 CONTENTS

NOTES

INTRODUCTION

This introduction makes no pretence at giving anything like a full account of Cyprian's life and times. Only the barest essentials of Cyprian's background and course of life up to the time when the letters take over are presented; this is intended to provide a minimum general context for appreciating the primary material which is the focus of the volume.

As the letters in the first volume, with four exceptions (*Epp.* 1–4), are all concerned with the persecution of Decius, I have provided a somewhat more detailed picture of events of the period in which that persecution occurred; but, again, I have judged it inappropriate to present in this work as complete an account as our records allow of the persecution. That would only deflect the reader from seeing for himself the more intimate and arresting details of the persecution which the letters themselves reveal. General topics more suitable for later volumes, such as Cyprian's relations with Rome and other churches, problems of sacramental discipline (penance, baptism), the episcopal sees of North Africa in this period and their incumbents, African synodal meetings in the 250s and their agenda, etc., are to be dealt with in the introduction to those volumes of the epistles where they seem most usefully placed.

THE LETTER COLLECTION

(i) General

For the history of the mid-third century of the Christian era, our extant literary sources are notoriously meagre and jejune. Cassius Dio, the consular Greek historian of the Roman Republic and the Roman Empire, had left off his history long ago in the glorious year of his second consulate, when he shared the consular *fasces* with the Emperor Severus Alexander in A.D. 229. Herodian, another Greek historian, who had himself been writing, for the most part, the history of his own times, had begun his chronicle with the death of Marcus Aurelius and the accession of Commodus, that is to say, with the year 180; but even he had left off his historical record with the portentous year of 238, the year that witnessed Pupienus, Balbinus and the three Gordians, all Emperors.

Thereafter, for better or for worse, we live with the company of the *Historia Augusta*, a series of biographies of the Caesars which are in fact ancient forgeries dating most probably from the late fourth century A.D. This Augustan History is our only major surviving guide down to the beginning of the reign of Philip the Arab (A.D. 244), and then even that most peculiar document (it is at times based on surprisingly sound material) breaks down entirely, only to begin again with the closing passages of the *vita* of Valerian.[1] That is to say, for the years 244 to 259, covering the period of the Emperors Philip, Decius, Gallus, and Valerian with his son Gallienus, we must rely for the most part, for our literary accounts of the political history, on those tantalizing shreds of evidence often shed so unconcernedly by Aurelius Victor, Zonaras and their allied company of compilators, epitomators and chronographers. One must even have recourse, appropriately enough, to the *Sibyllina Oracula*, blatant *post eventum* prophetic forgeries, the thirteenth book of which was composed at this season.[2]

Accordingly, obscurity lies deep over this period, but the gloom would be all the more profound did there not survive from within precisely these poorly documented years the writings of Cyprian of Carthage—some treatises, a dozen in number, a generous volume of *spuria* (many datable approximately to this age of Cyprian),[3] and most valuable of all for the historian, a substantial *corpus* of letters, eighty-two altogether. Most of these letters may be securely dated between the years 250 and late summer 258, when Cyprian died. A few may be earlier,[4] and needless to say, none may be later, save the four additional spurious letters.[5] The epistles span, in other words, the poorly documented reigns of Decius, Gallus, and part of the principate of Valerian-Gallienus. They are, therefore, precious historical documents.

But not historical only. Cyprian writes his letters from Roman North Africa and whilst for a man of his type, an educated Carthaginian property-owner, he is unusually, but not uniquely, a Christian, those letters nonetheless disclose a wide view of his mentality. We are observers of his values and attitudes, his habits of talking and arguing, his opinion of authority and institutional organisation, his sense of position, his general way of going about things. More valuably than immediate historical documents we are accorded by the letters an entrée into the social and mental world and can glimpse some of the spiritual horizons of an articulate mid-third century provincial Roman. That precious insight into the world of the mid-third century— what people in the society in which he moved were saying and thinking, what issues they considered uncontroversial, what topics they regarded as worthwhile to argue about—would have been obscured by a mind more creative, more original or more adventurous than Cyprian's. All the evidence converges to suggest that the reactions registered by Cyprian he inherited from predecessors or he shared with peers.

For the world we enter *via* the letters, though centred on Roman North Africa and Carthage in particular, is by no means confined within those limits. The official correspondence which Cyprian conducted is of notable breadth and frequency. Among the letters which we have figure communications with Christian communities in Spain,[6] in Gaul,[7] in Cappadocia[8] (all suggesting previous correspondence with these areas), and of course in Rome[9] and elsewhere in Italy.[10] As metropolitan of the

African Church he sends to Rome on one occasion a list of all the orthodox African bishops and their sees,[11] no doubt in order to keep the Roman records up-to-date, and also their address-list for communications. And Cyprian can write under the assumption that there exists uninterrupted ease of communications all around the Mediterranean, freely cross-referring to other public letters of his, presuming that they must have come the way of his correspondents.[12] Similarly he is prepared to claim of an open letter written by the Roman clergy that it "has been circulated throughout the entire world and has reached the knowledge of every church and of all the brethren."[13] The atmosphere of the letters whilst strongly redolent of the temper of Roman North Africa is not exclusive to those shores. Cyprian was writing not as an isolated figure of his times.

But the letters are not just social as well as historical documents. The scholar of the history of the Christian Church, and of religions generally, finds caught in the letters a picture of the life of the Christian religious community of the period, at many points tantalisingly imprecise and elusive but nevertheless of inestimable value.

As a religious institution the lines of authority within this Church can be traced (often tangled and confused) in its dealings with dissent, disobedience and dispute within the Christian ranks, whether collectively by Conciliar agreement or individually by episcopal judgment (answerable to God alone) as well as by intercommunication between the sister churches at once both conciliar and individual; in all this the stance taken towards and by the *ecclesia principalis* of Rome has invited much analysis, and disagreement. And the interpretation and development of the roles of the Church ministers, episcopal and clerical generally, can be viewed in the course of their evolution at a season when in the community at large political tempers were becoming increasingly authoritarian whilst, by contrast, imperial society was becoming increasingly fragmented provincially. It would not be surprising to discern signs of that tension and potential dislocation in the narrower compass of the Carthaginian church.

And as a religious society attitudes towards sin and purity, sex and celibacy, the occult and the sacramental, unwritten traditions and recorded scriptures, the liturgy and its ministers, property and possessions, suffering and persecution, the sacred fellowship and the profane outsiders, orthodoxy and heresy, charitable works for Christian brothers and pagan neighbors, are strikingly, and often surprisingly, illuminated.

(ii) Compilation

A few general remarks, first, about these epistles as a collection.

Not all the letters are of Cyprian's own hand. Some of the letters which prompted Cyprian's replies have also come down to us, amounting to sixteen letters in all, and providing, incidentally, some fine examples of ungrammatical and at times almost unintelligible vulgar Latin.[14] In addition, synodal or collective letters of the African Church tally six—they bear clearly some of the marks of the prelate who presided over both local council meetings of proconsular bishops and over gatherings of the full African synod drawn from Africa Proconsularis, Numidia, and the Mauretanias, viz., Cyprian of Carthage himself.[15]

The remaining sixty letters are all Cyprian's own work. Excepting synodal letters there are at least a dozen other letters actually cross-referenced by Cyprian himself, or referred to by others elsewhere, which are not extant;[16] and there appear to be a considerable number more which can be reasonably inferred from Cyprian's text or from his epistolary practice.[17] Manifestly, we do not have anything like the full archive of Cyprian's correspondence written during his term as bishop; neither would anyone editing even a selection drawn from his files have left such jagged and haphazard gaps in putting together consciously a collection for publication. And of the more personal letters which contemporary interpretations of duty and courtesy would have dictated that Cyprian in his class and position should have composed in large number, we have but one, chance-surviving, sample.[18] We are dealing, therefore, with no systematic or carefully prepared and arranged epistolary collection.

For it is quite clear that, on the one hand, there was well

established in the very generation after Cyprian's death, the general *corpus* of Cyprian's treatises, and that *corpus* survives intact. This we know from Pontius, the biographer and contemporary of Cyprian, whose *vita* of Cyprian survives as our first extant Christian biography; he lists all the treatises.[19] Similarly, in the so-called Cheltenham List of A.D. 359–365, a stichometric list of the contents of a manuscript of that date, the treatises are all there *cum indiculis versuum*,[20] as they are also in a sermon delivered by Augustine, one of a number he gave *de natale sancti Cypriani*.[21] The general manuscript tradition of the treatises was thus firmly established from the start.[22]

On the other hand, the *corpus* of the epistles appears to have been slow to gather definitive shape. The total of von Soden's list of manuscripts containing at least some piece of the writings of Cyprian amounted to the daunting figure of 151—and one can reasonably assume that his list (drawn up in 1904) is not exhaustive[23]—but even so not one manuscript contains the full number of our letters. What manuscripts do have a group of letters, have them with great diversity of number and of order. Only one, a late, fifteenth-century one, has all but one collected together.[24] The letter missing from that collection was published for the first time as recently as 1944; it survives in but one, fifteenth-century, manuscript from Norfolk.[25] The *explicit* only of this letter did, however, turn up in an earlier, eleventh-century, collection.[26] One is made to wonder whether further remnants of the Cyprianic correspondence may chance to be disclosed elsewhere.

It is also worth bearing in mind that what we have almost entirely from Cyprian and mostly from his correspondents are not private messages but public letters, written and designed from the start to be encyclical in the full sense, to be circulated and to be copied freely—and indeed Cyprian feels free to insist, gently but firmly, that Pope Cornelius disseminate and have read publicly the letters he sends as intended, and not suppress them.[27] There was, however, a certain amount of double-think in all this. For Cyprian could also express astonishment at Cornelius for even considering reading publicly in Rome a defamatory letter about Cyprian himself, written by one of

Cyprian's disaffected Carthaginian presbyters;[28] elsewhere, Cyprian reminds Cornelius that he did not hesitate about suppressing a letter from Cornelius' rival, the anti-pope Novatian. That letter, he avers, was too improperly unchaste in language to be heard by Christians and in church.[29] But generally, Cyprian takes pains to urge that copies are to be taken of his letters both by the clergy present in Carthage and by any visiting clergy who may turn up in the future, even, on one occasion, appointing a *lector* to act as supervisor of the operation,[30] and on another sending already prepared *exemplaria*, apparently intended to facilitate distribution.[31] And like most Romans of his class he kept a record of old letters, his own as well as others', ready at hand to have copies taken at need to be passed on to other correspondents.[32] At one time such an enclosure amounted to a dossier of no fewer than thirteen letters (all of which, as a result, we still have),[33] others amounted to nine letters, five, four, two,[34] and there were, similarly, *addenda* attached to letters that he received from others.[35] Such are the sources of the majority of the non-Cyprianic letters.

Paradoxically, the nonsurvival of letters of Cyprian's correspondents can also be explained by these practices of inclusion, circulation, and suppression. Here is one example. Cyprian had carefully circulated his own objections and answers to Pope Stephen's controversial baptismal policy, but somehow Cyprian did not quite get around to circulating Stephen's reply to that letter. One bishop was bold enough to ask Cyprian for a copy of that reply. He got his *exemplum*, but with a full ten-page covering supplement (of refutation) by Cyprian's own hand. That supplement survives—presumably Cyprian saw that it was circulated independently—but Stephen's letter, clearly generally suppressed, significantly does not.[36] So, too, with one of the few gaps discernible in the letters of this first volume. Cyprian approved of the general message to be found in letters sent to Carthage both by the Roman clergy and by the Roman confessors (*Ep.* 27.4), but, insultingly, the former message was pointedly addressed not to Cyprian but *ad clerum*, the latter to some Carthaginian confessors. Cyprian does not proceed to distribute copies of these letters (which do not survive) unlike the next letters from both the Roman clergy (*Ep.* 30) and the Roman confessors (*Ep.* 31) which are alike addressed to himself personally, and copies of which he proceeds to distribute with alacrity, (and which do survive).

In this maze of copy-keeping and circulating letters one clearly could not be too cautious. The Numidian bishop Antonianus was naive enough, for example, to write to Cyprian one version of his firmly opposed attitude towards the schismatic Novatian, a copy of which was to be forwarded to Pope Cornelius, and later on another and a now less certainly critical version, which was passed on to Cyprian through the services of a presbyter, Quintus. Cyprian in comparing these two inconsistent versions is spurred on to pen a vigorous twenty-page reply.[37]

After Cyprian's heroic death in September 258, his glory now sealed by martyrdom, we may surmise that his devotees would gather dossiers of their hero's treasured epistles for themselves, just as in the preceding century we learn from Polycarp of the Philippians gathering a collection of the correspondence of Ignatius of Antioch ("We send you, as you asked, the letters of Ignatius, which were sent to us by him, and others which we had by us.").[38] Or just as Eusebius, early in the fourth century, collected over a hundred letters written by his beloved Origen,[39] Cyprian's exact contemporary. But it would have been no light task to gather together Cyprian's correspondence, for several of the letters are as long as fully-fledged pamphlets or *libelli* (such as Letter 63 against the practice of celebrating the Eucharist with water unmixed with fermented wine or Letter 69 which is in part a defence of the efficacy of "clinical," or sick-bed, baptism).

Under such circumstances, the initial compilations would be both arduous and necessarily, to an extent, haphazard. And in their subsequent transmission, assiduity in searching out and recopying these letters would, naturally enough, be subject as well to the vagaries of later-day interests and controversies. The more popularly copied groups of letters, such as those to and from Rome, would be simply a reflection of later preoccupations.[40] The Donatists, likewise, selected and cherished certain letters which reflected their own particular sentiments.[41] The

fitful, erratic and extremely diverse and contaminated manuscript traditions of the letters, along with the (now) painfully
obvious gaps which need to be supplied in order to make a
coherent collection of material, are consistent with such postu-
lated conditions of compilation and transmission.

And *pace* Bayard, the collection does not seem to have been
complete by the late fourth century, in Augustine's day. Augustine found a reference by Crescens of Cirta to a letter of Cyprian
to Pope Stephen on the subject of rebaptism.[42] He searched his
copy of Cyprian, found the letter to Stephen, but complains, at
considerable length, that he couldn't find anything on that topic
of rebaptism there. From his description he was looking at our
Letter 68, and he was right to complain. But we happen to have
two letters of Cyprian to Stephen, and the second, our Letter 72,
is obviously the one Crescens had in mind, but it clearly did not
figure in Augustine's collection. It is ironical to think that
despite the vast volume of imperial literature that we have lost,
we are probably better supplied with Cyprian's epistles than
were many of the early Fathers of the Church.

Bayard[43] bases his case for a complete collection of the epistles on remarks made by Rufinus of Aquileia at the close of the
fourth century.[44] Rufinus observes that *sancti Cypriani martyris
solet omne epistolarum corpus in uno codice scribi*, and he goes on to
note that at Constantinople heretics were peddling such volumes of the complete *epistolae* with the heretical (Novatianic)
tract *De Trinitate* surreptitiously interpolated in the *codices*, and
they were peddling them among the poor at bargain prices to
entice them to buy the heresy baited with a generous amount of
the orthodox Cyprian.[45] (They must have been, we ought to
deduce, already in a Greek version.)[46] But here *epistolae*, as it
does in many of the subscriptions to our manuscripts, could
well mean merely *libelli*[47] and it is the complete collection of
Cyprian's treatises which is in all likelihood being referred to;
for these, as we have seen, were published in full.

(iii) Chronology

Given the way the letters have come down to us, with no
attempts having been made at presenting them in sequence

according to date of composition, their arrangement into chronological sequence becomes, for the modern editor, a highly significant, and vexed, problem, much depending on the internal evidence provided by those letters which we do have. But thanks to the diligent researches of a number of dedicated scholars over many generations,[48] the place of most, but not all, of the letters can, in fact, be confined within quite narrow limits. Before each letter I have discussed the question of its chronology relative to other letters in the collection and, where feasible, I have made a hazard at the approximate calendar date of the document.

What I do suggest is that the letters of this volume—and at least their introductory commentaries—should be read in the following order. Firstly Letters 1 to 4, being non-persecution (but not necessarily pre-persecution) documents. And then, in order, Letters 7; 5 and 6; 13 and 14; 11, 10 and 12; 15, 16 and 17; 18 and 19; 8 and 9; 20; 21, 22 and 23; 24 and 25; 26 and 27. From Letter 7 onwards, that will carry the reader through a reasonably intelligible sequence from very early 250 until high summer of that year; the arguments for this suggested reading order are, of course, presented in the commentary.

But before reading the letters, a little on their general context.

CYPRIAN AND CARTHAGE IN THE MID-THIRD CENTURY

The economy of the Roman world was fundamentally agrarian, and for the most part that agriculture produced a livelihood no higher than subsistence level. Under such general "underdeveloped" circumstances of the ancient world,[49] great urban complexes are remarkable exceptions, and in the mid-third century Carthage provided one of the four great and exceptional cities of the Roman world—along with Antioch, Alexandria, and Rome.[50] The vast tracks and estates up the river valleys and over the plains of the countryside, intensely developed and exploited to an unusual degree of sophistication, had for generations produced, thanks to abundant peasant labour and careful storage of the available rainfall for irrigating the land, rich surpluses of cereal crops and more recently, of oil for their aristocratic and imperial landowners.[51] The life of Rome was dependent on being supplied with such export surpluses, especially of grain, and the North African city which was their major outlet along a generally inhospitable coastline prospered. Despite the destructions suffered in the now far distant past, Carthage of the mid-third century was a city of flourishing physical aspect, most of which is now regrettably lost or undisclosed to the archaeologist, though indications are that as a sequel to a series of ultimately disastrous local revolts[52] the economic life of the city was in fact currently undergoing considerable difficulties and malaise (not unlike many contemporary areas of the empire).[53] The delicate economic infrastructure of the society, and financial confidence, were slow to recover after the disolocation and destruction suffered in the general turmoil. But despite the absence of its protecting legion, normally stationed in Numidia,[54] and thanks to the natural bulwark of mountains in the hinterland, the Aurès to the south and the Kabylie to the southwest, the city of Carthage itself remained with little sign of actual physical distress from this period of political and military, as well as economic, instability.[55] And at all events Cyprian voices no complaint about immediate dangers to the city nor of shortage of funds available for almsgiving and other charitable services for the indigent of the city of Carthage.

Heterogeneous the inhabitants undoubtedly were in this populous city—people whose traditions were of Punic provenance, immigrant Greeks,[56] a sizeable Jewish community,[57] a diversity of native Libyan tribesmen and languages[58] (though the indigenes were to be found mainly as nomads in the high country of the interior), along with the dominant Roman settlers now domiciled in Africa for over three centuries.[59] It is a fair guess that despite the city's generous public amenities and edifices (including colossal baths, *odeum*, theatre, vast circus, and magnificent amphitheatre), its artificial harbour with an imposing ring of colonnades[60] and a formally laid-out central area on the grandest scale, the bulk of the urban population nevertheless lived a precarious existence in shambling shanty-towns of mud-huts on the outskirts of the city and a relatively few only enjoyed the mansions, villas and pleasure gardens of the great. The city itself was dominated, literally and symbolically, by the palatial residence of the governor, the proconsul, up on the hill above the Forum, the Byrsa. Little would be needed to stir such a wretched and divided population to the point of rioting—as they were to do on several occasions against Cyprian.[61]

Rome had brought with her a class structure where good education, property and a say in government tended to remain the privilege of a select few. Cyprian was a man of such property and education,[62] and his secular acquaintances included men who belonged to the local governing circles; they came from families of curial, equestrian and senatorial station.[63] Cyprian's trial and martyr's death followed, accordingly, the course proper for an *honestior*, a man of the upper-classes (note the house arrest, despite the extreme gravity of the charge, and the method of execution); and his style at the very end—twenty-five gold coins (*aurei*) to be presented to his executioner[64]—continued to be in the manner of handsome public benefaction and patronage traditional in (and expected of) such a level of society. Cyprian was a man with a sense of his position, conscious of his role as a *persona insignis*, a figure of prominence.

The family of the man is, however, otherwise unknown and his nomenclature (*Caecilius Cyprianus qui et Thascius*)[65] remains of the obscurest. But the sort of property he possessed in Carthage—it included well-known urban *horti* (he can casually refer to them when writing to his clergy and laity as *horti nostri*)[66]—suggests strongly that he was from a local, established family of some wealth; such leisured property is most likely to have come by way of inheritance. Less plausible is the picture of Cyprian as a self-made man who has risen in society and acquired this estate by (let us say) a combination of parental sacrifice and ambition, native talent, and a wealthy patron—like Augustine's earlier career in the following century.

When we meet Cyprian in the 240s he is living on this estate in Carthage, he has won for himself (according to later, but not uninformed, sources)[67] reputation and renown as a *rhetor* in a society which prized highly oratorical skills and achievement—and Carthage was *the* centre for rhetorically-passionate Africa.[68] Late in that decade he is to appear, even though a very recent convert to Christianity, as a man of an authority and stature appropriate for replacing the recently deceased bishop Donatus; the Christian laity urged his candidature with enthusiastic, and successful, acclaim.[69] That suggests a man of some maturity—possibly, to hazard a guess, he was at the time at least into his forties[70]—used to holding a prominent place in his society. Certainly, later as bishop, he gives the appearance of dealing with his *plebs* (clients who had supported his candidacy as bishop) with much greater ease and assurance as their episcopal patron than he does with his more immediate clerical colleagues.

What information of any reliability we have—and it does not amount to much—points to Cyprian's secular life as *rhetor* being spent not so much in legal activities in court as an *advocatus* (though there is some evidence which could suggest this)[71] as in training hopeful devotees in the highly elaborate and stylized art of the public declamation of the time.[72] It would not be too fanciful to imagine for him as well the occasional engagement in oratorical contests, guest performances for panegyrics on public occasions, epideictic displays in private salons and *auditoria* or the like.[73] In the society of the day these talents and activities would not only win a man ephemeral applause but confirm him in a place of honour and distinction amongst his generation.

Cyprian had not married,[74] and his biographer suggests—no doubt idealistically but perhaps also not without some truth—that there was in him a scholarly dedication to the pursuit of higher learning and accomplishments.[75] Hindsight furthermore suggests that he shared with many of his pagan contemporaries an earnest moral mindedness, espousing exacting and sometimes rigorously unyielding, even puritanical, high principles of behaviour and manner. A strong sense of sin, of virtuous living, of moral imperatives, as well as an intense awareness in the reality of a spiritual world, were not notions exclusive to the adherents of Christianity, nor were they confined only to the more thoughtful and philosophic among the pagan members of this society.

By about the middle of the 240s, Cyprian, possessed of such a background, had become attracted to Christianity under the influence and friendship of an ageing Carthaginian presbyter Caecilianus.[76] Conversion, baptism, renunciation of his wordly estate, and advancement to clerical office, which involved withdrawal from his secular profession,[77] followed in swift succession, until by about Easter 249, and probably earlier, he had been installed as bishop of Carthage.[78] Some older clerics had openly opposed the appointment of this novice Christian and despite a public *refus de pouvoir* and gestures of generosity from the eventual victor towards the defeated, the animosity engendered by this opposition continued to rankle.[79] It sounds as if Cyprian was an unusually well placed and educated convert for this Church; he was too competent and prominent a figure to pass by in filling the vacant *cathedra* of Carthage. In contemporary Pontic Comana the townspeople are reported to have been looking for a new bishop from among "those who appeared to be outstanding in eloquence, birth and other distinguished qualities."[80] The long centuries to come are to witness the appointment of many a similar Church leader, who was also prominent in local society, graced with the qualities of leadership and those classically valued accomplishments of *studia et bonae artes*.[81]

Indeed, as also is to occur in later history, some of the clerical resentment to Cyprian's unusually rapid promotion may well have been roused precisely because of his superior class, education, and manner. To judge from the little evidence we have, the awkardly expressed Letter 24 from the African bishop Caldonius, the *sententiae* of the African bishops at the synod of 256, the somewhat gauchely over-ambitious *vita* by the Carthaginian deacon Pontius, Cyprian may well have found for company relatively few Christian clerics in Africa who could match his accomplishments (and Caldonius was his trusted confidant,[82] and Pontius his chosen deacon to share his exile).[83] Our closest contemporary social picture is of the Christians in the literary dialogue of Minucius Felix, the *Octavius,* which Cyprian appears to have read;[84] in every probability the protagonists came from

African Cirta or thereabouts—but they are of the laity and two of the three are depicted as domiciled in Rome.[85] In the absence of satisfactorily controlling evidence, it is easy to form an exaggerated perception of the social and cultural isolation which Cyprian may have needed to face in becoming a Christian; but it would be fair to assert that disagreement with his clergy over other issues could readily be sharpened if there were social differences. In an irretrievably class-conscious society it was not possible to overlook such class distinctions.

But, on the other side, some of the popular enthusiasm for Cyprian's promotion may have been not just for his eloquent tongue in public oratory and his qualifications for Church administration and leadership. This was a man of demonstrable dedication. The gesture of wishing to sell all his wordly goods for the benefit of the Christian poor—to rely on the testimony of Cyprian's biographer[86]—may indeed be in the tradition of the munificent nobility (as of the Gospel precepts), but it was nevertheless a personal act of humane charity as well as of total commitment: Cyprian would be selling his secular social status along with his patrimony.[87] For a remarkable feature about Cyprian is how fully a churchman he became in response to his new episcopal role, finding his total career (so far as we know) inside the Church, with his talents and energies fully absorbed in the duties of clerical office and ecclesiastical activities. Though others had lived such a life before him, Cyprian's letters allow us to see this new type of churchman clearly delineated for the first time.

Along with that absorption in Church affairs came, it would appear, a corresponding cultural and intellectual absorption; Cyprian was prepared to sell not only his patrimony but much of his cultural birthright as well. All the quotations, allusions, and verbal reminiscences of classical letters, the poets and writers of the past, which richly embellished the compositions of an accomplished rhetorician of the day are astonishingly absent from his churchman's prose, and even the traditional classical *exempla*, the rhetorical stock-in-trade for illustration and elaboration on a theme, are severely limited. This can only be the result of conscious rejection and restriction. Instead, Vergil and

Ovid, Cicero and Sallust are replaced by the "sacred letters" to which he devoted study even as a catechumen.[88] Despite the inelegance of quoting verbatim, and often, texts from a Latin version of the Bible which was painfully disharmonious with his own style, Cyprian consistently treats his biblical text with meticulous and exacting reverence; he avoids, by and large, any rewriting of his citation to suit his own paragraph, and even the oblique biblical reference or allusive phrase is relatively rare for one so steeped in the *lectio divina*. In the face of stylistic disadvantages his conscious choice is the direct biblical quotation, normally prefaced by some introductory formula.[89] He has joined a Church with a tradition of deep respect for the hallowedness of the sacred word, "the holy and adorable words of the Scriptures," as one of his contemporary African bishops describes his Bible.[90] Cyprian has joined a Church of *The* Book: symbolically, its first members who figure in our records over half a century before Cyprian became bishop, appear in a Carthaginian court bearing (like itinerant missionaries) *libri et epistulae Pauli viri iusti*;[91] and half a century later, its members who, in time of persecution, were thought to have surrendered the hallowed Book to the Roman authorities for destruction, are to be hounded ferociously and relentlessly.[92]

Religious conversion into this Church for a man of such *devotio*, such dedicated temperament, seems to have entailed a kind of linguistic conversion as well. By contrast with other African writers with similar rhetorical backgrounds, say a Minucius Felix a little earlier or an Arnobius or a Lactantius somewhat later, Cyprian is unusually lavish in the range and variety of words with a Christian formation or connotation which he liberally makes his own, not only the almost inevitable technical terms but sometimes ugly Christian neologisms and specialised usages that had been engendered in this close-knit and somewhat beleaguered and separate community. So closely and so wholeheartedly has he identified himself with his new society, and put his literary talents to its service.

For before the year 250 had begun he had already turned his vigorous pen to the composition of the apologetic essay, the *Ad Donatum*. Quite probably within the last twelve months he had composed the tractate *De habitu virginum* and, some have argued, the *De opere et eleemosynis* as well[93] (at all events, chronological questions aside, church discipline and moral purity, practical charity, and almsgiving are to signify dominating themes in Cyprian's thought and action). And he had been responsible for the compilation of the three books of biblical *testimonia*, the *Ad Quirinum*. Stylistic arguments have been advanced that a notable letter like Letter 63 (*De sacramento dominici calicis*) should be dated to this early period also.[94]

Overall, it is easy to give undue, and therefore misleading, emphasis to the authoritarian, if not autocratic, interpretation which Cyprian placed on his duties towards his subjects in his supreme *officium* as bishop, the *sacerdotii sublime fastigium* as he calls it.[95] That interpretation is hardly a surprising reaction to his episcopal role for a man of his background. For him, the natural model for the exercise of supreme authority was the Roman who held the *officium* of proconsul, governing the subjects in his *provincia* of Africa Proconsularis. For that proconsul, there was little delegation of real power in his administration to his *legati*, his subordinate assistants, and a surprising amount of personally-exercised authority, judgements, and decisions (after due consultation of the counsel proffered by his colleagues on his advisory staff). Cyprian conducts himself somewhat similarly in his *administratio divina* (as he terms it) amongst his subjects, the clergy and laity in his see of Carthage, and among his colleagues, the conferring bishops in his own *provincia* (as he describes it). Our unusually rich information about Cyprian reveals fully for the first time a dominating type of "metropolitan" incumbent which is to be by no means without parallel in the following centuries, but one is allowed to suspect that he may have had in fact contemporary counterparts elsewhere.

It is also easy to distance the man too far. The letters ought to prevent us from forgetting that we are studying not a theologian but a pastoralist who had to deal, by force of circumstances, with theological problems embedded in the practical decisions of his administration. The poor and the suffering of Carthage—as with victims of the plague[96]—and the financial back-up needed to support them and the clergy who were the ministers of his care are deep and real concerns of his. Cyprian's rapid promotion had soured relations with older clergy who had been moving more slowly and regularly up the rungs on the ladder of religious advancement; he brings to bear all his rhetorical flexibility and his politician's instincts—and they are considerable—in his endeavours to repair those relations. But, despite those endeavours, it is not long before there is to be disclosed the tension between, on the one hand, rigorist principles and standards, inherited from his ecclesiastical and his own moral traditions, and, on the other hand, a laudable spiritual desire for upholding the bond of charity in his community (as well as understandable practical considerations for restoring unity and harmony).[97] Cyprian becomes a very human figure caught between contrary pressures and struggling to achieve an acceptable compromise. In all this, concerned for the preservation of his own dignity as *praepositus* he undoubtedly was—such was the man, and the times—but the reality and intensity of his *concern* for the church and its members which it was his duty to serve as its *praepositus servus* is forcefully revealed by these letters. This is a man who, whatever else, *cared*, whilst upholding that supremely Roman virtue of *pietas*, a familial loyalty towards (Cyprian would not wince so to express it[98]) God, his Father and his Mother, the Church, as well as towards the sons entrusted to his tutelage.

Neither ought we to forget that we are studying in the letters a Christian who lives in the third century, an age of increasing superstition generally and of growing fondness for the occult; a Christian, moreover, who has joined a Church where the seeds of Montanism had found congenial ground. Despite his skill and drive as a practical administrator, Cyprian appears to act, strangely, but on the testimony of his own words, not infrequently at the behest and monition of visions, divine signs, and dreams—and so it appears, from the epistles, do others.[99] Sometimes in this one can legitimately suspect literary or biblical convention. Cyprian, for example, can describe his flight in the persecution of Decius as being due to divine monition (after the style, say, of the flight into Egypt or the homeward route of the Three Kings).[100] But elsewhere, in two passages, he lists several very sound and practical considerations which induced him to flee—without any talk of occult inspiration. In talking in terms of divine monition, therefore, he may possibly have been using, at times, a "mythologizing" manner of speaking.

But that this was not always simply a matter of *modus dicendi* is shown by Letter 66. This is one of the comparatively rare occasions in the correspondence when Cyprian permits himself the pleasure of rhetorical vituperation[101] (though he shows he had clearly a good hand for it), and this is the only occasion when he fails to close his letter with a cliché of epistolary politesse. And this is precisely when the power and reliability of dreams—and, in particular, of his own episcopal *somnia* and *visiones*—have been attacked.[102] That matter affected him vitally; others may indeed receive inspiration but as the bishop, the chosen of God and of God's people, he can expect to receive in this way veridical, divine guidance in his decisions as bishop. It is now explicable that the age which produced such a religious mentality should also be marked by the first two general persecutions against Christianity.

THE PERSECUTION OF DECIUS

(i) Background

When people turn their thoughts to the Roman Empire of the mid-third century, there is often conjured up before them visions of military catastrophe, barbarian invasion, Persian inroads, political instability, a riot of pretenders, urban unrest, monetary collapse, agrarian chaos along with natural disasters of flood, famine, earthquake and plague. As Gibbon describes it: "The whole period was one uninterrupted series of confusion and calamity."[103] These sorry, and sometimes desperate, events undoubtedly occurred—but not all at once, nor all the time, nor affecting every area. The society did suffer, but the sequel was to show that the damage was not beyond repair. Life went on. And it must be borne in mind that our sources for the period tend towards eschatological expectations and perspectives, their authors emphasizing what they were keen to perceive;[104] some (but by no means all) of the "crisis" of the mid-third century is in the mind of the beholder.[105]

And it is possible to make it all begin too early. Despite increasing problems of internal stability and continuity at the centre of government and the emergence of more obvious tensions and strains between, on the one hand, the emperor and his imperial court (more often now away in the frontier lands), and, on the other hand, the army (often now attached to particular areas), as well as the senate back in Rome, nevertheless the average provincial in the 240s may have viewed his life as being basically little changed from that lived by his father or for that matter his grandfather. Times may indeed have been harder— revolts and pretenders, frontier inroads and untrustworthy coinage do not stimulate general trade and bolster business confidence[106]—but when, towards the end of the decade of the 240s (to be precise, on April 21, 248), the millenial games of Rome were celebrated, why should our Roman citizen have reason to believe that the completion of a second millenium of Rome's existence was beyond the realms of feasibility? After Philip the Arab and his son had offered celebration in Rome with solemn ritual and jubilee, along with the spectacular sacrifice of animals and a grand *venatio* of exotic beasts in the Circus Maximus, and with three nights devoted to theatrical pageants in the Campus Martius,[107] there was public outburst and parade of a spirit of renewal and renascence, and the legends of *saeculum novum*, *Roma aeterna*, *restitutor saeculorum*, the Phoenix image, among others, significantly make their appearance on the propaganda of the imperial coinage.[108]

(ii) The Emperor Decius

When Decius made his entrance into Rome as the new emperor in the last months of the following year, one of the most urgent tasks confronting him was to confirm his claim to the imperial power.[109] As a widely experienced and senior consular, he may have found the ranks of the Senate sympathetically disposed, but more general and popular support might be won by fostering that upsurge in spirit which had greeted Rome's new millenium. His issue of the extraordinary series of Antoniniani, honouring many of the *Divi*, the divinized emperors of the past age,[110] is a declaration of the values he intended to uphold: this new emperor is to follow in the footsteps of the emperors who had served the Empire and its people well in the bygone millenium. The days of glory are beginning all over again.

The emperor is indeed blessed with an elder son who can be promptly despatched northwards to confront with military valour the latest frontier threat to the security of Rome. He is himself a provincial from the Danubian area, his *patria*, Sirmium (or to be more exact, the obscure *vicus* of Budalia), being in a martial zone of troops and veteran colonies, its inhabitants accustomed to the virtues of imperial patriotism and the service of Rome.[111] He takes the name Traianus, who was by now confirmed in the literary tradition as both *optimus princeps* and the supreme *vir militaris* among the emperors.[112]

In the distant past, the people of Rome had been bidden to come forward as a body to throng all the temples and shrines of the tutelary deities of the state, to win at a time of crisis the *pax deorum*.[113] Though we cannot get inside the man, we can imagine that orders were sent out for an announcement to be made at the beginning of the new year[114] that all the inhabitants of the new Rome of the second thousand-years, that is to say, the whole Roman world, are to make sacrifice to the gods, thereby placating the divinities who alone have the power to protect from danger, and indeed to bless with peace and victories, the wide-flung Empire. Besides, a series of brilliant military victories, won under the new emperor's sacred auspices, would consolidate wonderfully his claim to the imperial purple in the military-minded Roman world of power.

This religious rally was a decidedly old-fashioned gesture. To judge from the glimpses we catch of Decius in the *Historia Augusta*, that document, at least, made him out to be in such an image,[115] and, besides, provincials were the notorious depositories of the ancient ways; but the general notion of the need to secure the *pax deorum* in order to secure the state's prosperity was deep-seated in Roman religious tradition. And contemporary thought could emphasise as well that worshippers of new-fangled divinities were the source of civil disobedience, conspiracies, and revolutions; loyal subjects adhere to the traditional rites.[116] Jews would be exempted from any such imperial orders on religious matters; that was, by now, the official and traditional attitude towards their bizarre but ancient rituals.[117] Christians, however, were notorious for absenting themselves from the public ceremonials by which the *pax deorum* was attained, and they had neither the antiquity nor the racial integrity that Romans understood and appreciated to exempt them. If the rally was to be really effective the leaders of these dissident Christian communities would need to be sought out so that they would bring their flocks with them to the public altars of the gods of Empire (their own god they might continue to worship).[118] Within a matter of weeks of the year 250, Fabian, bishop of Rome, was dead,[119] Cyprian, in Carthage, had withdrawn into hiding in the face of public outcry and rioting, his person and his goods proscribed,[120] and in Alexandria, a *frumentarius* was dispatched to seek out the bishop, Dionysius, the selfsame hour that the imperial proclamation was issued by the prefect, Appius Sabinus.[121] The conclusion seems inescapable that authorities were aware that in their communities there were "atheists" who, by definition, denounced the gods of Empire and could be expected, accordingly, to resist complying with the emperor's orders to do them honour. It does not have to follow, however, that such "atheists" were the immediate target of the legislation, only that they incurred pressure and then penalties by their refusal to obey it. And it goes too far against the evidence in the opposite direction to posit that when the orders were issued the existence of Christians had been overlooked entirely—the prompt pressure on Christians to comply, with the emperor himself in Rome, it can be argued, conducting the test-trial of an initial recusant, runs counter to this suggestion also.[122] It is worth emphasizing again the positive thinking and religious values behind the orders: the universal rally of the inhabitants of the Roman world was conceived on the most generous of scales. Throughout the length and breadth

of the empire men were to win the favour of the tutelary gods of
that empire. And it was a notion that mattered; it was worth
defending, in the event, by the brutal weapons of exile, confiscation, torture, imprisonment, privations, and even death. This
was no idle undertaking.

We need not be detained too seriously by the motivation
ascribed to Decius by Eusebius and further elaborated in later
sources, Decius being activated (according to this reading) by
personal animosity against Philip and his son who had supported (or worse) the Christian cause.[123] It is difficult to find any
circumstantial evidence to uphold the alleged Christian sympathies of Philip;[124] it is hard, therefore, to accept, in turn, the
reaction to such sympathies accredited to Decius. Ancient his-
toriography was strongly inclined to discern personal caprice
(beyond documentation) behind major historical events. Indeed,
it is possible to suspect that, intially, the Christian sympathies of
Philip were discovered precisely in order to account for the
facts of Decius' persecution; at a second stage in the circular
argument, the fact of Philip's Christian sympathies, so deduced,
could be exploited to account for Decius' actions as persecutor.
We are in no position to deny outright such private hostility on
the part of Decius, but neither ought we, as a matter of method,
to rely on Eusebius' testimony for it.[125]

(iii) The Orders

We have precise certainty neither of the date nor of the terms
contained in Decius' imperial edict.[126]

The former can be narrowed down to the last weeks of 249 or
the opening weeks of 250 when Decius was present in Rome. To
be more precise is not possible. The earliest known victim is
Pope Fabian, and he was dead by 20 January 250. The annually
celebrated sacrifices for the emperor's personal welfare, the *vota
sollemnia*, which were celebrated throughout the Empire on 3
January, would make an attractive (though speculative) context
for the proclamation of a universal sacrifice 'to the gods.'[127] It is
worth noting, that contrary to what the evidence of Decius'
coinage might suggest—the series of Antoniniani honouring

many of the *Divi,* the deified emperors—the emperor-cult was not directly involved in this persecution; "the gods" were left unspecified.[128]

Nevertheless, some attempts have been essayed to find evidence in the plenitudinous rhetoric of Cyprian for a date earlier than January 250, for the trial of Celerinus, which, on Cyprian's testimony, took place in Rome at the onset of the persecution (*inter persecutionis initia ferventia*).[129] In a lyrical description of the imprisonment of Celerinus' companions (the presbyters Moyses and Maximus, the deacons Nicostratus and Rufinus, and Urbanus, Sidonius, Macarius),[130] Cyprian describes, beginning with winter, the yearly cycle of the seasons that has passed (and they have not seen) and the spiritual harvests they have garnered during those seasons. He begins: *Ecce dignitas caelestis in vobis honoris annui claritate signata est et iam revertentis anni volubilem circulum victricis gloriae diuturnitate transgressa est. Inluminabat mundum sol oriens et luna decurrens: sed vobis idem qui solem fecit et lunam maius in carcere lumen fuit. . . .*[131]

Sol oriens has been taken as specific, i.e., the winter solstice; 21 December, 249, therefore, was the date involved.[132] *Luna decurrens* has also been taken as specific; there was a new moon on 21 December, 249, at 3.22 Greenwich Mean Time. Therefore, there was a *luna decurrens* during 8–20 December, and this was the date of their imprisonment.[133]

Both theories err in mistaking the rhetorical nature of the passage and the rhythm of thought. The sun outside the prison was *oriens:* it rose (and set); the moon outside was *decurrens:* it waned (and waxed). Whereas the Christian prisoners, though incarcerated in physical darkness, were bathed in perpetual radiance, in the *aeterna illa et candida luce* of Christ. Precise meteorological facts were not at all in Cyprian's mind; contrasting rhetorical effects were.[134]

When the Emperor Decius issued his edict bidding an act of sacrifice to be made to the gods, who were the people enjoined to perform this rite? Frequently, in modern accounts, those involved are referred to as "all citizens"[135] or "all the free population"[136] of the Empire—and since the promulgation of the *Constitutio Antoniniana*, free inhabitants of the Empire were *ipso facto* Roman citizens.[137]

For many years it was thought that there was primary documentation which refuted this claim. From Egypt there have come to light, so far, 44 *libelli*, or certificates of sacrifice, issued by the supervising officials to those who conformed to the demands of the edict of Decius: they are dated between 12 June and 14 July, 250.[138] One of these certificates appeared to concern a certain Inaro (παρ' Ἰνάρους Ἄκις)[139] who, alone of the main petitioners of the *libelli*, did not show the Aurelian *gentilicium* (though it ought to be observed that in these *libelli* wives and children not infrequently appear without that formal title also).[140] The conclusion was drawn that not only Roman citizens were involved: the controversial Egyptian subclass of unenfranchised *dediticii* were also concerned.[141] But that claim rested on insecure foundations: the papyrus has subsequently been reinterpreted to read π (αρὰ) Αὐρηλίου Σάκις,[142] and it therefore concerns yet another Aurelius, a Roman citizen.

On this question, the evidence of the contemporary writings of Cyprian ought not to be overlooked. And the impression which one certainly draws from his words is that *all inhabitants* of the Empire were involved, regardless of sex, age, and citizen-status.[143]

Cyprian talks scathingly of the unspecific wording of the certificates of forgiveness (*communicet ille cum suis*) which were issued by the confessor Lucian and his followers to Christians who had lapsed during the persecution: . . . *possunt nobis et viceni et triceni et amplius offerri qui propinqui et adfines et liberti ac domestici esse adseverentur eius qui accepit libellum.*[144] This implies firmly and clearly that *liberti* and *domestici* had been involved in the sacrificial proceedings enjoined by Decius' edict; otherwise they would not figure as lapsed Christians anxious to secure a return to communion.

Similarly Cyprian singles out the extenuating case of those Christians who had sacrificed in person as proxy for many others (who had absented themselves)—thus, in charity, endangering but one soul on behalf of many: *qui ipse pro cunctis ad discrimen accedens uxorem et liberos et domum totam periculi sui pactione protexit.*[145] Here *domum totam*, like *liberti ac domestici*, ought to allow the inference that not merely the "free inhabitants" of the empire but the servile classes as well were involved.[146]

More precise one cannot be, but it is still worth adding that it was Cyprian's perception that the effects of the orders were universally experienced (*totius orbis haec causa est*)[147] and that we have recorded, by way of corroboration, evidence of the persecution for Spain, Gaul, Italy, Sicily, Africa, Egypt, Palestine, Syria, Pontus and almost certainly Asia (Pionius).

At least we are in no doubt that the orders required of such inhabitants that they "pour libation, make sacrifice and taste of the sacrificial victims" in honour of the gods;[148] we have one example where an offering of incense was an acceptable substitute.[149]

Our very earliest evidence for 250 happens to make no mention of the issuing of certificates (*libelli*) to those who so sacrificed, but that they were issued generally in the course of 250 emerges clearly from the evidence (Spain, Rome, Africa, Egypt). Some have concluded that these certificates belong, therefore, to a later stage in the persecution; they are "an afterthought, a final device in the destruction of the Christian Church,"[150] designed specifically as a means of detecting Christian suspects. But if this is true, the date for their introduction cannot be postponed for very long. The lady in Rome who bribed her way out of sacrificing in Letter 21 did so before Easter in 250, that is to say, before the end of the first week in April. She was still guilty of a sin which excluded her from Christian communion: we must presume she had bought or signed an incriminating document.[151] By the following month Cyprian is distinguishing grades of apostasy (those who pollute their hands and lips with pagan sacrifice, those who pollute their consciences with *nefandi libelli*), but he introduces the subject casually and not as any novel change in the situation.[152] Indeed, from Letter 20 it is plain that we have no reason to suspect that we have any gaps in Cyprian's correspondence to his clergy and people for the first half of 250; nowhere in this correspondence is there any hint of

the sudden new wave of perils which any *new* imperial orders
requiring certification would have brought to hitherto unmolested Christians. We must conclude that by the time Cyprian
starts up his correspondence with Letter 7 from his place of
concealment, certification was part of the routine of this persecution.

On this question the dates of the Egyptian *libelli* discovered
have been invoked for support; they are not issued until June–
July of 250. It is argued, therefore, that they belong to a second
and more intensive stage in Decius' persecution when such
certificates were required.[153]

But if one considers the locality of the known *libelli* (Theadelphia, Alexandru Nesus, Philadelphia, Oxyrhynchus, Arsinoe,
Narmouthis), the dates in Egypt ought in fact to occasion no
great surprise nor any special explanation. The imperial orders
had to travel in mid-winter conditions to Alexandria (perhaps
two months or more out from Rome)[154] and then laboriously up
country (under ordinary circumstances, slowly, by river). A
delay of some three to four months would be quite appropriate
for the advent of the orders in this area, and it could well be
longer.[155] Then, it would appear, the local authorities had to
agree upon their own *dies praestitutus* for the sacrifices enjoined
in the imperial orders; they simply chose the bureaucratically
convenient season, perhaps about a month later, after the activities of harvesting and before the annual inundation.[156] It is easy
to overlook how lengthy the delivery of even urgent and imperial communications could be under ancient conditions of travel.[157] But there is one corollary that might be drawn, however.
Christians up in this locality could well have had advance warning of the coming trial from their brethren down on the coast,
and had every opportunity to make themselves scarce. This
reduces considerably the likelihood of finding any apostate
Christians among the finds of the Egyptian *libelli*. (Compare
Letter 80, later in the decade: Cyprian's agents could get to him
precise and detailed information about Valerian's "Second Rescript" before the official, imperial letter had reached the Proconsul himself, and Cyprian's secure information had itself been
preceded by rumour of further troubles.[158] Cyprian's letter is

designed to disseminate widely among the North African Christians word of the impending *agon* in advance of its official promulgation.)

(iv) Implementation of the orders

In making his sweeping edict Decius may have given little serious forethought to the practical administration of his orders in, say, the backwoods of Britannia or the wilds of Mauretania: such practical problems were to be left to the local administration in the provincial *civitates* to be dealt with in such way as they could. And the problems must have been considerable.

Our impression is of variously composed local commissioners who were empanelled to supervise the sacrificial actions and who by their signature certified the veracity of the *libellus* presented to them by the petitioners. In the large city of Carthage, for example, the examining board, or most probably, boards[159] consisted of "five prominent citizens joined to the city magistrates" (*quinque primores . . . magistratibus . . . copulati*)[160] whereas in the smaller African town of Capsa a single magistrate appears to have been responsible for the operation of the edict.[161] In Spain (Emerita in Lusitania?),[162] Bishop Martialis appeared before a *procurator ducenarius*,[163] (although this may not be an initial declaration before the official appointed to supervise the sacrifices but a case of appeal); at Smyrna, in Asia, the commission appears to have been composed of "the temple steward Polemon and those appointed with him";[164] in the Egyptian villages the panels range, on our extant documents, from two commissioners plus a secretary to a single local magistrate (*prytanis*).[165] No doubt in larger Egyptian centres more elaborate panels were established, as at Carthage.

Along with the appointment of a commission suitable for the locality, a final date had to be set by which time the local inhabitants were to have presented themselves for their act of sacrifice and for their declaration that they had "always and without interruption sacrificed to the gods."[166] Local conditions will have dictated differing dates and periods. In Carthage, our impression is that the crucial date had come and gone by at least mid-April of 250 and probably some time before that date;[167]

thereafter the commission's work may have been largely confined to dealing with defectors, or late-comers, brought before their attention. The recalcitrant they discovered would have to be referred to a higher magistrate for trial (in Carthage, the proconsul). The evidence allows the suggestion—but does not, of course, establish it—that after the lapse of twelve months from the date set locally for the sacrificial rites, the various commissions were dissolved. When that occurred the persecution was thus effectively over; the dwindling activities of the local commissions in the last months of their life thereby gave the impression that the persecution merely petered out. Before the end of March 251 Cyprian could be publicly planning to return to Carthage and to hold a Council meeting attended by fellow bishops similarly at liberty. Even so, the release of any Christians still imprisoned and the recall of the exiled will have required, in addition, deliberate and separate official action.[168] And this was well in advance of Decius' death in June 251.

Our sources allow us to glimpse scenes of these commissions at work. We see the appointed magistrates flocked by crowds anxious to prove (correctly or not) their religious loyalties;[169] at times among the crowds Christians of prominent station are pushed forward, urged on by pagan inciters to demonstrate their compliance.[170] Smoking altars are set up around the Forum to help cope with the numbers, but characteristically, in the larger and romanised town centres, long lines of slowly moving processions wind their way up to the altars set before the Capitoline temple, traditionally dedicated to Jupiter, Juno, and Minerva.[171] When the pilgrim reaches an altar, he places on it a portion of ritual meat in offering, pours there a little wine in libation, and tastes a morsel of the sacrificial meats provided. (We hear of some apostates so eager to establish their pagan loyalties that they brought their own *hostia* and *victima* with them; and we have reference to one group of *thurificati*, who burnt incense rather than offered sacrifice).[172] Our pilgrim now presents his *libellus* (possibly in duplicate)[173] to the commission; it is patterned, by and large, to a standard formula and often, for the illiterate—or the speaker of a native language only—prepared for him by a local notary.[174] It is read out,[175] the petitioner acknowledges it as his own,[176] and one or more of the commissioners then duly sign it as witnesses in the appropriate place on the document.[177]

The officials can also be observed in more clandestine activities.

Bribery was a common social plague of the Later Roman Empire,[178] and the Codes reveal that the authorities strove, but vainly, in the fourth century, to regulate (for they were unable to prohibit) what had become by then customary *sportulae*— even down to a gratuity paid to the tax-gatherer for his pains in collecting one's taxes.[179] The persecution of Decius reveals the same social trend earlier, in the mid-third century.

For during that persecution what very many Christians did was not to perform the actual pagan rites enjoined upon them but to bribe the official or officials concerned, and purchase their *libellus*. They could thereby secure immunity from the edict's penalties, and, they thought, retain their Christian faith unimpaired.[180]

The pagan magistrates were no doubt accustomed to such arrangements. And it seems clear that in bribing their officials these Christians also acted with little hesitation. Writing a good generation or so earlier, Tertullian testifies that bribing one's way out of the clutches of a persecutor was common practice for a Christian, and one which, with his rigorous temperament, he personally disapproved of.[181] Clearly others did not.

In the minds of the *libellatici*, or purchasers of *libelli*, in the persecution of Decius, there was simply not much difference between passing money over to a *praeses* or to an intending *delator*, and thus securing freedom from threatened molestation (as Tertullian testifies Christians had done in the past), and passing over money, either in person or through a deputy,[182] to a local official thus securing a *libellus* and thereby freedom from molestation from Decius' edict.

But to the legally-minded ecclesiastical authorities, at least in the West, what was purchased was significant (for the East our sources are comparatively meagre).[183] For a Christian it was tantamount to a formal declaration of apostasy, and by acknowledging a *libellus* as his own a Christian was, technically, guilty of denying his faith.[184] He joined the ranks of the *lapsi*, the fallen. By the time Cyprian came to compose Letter 15 in about May of 250, he was painfully aware of a significant, and importunate, group of these purchasers of *libelli* present in Carthage.

In accounts of this persecution frequent mention is made of the use by the commissions of local taxation registers and census returns for the administration of the edict.[185] But it is more than doubtful whether the servile population would be included in most census takings.[186] And as for the registers for the *tributum capitis*, the most general tax, slaves again would not figure, as they were exempt; and local variations probably ensured that these registers were incomplete for the free population—the tax might apply in one area to males only, in another to citizens between the ages of puberty and 65, and so on.[187] The tax registers, therefore, could not always be relied upon to provide a full list of local citizens.[188] And there is no word of special lists being compiled for the occasion.[189]

In Egypt, at any rate, which had, by Roman standards, an exceptionally well-developed bureaucracy, it is clear that there was room for people to slip through the official nets.

From the extant *libelli* it appears that people had no need to return to their village of registration, as they were required to do in the periodic 14-year census in that province. At least seven petitioners (with their dependants) receive *libelli* whilst visiting another village.[190] That suggests that the census-rolls may not have been checked at all—and if they had been, the subsequent cross-checking of other rolls throughout the province in order to detect absentees would have been remarkably slow, cumbersome, and inefficient, and such a procedure would certainly have allowed ample opportunity to recusants to make good their escape.

Here the contemporary evidence of Dionysius of Alexandria might be invoked.[191] He describes the crowded sacrificial scene in Alexandria. People were called by name (ὀνομαστί τε καλούμενοι) to approach the altars. Were the magistrates calling from the census-rolls? Possibly not, for as we have observed, one might sacrifice not in one's place of census-registration. The calling-by-name could, therefore, be purely organizational when large numbers were involved (as would be the case in the populous city of Alexandria).[192] It may be that on arrival at the appointed place people submitted their names and then they waited around for their turn. The name-calling was merely to obviate confusion or lengthy queues.[193]

In order to escape detection by authorities, or delation by neighbours, there appears to have been a concomitant and a widespread refugee movement.[194] Bishops fled from distant provinces to be lost in the crowds of Rome;[195] and we hear, for example, of 65 refugees from Carthage who were cared for by the two sisters of Celerinus in Rome.[196] In turn, Christian refugees fled to the crowds of Carthage also; they required special funds for their needs,[197] and they might find shelter in Christian homes, as displaced fugitives and exiles (*extorres et profugi*), in large numbers.[198] Gregory Thaumaturgus took to the safety of the Pontic hills;[199] and likewise many Egyptians fled to "the Arabian mountain" (τὸ Ἀράβιον ὄρος)[200] for refuge, and subsequent perils.

When the persecution died down Cyprian could muster for his African Council, held in the first half of 251, a "copious number of bishops" and these bishops were "whole in soul and body" (*Ep.* 55.6.1). The charity of hospitable fellow-Christians had ensured that even the main figures in the Church, the bishops, had managed to escape in safety and without spiritual compromise. There is little evidence to suggest that any systematic search was made for them. The authorities appear to have relied on delation as the main weapon for subsequent detection; and if inhabitants were poor, insignificant, and unobtrusive, they were most unlikely to be the victims of delation. And very many Christians *were* poor and insignificant, and they escaped. They were the *stantes*, the steadfast; they are the silent, and characteristic, heroes of the persecution of Decius.[201]

This may explain why Cyprian says (or at least does not deny) that he fled because he was an *insignis persona*, an eminent figure,[202] and why Cyprian says his clergy can carry on their work in Carthage because they are not *insignes personae*, that is to say, if they are prudently *mites* and *humiles*, *quieti* and *taciturni*, if their behaviour does not excite attention.[203]

Even if there were lists which contained the names of all inhabitants, citizen and slave, and even if these rolls were checked by the panels of supervising officials, the notoriously poor police facilities of the Roman Empire would mean many could escape; and this they clearly did. It is little wonder that in the next general persecution, that of Valerian, higher clergy, senators, matrons, knights and *Caesariani* are specifically victimized;[204] but the general mass of Christians, both lay and minor clerical, were passed over.[205] To persecute them systematically was, it had been learnt from this persecution of Decius, administratively too difficult.

(v) The victims

When a recusant was detected by or reported to a commission, when a well-known Christian was arrested by searching soldiers or was hounded by his neighbours to sacrifice and publicly refused, when an enthusiastic Christian defiantly flaunted his refusal to comply, or when a person who had initially sacrificed subsequently presented himself voluntarily in order to repudiate his earlier actions, then the task of the local officials was clear. After verifying the facts, and possibly putting some pressure on the recalcitrant to relent,[206] they referred the case to the local governor, to be dealt with as he came on the rounds of his assize *conventus*. For however tempted they might be in such a case to act *ultra vires*,[207] the matter was strictly beyond the legal competence of such minor magistrates; the penalties liable (not laid down perhaps with specificity) could be capital.[208] After his initial ordeal, and confession, the Christian could face a period in prison, awaiting trial, followed by appearance before the governor's tribunal and eventual sentence. At the trial the judge might exercise his rightful discretion and dismiss the case,[209] or the accused might be sentenced to some form of exile (along with confiscation of his property).[210] However, as apostates (to honour the gods) were wanted rather than martyrs, torture and further periods in prison under conditions of varying stringency might be imposed. Under such circumstances obstinacy might be repaid in the end by death in prison,[211] or, in relatively rare cases, by a death sentence, or by eventual dismissal as a hopeless case. Much will have depended on local conditions (for example, public outcry against the Christians, which it was the course of prudence to assuage), the disposition of the governor himself, and the status, age, sex, and demeanour of the recusants themselves.[212] Though incontestably a period of intense anxiety and extreme apprehension for most confessing Christians, the persecution of Decius was in fact less lurid than many of the martyr *Acta* might lead us to believe.

Eastern Provinces

It is difficult to assess how far we may with any assurance extrapolate from our surviving evidence to undocumented areas. Nevertheless, patterns are discernible even in such erratic evidence as we do have.[213]

Concerning the area about which he might best be informed, and about events that occurred only about a decade perhaps before his own birth, Eusebius can report that the bishops of Antioch in Syria (Babylas) and of Jerusalem in Palestine (the aged Alexander) both died in prison as unrepentant confessors.[214] Origen (domiciled in Palestinian Caesarea) survived his long months of imprisonment; despite the dungeons, tortures, chains and rack, which Eusebius found described in detail in numerous letters of Origen's, he nevertheless outlived the emperor Decius.[215] We are left to wonder whether there can have been in this general area any other resistance heroes the memory of whom had faded so quickly, within half a century, in the local church tradition.[216] The absence of the death penalty is noteworthy.

Further northwards in Smyrna (province of Asia), we encounter the arrest on February 23, 250, of a group of Christians discovered praying together in a house (a churchhouse?),[217] namely the presbyter Pionius, together with another presbyter (Limnos) and three of the laity (Sabina, Asclepiades, and Macedonia);[218] we observe their refusal to sacrifice after appearing before the commission in the city's forum, and their incarceration. In the face of provocation and pressures from officials, soldiers and populace of Smyrna alike, they adamantly await the

arrival of the proconsul.[219] Trial and tortures end with Pionius'
condemnation to death (by fire) on March 12, 250, along with a
Marcionite Christian. We are not told of the fate of his other
companions, nor of the three others they discover already in
prison. Here the local citizenry voice the threat of death—or
females to the brothels[220]—at the outset; there prevails an atmosphere charged with intense religious hostility. In such a setting
the proconsul judges in the end that little quarter should be
given, nor was it expected. Pionius' dialogue with the proconsul who vainly urges the Christian to offer sacrifice to whatso-
ever deity he cares to have in mind is a revealing vignette of this
persecution.[221]

Up in the more northerly district of Pontus the stress in the
vague and fulsomely rhetorical narrative of Gregory of Nyssa
(in his life of Gregory Thaumaturgus) is on the search for
Christian fugitives, arrests, imprisonments and tortures.[222] One
martyr's name only is given, Troadius (a young man of prominent station), and he was seen in a miraculous vision dying
"after many tortures";[223] this does not sound like execution but
death as a result of tortures applied to induce apostasy.

The remaining Eastern evidence comes from Egypt and derives from a first-hand account—excerpts from two letters by
Dionysius, bishop of Alexandria at the time, as preserved by
good fortune in Eusebius.[224] In a few brief pages we meet (for
Alexandria), five "volunteer martyrs" (Ammon, Zeus, Ptolemy,
Ingenuus—all soldiers—and Theophilus), five Christians sentenced to death by fire (Macar, Hero, Ater, Isidore and Neme-
sion), four by quicklime (Julian, Cronion, Epimachus and
Alexander), four by beheading or the sword (Besas, Ammonarion, Mercuria, Dionysia)—altogether eighteen named Alexandrian victims, plus the instance of a hired steward (Ischyrion)
beaten to death by his outraged employer, a government official
(outside Alexandria). Throughout, statements and illustrations
abound of desperate fugitives and refugees, prisoners heroically
enduring tortures, and the angry mob violently harrassing notorious Christians (the wealthy and the prominent).[225] What
has to be recalled here is the religious atmosphere that has been
prevailing in Alexandria. The previous year had seen a full-scale

and savage religious pogrom against the Christians, not an entirely unusual sort of phenomenon for that troubled city, complete with lynching (Serapion), burning (Apollonia), stoning (Metras, Quinta), and the looting of Christians' property. That smouldering mood of bigotry and virulent hostility was resuscitated by the advent of Decius' edict and appears to be reflected in the apparently high number of Alexandrian victims condemned to death for their religious intransigence. How far this mood prevailed in Egypt generally outside the city of Alexandria we do not know, but we do have Dionysius' general word for it that "very many others throughout the cities and villages were torn to pieces by the heathen."[226] The forty-four *libelli* surviving from the rubbish dumps of the towns and villages of upper Egypt begin to acquire a moving, and human, context.[227]

Western Provinces

Although our evidence from Spain and Gaul implies that the edict of Decius was enforced there,[228] we do not chance to have in our meagre records certain knowledge of Decian martyrs from these localities. The same is true for Sicily,[229] whereas an odd note seems to preserve the name of two Decian victims in Campania (Capua)—Augustine and Felicity.[230]

In Rome, however, pope Fabian certainly died a martyr's death, in late January of 250 A.D.[231] But no detailed account survives of his *gloriosus exitus;*[232] it may have been due to torture, or simply the sudden shock of the adversities of Roman prison life. Thereafter, though imprisonment, privations, and tortures were undoubtedly the lot of a number of Christians arrested in Rome, we have to wait very many months before there is any word of Christian deaths. There are indeed none by the time Cyprian wrote Letter 28 (? August/September 250),[233] but some had occurred by Letter 37 (§3; winter of 250/251). The Roman presbyter Moyses died subsequent to that letter, after a confinement lasting some eleven months;[234] many of his companions lived on to enjoy release from their prison only a short while later.[235] Here, in what was unquestionably the largest Christian community in the West, defiant Christians are not automatically punished with death. The pattern matches much of our other evidence. Christians were not being extirpated, only being induced, by variable means and at variable levels of intensity, to conform, and even then some of those apprehended were simply dismissed in despair.

The rich details provided by the pages of Cyprian present much the same picture for Africa: flight, trials, exiles, confiscations, imprisonments, tortures—and a mob lynching[236]—are all there to be sure, with all their attendant fears and horrors, but deaths are relatively few and none is certainly by way of legal condemnation. The best commentary is to read Letter 22 which supplies all of the named victims (17 all told) apart from the pair Castus and Aemilius who died undergoing tortures and very probably at this period.[237] But it remains a humbling reminder of our ignorance, and of the haphazard nature of our testimony, that had Cyprian not had occasion to include a copy of Letter 22 with his correspondence, we would have been left largely unaware in any detailed and personalized way of the harsh realities of the sufferings being endured in Carthage.

Overall, to judge from the list of the victims we know, certainly by no means all Christians "died in prisons dark, by dungeon, fire and sword." Far from it. But the memory of the nightmare, if not of the details, of this persecution lived vividly on, and rightly so. We can guess that Decius would have been surprised by his posthumous reputation; matters of state more pressing and distracting than the fate of a relatively few Christians had claimed most of his attention and energies during his brief principate. But as for his religious programme generally, he may even have regarded it as not unsuccessful. After all, so many pagans as well as lapsing Christians throughout the Empire had in some measure done honour to the Empire's gods.

The Clergy of Carthage

If we are to appreciate fully Cyprian's relations with his own clergy—for we meet a number of his clerics, and problems with these clerics, already in the first volume of letters—it is important for our understanding to have an idea of the numbers involved.[238] Unfortunately we are denied certainty that we have recorded anything like a reasonably full list of Cyprian's *clerus.* Some categories, for example those of deacon and subdeacon, may indeed be more or less fully represented precisely because, as messengers and ministers of charity, they have reason to appear by name with greater frequency than others in certain of the letters; whereas of the remaining grades, for example that of presbyter, we may, or may not, possess a representative sample.

From the table below, it can be seen that for the decade of Cyprian's episcopate, we have the names of some five or six deacons and for the same period of some six to eight subdeacons. It would be reasonable to deduce from these figures that Cyprian's church probably possessed an establishment of the standard maximum number of deacons, viz., seven at any one time, and therefore of their assistants as well, the subdeacons. In contemporary Rome there was a similar establishment of seven for each division. This number need not tell us much about the relative size of the Carthaginian church, only that its activities (liturgical and charitable) merited the appointment of the full number of deacons and subdeacons.[239]

Of the minor grades, six only acolytes appear (42 in Rome); there is mention of up to five lectors and of one exorcist (52 in this group, including "door-keepers," in Rome.)[240] As for presbyters, the number in Rome was 46, whilst our Carthaginian evidence provides twelve presbyters in all at a maximum, and of those twelve one is highly doubtful (Tertullus),[241] one is debatable (Gaius Didensis), one is enrolled in the course of 250 or in early 251 (Numidicus), one appears only as Cyprian is about to die (Julianus).[242]

If it is the case that the sample of the minor clerical grades of acolyte, lector and exorcist is a fair one for Carthage—about one seventh or eighth of the equivalent Roman staff—then, by contrast with the Roman *presbyterium,* we might conjecture a parallel ratio, namely something between six to eight presbyters in Carthage at any one time. That conjecture might get some confirmation from the fact that acolytes and presbyters are likely to be about the same in number. At the time of writing

Letter 43 Cyprian has five dissident presbyters and (it would appear) three presbyters only upon whom he can rely for devoted loyalty[243]—a total of eight. If that deduction is valid, and it is open to doubts, then when Cyprian is writing Letters 16, 18, and 19 to his clergy, we would need to realize that of the eight presbyters deduced from Letter 43, Rogatianus was still away in exile, Numidicus was yet to be enrolled (did he replace a deceased Sergius?),[244] and, after allowing for five presbyters in open dispute with Cyprian, the *fidelissimus atque integerrimus* Virtius only is left. This being so, we can appreciate the desperateness of Cyprian's attempt in these letters to retain some control over his leading clergy. The five presbyters in dispute with Cyprian were certainly old opponents at his election as bishop; we would then need to realize also that the majority of the *presbyterium* had objected, and objected publicly, to his appointment. No wonder Cyprian courted his *plebs* so assiduously.

But whilst an argument can be made that all this could have been the case, it has regrettably to be remembered that the basis upon which this reconstruction is built is entirely fragile. For the deduction from Letter 43 that Carthage normally had eight presbyters only may be erroneous. The calculation does not make allowance for two points. One, that a number (unspecified) of Carthaginian presbyters had recently lapsed in the course of the persecution of Decius and that these lapsed presbyters are distinct from the five opponents who, whatever else they are termed, are nowhere described as *sacrificati* or *libellatici;* Cyprian's language suggests, misleadingly or not, that the number of lapsed presbyters was not negligible. Two, that the three, Virtius, Rogatianus and Numidicus, certainly appear in Letter 43 as the only loyal and upright presbyters at present in Carthage, but have others still to return from hiding like Cyprian himself? The presbyter Primitivus, for example, is soon on the scene, entrusted with delicate diplomatic negotiations; he appears to be Carthaginian. Impressions certainly are that the church in Carthage should approximate in size more closely to the church in Rome than our present statistical evidence permits us to assert; but it is well to remember that such general impressionistic reactions may simply be misleading.[245] Given

CYPRIAN'S CLERGY

Note: Only the first reference to the person in the correspondence is given; any other references will be found gathered in the notes on the passages cited.

Presbyters	Deacons	Sub-deacons	Acolytes	Exorcists	Lectors
• Donatus, *Ep.* 14.4	• ? deacon of Gaius Didensis, *Ep.* 34.1	• ? Crementius, *Ep.* 8.1.1	• Naricus, *Ep.* 7.2	• anonymous, *Ep.* 23	• Saturus, *Ep.* 29.1.2
• Fortunatus, *Ep.* 14.4		• Fortunatus, *Ep.* 34.4.1	• Nicephorus, *Ep.* 45.4.3		• ? Satyrus, *Ep.* 32.1.2 (possibly to be identified with Saturus)
• Novatus, *Ep.* 14.4	• ? Augendus, *Ep.* 41.2.2	• Philumenus, *Ep.* 34.4.1			
• Gordius, *Ep.* 14.4	• ? Felicissimus, *Ep.* 41.1.1	• ? Fortunatus, *Ep.* 36.1.1	• Favorinus, *Ep.* 34.4.1 • ? Saturus, *Ep.* 59.1.1		• Aurelius, *Ep.* 27.1.2
• ? Gaius Didensis, *Ep.* 34.1	• Victor, *Ep.* 13.7	• Mettius, *Ep.* 45.4.3	• Lucanus, *Ep.* 77.3.2		• Celerinus, *Ep.* 21

• Rogatianus, Ep. 6	• Rogatianus, Ep. 75.1.1	• Optatus, Ep. 29.1.2	• Maximus, Ep. 77.3.2		• anonymous, Ep. 23
• Sergius, Ep. 6	• Pontius, Jerome, De viris illus. 68		• Amantius, Ep. 77.3.2		
• Numidicus, Ep. 40		• Herennianus, Ep. 77.3.2			
• Virtius, Ep. 43.1.1		• Julianus, Act. Cyp. 5.5			
• Primitivus, Ep. 44.2.1					
• Julianus, Act. Cyp. 5.5					
• ? Tertullus, Ep. 12.2.1					
Totals: up to 12	up to 6	up to 8	up to 7	1	up to 5

43

the fitful and erratic nature of our evidence, we just do not have enough material from which we can form a really secure picture of Cyprian's *clerus*. (Perhaps, for consolation, we should recall that even if we had reliable clerical statistics we would still not be in a position to gauge from them the actual size of the Christian congregation of Carthage). Neither is it possible to form any picture of the meeting place where this clergy took their seat with Cyprian in their midst, along with the assembled *plebs*. Presumably it was large enough to accommodate the periodic, apparently annual, council meetings of the African Church, where at least 90 bishops could gather along with attendant presbyters and deacons,[246] and a large body of the laity. All we can say is that a church with a place of assembly accommodating up to several hundred people could not escape general attention, nor could an annual gathering of travellers coming in for these council meetings from Mauretania, Numidia, Tripolitania as well as all over Africa Proconsularis remain an unnoticed event in Carthage. This was no underground church, but well-known to the government officials, with Cyprian as its locally prominent *praepositus*.

EDITIONS, TRANSLATIONS AND BIBLIOGRAPHY

Finally, a word or two about the nature of this commentary, the text followed and the bibliographical aids on Cyprian.

Cyprian is a seminal author and a major witness, prior to the fourth century, of early Latin Christianity; to explore all of the tangential aspects for which his writings are such an important source would be to make this commentary self-defeating. The aim, then, has been to provide (as briefly as could be managed) an understanding of the broader social and historical setting of these documents, and, above all and more narrowly, to explicate the text itself that is before the reader. Of course that task does necessarily involve touching upon sacramental and ecclesiastical matters, but, by election, these do not figure as the central issues of this commentary. If the observations assist in the comprehen-

CHRONOLOGICAL TABLE

A synoptic view of the decade of Cyprian's episcopate. Minor emperors and pretenders are omitted.

Year	Imperial	Papal	Easter Sunday[247]	Cyprian
248			March 26	• Bishop Donatus died • Elected bishop second half 248/early 249 • ? *De habitu virg.*
249	Philip died ? Sept./Decius emperor		April 15	• ? *De opere* • *Test. (ad Quir.)*
250		Fabian mart. Jan 20	April 7	• In hiding from early 250 • ? *Ad Fortunat.* • ? *De dom. orat.*
251	• Decius died June • Gallus emperor (with Hostillian, and then with Volusianus)	Cornelius elected in spring (March)	March 23	• Return to Carthage after Easter • *De lapsis* • *De unitate*
252			April 11	• *Ad Demet.* • *De mort.*
253	• Gallus died midyear • Aemilianus emperor for several months (summer) • Valerian and Gallienus emperors (Sept.)	• Cornelius died early June • Lucius elected late June	April 3	

254	• Lucius died early March • Stephen elected mid-May	April 23	
255		April 8	
256		March 30	• *De bono pat.* • ? *De zelo*
257	• Stephen died early Aug. • Xystus II elected ? late Aug.	April 19	Exiled to Curubis, Aug. 30
258	• Xystus II mart. Aug. 6	April 11	mart. Sept. 14

sion of Cyprian's message (and that of the other correspondents) and in an appreciation of the train of argument which the letters present, they will serve their intended function well enough.

Accordingly, students of theological history and ecclesiological theory are going to be, I fear, ill-served. But they may possibly find here and there some material which they can turn to use for their own researches. Unlike students of the text of the Bible, they will be wholly disappointed. As a matter of policy, I have deliberately eschewed comment on Cyprian's biblical text and its relationship with other early Latin versions: that is a specialist's field for which I do not pretend to offer anything that cannot be discovered from the standard works of reference and sources of information.

I have been constrained to follow the standard text—Hartel's—and its *apparatus criticus* (CSEL 3.2, 1871; there is a Johnson Reprint, New York, 1965). I have tried to do my best with what Hartel provides, but when I am despairing or doubtful I say so. Unfortunately the *Corpus Christianorum* edition of the letters, a Herculean task, is not yet complete (in the able hands of Dr. G. F. Diercks). In other words, what is here presented has to be regarded as a working translation and commentary of the Hartel text (the order of the letters is therefore left as Hartel has presented them); one day it will doubtless need to be emended at many points both in the translation and in the commentary when a more satisfactory text has been established for each of the letters, and the time is long overdue for a new (and less misleading) ordering of the letters.

I have, naturally enough, consulted all the other printed texts I could locate (not always, I must confess, with much profit)—those of Erasmus (Basel, 1521), Manutius (Rome, 1563), Pamelius (Antwerp, 1568), Rigaltius (Paris, 1648), Pearson and Fell (Bremen printing, 1690), Baluzius-Maran (in the reprinted version of ML 4, 1844), Goldhorn (Leipzig, 1838), and Bayard (repr., Paris, vol. 1, 1962; vol. 2, 1961). And I have read with care but, regretfully, again with only minor rewards, such explanatory notes as are provided in some of the earlier editions (adding Routh, *Reliquiae Sacrae*, 2nd ed., vol. 3, Oxford, 1846, which contains some commentary also). Most of these comments are in fact reprinted in various parts of ML3 and 4. Here I must cite, *honoris causa*, the splendid edition of Pearson and Fell, which, along with the *Annales Cyprianici* of Pearson and the thirteen *Dissertationes* of Dodwell which it contains, comes nearest to providing the only existing general commentary on these letters—and much has been written in the intervening three centuries since it was first printed in 1682!

Of the previous translations in English by far and away the most distinguished for elegance and accuracy is that of H. Carey (Oxford, 1844). It is, of course, long out of date for providing a translation in a contemporary style of English, but in my (sometimes desperate) struggle to keep as closely to the text whilst at the same time providing a version couched in something like modern English, it has still been my most useful aid for capturing the eluding turn of phrase. One has to go as far back as N. Marshall (London, 1717) for what I would regard as the next most successful English translation. The commonly used and most generally accessible version of R. E. Wallis (Edinburgh, 1868 in the Ante-Nicene Christian Library) as well as that of R. B. Donna (Washington, 1964 in the Fathers of the Church series), have, I regret to have to admit, on most occasions helped only to sharpen my perception of misinterpretations and obscurities. The same would be true of the *Selected Epistles* of T. A. Lacey (London, 1922), with inaccuracies regrettably added to the canon of misdemeanours. Of all the translations in foreign languages I owe most to that of Bayard for help in reaching an understanding of what the Latin is wanting to say; Bayard has always been on my desk when roughing out the first draft and its stamp has never quite been effaced by the time the final text has been arrived at.

Here I feel constrained to emphasize my considered approach—correct or incorrect—to the task of translating. Obscurity and awkwardness I am only too well aware remain in the translation which I present, but I have judged that this is a price which ought to be paid for the reward of keeping to the text as closely as I could manage in current English idiom. A racier and more interpretative version would have been much easier to compose, and to read—but even less of Cyprian and more of my own intrusive reading of the text would have remained; I have been anxious not to distance Cyprian even further than necessary from his English-speaking reader.

Students of Cyprian are well served with aids for directing them to the immense secondary literature relevant for a fuller understanding of many points in the letters. J. Quasten, *Patrology*, vol. 2, 340 ff., provides ample coverage up to the date of publication (1953) to start one on the track after most questions; more recently and fully, the catalogue assembled in the first volume of the Cyprian *Corpus Christianorum* takes one up to the year 1972, and the annual publications of *L'année philologique*, *Bibliographia Patristica*, the quarterly issues of *Bulletin Signalétique*, *part 527* (plus an annual index), devoted to "Sciences Religieuses," as well as the regular supplement to the issues of *Revue d'histoire ecclésiastique*, among other bibliographical guides, will ensure that the most obvious titles after that date do not escape the notice of the diligent searcher.

*   *   *

I can't express how deeply I appreciate the forebearance of my wife and family over the many years during which I have pursued this topic. It cannot have been easy living with a person who has shown reluctance in being distracted from an absorbing mental world (and a fascinating companion) into the noisy realities of everyday familial life. They, and equally kindly University colleagues, will doubtless be relieved when the remaining volumes are fully complete. The Institute of Classical Studies in London provided in 1973 a period of blissful quiet, and volume one owes its final existence to that gratefully accepted year of undemanding hospitality. It remains a pious hope of mine that the remaining volumes will follow in quick succession. (The typescript for the final volume was completed during 1982.)

Dr. G. F. Diercks has kindly communicated to me new readings on the text of the letters which he is proposing for his edition of the letters. This kindness has helped clarify my understanding of the text at a number of points, and I am most appreciative.

My final word must be reserved for Fr. M. Bévenot, S.J. and Dr. S. L. Greenslade; with an exemplary display of scholarship combined with charity, they courteously read much of my manuscript, squandering many hours which they could have otherwise devoted to their own valuable work, and they offered on it their scholarly advice and searching criticism—and many thoughtful and timely corrections. I can only regret that both are no longer alive to read this grateful acknowledgement.

* * *

These volumes on the letters of Cyprian are dedicated to the memory of my son, Peter, who died at the age of fourteen years. My family had accompanied me to Cambridge in England so that I might continue this work on Cyprian, and there his fatal traffic accident occurred in August 1979. *Lux perpetua luceat ei.*

LETTER 1

Cyprian sends greetings to the presbyters, deacons and laity dwelling at Furnos.[1]

1.1 I and those colleagues of mine who were present[2] and our fellow presbyters who sat in council with us[3] were deeply shocked, my very dear brothers, when we learnt that our brother Geminius Victor,[4] on departing this world,[5] nominated in his will Geminius Faustinus, a presbyter, as guardian.[6] And this, despite the fact that some time ago[7] it was laid down at a council of bishops[8] that no-one should appoint in his will any person from among the clergy and ministers of God[9] to be guardian or trustee,[10] the reason being that everyone honoured with the sacred priesthood and appointed to clerical office[11] ought to dedicate himself exclusively to altar and sacrifices[12] and devote himself entirely to prayer and supplication.[13] For it is written: *No soldier fighting in God's service entangles himself in the anxieties of this world, thereby enabling himself to be free to please Him who enlisted him.*[14]

1.2 This saying applies to all mankind. But how much more ought men not be entangled in the anxieties and snares of this world who are engaged in sacred and spiritual matters and who are not therefore free to withdraw from the Church and devote themselves to earthly and worldly affairs.[15]

This rule for the ordering of religion was observed in time past by the Levites under the Law.[16] Thus, when the eleven tribes were dividing up and sharing out ownership of the land, the tribe of Levi, dedicated as it was to temple, altar and sacred offices, received no allotment in that distribution—whereas the others turned to the cultivation of the land, they cultivated the favour of God exclusively and for their support and sustenance they received from the eleven tribes a tenth portion of the fruits of the soil.[17] All this was done according to the arrangement and ordinance of God, so that those who were engaged in the works of God should not in any way be distracted nor should they be compelled to turn their thoughts or energies to worldly affairs.

This is the arrangement and rule which applies to our clergy even to-day: those who are advanced in the Church of God by clerical appointment[18] are not to be distracted in any way from their sacred duties; they are not to become entangled in the anxieties and worries of this world but rather, receiving as they do in the gifts and donations of their brethren[19] the tenth portion, as it were, of the fruits of the earth,[20] they are not to withdraw from the altar and sacrifices but day and night are to be dedicated to heavenly and spiritual concerns.[21]

2.1 The bishops who preceded us[22] after holy deliberation on this question[23] decreed the following salutary provisions for the future: no brother should nominate on his death one of the clergy as guardian or trustee, and should anyone do this the offering should not be made on his behalf[24] nor should the sacrifice be celebrated for his repose.[25] For he does not deserve to be named at the altar of God in the prayer of the bishop[26] seeing that he was prepared to distract away from that altar bishops and ministers of religion.

2.2 And so, since Victor has had the temerity to appoint Geminius Faustinus, a presbyter, as guardian, contrary to the rule lately[27] laid down by the bishops in council, it is not right that in your community the offering should be made for his repose or that any prayers of supplication should be made on his behalf in your church.[28] In this way we may uphold a decree enacted by bishops and dictated at once by religion and by necessity, and at the same time we may establish a warning to the rest of our brothers not to entice away to worldly anxieties bishops and ministers of God who are dedicated to the service of His altar and church. If we exact punishment for the offence which has now occurred we will ensure for the future that this will not be repeated in the case of our clergy.

I wish that you, my very dear brothers, may ever fare well.

LETTER 2

Cyprian sends greetings to his brother Eucratius.[1]

1.1 My dearest brother, out of the love which you bear me and the respect in which we hold each other, you have thought fit to consult me for my opinion concerning a certain actor.[2] Though resident in your community[3] he still persists in his disgraceful profession; and you ask whether such a man ought to remain in communion with us, for as master and teacher not in the education but in the corruption of young boys[4] he is instilling the evil he has learnt himself into others as well.

1.2 On this question, my personal view is that it is not in keeping with the reverence due to the majesty of God and with the observance of the gospel teachings for the honour and respect of the Church to be polluted by contamination at once so degraded and so scandalous.

Even in the Law men are forbidden to put on women's clothing and if they do so they are judged accursed.[5] It must, accordingly, be a far worse offence not merely to dress in women's clothes but, by acting, to depict in the course of teaching this immoral art, the degraded, the degenerate and the effeminate.[6]

2.1 No-one should plead in excuse that he personally has given up the stage, whilst nonetheless he continues to teach others. He cannot be considered to have retired if he puts others in his stead and replaces his own single person by a number of substitutes; for he is teaching and instructing men, contrary to the ordinance of God, how to be debased into women and how, through art, to change their sex and thus by the sinful actions of their perverted and degenerate bodies to give gratification to the devil who despoils the handiwork of God.

2.2 If such an instructor pleads poverty and straitened circumstances, his needs can be alleviated along with those of others who are supported by the provisions of the Church—on condition, of course, that he can be satisfied with more frugal, and harmless, fare[7] and does not consider that he ought to be bought off by means of a pension, so as to break away from his sins, for he is the one to benefit from such a break, not us.[8] But suppose he seeks from this profession all the gain he wants; what sort of profit is it to snatch men away from the banquet of Abraham, Isaac, and Jacob,[9] and after glutting them in this world on an evil and vicious diet to lead them off to the extreme torments of never-ending hunger and thirst?

2.3 Accordingly, you should do your utmost to call him away from this depraved and shameful profession to the way of innocence and to the hope of his true life; let him be satisfied with the nourishment provided by the Church, more sparing to be sure but salutary.[10] But if your church is unable to meet the cost of maintaining those in need,[11] he can transfer himself to us and receive here what is necessary for him in the way of food and clothing.[12] Instead of teaching others outside the Church lessons that lead to death, he can learn himself within the Church lessons that lead to salvation.

I wish that you, my dearest son,[13] may ever fare well.

LETTER 3

Cyprian sends greetings to his brother Rogatianus.[1]

1.1 I and those colleagues who were present[2] were deeply shocked and disturbed to read your letter, my dearest brother, in which you complain that you have been harassed by the insolent and contemptuous conduct of your deacon who has disregarded your dignity as bishop and left unheeded the duties of his own station.[3]

For your part, you have shown us honour and acted with your customary humility in choosing to lay before us your complaint about him, whereas you possessed the right, by the power and authority of your episcopal chair,[4] to exact immediate punishment from him; you could have rested assured that all of us your colleagues would welcome whatever action you took by virtue of your episcopal power against this insolent deacon of yours. In fact, you have injunctions from God concerning men of this character, since, in Deuteronomy, the Lord our God says: *And whatever man acts with such arrogance that he pays no heed to the priest or the judge, whoever he may be in those days, that man shall die, and when all the people hear of it, they will be afraid and will desist, henceforth, from their wickedness.*[5]

1.2 There is another text which demonstrates to us that these words of God were uttered with all His true and solemn majesty in order to secure honour and vindication for His priests. When three of the temple servants,[6] Core, Dathan, and Abiron, had the arrogant presumption to lift up their heads and act in opposition to Aaron the priest and set themselves on an equal footing with that priest, their appointed leader,[7] the earth opened up, swallowed and devoured them and they were punished forthwith for their insolence and sacrilege. And they were not alone: two hundred and fifty others as well who were their companions in rebellion were consumed by the fire that burst forth by the power of the Lord,[8] thereby proving that priests of God are vindicated by Him who makes priests.[9]

Furthermore, when, in the Book of Kings, the Jewish people held Samuel their priest in scorn because of his age—as you now have been—the Lord cried out in anger and said: *They have not despised you, they have despised me.* And as vengeance for this, He raised up Saul to be their King to beset them with grave hardships and to tread underfoot and oppress this arrogant nation with all kinds of insult and punishment. In this way through divine retribution the priest was avenged for the scorn in which this arrogant nation had held him.[10]

2.1 In his turn Solomon, under the influence of the Holy Spirit, testifies and demonstrates the nature of the priest's authority and power, by these words: *Fear God with all your soul and reverence His priests.* And again: *Honour God with all your soul and pay honour to His priests.*[11] The blessed Apostle bore these precepts in mind when, as we read in the Acts of the Apostles, these words were spoken to him: *Do you thus insult and revile God's priest?* For he answered and said: *I was unaware, my brothers, that he is the high priest. For it is written: You shall not insult the leader of your people.*[12]

2.2 Moreover, Our Lord Himself, Jesus Christ, though our King, our Judge and our God, right up to the day of His passion[13] continued to show honour to the pontiffs and high priests, even when, for their part, they continued to show neither fear of God nor acknowledgement of Christ. Thus, when He had cleansed the leper, He said to him: *Go and show yourself to the priest and make the appointed offering.*[14] Acting with the humility whereby He taught us also to be humble, He continued to call him a priest whom He knew to be sacrilegious. Likewise, in the very course of His passion, when He had been struck on His face and it was said to Him: *Is this the way you reply to the high priest?* He uttered no word of abuse against the person of the high priest, but rather He defended His own innocence, saying: *If I have spoken ill, reprove me for the ill; but if I have spoken well, why do you strike me?*[15]

He acted in all this with humility and forebearance just so that we might have a model of humility and forebearance; and by behaving in this manner Himself towards priests who were false, He taught that priests who are true should receive their full and rightful reverence.

3.1 For their part, deacons should bear in mind that it was the Lord who chose Apostles, that is to say, bishops and appointed leaders,[16] whereas it was the Apostles who, after the ascension of our Lord into heaven, established deacons to assist the Church and themselves, in their office of bishop.[17] Are *we* really in a position to rebel in any way against God who makes us bishops? Equally is it possible for deacons to rebel against us who make them deacons?

3.2 Therefore, it is proper that the deacon of whom you write should do penance for his outrageous conduct, thereby acknowledging the reverence due to his bishop and making amends, with full humility, to the bishop, his appointed leader.

In this sort of behaviour, indeed, pleasing themselves and treating their appointed leaders with arrogant contempt and scorn, in this lie the origins of heretics, the source for the onslaughts of evil-minded schismatics.[18] This is how men come to abandon the Church, set up an unholy altar outside that Church and rebel against the peace of Christ and the establishment and unity appointed by God.[19]

3.3 Should he harass and provoke you further with his inso-

lent behaviour, you should exercise against him the powers of
your office, either by deposing him or by excommunicating
him. The Apostle Paul, writing to Timothy, said: *Let no man
despise you for your youth.*[20] Your colleagues have, accordingly,
all the more reason for saying to you: Let no man despise you
for your age.[21]

3.4 You write that there is a certain person who is in league
with this same deacon of yours and a partner in his arrogance
and rebellion. This man, too, and any others who prove to be
like them and act in opposition to a bishop of God, you have
power to curb[22] or to excommunicate.

But what we really urge and advise is that they rather acknowledge their offence, make amends, and thereby permit us
to keep to our own intention—for our wish and desire is to
overcome by kindly forebearance the insults and outrages of
individual offenders in preference to exacting punishment by
virtue of our episcopal powers.

I wish that you, my very dear brother, may ever fare well.

LETTER 4

Cyprian, Caecilius, Victor, Sedatus and Tertullus,[1] *together
with the presbyters who were present,*[2] *send greetings to their brother
Pomponius.*[3]

1.1 Our dearest brother, we have read your letter which you
sent by our brother Paconius: in it you urgently request that we
write back to you stating our views on the question of these
virgins, who, it has been discovered, despite the fact that they
once made the firm resolve[4] to preserve with unwavering steadfastness their chaste state,[5] have subsequently shared the same
bed with men (one of these, you note, being a deacon). They
admit to having slept with men, but it is also true that they
insist on their virginity.[6]

1.2 As you desire our advice on this matter, we want you to
know that we do not depart from the precepts handed down by

the evangelists and the apostles[7] which prescribe that we take counsel with courage and firmness for the well-being of our brothers and sisters, and that we uphold the discipline of the Church[8] by every means we find useful and conducive to salvation. For our Lord Himself declares: *And I will give you shepherds according to my heart's desire, and they will pasture you with discipline.*[9] And again it is written: *Wretched is he who rejects discipline.*[10] In the Psalms, too, the Holy Spirit instructs us as follows: *Keep discipline lest God chance to be wrath and you perish from the right way beneath the sudden blast of His anger.*[11]

2.1   And so, our dearest brother, our foremost endeavour, for leaders and for laity alike,[12] must be, fearing God as we do, to adhere with the utmost scrupulousness to these divine ordinances on discipline and not allow our brothers to go astray and live according to their personal caprice and whims.[13] Acting faithfully to these precepts[14] we should take counsel for the life of each person;[15] we should not allow virgins to dwell with men—I do not mean sleep together, but they should not even live together. Not only is there the weakness of their sex,[16] but they are at a still vulnerable age[17] and ought to be guided completely by our direction and control. Otherwise the devil may be given an opportunity to do them harm as he lies in ambush, on the watch to wreak havoc amongst us. As the Apostle also says: *Give no opportunity to the devil.*[18]

2.2 Vigilantly must the ship be freed from the dangerous shoals lest it be smashed amongst the reefs and rocks; speedily must you rescue your belongings from the conflagration before they are overwhelmed by the flames and burnt to ashes. No-one very close to danger is safe for long.[18a] Equally the servant of God who has entangled himself in the snares of the devil will find himself unable to escape from the devil himself. In cases like this we must intervene with promptness, so that they may be separated while they can still be separated unharmed;[19] it will not be possible to part them subsequently, even if we do intervene, once they have been united by a common sense of guilt.[20]

2.3 Accordingly, we see how many men are thus coming to

dreadful ruin, whilst it causes us extreme distress to observe that very many virgins are being corrupted by unlawful and perilous associations of this kind. If they were fully sincere in dedicating themselves to Christ, then they ought to persevere in their modesty and chastity without giving rise to any sort of gossip, and thus with constancy and steadfastness await the reward of their virginity.[21] If, on the other hand, they are unwilling or unable to persevere, then it is better that they should marry than fall into the fire by their sins.[22] Clearly they must avoid causing any scandal for their brothers and sisters, since it is written: *If the food scandalizes my brother, I will not eat of meat while this world lasts, for fear I may cause him scandal.*[23]

3.1 No-one should imagine that she can defend herself with the plea that it can be proven by examination whether she is a virgin,[24] since the hand and the eye of midwives may frequently be mistaken and, besides, even if she is found to be an unsullied virgin in her private parts, she could have sinned all the same in some other part of her person which can be sullied and yet cannot be examined. There can be no doubt that a great deal of shameful and sinful conduct is admitted by the mere fact of going to bed together, of embracing, of talking together, of kissing, and—disgraceful and disgusting conduct—of two people lying and sleeping together.

3.2 If a husband should come along and see his own wife lying with another man, is he not outraged, is he not incensed, in grief and jealousy perhaps even seizing a sword in his hand?[25] Christ is our Lord[26] and our Judge: when He observes His own virgin who has been vowed to Him and dedicated to His holy estate[27] lying with another man, imagine His rage and His fury and the punishments He threatens to exact for such unchaste associations.[28]

3.3 It is our duty to take pains to ensure by every possible means that every one of our brothers can escape His spiritual sword and the approaching day of His judgment. All are obliged to uphold the discipline without fail: all the more is this duty incumbent upon church leaders and deacons in that they should provide others with teaching and example by the way in which they live and behave. How can they be overseers of innocence and chastity if they are indeed the very source and origin of corruption and instruction in vice?

4.1 Accordingly, my dearest brother, you have shown wisdom and firmness in excommunicating the deacon who has stayed with a virgin on a number of occasions, as well as the other men who were in the habit of sleeping with the virgins.[29] If these virgins have done penance for their unlawful intimacy and have broken off their relationships, they should be, first of all,[30] submitted to a careful examination by midwives, and if they are found to be virgin, they should be received into the Church and admitted to communion[31]—with this warning, however, that if at a later date they return to these same men or if they dwell with them in the same house and under the same roof, they will be censured more severely and will be cast out, and will not be readily readmitted to the Church for any such misconduct in the future.[32]

If, on the other hand, it is discovered that any of them has been corrupted, she should do full penance.[33] The crime she has committed is not against a husband; she has committed adultery against Christ, and, therefore, only when there has elapsed what is judged an appropriate period[34] and she has publicly confessed,[35] may she return to the Church.

4.2 But if they continue to be obstinate and refuse to be separated from each other, they can rest assured that such persistence in impurity on their part entails that we can never admit them into the Church: our fear is that by their sins they may point the way to ruination for others.

And they should not think that there is still hope of life and salvation for them if they have refused to obey their bishops and priests. For the Lord our God says in Deuteronomy: *And whatever man acts with such arrogance that he pays no heed to the priest or judge, whoever he may be in those days, that man shall die, and when all the people hear of it, they will be afraid and will desist, henceforth, from their wicked actions.*[36] God enjoined that those who did not obey His priests should be put to death and for the disobedient He fixed the time of His judgment.

4.3 In those days men did indeed die by the sword, for the

custom of physical circumcision still continued also. But today the faithful servants of God have come to practise a circumcision that is spiritual, and it is, therefore, with a spiritual sword that the insolent and the arrogant are slain—by being cast out of the Church. For they cannot find life outside the Church, since there is only one house of God and no-one can find salvation except within the Church.[37] That the unruly perish when they do not heed or obey the saving precepts, the sacred scriptures confirm with these words: *The unruly loves not the one who rebukes him but those who hate reproaches will meet a shameful death.*[38]

5.1 Accordingly, our dearest brother, you must ensure that the unruly do not die or perish, by guiding the brethren, as best you can, with saving advice and by taking counsel for the salvation of each individually. Strait and narrow is the way by which we enter into life,[39] but great, exceedingly great, is our reward when we reach our glory. They who have once *castrated themselves for the sake of the kingdom of heaven*[40] must endeavour to please God in all things; they must not fail to pay heed to the bishops of God,[41] they must not make of themselves a cause for scandal to their brethren throughout the Church.

5.2 And even if it might appear that we are causing them distress for the moment, we should not be deterred from giving our saving admonition and advice, in the knowledge that the Apostle also said: *Have I then become your enemy by declaring the truth to you?*[42] If they do obey us, we shall be delighted: through the influence of our words we have set them firmly on the path of salvation.[43] But it may be that some perverse brethren refuse to obey. Now the Apostle says: *If I wanted to please men, I would not be a servant of Christ.*[44] Accordingly, if we fail to persuade them to become pleasing to Christ, at least we should do our best to be pleasing to Christ our Lord and to our God, by keeping His precepts.

I wish that you, my most dear and cherished brother, may ever fare well in the Lord.[45]

LETTER 5

Cyprian sends greetings to the presbyters and the deacons, his dearest brothers.[1]

1.1 I send greetings to you, my dearest brothers, safe as I am by the grace of God,[2] and I rejoice to learn that for your part you, too, are all completely safe.[3] The circumstances of my present position do not allow me to be there with you at the moment; and I, therefore, ask of you, in accordance with your faith and devotion, to discharge in Carthage[4] not only your duties but mine as well, ensuring thereby that discipline and zeal are fully maintained.[5]

1.2 I ask that there be nothing wanting in furnishing supplies to those who have confessed the Lord with words of glory[6] and who are now to be found in prison,[7] as equally to those who are suffering from need and want but yet continue faithful in the Lord.[8] For all the funds collected have been distributed amongst the clergy in Carthage[9] precisely to meet emergencies of this kind, thus putting a number in the position to ease individual cases of hardship and necessity.[10]

2.1 I also ask that you exercise every care and attention to ensure the general peace.[11] I know that our brethren in their charity are very anxious to visit and meet the noble confessors whom God has already blessed with so brilliant and glorious a beginning,[12] but all the same I consider they should act with caution, avoiding visits in crowds and meeting in large numbers together for fear that this may provoke ill-feeling and they may be refused all access to them: if we are greedy and never satisfied in our demands, we run the risk of losing everything.

And so take counsel and care that moderation makes visiting safer; in particular the presbyters who celebrate the offering there before the confessors should take it in turns to go individually, accompanied each by a different deacon,[13] because the risk of resentment is diminished if the people who visit and meet together[14] change and vary. In all things we ought to act with meekness and humility as befits the servants of God, accommodating ourselves to the circumstances[15] and taking precautions to ensure the general peace and the well-being of our people.

I wish that you, my most dear and cherished brothers, may ever fare well. Be mindful of us and send our greetings to all of our brothers. My deacon sends his greetings to you[16] as do all who are with me.[17] Farewell.

LETTER 6

Cyprian sends everlasting greetings in God to Sergius, Rogatianus, and the other confessors.[1]

1.1 I send greetings to you, my dearest brothers. I, too, long to have the joy of seeing you[2]—if only present circumstances allowed me to come to you.[3] There is nothing which could give me greater joy nor satisfy more my longing than at this moment to be embracing you, clasped by those hands of yours which have preserved their faith in the Lord with purity and innocence, and have scornfully rejected the sacrilegious acts of compliance.[4] There is nothing which could give me greater pleasure or more noble delight than at this moment to be kissing those lips of yours which have confessed the Lord with words of glory[5] and actually to be looked upon by those eyes of yours which have looked down in scorn on this world and have shown themselves worthy of looking upon God.

1.2 But as it is not possible to share in this joy together, I am sending this letter in my stead to be heard by your ears, to be seen by your eyes.[6] I send my congratulations to you, as well as my exhortations that you persevere with steadfast courage in your glorious and holy confession. You have entered upon the pathway of the Lord's blessings. May you press forward along it with spiritual valour so that you may gain your crown, having as your guard and guide the Lord who said: *And see, I am with you all days, even to the end of the world.*[7]

Blessed is the prison which your presence has filled with light;[8] blessed is the prison which sends men of God to heaven. I hail such darkness which outshines the sun itself, which is more radiant than this light of the world, darkness where now temples of God have been raised[9] and your limbs have been hallowed by holy confession.

2.1 There should now be found in your hearts and minds nothing but those divine precepts and heavenly ordinances whereby the Holy Spirit has ever encouraged us to endure sufferings.[10] No-one should have his thoughts upon death, but upon deathlessness, nor upon temporary afflictions but upon everlasting glory, since it is written: *Precious in the sight of God is the death of His righteous ones.*[11] And again: *An afflicted spirit is a sacrifice to God, a heart humbled and broken God does not despise.*[12] And again the holy Scriptures speak of the torments which hallow martyrs of God and sanctify them by the very test of suffering: *Even if they have endured torments in the presence of men, yet are their hopes full of immortality; and though distressed in a few things, in many things they will be richly rewarded, for God has tried them and found them worthy of Himself. Like gold in the furnace He has tested them and like a burnt offering He has welcomed them. And in due time He will show regard for them: they will judge nations and be lord over peoples and their Lord will reign for ever.*[13]

And so when you reflect that you will be judges, that you will reign, with Christ the Lord,[14] you must inevitably rejoice, you must spurn the tortures of the moment[15] for joy at what is to be; you know that it was so ordered from the beginning of the universe that here Righteousness should struggle and wrestle in this world, for at the very beginning the righteous man Abel was slain and thereafter all those righteous men have been slain, both the Prophets and the Apostles whom He sent forth.[16]

To all of these the Lord has set an example even in His own person. He has taught that only they reach His kingdom who have followed Him along His own pathway, by these words: *He who loves his life in this world, will lose it, and he who hates his life in this world will preserve it unto life everlasting.*[17] And again: *Fear not those who kill the body but cannot kill the soul. But rather dread him who can kill both body and soul in hell.*[18]

Paul, too, exhorts that as we desire to gain the Lord's promises, so we must imitate the Lord in all things. *We are,* he says, *sons of God: but if sons, heirs of God also and joint-heirs with Christ—if, indeed, we share in His sufferings so that we may share in His glory.*[19] And he goes on to make a comparison between present time and future splendor with these words: *The sufferings of these times are not to be compared with the splendor that is to come which will be revealed in us.*[20] With our thoughts set on this glory and splendor, it is fitting for us that we endure all manner of tribulation and persecution; for although many are the tribulations of the righteous, yet they are delivered from them all who have their faith in God.[21]

3.1 Blessed, too, are the women who are there with you as partners in your glorious confession;[22] by holding fast to their faith in the Lord and by displaying valour above their sex[23] not only are they personally close to winning their crowns but by their steadfastness they have set an example to the rest of womankind as well.

That there might be nothing lacking in the glory of your company, so that there with you every age and sex might be honoured, God in His goodness has allied with you in glorious confession young boys as well;[24] to us He has made manifest deeds such as those illustrious youths Ananias, Azarias, and Misael once did.[25] When they were shut up in the furnace, the fire drew back from them and the flames yielded them a place of refreshment,[26] for the Lord was present with them proving that against His confessors and martyrs the heat of hellfire could have no power but that those who believed in God would continue ever safe and in every way secure.

I ask you in your piety to ponder carefully the faith which those boys possessed, a faith which could win God's favour so fully. Ready to undergo anything, as we all ought to be, they said to the King: *King Nabuchodonosor, there is no need for us to reply to you on this matter. For the God whom we serve has the power to rescue us from the blazing flames of the furnace, and He will deliver us, O King, out of your hands. And even if He does not, let it be known to you that we do not serve your gods neither do we worship the golden statue which you have erected.*[27]

Though they not only believed but, such was their faith, knew that they could be delivered even from their present sufferings, yet they would not boast of this nor lay claim to it for themselves; so they added the words 'even if He does not' lest, without the supporting testimony of suffering, the force of their confession might be diminished.[28] They went on to say that God can do all things but that nevertheless what they had faith in was not that they were going to be set free then and there[29] but they were rather thinking of the glory of their eternal safety and deliverance.

4. Such is the faith which we too must preserve and contemplate night and day, with our whole hearts prepared for God, scorning things of the moment and with our thoughts directed entirely on the future—the delights of the everlasting kingdom, the embrace and kiss of the Lord,[30] the sight of God.

Thus in every way you may follow in the footsteps of the presbyter Rogatianus, aged and glorious as he is: by his courageous piety and the grace of God he is blazing for you a pathway that leads to the glory of our time. In company with our brother, the ever calm and prudent Felicissimus,[31] he sustained the people's first savage attack;[32] he prepared in advance a lodging-place for you in prison, and now he continues to march on ahead, to mark out, as it were, the ground for you.[33]

Our prayers are unceasing, begging the Lord that your witness may be perfected. You have taken the first steps that lead to the lofty heights. May those whom He has made into confessors He make also into crowned martyrs.

I wish that you, my dearest and most blessed brothers, may ever fare well in the Lord and that you may attain the glory of the heavenly crown.

LETTER 7

Cyprian sends greetings to the presbyters and deacons, his dearest brothers.

1. I send greetings to you, my dearest brothers, by the grace of God in safety[1] but anxious to return soon to you and thus assuage my longing as well as yours and that of all our brothers.[2] All the same, it is my duty to look to the general peace of the community and, for the moment, I must accordingly remain separated from you, however low that makes my spirits. What I fear is that my presence may provoke an outburst of violence and resentment among the pagans[3] and we become thereby responsible for the peace being broken,[4] whereas it is particularly a duty of ours to ensure that everyone is left undisturbed.

And so I will come to you only when you write that affairs have been settled[5] and I ought to come, or if, before then, the Lord should vouchsafe a sign to me.[6] Where else, I ask, could I be with greater propriety or joy than in the place where it was the will of God that I should come to believe and grow?[7]

2. I urge that you be scrupulous in your care for the widows,[8] the sick, and all the poor,[9] and further, that you meet the financial needs of any strangers who are in want[10] out of my own personal funds[11] which I have left in the care of our fellow presbyter Rogatianus.[12] In case these funds have already been completely expended, I am sending to Rogatianus by the acolyte Naricus[13] a further sum, to ensure that the work of charity amongst those in difficulties may be carried out the more generously and readily.

I wish that you, my dearest brothers, may ever fare well.

LETTER 8

1.1 The subdeacon Crementius[1] has come to us from you on certain business.[2] We have learnt from him that the blessed pope Cyprian[3] has gone into retirement[4] and that it is maintained that he is certainly right to have done so for the special reason that he is a person of prominence.[5]

But the fact is the contest is now at hand which God has allowed to take place in the world, a combat between the adversary and his servants.[6] It is His will that this struggle should make manifest to angels and men that the victor receives his crown[7] but that the vanquished brings on himself as his prize the sentence which has been made manifest to us.[8]

Now we are clearly the church leaders[9] and it is accordingly our duty to keep watch over the flock, acting in the place of our shepherds; and so, if it is found that we are neglectful, the same words will be said to us as were spoken to our predecessors[10] who were such neglectful leaders, namely, that "the lost we have not sought, the strayed we have not brought back, the lame we have not bound, but their milk we have eaten and with their wool we have been clothed."[11]

1.2 Moreover, this is a lesson which the Lord Himself teaches us, fulfilling what was written in the Law and the Prophets. In His own words: *I am the good shepherd; I lay down my life for my sheep. But as for the hireling shepherd, whose own the sheep are not, when he sees the wolf coming he abandons them and flees and the wolf scatters the flock.*[12] Furthermore He said to Simon: *Do you love me? He replied: I do. He said to him: Feed my sheep.*[13] And we can see that these words were fulfilled by the very manner of his death,[14] and the rest of the disciples acted likewise.[15]

2.1 And so, dearly beloved brothers, our desire is that you are found to be not hireling but good shepherds. You are aware that there is the risk of extreme peril should you fail to exhort our brothers to stand steadfast in the faith;[16] otherwise they may rush headlong into idolatry[17] and be totally ruined.

2.2 And it is not by words alone that we exhort you to do this. You will be able to learn from the many travellers who come to you from us[18] that, with the help of God, all these things we not only have done ourselves but we continue to do them with unremitting zeal in the face of worldly dangers. For we keep before our eyes fear of God and everlasting punishments, rather than fear of men and brief-lived sufferings. We do not abandon our brothers but we exhort them to stand firm in the faith and, as is their duty, to be in readiness to walk with the Lord.[19]

2.3 In fact, some were actually on their way up to perform the compulsory ceremonies when we called them back.[20] The Church stands courageously and firmly in the faith, despite the fact that some people have fallen,[21] overwhelmed by sheer terror, whether because they were persons of prominence[22] or because they were seized by fear of men. It is true that they have been separated from us but we have not forsaken them; rather we have exhorted and we do exhort them to do penance, in the hopes that somehow they may be able to win pardon from Him who is able to bestow it. Otherwise our fear is that if they are deserted by us, they may become more sinful still.[23]

3.1 You see, therefore, dear brothers, that it is your duty also to act likewise, so that even in the case of those who have fallen, you may, by your encouragement, reform their hearts, and thus, if they are arrested a second time, they may become confessors and thereby be able to set right their former error.[24]

There are, besides, other duties incumbent upon you, which we here mention also. Thus, should illness seize those who have fallen in this encounter, then, provided that they are doing penance for their action and are anxious for communion,[24a] it is certainly right to bring them comfort.[25] It is certainly right also that there should be people to attend to the needs of widows and others in distress who are unable to support themselves,[26] likewise of those who are in prison or who have been driven from their own homes.[27] Furthermore, catechumens who fall ill, ought not to be cheated of their hopes, but they should be brought comfort.[28]

3.2 And, in particular, if the bodies of the martyrs or of the others are left unburied, severe danger threatens those whose duty it is to do this work.[29] Accordingly, whoever amongst you on whatever occasion carries out this task, he is accounted, we are sure, a good servant and, therefore, as he has been faithful over little, he will be set in authority over ten cities.[30]

May God who gives all things to those who hope in Him grant that we may all be found engaged in these good works.

3.3 The brethren who are in chains send their greetings to you, likewise the presbyters and the whole Church[31] who keeps watch herself with unresting care over all who call upon the name of the Lord. And for ourselves, we ask that you, in your turn, be mindful of us.

3.4 For your information, Bassianus has arrived.[32] We also ask of you, zealous as you are to serve God, to send copies of this letter to as many as you can, as suitable opportunities occur, or to compose letters of your own or send a messenger,[33] so that they may stand courageous and steadfast in the faith.

We wish that you, dearly beloved brothers, may ever fare well.

LETTER 9

Cyprian sends greetings to his brothers, the presbyters and deacons dwelling in Rome.[1]

1.1 There had been, my dearly beloved brothers, unsubstantial rumour here amongst us that my colleague,[2] that good man, had departed this life. Whilst we still did not know what to believe, I received the letter which you sent me by the hands of the subdeacon Crementius.[3] This informed me in the fullest detail about his glorious end,[4] and I was overjoyed at the thought that the untarnished character of his administration[5] had been graced with the honour and fulfilment that it merited.

1.2 I congratulate you also most warmly for fostering his memory with such a distinguished and splendid testimonial. Through your good services we are consequently made aware of facts which redound to your glory through the memory of your leader and which at the same time provide us with a model of faith and virtue. There is great danger that the collapse of a leader may lead to the downfall of his followers;[6] but, by the same token, there is great profit and aid to salvation should a bishop show his brothers by his unshakeable faith that he deserves to be imitated.[7]

2.1 I have also read a letter[8] in which it was not specifically stated who were the persons who wrote it or who were the persons to whom it was written.[9] And the handwriting in this same letter[10] as well as the contents and the actual paper[11] have led me to suspect that something may either have been withdrawn from the genuine version or have been altered in it.[12] And so I am returning to you the original letter;[13] you will then be able to recognize whether it is the same letter which you gave to the subdeacon Crementius to deliver.[14]

2.2 For it is an extremely grave matter if the truth of an ecclesiastical letter has been corrupted by any falsehood or fraud.[15]

That we may know this, therefore, examine the handwriting and the concluding greetings[16] to see whether they are yours and write back to us what is the truth of the matter.

I wish that you, my dearly beloved brothers, may ever fare well.

LETTER 10

Cyprian sends immortal salutations in God the Father to the martyrs and confessors of Jesus Christ our Lord.[1]

1.1 I am overwhelmed with joy and gladness, my brothers most brave and most blessed,[2] for I have learned of your faith and your fortitude. In these virtues our Mother the Church[3] takes great pride—just as she indeed took pride recently[4] when those who remained resolute in their confession incurred the punishment which drove the confessors of Christ into exile.[5]

But confession now, with its sufferings, demands greater courage,[6] yet it confers, correspondingly, brighter renown and nobler honour. The combat has increased, and with it the glory of the combatants. You have not hung back from the battlefront from fear of the tortures; rather the tortures have themselves incited you on to join the battlefront. Courageous, steadfast, you have advanced with generous self-sacrifice[7] into the very heart of the fighting.

1.2 Some of your number, I hear, have already received their crowns; others are very close to winning their crowns of victory;[8] and everyone immured there in prison in your glorious ranks is animated with the one and the same ardour and valour for the fray, as becomes soldiers of Christ in the encampment of God. No blandishments should seduce the unsullied steadfastness of our faith, nor threats terrify, nor tortures and torments overwhelm, for greater is He who is within us than he who is in the world:[9] the divine protection has greater power to raise us up than earthly anguish can avail to cast us down.[10] This fact has been proved by the glorious contest of our brothers. In leading the vanguard to victory over tortures they have given the others a model in fortitude and faith; they fought at the battlefront until the very battleline collapsed, vanquished.

2.1 How am I to find words of praise to extol you, most courageous brothers? Can I add to the lustre of your valiant hearts and to the constancy of your faith by phrases of panegyric? You have endured to the point of perfecting your glory the severest of interrogations,[11] without giving in to the tortures; rather they have given in to you. The torments would not give an end to the pain; crowns of victory have. The harsh butchery has lasted long not in order that those stalwart in faith might be overthrown but that men of God might be sent all the more swiftly to their Lord.[12]

2.2 The throng of by-standers watched in wonderment this heavenly, this spiritual contest of God, this battle of Christ; they witnessed His servants stand their ground unfettered in voice, unsullied in heart, superhuman in valour. Though all exposed to the weapons of this world, these believers were clad in the armour of faith.[13] The tortured stood their ground more resolutely than their torturers; and their limbs, battered and butchered as they were, vanquished the instruments of torment as they battered and butchered them. Impregnable faith could not be stormed by the lengthy repetition of savage blows, even though, with the framework of their vitals torn apart, the servants of God no longer had limbs to offer to their torturers but wounds only. There flowed blood such as to quench the blaze of persecution, to quiet with its glorious flood the flames and fires of hell.[14]

2.3 Noble indeed and magnificent was that spectacle of the Lord,[15] made truly welcome to the eyes of God through the fealty and dedication of His soldier[16]—just as is written in the Psalms where the Holy Spirit both speaks to us and admonishes us: *Precious in the sight of God is the death of His righteous ones.*[17] Precious is this death which has purchased deathlessness at the price of one's own blood, which has received a crown from God for the supreme act of valour.

3. Christ exulted to be there, among such servants of His; He rejoiced to fight to victory in their midst, guarding their faith and giving to believers as much as the recipient believes he is receiving.[18] He was present at His own contest; to the warriors and champions of His name He gave spirit, strength, and support. And He who for us was once victorious over death, is now in us over it ever victorious. As He said: *When they deliver you up, give no thought as to what you are to say; for it shall be granted you at that hour what you are to say. It is not you who speak but it is the spirit of your Father who speaks within you.*[19]

4.1 The present battle has given proof of this. A voice filled with the Holy Spirit broke forth from the martyr's lips when the most blessed Mappalicus, in the midst of his torments, cried out to the proconsul:[20] "The contest you will see tomorrow." And the words he spoke giving witness to his fortitude and his faith, the Lord has fulfilled. A heavenly contest was staged, and the servant of God did win his crown, striving in the contest which he had promised.

4.2 This is the contest which the prophet Isaiah foretold of old when he said: *There will be for you no mean struggle with men for it is God who provides the contest.* And he added these words in order to reveal what this contest was going to be: *See, a virgin will conceive in her womb and she will bring forth a son and his name you will call Emmanuel.*[21] This is the contest of our faith, wherein we do battle, wherein we conquer, wherein we are crowned.

4.3 This is the contest which the blessed Apostle Paul has also revealed to us, the contest in which we are to run and to attain to a crown of glory. *Do you not know,* he says, *that of those who run in a race, all indeed run but one only receives the palm. So run that you may win it. In their case their object is to receive a corruptible crown, but ours an incorruptible.*[22] Likewise he revealed his own contest and he promised he would soon be a victim offered to the Lord, with these words: *Now I am poured out in libation and the time is at hand when I am to be taken up. I have fought the good fight, I have finished the race, I have kept the faith. Now there is left for me a crown of righteousness which the Lord, the righteous Judge, will give me on that Day, and not to me only, but to all who have loved His coming.*[23]

And so, this contest, predicted of old by the prophets, presented by the Lord, performed by the apostles,[24] Mappalicus in his own name and that of his colleagues[25] promised anew[26] to the proconsul. Nor did his voice of faith fail in its promise. The fight he pledged he has staged, the palm he deserved he has received.

4.4 My prayer and my exhortation is that the rest of you follow him, now a most blessed martyr, and the others who were his partners in the same conflict and his companions, who proved themselves in faith steadfast, in pain long-suffering, in interrogation victorious.[27] May those who have been united by lodging together in prison and by the bond of confession, be thus united also in the culmination of their courage,[28] winning together their heavenly crowns. Hence, I pray that as our Mother the Church bewails the downfall and the death of very many, by your joy you may dry her tears, and by the challenge of your example you may confirm the resolution of the rest who yet remain standing.[29] If the battle-front shall call you, if the day of your conflict shall come, fight the battle bravely, wage the war resolutely, knowing full well that you wage it beneath the immediate gaze of the Lord,[30] that by confessing His name you attain to His glory. For He is not one merely to look upon His servants; He wrestles Himself within us, He joins battle Himself, in the blows of our contest He Himself both gives and wins the crowns.[31]

5.1 Now should the mercy of God chance to bring peace before the day of your combat, your resolve remains still unsullied, your conscience ever glorious: no-one among you should feel downcast believing that he is inferior to those who, ahead of you, have spurned and vanquished this world, have endured their tortures to the end, and so have gone to the Lord by the paths of glory. For the Lord searches our hearts and our minds;[32] He perceives what is secret, He beholds what is hidden. To have Him alone as witness—He will be the Judge—is enough to earn the crown from Him.

5.2 Either course, therefore, my dearly beloved brothers, equally confers nobility and glory. By the one, the surer way, you hasten to the Lord by the completion of your victory; by the other, the more joyful way, after gaining your glory you obtain a reprieve[33] and flourish in the praises of the Church.

Blessed indeed is our Church, illumined in this way by the honour of the grace of God, rendered radiant in our days by the glorious blood of martyrs. In the past she was clad in white through the good works of our brothers; now she is arrayed in crimson through the blood of her martyrs. Amongst her blossoms she lacks neither the lily nor the rose.[34] Let each man now strive for the highest honour in either estate. Let them win crowns—white for good works, crimson for sufferings. In the heavenly fortress both peace and warfare have their own flowers, so that with them the soldier of Christ may be garlanded in glory.

I wish that you, my brothers most brave and most blessed, may ever fare well in the Lord and be mindful of us. Farewell.

LETTER 11

Cyprian sends greetings to his brothers, the presbyters and deacons.[1]

1.1 I am aware, my dearly beloved brothers, that—such is the fear which all of us owe to God—you, too, in Carthage[2] are urgent and importunate in constant prayer and earnest entreaty. Even so, notwithstanding your piety and solicitude, I send to you my personal exhortations as well that, in order to placate and appease our God, we should mourn not with voice only, but also with fasting and tears and every form of supplication.

1.2 For we must face the fact and acknowledge it that the raging devastation of this persecution which has ravaged the major part of our flock,[3] and continues still to ravage it,[4] has come upon us for our sins; we have not been keeping to the way of the Lord, we have not been observing the heavenly commandments given us for our salvation. Our Lord has done the will of the Father, but for our part, we do not do the will of God. Instead, property and profit we strive for,[5] pride we pursue, our time we devote to rivalry and dissension,[6] innocence and faith we neglect, the world we renounce with words only, not deeds,[7] each person pleasing himself alone and displeasing everyone else.[7a]

And so we are being given the thrashing which we deserve. As it is written, *The servant who recognizes the will of his master and has not obeyed his will, will be thrashed many times.*[8]

1.3 What blows, what flogging do we in fact not deserve when even confessors, who ought to have set an example of good conduct to others, fail to keep discipline.[9] Hence, there being certain confessors swollen with immodest and insolent vainglory in their confession,[10] the tortures have come,[11] and tortures without any cessation of the torturer, without the release of condemnation,[12] without the solace of death, tortures which do not readily let their victims go to their crown but which wrench for as long as it takes to break a man;[13] the only exception being any one who should have departed—through God's mercy taken away in the very midst of his torments and gaining glory, not because the torturing had come to an end, but by the quickness of his death.[14]

2.1 These sufferings we are undergoing for our iniquities and our deserts, just as God forewarned with these words of stricture:[15] *If they abandon My law and in My judgements they do not walk, if they violate My precepts and My ordinances they do not observe, I will visit their wicked deeds with the rod and with the lash their iniquities.*[16] And that is why we are feeling these rods and lashes, for we neither please God by our good deeds nor render satisfaction to Him for our sins.

2.2 From the depths of our heart and with our whole soul let us then ask for the mercy of God,[17] for He went on to say

Himself: *But my mercy I will not scatter away from them.*[18] Let us seek, and we receive. And if we experience slowness and delay in receiving—our offences are grave indeed—let us knock, because to him who knocks it is opened; that is, provided we knock at the door with our entreaties and cries and tears[19]—we must be incessant and importunate in making them—and provided that we are united together in making our prayer.[20]

3.1 You ought to know what has particularly induced, indeed driven, me to write this letter to you. The Lord thought fit to manifest and reveal a vision.[21] In it, these words were spoken: "Ask and you shall have." And then the congregation standing by[22] was enjoined to ask on behalf of certain people pointed out to them, but in putting their request their voices were discordant, their wills conflicting; and He who had said "ask and you shall have" was exceedingly displeased at the fact that the people were divided and at variance, and that amongst the brethren there was no one, uniform agreement and harmonious concord. And this, despite the fact that it is written: *God who makes men dwell united together in a house,*[23] and even though we read in the Acts of the Apostles: *The multitude of those who believed were of one heart and mind.*[24] Likewise the Lord has commanded with His own lips: *This is My commandment, that you love one another,*[25] and again: *But I say to you that if two of you are in agreement on earth in seeking any matter, it shall be granted to you by My Father who is in heaven.*[26] Now, if two, united together, have such power, what could be accomplished if all should be united together?

3.2 Had there been agreement amongst all the brethren, in conformity with the peace which the Lord has given us,[27] we would long ago[28] have gained from our merciful God what we are seeking, neither would we now have been tossed for so long on these waves which jeopardize our faith and our salvation. In fact, these evils would not have befallen our community had they all been of one mind together.

4.1 Now this was also revealed: the father of a household was seated, with a young man[29] sitting on his right. This young man looked worried and somewhat aggrieved as well as distressed, as he sat mournfully holding his chin in his hand.[30] But there was another person standing on the left side; he was carrying a net and he kept threatening to cast it and ensnare the crowd of by-standers. And when the person who saw this vision wondered what this meant, he was told that the young man who was sitting like that on the right was grieving and sorrowful at the neglect of his precepts, whereas the one on the left was jubilant at being given the opportunity of obtaining from the father of the household leave to rage and destroy.

4.2 This revelation was made long ago before the present devastating storm arose. And we see now fulfilled what was then revealed: so long as we hold in scorn the precepts of the Lord, so long as we do not observe the saving ordinances of the law which He has given, the enemy gains power to do harm and with a cast of his net holds us enmeshed, too ill-armed and off-guard to repel him.

5.1 We must be urgent in prayer and raise our mournful cries with incessant supplication. For I must tell you, my very dear brothers, that not so long ago[31] in a vision this reproach was also made to us.[32] We are slumbering in our supplications, I was told; we are not watchful in prayer. It is undoubtedly true that God loves the man whom He chastens.[33] When He chastens, He chastens in order to improve him, and He improves him in order to save him. We must, therefore, cast off and burst the bonds of sleep and pray with urgency and watchfulness, as the Apostle Paul enjoins us: *Be urgent and watchful in prayer.*[34] Not only did the apostles never cease to pray day and night, but the Lord Himself, too, the teacher of our rule of life, the Way for us to imitate,[35] prayed often, and watchfully. As we read in the Gospel: *He went out on to the mountain to pray and spent the whole night in prayer with God.*[36]

5.2 There can be no doubt that when He prayed He was praying for us, for He was not a sinner Himself, but He bore our sins.[37] So earnestly did He seek to intercede for us, as we read in another passage:[38] *And the Lord said to Peter: Behold Satan has demanded to sift all of you like wheat. But for you, Peter, I have pleaded that your faith fail not.*[39]

Now if He goes to such pains for us and for our transgressions, watching and praying, it follows that we ought all the more to be urgent in prayer and supplication, firstly making our plea to the Lord Himself, and then, through Him, making our amends to God the Father.

5.3 Jesus Christ our Lord and God we have as advocate and intercessor[40] for our sins, on condition that we are repentant of our sins in the past, that we confess and acknowledge[41] our transgressions whereby at present we offend the Lord, that we pledge that for the future at least we will walk in His ways and fear His commandments.

The Father is both chastening and protecting us, if, that is, we stand steadfast in the faith, in spite of trials and tribulations, firmly clinging to His Christ—as it is written: *Who shall separate us from the love of Christ? Shall trial or tribulation or persecution or hunger or nakedness or peril or sword?*[42] None of these can separate those who believe, none can prize away those who cling to His body and blood. This persecution is a way of sifting and searching our sinfulness;[43] God would have us threshed[44] and tested as He has always tested His own. But it is nevertheless true to say that in His tests never has He failed to give support to those who believe.

6.1 Finally, even the least of His servants, set as he is in the midst of very many transgressions and undeserving of His favour, He favoured nevertheless in His goodness towards us with these instructions: Tell him, he said,[45] not to be anxious, for there is going to be peace, but there is, meantime, a short delay, for some are left still to be tested.

6.2 And further, through God's favour, we are admonished to be abstemious in diet and sober in drink.[46] I have no doubt that this is to prevent hearts now uplifted with heavenly strength from being emasculated by worldly allurements or souls from being less watchful in prayer and petition by being weighed down with lavish feasting.

7.1 I had no right to keep these particular matters concealed or to confine knowledge of them to myself alone; for they can serve to govern and guide each one of us. In your turn, you ought not to keep this letter concealed among yourselves but you should make it available to the brethren to read.[47] To obstruct those things by which God has favoured us with admonishment and instruction is the action of someone who would not have his own brother receive admonishment and instruction.

7.2 They must know that we are being put to the test by our Lord; they must not fall away, under the impact of the present persecution, from that faith whereby we once came to believe in Him. Each man, recognizing his own faults, should even now put off the habits of the old self.[48] *No-one who looks back, once having put his hand to the plough, is fit for the kingdom of God.*[49] And Lot's wife, on being freed, looked back in defiance of her instructions and forfeited her deliverance.[50] We must not turn towards the things which lie behind, to which the devil calls us back, but towards the things which lie ahead, to which Christ calls us. Let us lift up our eyes towards heaven lest we are beguiled by the delights and allurements of the earth.

7.3 Every one of us should pray to God not for himself only, but for all his brothers, just as the Lord taught us to pray. His instructions are not for each of us to pray privately but He bade that when we pray we should do so with united hearts in communal prayer for everyone. If the Lord shall observe that we are humble and peaceable, joined in union together, fearful of His wrath, chastened and amended by the present sufferings, He will make us safe from the assaults of the enemy. When discipline has led the way, forgiveness will follow.

8. What we must do is to beg the Lord with united and unidivided hearts, without pause in our entreaty, with confidence that we shall receive, seeking to appease Him with cries and tears as befits those who find themselves amidst the lamentations of the fallen and the trembling of the remnant still left, amidst the host of those who lie faint and savaged and the tiny band of those who stand firm.[51] We must petition that peace be promptly restored, that help be quickly brought to our places of concealment and peril,[52] that those things be fulfilled which the Lord vouchsafes to reveal to His servants[53]—the restoration of His church, the certitude of our salvation, bright skies after rain, after darkness light, after wild storms a gentle calm. We must beg that the Father send His loving aid to His children, that God in His majesty perform as so often, His wondrous

works[54] whereby the blasphemy of the persecutors may be confounded, the repentance of the fallen may be restored,[55] and the courageous and unwavering faith of the persevering may be glorified.[56]

I wish that you, my dearly beloved brothers, may ever fare well and be mindful of us. Greet the brethren in my name and urge them to be mindful of us. Farewell.

LETTER 12

Cyprian sends greetings to the presbyters and deacons, his brothers.

1.1 I am well aware, my dearest brothers, that I have repeatedly urged you in my letters[1] to pay every care and attention to those who have confessed the Lord with words of glory[2] and who are now to be found in prison. Nevertheless, I enjoin you again and again not to be wanting in any way in caring for those whose glory is itself not in any way wanting. I only wish that the circumstances of my position and station[3] allowed me to be with you now in person; I would gladly and readily undertake my accustomed duties and fulfil all the offices of charity[4] towards our courageous brothers. As it is, I ask that you take good care to act in my stead, discharging my role,[5] and doing everything that ought to be done for those whom God in His goodness has blessed with such splendor for their meritorious acts of faith and valour.

1.2 You should pay special care and solicitude also to the bodies of all those who, without being tortured, nevertheless die in prison, departing this life in glory.[6] They are inferior neither in valour nor in honour, so that they, too, should be added to the company of the blessed martyrs.[7] They have endured, in so far as they were able, whatever they were prepared and ready to endure. A man who, under the eyes of God, has offered himself to torture and to death, has in fact suffered whatever he was willing to suffer.[8] He did not fail the tortures; they failed him.

1.3 *Whoever has confessed Me before men, I shall confess before My Father*, says the Lord.[9] They have confessed. *Whoever has endured right to the end, shall be saved*,[10] says the Lord. They have endured, and right to the end they have borne unsullied and unspotted their meritorious deeds of valour. Again it is written: *Be faithful unto death and I will give you the crown of life*.[11] They have persevered faithful unto death, unshakeable and invincible. When to willingness on our part and confession amid chains and prison there is added the conclusion of death, then the glory of martyrdom has been perfected.

2.1 Accordingly, you should keep note of the days on which they depart this life; we will then be able to include the celebration of their memories in our commemoration of the martyrs.[12] In any case, our most faithful and devoted brother Tertullus,[13] besides all the other services of charity which he performs with his customary zeal and concern—and that includes equal diligence concerning the bodies of the dead in Carthage[14]—has written and continues to write, letting me know the days on which our blessed brothers in prison depart in glory from this life and enter into immortality. And here in their memory we celebrate the offerings and sacrifices[15] which, under God's protection, we shall soon celebrate there with you.[16]

2.2 As I have by now frequently written,[17] be unsparing also in the care and attention you give to the poor—that is to say, the poor who, standing steadfast in the faith and fighting valiantly on our side, have not deserted the battlements of Christ.[18] They are now deserving of even greater love and concern from us, for they have been neither constrained by poverty[19] nor overthrown by the storm of persecution, but by remaining faithful servants of the Lord they have, besides, set the rest of the poor an example of faith.

I wish that you, my most dear and cherished brothers, may ever fare well and be mindful of us. Greet our brothers in my name. Farewell.

LETTER 13

Cyprian sends greetings to his brothers, Rogatianus the presbyter, and the other confessors.[1]

1. It is some time since I wrote to you,[2] my very dear and courageous brothers. In my letter I expressed great delight and jubilation at your faith and valour. And now again, the first greetings that come to my lips are words of repeated and incessant joy and praise at the glory of your name. For what greater or finer prayer could I make than to see, as I do now, the flock of Christ resplendent with the honour of your confession. At this all of the brethren have need to rejoice, it is true, but in this general rejoicing the bishop has the largest share; for the glory of the Church is the glory of its leader.[3] And the grief we suffer over those who have been overthrown by the hostile storm is balanced by the gladness we enjoy over you, against whom the devil has been unable to prevail.

2.1 Yet we do urge you, by the faith which we share, by the true and sincere love we feel for you in our hearts, to take care that just as you have defeated the enemy in this initial encounter,[4] you continue to uphold your glory with a courageous and enduring valour. We are still in this world, we are still in the fighting line, we do battle each day for our lives. You must make every effort to ensure that what has started in this way, continues also to grow, that what you have commenced with such a happy beginning may be brought in you to its perfection. It is a slight thing to have had the capacity to gain something; it is far greater to be able to keep what you have gained. In the same way it is not just by receiving but by preserving our faith itself and our saving birth that we are brought to life. The mere act of acquisition does not immediately save a man for God, but perseverance to the end.

2.2 This is a lesson which the Lord has taught us on His own authority with these words: *Look, you have been made whole. Sin no more lest something worse befall you.*[5] Imagine the Lord now saying this also to His confessor: "Look, you have been made a confessor. Sin no more lest something worse befall you." When

Solomon and Saul and many others ceased to walk in the pathways of the Lord, they were unable to keep the grace that had been given to them; as they abandoned the teachings of the Lord, so His grace abandoned them.[6]

3.1 We must persevere along the straight and narrow road of honour and glory.[7] It befits every Christian to be peaceable and humble and to show that tranquillity that comes from right living, in accordance with the word of God who has regard for no man unless he is humble and peaceable and trembles at His teachings.[8] All the more is it obligatory for you confessors to observe and fulfil this precept, for you have been made an example for the rest of the brethren; everyone ought to be stimulated to follow in their lives and actions the manner of your conduct.

3.2 The Jews have become alienated from God, for it is due to them that the name of God is blasphemed among the Gentiles;[9] whereas, by the same token, they are dear to God whose obedience and noble witness bring praise upon the name of the Lord. As the Lord spoke in warning in these words of Scripture: *Let your light shine before men that they may see your good works and glorify your Father who is in heaven.*[10] And the Apostle Paul says: *Shine like beacons in the world.*[11] Likewise Peter urges: *Like pilgrims and strangers refrain from carnal desires which war against the soul, maintaining good conduct among the Gentiles, so that whilst they disparage you as evil-doers they may see your good works and glorify the Lord.*[12]

These are precepts which the majority of you, to my joy, do in fact heed; you have been blessed and honoured by the very act of your confession, and by virtuous and peaceable conduct you are guarding and preserving your glory.

4.1 But I do hear that there are some who are corrupting your company[13] and by their evil conduct are destroying the credit of your distinguished reputation. As lovers and guardians of your own reputation, you have a duty to rebuke them yourselves and to restrain and to correct them. For it brings great disgrace to your name when there are faults committed either by someone spending his days in drunkenness and debauchery[14] or by someone returning to the country from which he has been banished[15] (so that he dies, if he is caught, now not as a Christian but as a criminal).[16]

4.2 And I hear also that there are some who are swollen and inflated with pride, even though it is written: *Be not high-minded but fear. For if the Lord spared not the natural branches, it may be He will not spare you either.*[17] Our Lord *was led like a sheep to the sacrifice, and as a lamb before its shearers is silent, He opened not His mouth.*[18] *I am not,* He says, *rebellious neither do I gainsay. My back I have given to the scourges, My cheeks to their blows. My face I have not turned away from the foulness of their spittle.*[19]

4.3 Is there anyone now living through Him and in Him[20] who dares to feel proud and exalt himself, being unmindful both of the deeds which He accomplished and of the commandments which He handed down to us either through Himself or through His apostles? If it is the case that the servant is not greater than his master,[21] then those who follow the Lord ought to imitate His footsteps humbly, peaceably and silently. For the more lowly a man shall be the more exalted shall he become. As the Lord says: *He who has been least among you, he shall be great.*[22]

5.1 There is another matter which must appear appalling to you and which caused us to be deeply disturbed and distressed when we learnt of it. There are even those who pollute by shameful and scandalous cohabitation temples of God,[23] members sanctified and enlightened anew after confession,[24] promiscuously sharing their beds with women; even if there may be no defilement on their consciences, it is in itself a very grave sin to cause scandal themselves and to be the source of an example which may lead to the downfall of others.[25]

5.2 Furthermore, there ought to be no quarrelling and rivalry amongst you.[26] For the Lord has left His peace to us,[27] and it is also written: *You should love your neighbour as yourself. But if you carp at and find fault with each other, you run the risk of destroying each other.*[28] You, too, I beg you, should refrain from wrangling and back-biting, for those who back-bite will not obtain the kingdom of God.[29] Not only that. The tongue which has confessed Christ must be kept pure and unharmed and preserve its honour. The man who speaks words of peace and goodness and justice following the precepts of Christ, he is the one who confesses Christ each day.[30]

5.3 Once we renounced the world when we were baptized.[31] But to-day we really renounce the world: tried and tested by God, abandoning everything that is ours,[32] we have followed the Lord and we take our stand and live our lives by faith and fear in Him.

6. We must fortify our strength by mutual exhortation, and progress further in the way of the Lord. When in His mercy He has brought the peace which He solemnly promised He would bring,[33] we may thus return to the Church,[34] new and, in a sense, changed men; our brothers and the pagans alike, when they welcome us, will find us corrected and reformed in every way, and those who formerly felt admiration for the glory of our valour will now admire the discipline of our lives.

7. To our clergy I wrote very explicitly both recently when you were still in prison[35] and I have written to them similarly again now.[36] I have asked that you be supplied with everything you find needful in the way of food and clothing. Nevertheless I am also sending to you myself 250 sesterces from the meagre resources which I brought with me[37] (this is in addition to another 250 sesterces which I sent previously).[38] Victor the deacon and former lector who is with me here is also sending you 175.[39] And I am delighted to hear that in their charity our brothers vie with each other in large numbers to alleviate your difficulties with contributions of their own.[40]

I wish that you, my dearly beloved brother, may ever fare well.[41]

LETTER 14

Cyprian sends greetings to the presbyters and deacons, his brothers.[1]

1.1 I had certainly hoped, my dearly beloved brothers, that the greetings I might send by letter should find the whole of our clergy safe and sound.[2] But this hostile tempest has overwhelmed not only the majority of our people[3]—what has caused us the greatest distress of all is that it has involved in its devastating wake even a portion of the clergy.[4] And so we pray to the Lord that just as you now are, as we know, standing firm in faith and fortitude, so too in the future we may send our greetings to you still standing, thanks to the mercy of God.

1.2 There are, I am aware, urgent reasons why I should come to you in all haste myself. Not only is there my ardent yearning for you; this is the object of my most earnest prayers. But we would also be able, taking counsel in large numbers,[5] together to discuss, weigh and determine questions related to the government of the Church; the well-being of our community demands answers to them.[6] In spite of this, it has seemed better advised to continue, for the time being, quietly in my place of hiding.[7] My decision has been made out of concern for a variety of considerations, and they involve the peace and safety of us all.[8] Our very dear brother Tertullus will explain all this to you.[9] He it is who counselled me on this course of action[10]—behaviour characteristic of the earnest zeal he bestows upon the works of God; he urged that I should act with prudence and restraint, that I should not rashly commit myself to public view, more particularly in that place where I have been sought and shouted for so often.[11]

2.1 I am relying, therefore, on your charity and devotion[12] which I know so well. By this letter I both exhort and charge you that as your presence in Carthage causes no offence and occasions hardly any danger,[13] you should perform in my stead those offices which are necessary for the administration of the church.[14]

The poor, in the meantime, must be cared for to the extent that it is possible and in whatever way that it is possible, provided, that is, they remain standing with faith unshaken and have not forsaken the flock of Christ.[15] You should take earnest care that they are provided with the means for alleviating their poverty; otherwise necessity may force them to do in their difficulties actions which faith prevented them from doing in the storm.[16]

2.2 To the glorious confessors likewise you must devote especial care. I know that very many of them have been supported by the devotion and charity of our brethren.[17] Nevertheless there may be some in need of clothing or provisions; they should be supplied with whatever is necessary, as I also wrote to you previously when they were still in prison.[18] But there must be this proviso: through you they must be informed, instructed, and taught what the discipline of the Church, based on the teaching authority of the Scriptures, requires of them. They must conduct themselves humbly, modestly, and peaceably.[19] In this way, they may preserve the honour of their name—after uttering words of glory they may also live lives of glory. And by serving the Lord well in all things and perfecting their renown they may thereby render themselves worthy of attaining their celestial crown. For there remains more, over and above what appears to have been completed.[20] As it is written: *Praise not any man before his death.*[21] And again: *Be faithful unto death and I will grant you the crown of life.*[22] The Lord also says: *He who has endured until the end, he will be saved.*[23]

2.3 They should imitate the Lord, who as the time of His passion drew near became not more proud but more humble. It was then that He washed the feet of His own disciples, saying: *If I, your Lord and Master, have washed your feet, you ought also to wash the feet of others. I have set an example for you, so that as I have done you also should do to others.*[24] Likewise, they should follow the teachings of the Apostle Paul. Having been imprisoned many times, scourged and exposed to the beasts, he continued to be in all things meek and humble; not even after the third heaven and paradise did he make any arrogant claims for himself.[25] As he said himself: *We have not eaten bread from another without payment; instead, in labour and weariness we have toiled by day and by night lest we become a burden to any of you.*[26]

3.1 Bring each of these lessons home to our brothers, I beg of you. He who has humbled himself will be exalted.[27] Now is the time, therefore, for them to be all the more afraid of the snares of the adversary—the more courageous a man is the more savagely he attacks him; the very fact of defeat renders him more fierce in his efforts to vanquish his victor. The Lord will make it possible for me also[28] both to see them and, by saving words of exhortation, to confirm their hearts in the resolve to preserve the glory they have won.

3.2 For it distresses me to learn that there are some who are running about, conducting themselves viciously and arrogantly; they give themselves over to frivolities and quarrelling,[29] polluting the members of Christ, even after their confession of Christ, by acts of unlawful cohabitation,[30] refusing to be ruled by the deacons or presbyters,[31] and causing the honour and glory of the many good confessors to be disfigured by the depraved and evil lives of a few. These few have need to fear the others lest, condemned by their testimony and judgment, they may be excluded from their society. For he is in the end a genuine and glorious confessor who after his confession does not cause the Church to blush but to boast.

4. I refer now to the question raised by our fellow presbyters Donatus, Fortunatus, Novatus, and Gordius in their letter to me.[32] I can make no reply on my own, for it has been a resolve of mine, right from the beginning of my episcopate, to do nothing on my own private judgment without your counsel and the consent of the people.[33] But so soon as by God's favour I have come to you, we will then discuss in council together, as the respect we have for each other demands, what has been done or what is to be done.[34]

I wish that you, my most dear and cherished brothers, may ever fare well. Be mindful of me and send warm greetings from me to the brethren that may be with you;[35] urge them to be mindful of us. Farewell.

LETTER 15

Cyprian sends greetings to the martyrs and confessors, his dearest brothers.[1]

1.1 The anxious cares of our office[2] and the fear of God[3] leave us no choice but to send to you, most valiant and most blessed martyrs,[4] words of admonishment by this letter of ours. Those who with such dedication and valour preserve the faith of the Lord, ought also to observe the law and discipline of the Lord.[5] It is the duty of every soldier of Christ to stand by his general's orders; so much the more is it fitting that you should show special diligence in your obedience to His orders, in that you have become for others a model both in valour and in the fear of God.

1.2 I had certainly been under the impression that the presbyters and deacons who are there present in Carthage[6] were providing you with the fullest advice and instruction in the law of the gospel, just as was always the practice in times past under our predecessors.[7] In making their visits to prison the deacons would moderate the requests of the martyrs[8] by counsel of their own and by precepts of the Scriptures. But as things are now, I am most gravely distressed to learn that in Carthage the holy precepts are not being presented to your attention; not only that, but they are actually being impeded. The result is that those actions which you are taking yourselves and which manifest both due circumspection towards God and respect towards the bishop of God, those actions are being undermined by certain presbyters who behave without a thought for fear of God or respect for their bishop.[9]

You have addressed a letter to me in which you petition that your requests might be examined and that peace be granted to certain of the fallen as soon as the persecution is over and we can meet together with the clergy and reassemble.[10] Whereas they,[11] acting contrary to the law of the gospel, contrary also to your own respectful petition, before penance has been done, before confession of the most serious and grievous of sins has been made,[12] before there has been the imposition of hands by the bishop and clergy in token of reconciliation,[13] they have the audacity to make the offering on their behalf and give them the Eucharist,[14] that is to say, to profane the sacred body of the Lord. And this in spite of the words of Scripture: *He who has eaten the bread or drunk the cup of the Lord unworthily, will be guilty of the body and the blood of the Lord.*[15]

2.1 For this the fallen can certainly be pardoned. Who would not, when dead, hasten to be brought to life? Who would not make speed to gain his own salvation? But it is the duty of the appointed leaders[16] to adhere to the commandments and give instructions to both the hasty and the ignorant. Otherwise there is the danger that those who ought to be shepherds of their flock may become their butchers. To grant concessions which lead to destruction is to deceive. This is not the way to lift the fallen to his feet; rather, by offending God,[17] he is being driven towards total ruin.

2.2 And so let those who ought themselves to have been the teachers be taught at least by you.[18] They should keep your petitions and requests for the bishop, awaiting the seasonable time (when peace has been restored) for granting the peace which you request.[19] The mother needs first to receive peace from the Lord and then the question of peace for her sons can be considered, in the way that you desire.[20]

3.1 I also hear, my most dear and courageous brothers, that there are certain people who are shamelessly pestering you; they do violence and outrage to your modesty.[21] I beg of you, therefore, by every form of entreaty I can, to be heedful of the gospel and to bear in mind the nature and the extent of the concessions granted in the past by your predecessors in martyrdom,[22] as well as the anxious care which they showed in all things. You, too, should show anxious care and prudence in weighing the requests of those who petition you. As the Lord's friends, destined hereafter to sit in judgment with Him,[23] you must examine the conduct, the meritorious deeds and deserts of each individually,[24] considering the kinds of sin they have committed and their gravity.[25] For my apprehension is that if you promise or we do something that is hasty and unworthy, our church may have cause to blush even before the very pagans.[26]

3.2 We are the subject of divine visitations.[27] In them we are frequently being castigated and admonished to ensure that the commandments of the Lord remain free from corruption or violation. I am indeed aware that amongst you in Carthage this is still the case also, I mean that a great many of you as well receive instruction from God's stern words to preserve the discipline of the Church.[28] And this could be achieved universally, if you submit to prayerful scrutiny the requests put to you, at the same time recognizing and curbing those who make personal exceptions in the distribution of your blessings either in order to curry favour or with an eye for profiteering from this unlawful traffic.[29]

4. On this question I have written to the clergy as well as to the laity, both of which letters I have instructed should be read to you.[30]

But there is a further matter of which you ought to take careful cognizance and correct.[31] You must specify by name the persons to whom you desire peace should be granted. For I hear that there are certificates being drawn up for certain people in the form: "Let So-and-So be admitted to communion along with his household." This is an action completely without precedent among the martyrs[32]—and its effect will be that such vague and indefinite certificates will heap odium upon me in the future. For the words "So-and-So along with his household" fling the door wide open: there can present themselves to us twenty and thirty and more at a time who claim to be the relations, in-laws, freedmen or domestics of the person who received the certificate.[33] And this is why I ask that you specify by name in your certificates only those whom you see personally, whom you know and whose repentance you observe to have almost reached the point of making amends.[34] In this way the letters you direct to us may be in harmony with faith and discipline.

I wish that you, my most brave and most beloved[35] brothers, may ever fare well in the Lord and be mindful of us. Farewell.

LETTER 16

Cyprian sends greetings to his brothers, the presbyters and deacons.[1]

1.1 I have long held my patience, beloved brothers, in the belief that modest silence on our part might be of help to advance the general peace.[2] But the fact is that there are certain people[3] who are doing their best by their rash behaviour and unrestrained and reckless presumption to undermine the honour of the martyrs, the humility of the confessors, and the peacefulness of our entire people. In such circumstances it is our duty no longer to hold our peace; otherwise undue reticence may lead to peril for the people and for ourselves[4] alike.

1.2 What peril indeed have we not reason to fear when the Lord is so offended,[5] seeing that some of the presbyters, being mindful neither of the gospel nor of their own position[6] and, moreover, paying heed neither to the future judgment of the Lord nor to the bishop at present placed in charge over them,[7] are doing something that was totally unknown under our predecessors[8]—with insult and scorn for their bishop they arrogate entire authority to themselves?[9]

2.1 I only wish that while they were arrogating every power to themselves, they were not at the same time wrecking the salvation of our brothers.[10] Insults to our episcopal dignity I could ignore and endure, just as I have always ignored and endured them.[11] But this is not now the time for ignoring them when our brothers are being deceived by certain people among you. Without a thought for restoring salvation, they wish only to win popular acclaim—and they end up instead being a stumbling-block to the fallen.

2.2 That the wrong which the persecution has forced the fallen to commit is most heinous, even they who committed it are themselves aware. For our Lord and judge has said: *He who has confessed Me before men, I too will confess him before My Father who is in heaven; but he who has denied Me, I will deny him also.*[12] And again He has said: *All sins will be forgiven to the sons of men, even blasphemies. But whoever has blasphemed against the Holy*

Spirit, does not receive forgiveness but he is guilty of an everlasting sin.[13] Likewise the blessed Apostle has said: *You cannot drink the cup of the Lord and the cup of demons. You cannot partake of the table of the Lord and of the table of demons.*[14]

2.3 Whoever withholds these truths from our brothers is deceiving men who are in misery. Those who otherwise by doing genuine penance could now be making amends, through their prayers and good works,[15] to God who is their merciful Father,[16] are now being led astray to their greater ruin; they could be raising themselves up but instead they are falling further still.

In the case of less serious sins, sinners do penance for the appropriate period[17] and in accordance with the regular stages in the Church's discipline they come forward to make public confession and through the imposition of hands by the bishop and clergy they receive the right to be admitted to communion. But in the present circumstances, at a premature season, whilst the persecution still persists and before peace has yet been restored to the Church herself, they are being admitted to communion and the offering is being made in their name;[18] and when they have yet to do penance, when they have yet to make confession, when they have yet to have the hands of the bishop and clergy laid upon them, they are being given the Eucharist, even though it is written: *He who has eaten the bread or drunk the cup of the Lord unworthily, will be guilty of the body and the blood of the Lord.*[19]

3.1 But in this case it is not a question of blaming those who have failed to keep to the law of Scripture. Rather they will be blamed who, though in charge, fail to present these truths to their brothers so that, instructed by their leaders, they may do all things in the fear of God and following the ordinances which He has given and prescribed.[20]

3.2 The consequence is that they are exposing the blessed martyrs to ill-will and they are bringing these glorious servants of God into conflict with the bishop of God.[21]

For, on the one hand, these martyrs, being mindful of our position, have directed to me a letter, petitioning that their requests should be examined and peace be granted, but only when our mother herself should have first gained peace through the Lord's mercy and we have been brought back to God's Church through His protection. Whereas, on the other hand, these people, sweeping aside the respect which the blessed martyrs along with the confessors reserve for us, with nothing but scorn for the law and ordinance of the Lord which these same martyrs and confessors enjoin should be kept,[22] before fear of persecution is extinguished, before our return, practically before the martyrs even breathe their last,[23] these people join in communion with the fallen, they make the offering and to them they give the Eucharist.[24]

And yet, even if the martyrs amid the fervour of their glory were to pay scant regard to the Scripture and to go too far in their wishes contrary to the law of the Lord, nevertheless it would still be the duty of the presbyters and deacons to present them with guiding counsel, just as always happened in the past.[25]

4.1 And that is why God in His strictness[26] does not cease to rebuke us, by day and night. For in addition to visions of the night,[27] during the day also innocent young boys, who are here with us,[28] are being filled with the Holy Spirit, and in ecstasy they see with their eyes and they hear and they speak the words of warning and instruction which the Lord in His goodness gives to us.[29] And you shall hear all of these things when the Lord who bade me withdraw has brought me back to you.[30]

4.2 Meantime these particular people among you who are rash, impetuous, and arrogant, if they have no regard for man, ought to have at least fear of God.[31] They should be aware that if they persist further in this same mode of behaviour, I shall make use of that admonition which the Lord bids me use, namely, that they should be temporarily[32] prohibited from making the offering[33] until they can plead their case before us,[34] before the confessors themselves,[35] and before all the people as soon as with the Lord's permission we are gathered again to the bosom of our Mother the Church.

On this matter I have written letters to the martyrs and confessors, and to the people, both of which letters I have instructed are to be read to you.[36]

I wish that you, my most beloved and cherished brothers, may ever fare well in the Lord and be mindful of us. Farewell.

LETTER 17

Cyprian sends greetings to his brothers among the laity.[1]

1.1 There is no need for me to be told, my dearest brothers, that you are pained and distressed over the downfall of our brethren. I too, like you, am pained and distressed for each one of them, and I am suffering and feeling what the blessed Apostle describes: *Who is weak and am I not weak? Who is made to stumble and do I not burn with indignation?*[2] And again he has claimed in his epistle: *If one member suffers, the other members also share in the suffering; and if one member rejoices, the other members share in the rejoicing.*[3]

I share in the suffering, I share in the pain of our brothers; as they fell, laid low before the fury of the persecution, they tore away part of our own vitals with them, and by their wounds they inflicted a like pain on us. These are wounds which can indeed be healed by the power of our merciful God.[4]

1.2 All the same, my view is that we ought not to be hasty or do anything incautiously or hurriedly; otherwise there is the risk that if we usurp peace rashly, we may rouse God's displeasure and wrath all the more severely.[5]

The blessed martyrs have sent us a letter about certain people, asking that their requests should be examined.[6] After the Lord has first restored peace to us all and, as soon as we have returned to the Church, these requests will be examined individually, in your presence and with the help of your judgment.[7]

2.1 In spite of this, I am told that there are certain of the presbyters who are neither mindful of the gospel nor do they heed what the martyrs have written to us: they do not preserve for their bishop the respect due to his sacred office and to his throne,[8] but they have already begun to join in communion with the fallen, offering the sacrifice on their behalf and giving them the Eucharist, whereas they ought to go through the proper stages to reach this end. For in the case of less serious sins, not committed directly against God,[9] a man does penance for an appropriate period; the penitent then must make public confession after his life has been examined; and nobody can be admitted to communion without first having had hands laid on him by the bishop and clergy. It follows that in the case of these most serious and grievous of sins we must comply with every observance, with all the greater reserve and restraint, in conformity with the discipline of the Lord.

2.2 This is indeed the counsel which the presbyters and deacons ought to have given to our people,[10] thereby cherishing the flock entrusted to their care and directing them, by means of the teaching of God, on to the way whereby they might beg for the recovery of their salvation. I know personally the peace-loving as well as the God-fearing disposition of our people;[11] I know that they would be keeping watch, making amends to God and beseeching His pardon, had they not been led astray by certain of the presbyters who wanted to win their favour.[12]

3.1 Accordingly, you at least must guide the fallen individually and your restraining counsel must temper their attitudes to conform with God's precepts. No-one should pick sour fruit, before the proper season. No-one, when his ship has been buffeted and holed by the waves, should entrust it again to the deep, before he has had it carefully repaired.[13] No-one should be in a hurry to take up and put on a torn tunic, before he has seen that it has been mended by a skilled craftsman and has got it back after treatment by the fuller.

3.2 I beg them to pay patient heed to our advice: wait for our return. Then, when, through God's mercy, we have come to you and the bishops have been called together,[14] a large number of us will be able to examine the letter of the blessed martyrs and their requests, acting in conformity with the discipline of the Lord and in the presence of the confessors,[15] and in accordance, also, with your judgment.

On this matter I have written both to the clergy and to the martyrs and confessors, both of which letters I have instructed should be read to you.

I wish that you, my most dear and cherished brothers, may ever fare well in the Lord and be mindful of us. Farewell.

LETTER 18

Cyprian sends greetings to the presbyters and deacons, his brothers.[1]

1.1 I am astonished, my dear brothers, that you have made no reply in answer to the numerous letters of mine which I have sent to you on many occasions.[2] And yet the welfare and needs of our community would best be regulated if we could give accurate counsel on the management of affairs after receiving information from you.

1.2 However, I see that there is as yet no opportunity for me to come to you and summer has already begun, a season which plagues with constant and serious illnesses.[3] It is my view, therefore, that we must bring some relief to our brothers.[4]

In the case of those who have received certificates from the martyrs and can, consequently, be helped by those martyrs' privileged position before God,[5] should they be seized by some sickness or dangerous illness, they need not wait for our presence,[6] but they may make confession of their sin before any presbyter in person, or if a presbyter cannot be found and their end is coming fast, even before a deacon.[7] In this way, after hands have been laid upon them in forgiveness,[8] they may come to the Lord with that peace which, in their letter to us,[9] the martyrs requested should be granted to them.

2.1 The remainder of our people who have fallen you must comfort and cherish by your presence[10] and your compassion lest they forsake their faith in the Lord and His mercy. For they will not be left deprived of the Lord's aid and assistance, if, with meekness and humility, they genuinely do penance and persevere in honourable reputation;[11] they, too, will be cared for by the remedy God provides.

2.2 Over the catechumens[12] as well you must keep unfailing watch in the case of any of them who is overtaken by serious illness and is close to death. The mercy of God should not be denied those who call upon the grace of God.[13]

I wish that you, my dear brothers, may ever fare well and be mindful of us. Send greetings on my behalf to all of our brothers and bid them be mindful of us. Farewell.

LETTER 19

Cyprian sends greetings to the presbyters and deacons, his brothers.[1]

1. I have read your letter,[2] my dearest brothers, in which you write that you are not failing to give our brethren your saving counsel,[3] bidding them lay aside all rash haste and show towards God truly religious patience. In this way, when by God's mercy we have come together, we will be able to discuss every aspect of the problem in conformity with the discipline of the Church.[4] For it should especially be borne in mind that it is written: *Remember whence you have fallen and do penance.*[5] Now he does penance who being mindful of this precept of God is meek, and patient, and obedient to the bishops of God,[6] and he thereby earns the Lord's favour by his acts of submission and his just works.

2.1 However, you indicate that there are certain people who cannot be restrained; they are importunately pressing for prompt reception into communion. And you ask that I give you a ruling on this matter. I think I wrote to you at sufficient length on this subject in my last letter to you.[7] I said that in the case of those who have received a certificate from the martyrs and who can accordingly receive from them aid and assistance before God over their sins, if it happens that they are beset by some dangerous illness, they should make their confession and you should lay hands on them in forgiveness, and thus they may be sent on to the Lord possessing that peace which the martyrs had promised to them.[8]

But as for the others who have not received any certificate from the martyrs and are stirring up resentment,[9] they must wait until, thanks to the Lord's protection, there is first general peace for the Church herself, since this is a question which does not affect just a few or one church only or one province but it concerns the entire world.[10]

2.2 For it befits the modesty, discipline and the very way of life we should all live[11] that we leaders[12] should assemble in company with the clergy, and in the presence as well of the laity who stand steadfast—to them also honour is due for their faith and their fear of the Lord[13]—and thus we may be able jointly to settle all matters by taking sacred counsel together.[14]

2.3 On the other hand, is it not contrary to all that is sacred and is it not fraught with peril precisely for those who are in such haste that whereas those who have been exiled and driven from their native land and stripped of all their possessions have not yet returned to their Church,[15] yet some of the fallen should want to press forward so as to precede even the confessors and to enter the Church ahead of them?[16] If they are in such excessive haste, they have what they are demanding within their own power—in fact present circumstances generously provide them with more than they demand. The battle is still being fought; each day the contest is being staged. If they are genuinely and resolutely repentant of their fault and if the fervour of their faith is overpoweringly strong, he who cannot be deferred can be crowned.[17]

I wish that you, my dearest brothers, may ever fare well and be mindful of us. Send greetings on my behalf to all the community and bid them be mindful of us. Farewell.

LETTER 20

Cyprian sends greetings to his brothers, the presbyters and deacons dwelling in Rome.[1]

1.1 I have discovered, beloved brethren, that the reports being made to you on our actions both past and present are not completely candid and accurate.[2] I have therefore considered it necessary to write to you this letter in order that I might render to you an account of our conduct, our maintenance of Church discipline, and our zeal.[3]

1.2 Right at the very first onset of the troubles, when the populace clamoured for me violently and repeatedly,[4] I followed the directives and instructions of the Lord[5] and withdrew for the time being.[6] I was thinking not so much of my own safety as the general peace of our brethren; I was concerned that if I brazenly continued to show myself in Carthage I might aggravate even further the disturbance that had begun.[7] And yet, though absent in body, I have not faltered in spirit,[8] action, or the advice I have given, endeavouring to look after the interests of our brothers in conformity with the Lord's precepts in so far as my meagre abilities have allowed.

2.1 As for what I have done, the letters which I sent as occasion required—thirteen in all—will tell you. Of these I am enclosing copies.

In these letters you will find from me counsel for the clergy,[9] exhortation for the confessors,[10] rebuke when required for the exiled,[11] and an urgent appeal to the entire community that they should beseech the mercy of God.[12] Under the Lord's inspiration[13] we have striven to the utmost of our meagre talents, in accordance with the law of faith and the fear of God.

2.2 But after the advent of tortures[14] our words reached as far as the prisons in order to bring strength and solace to our brothers who either had already been tortured or were still imprisoned waiting to be tortured.[15] Furthermore, I discovered that those who had stained their hands and lips with sacrilegious contagion or had none the less contaminated their consciences with impious certificates[16] were everywhere soliciting the martyrs, and they were endeavouring to corrupt the confessors, as well, flattering and importuning them with their entreaties.[17] The result was that with no distinctions drawn, with no inquiry made into each case separately, thousands of certificates were being issued every day, contrary to the law of the gospel.[18]

In view of this, I composed a letter in which, so far as I could, I tried by my counsel to call the martyrs and confessors back to the Lord's precepts.[19]

2.3 Likewise, in the case of the presbyters and deacons, I did not fail to act with the full vigour of my episcopal authority in order to check, by our intervention, certain individuals among them; too little mindful of the Church's discipline, they were acting with a rash and impetuous haste and had already begun to join in communion with the fallen.[20] The laity, too, we reassured to the best of our endeavour[21] and we gave them instruction so that the Church's discipline might be maintained.

3.1 Subsequently certain of the fallen, whether of their own accord or incited by someone else, began to make wild demands and charged forth striving to extort for themselves, by means of violent attack, the peace which had been promised to them by the martyrs and confessors. On this question I actually wrote two letters to the clergy and I gave orders that my letters should be read to them.[22] In order in some way to mitigate for the time being their violence,[23] I said that in the case of any who were in receipt of a certificate from the martyrs and were about to depart from this life, they should make their confession and after hands had been laid on them in forgiveness they should be sent on to the Lord in possession of that peace promised to them by the martyrs.[24] On this matter I neither laid down a law nor rashly set myself up as an authority.[25]

3.2 But I did think that respect should be shown to the martyrs whereas those who were striving so violently to create total chaos should be restrained. And furthermore I have read your message which you recently[26] sent to our clergy by the hands of the subdeacon Crementius.[27] You counselled that comfort should be given to those who fell ill after their lapse and, being penitent, were anxious to be admitted to communion.[28] I have, therefore, decided that I too should take my stand alongside your opinion, thereby avoiding that our actions, which ought to be united and in harmony on every issue, might differ in any respect.[29]

3.3 Besides, as regards the remainder, I have given instructions that even though they may have received a certificate from the martyrs they should be deferred until we are personally present. Then, when peace has been restored to us by the Lord, we church leaders can meet together in a large gathering,[30] and after exchanging views with you also, we will be able to arrange or amend all the various issues.[31]

I wish that you, beloved brothers, may ever fare well.

LETTER 21

Celerinus to Lucianus.[1]

1.1 As I write to you, my honoured brother,[2] I am both happy and sad.

I am happy, for I have heard that you have been apprehended for the sake of the name of our Lord Jesus Christ our Saviour[3] and that His name you have confessed before the magistrates of this world.[4] But I am also sad, for I have failed to receive any letters at all from you ever since the time I saw you off.[5] Indeed, I am at this moment weighed down by a twofold sadness; this is because though you were aware that Montanus, our common brother, was going to come to me from the prison where you are,[6] you still sent no word to me about how you are and what is happening to you.

But this is something which often happens in the case of the servants of God, especially those who are in the process of confessing Christ.[7]

1.2 I know that all such people cease to give a thought to the affairs of this world, for their hopes are set on a heavenly crown; as I have myself remarked, it may possibly have slipped your mind to write to me. It may also be true that you might actually term me, even given my very lowly position, your own brother—if indeed I, Celerinus, have proved worthy to be so named[8]—nonetheless, for my part, when I too flourished in the flower of confession,[9] I continued to remember the very oldest of my brothers, and by my letters I reminded them that my old affection[10] for them continued still with me and mine.

1.3 Yet, my dearest friend, I do ask of the Lord that you be bathed in that sacred blood[11] for the sake of the name of Jesus Christ our Lord before this letter of mine reaches you in this world; or failing that, if it does now reach you, I ask that you write to me in reply to it. So may He crown you whose name you have confessed. For I do believe that even though we may fail to see each other in this world, nevertheless in the future[12] we shall embrace each other in greeting before the presence of Christ. Please ask that I too may be worthy to receive my crown along with your company.[13]

2.1 I must tell you that I am in the gravest distress, and I keep remembering, day and night, our old affection, just as if you were here present with me. God alone knows it. And that is why I am now asking that you accede to my request and share in my grief over the death of my sister[14] who in this time of devastation has fallen from Christ. For, as appears quite evident to us, she offered sacrifice, and has roused the anger of the Lord. For this action of hers I was in tears day and night, during the joyful season of Easter; I have been spending my days mourning, in sackcloth and ashes,[15] and have continued to do so up to this day—until such time as, through your intercession or through the intercession of my honoured masters who have received their crowns and whose aid I ask you to invoke,[16] our Lord Jesus Christ in His compassion has come to the help and rescue of so disastrous a shipwreck.[17]

2.2 For I remember your old affection; I am sure that you will grieve, as everyone does, for our sisters—you too know them well—I mean, Numeria and Candida.[18] Is it not our duty to keep vigil for their sin, since they have us as brothers? They have been doing penance and good works amongst our colleagues, exiles who have come from you[19]—these will tell you themselves about their works of charity. In view of this I do indeed believe that Christ will now pardon them if you, His martyrs, ask Him.[20]

3.1 For I have heard that you have undertaken to be minister to those who are in the flower of confession.[21] What joy for you to realize the hopes which you have always yearned for, even though you sleep upon the ground.[22] You have wanted for His name's sake to be sent to prison; and that is now your lot. As it is written: *May the Lord grant to you according to your heart's desire.*[23] And now, I understand, you have become God's priest over them, their minister.[24]

3.2 I ask, therefore, my honoured friend, and I entreat through our Lord Jesus Christ, that you place my petition before the rest of your colleagues, your brothers and my honoured masters, and ask of them that whosoever of your number is first to receive his crown, should forgive these sisters of ours, Numeria and Candida, of such a sin.

Etecusa, in fact, I have always called by this name of Numeria—God is our witness—for in order to avoid offering the sacrifice she numbered out gifts.[25] It appears that she went up only as far as the Three Fates and then came down again.[26] So I am sure she did not sacrifice.

Their case has already been heard and our Church leaders[27] have bidden that they continue as they are for the time being until a bishop is appointed.[28] But we do beg that to your utmost, through your holy prayers and entreaties in which we put our trust, for you are not only the friends but witnesses of Christ, we beg that you pardon them completely.[29]

4.1 And so I ask you, Lucianus, my dearest and honoured friend, to be mindful of me and to accede to my request. So may Christ bestow that holy crown which He has in fact presented to you not only for your confession but also for your holiness of life, a crown for which you have always striven, showing yourself ever a model and a witness for the saints. But I do urge that you place my petition on this matter before all my honoured masters, your brothers, so that my sisters may receive help from you all.[30] For, my honoured brother, I must tell you that I am not the only one to put this request on their behalf, but Statius and

Severianus do so as well, and indeed all the confessors who have come here from where you are.[31] To meet them my sisters have gone down to the harbour in person and have escorted them up to the city;[32] they have seen to the needs of sixty-five and have looked after them in every way right up to the present time. All of them are in their care.[33]

4.2 But there is no need for me to burden further that holy heart of yours, for I know how eager you are to do works of charity.

Macarius sends his greetings to you, along with his sisters Cornelia and Emerita; he is overjoyed at the glorious flower of your confession and that of all of the brethren.[34] He is joined by Saturninus who has himself also wrestled with the devil,[35] who has also bravely confessed the name of Christ, who has also bravely confessed in Carthage under the torture of the claws, who here also earnestly begs and entreats this.[36] Greetings are sent to you by your brethren Calpurnius and Maria,[37] and all the saints our brothers.

And I must point out to you that I have written this letter also for my honoured masters, your brothers; I ask that you be so good as to read it to them.[38]

LETTER 22

Lucianus sends greetings in Christ to the honoured Celerinus, if I have proved worthy to be called his colleague.[1]

1.1 My dearly beloved and honoured brother, I have to hand your letter. You have distressed me so much by it that your distress almost drove away my great joy in reading after so long a time the letter I too have been eager to receive.[2] In your letter you thought fit to remember me, and thanks to your great humility it gave me great delight to read these words of yours to me: "if I have proved worthy to be named your brother"[3]—and that of a man such as I am who has confessed the name of God, in fear, and before petty officials.[4] Whereas you, by God's will, have not merely made your confession: in so doing you terrified away the great serpent himself, the forerunner of Antichrist[5] with those words and inspired utterances[6] by which I know that you, being a true lover of the faith and zealous for the teaching of Christ, have conquered the adversary; I am overjoyed to learn that you have acquitted yourself with such ardour.[7]

1.2 But now, my very dear friend—you deserve to be reckoned already among the martyrs[8]—it was your intention to distress us by your letter.[9] You have told me about our sisters— oh, how I wish it were possible to mention them apart from the great offence they have committed. Certainly we would not be overcome by such tears as we are now.

2.1 You ought to know what has happened to us. When the blessed martyr Paulus was still in the body,[10] he summoned me and said to me: "Lucianus, before Christ I say to you that should anyone seek peace from you after I have been called away,[11] grant it in my name." And moreover everyone of us whom the Lord has deigned to call away in this time of great tribulation, we have all together issued a joint letter granting peace to everyone together.[12]

You see, therefore, my brother, how we have decided upon this in favour of everyone in part because Paulus bade me do so. This decision we made when—before our present state of distress—we were ordered to die by hunger and thirst in accordance with the emperor's command.[13] We were shut up in two cells, but the emperor achieved nothing by the hunger and thirst.[14] Moreover, we were crammed together and the resultant heat was so overwhelming that no-one could endure it.[15] But now we have been brought up into full daylight.[16]

2.2 And so, my very dear brother, send our greetings to Numeria and Candida. [We grant them peace][17] in accordance with the command of Paulus and of the other martyrs whose names I add: Bassus (died in the mines),[18] Mappalicus (under interrogation),[19] Fortunio (in prison), Paulus (after interrogation), Fortunata, Victorinus, Victor, Herennius, Credula, Hereda, Donatus, Firmus, Venustus, Fructus, Iulia, Martialis, and Ariston[20]—all by God's will starved to death in prison. You will hear that we too will be joining their company within a matter of days. For it is now eight days—up to the time I write to you—since we have been shut up again. And for the five days previous to that[21] we received but a small amount of bread and a ration of water.[22]

And so, my brother, my petition is just as I put it now,[23] that as soon as the Lord has granted peace to the Church herself, they may receive peace in accordance with the command of Paulus and, as we have decided, after their case has been laid before the bishop and they have made their confession. And this is not only for these sisters but for all those sisters who you know are dear to us.[24]

3.1 All of my colleagues send greetings to you. Send our greetings to the confessors of the Lord who are there with you and whose names you have indicated, amongst whom are Saturninus and his companions—he is a colleague of mine also[25]—and Maris, Collecta and Emerita,[26] Calpurnius and Maria, Sabina, Spesina and the sisters Januaria, Dativa, and Donata.[27] We send greetings to Saturus and his family, to Bassianus and to all of the clergy,[28] to Uranius, Alexius, Quintianus, Colonica—to everyone, please, whose names I have not written, for I am so weary; so they ought to pardon me. I hope that you fare well, and Alexius and Getulicus and the brothers Argentarius and their sisters.[29] My sisters Januaria and Sophia, whom I commend to you, send their greetings to you.[30]

LETTER 23

All the confessors send greetings to pope Cyprian.[1]

This is to inform you that all of us have together[2] granted peace to those whose conduct since their fault you shall find, upon examination, to be satisfactory.[3] It is our wish that you should make this resolution known to other bishops also,[4] and it is our desire that you should be at peace with the holy martyrs.[5] Written by Lucianus, in the presence of an exorcist and a lector from the clergy.[6]

LETTER 24

Caldonius sends greetings to Cyprian and his fellow presbyters at Carthage.[1]

1.1 Our present grave circumstances demand that we do not lightly grant reconciliation. And, therefore, I considered I ought to write to you about the case of those individuals who first sacrificed but then when they were tested a second time, were sent into exile.[2] In my view they have washed away their former fault in that they forsake homes and possessions and, repenting, follow Christ.[3]

This is the case with Felix who was an assistant to the presbyters in the time of Decimus.[4] He was chained next to me (I, therefore, know this Felix particularly well)[5] and along with Victoria his wife and Lucius they have been exiled for their loyal faith, abandoning their possessions which are now held by the treasury.[6] Moreover, in the course of this same persecution,[7] a woman by the name of Bona was dragged by her husband to offer sacrifice; she did not sully her conscience but they, by holding her hands, thus made the sacrifice themselves.[8] She then started to cry out in protest herself: "I did not do it; you have done it." And so she, too, was exiled.

1.2 All of these have together been petitioning me for reconciliation.[9] They urge: "We have recovered the faith which we had lost; in repentance we have publicly confessed Christ." Although it is my view that they deserve to receive reconciliation, I have deferred their case in order to consult you; I do not want to appear to act with any rash presumption. If, therefore, you have come to any decision in council together, write to me.[10]

Send our greetings to our brothers, as ours send theirs to you. I wish you a very happy farewell.

LETTER 25

Cyprian sends greetings to his brother Caldonius.

1.1 We have to hand, my very dear brother, your letter which displayed great good sense as well as deep integrity and faith. Nor are we surprised to find you acting in all matters with discretion and prudence, experienced and well versed as you are in the Lord's Scriptures.[1]

On the question of imparting peace to our brothers, your judgement is correct. They have in fact restored peace to themselves by their genuine repentance and glorious confession of the Lord. They have justified themselves by their own words, by which they had earlier damned themselves;[2] they have washed away all their sin and, with the Lord assisting at their side, they have effaced their former stain by their subsequent display of courage. They ought not, therefore, to continue to lie any longer prostrate, as it were, under the power of the devil; by being banished and stripped of all their possessions,[3] they have raised themselves up on their feet and have taken their stand with Christ.[4]

1.2 I can only wish that in the same way the others might repent after their fall and be restored to their former state. At present, with rash and importunate demands, they are endeavouring to extort reconciliation from us.[5] To inform you how we have dealt with them, I am sending you a dossier containing five letters which I wrote to our clergy and to the laity and to the martyrs and confessors as well.[6] These letters have been sent to very many of our colleagues and have met with their approval;[7] they have written back saying that they also align themselves with this same policy of ours, in conformity with the catholic faith.[8]

Would you also pass on this document to as many colleagues of ours as you can, so that we may all adhere to the one course of action and to the one agreed policy in conformity with the precepts of the Lord.

I wish that you, my very dear brother, may ever fare well.

LETTER 26

Cyprian sends greetings to his brothers, the presbyters and deacons.[1]

1.1 The Lord speaks and says: *On whom will I cast my eyes if not on the man who is humble and peaceable and who trembles at my words?*[2] That is how we all ought to be, but in a special way this applies to those who, after their grievous fall, must strive to earn the Lord's favour by means of true repentance and complete humility.

But I have read a letter from all the confessors; it was their wish that I make this letter known to all of my colleagues and that the peace they have granted should be bestowed on those whose conduct since their fault we shall find, upon examination, to be satisfactory.[3]

1.2 This is a matter which involves the counsel and opinions of us all; I would not dare to prejudge such an issue nor to take on myself alone a decision which is everyone's concern. In the meanwhile, therefore, we ought to stand by the letters I last wrote to you.[4] I have already sent a copy of them to many of my colleagues also; and they have written at length to say[5] that they agree with our determination and that there should be no departure from it[6] until peace has been restored to us by the Lord and we are thus able to gather together and investigate each case separately.[7]

1.3 Moreover, I am appending to my letter a copy of two letters so that you may be informed as to what my colleague Caldonius has written to me and what I have said to him in reply.[8]

1.4 I ask that you read all this correspondence to our brothers that they may be rendered all the more inclined to patience and avoid adding to their former sin yet another. Which they will do if they will not allow us to be obedient to the gospel or will not have their cases investigated in accordance with the letter from all the confessors.[9]

I wish that you, my very dear brothers, may fare well and be mindful of us. Send greetings to all of our brothers.

LETTER 27

Cyprian sends greetings to his brothers, the presbyters and deacons dwelling in Rome.

1.1 I wrote to you, my very dear brothers, a letter in which I gave a description of our conduct and rendered an account of our zeal and our maintenance of Church discipline, paltry though those efforts may be.[1] But now something else has occurred which should also not be left concealed from you.

Our brother Lucianus is himself one of the confessors; his faith, to be sure, is ardent, his courage stout, but being very ill-grounded in reading the Lord's Scriptures he has ventured upon some very foolish activities.[2] For some time he has been styling himself as leader,[3] distributing certificates *en bloc* to large numbers in the name of Paulus[4] but written in his own hand. Whereas the martyr Mappalicus,[5] a prudent and restrained man, mindful of the law and Church discipline, composed no letters in opposition to the gospel, but he was moved only by familial piety to issue instructions that peace be granted to his own mother and sister[6] who had fallen; Saturninus, too, whilst he was still in prison after he had been tortured, issued no letters of that sort.[7]

1.2 But Lucianus, not only whilst Paulus was still in prison, distributed to all and sundry certificates written in his own hand in the name of Paulus, but even after the latter's death he has continued to do these same things under the name of Paulus. His claim is that in this he is following the instructions given to him by Paulus[8]—he does not know that he ought to obey the Lord rather than a fellow servant![9] Many certificates have been issued in the name of Aurelius, also, a young man who has endured tortures;[10] they have been written out in the hand of this same Lucianus, on the grounds that Aurelius is illiterate.[11]

2.1 To try to put some brake on this activity, I wrote a letter to them which I sent to you attached to my previous letter.[12] In that letter I unceasingly urged and counselled them to be mindful of the law and gospel of the Lord.

After that letter, as if acting with greater moderation and

restraint, Lucianus wrote a letter in the name of all the confessors.[13] By that letter he undermined well nigh every bond of faith, and fear of God, and command of the Lord, and the sanctity and stability of the gospel teachings. For he wrote in the name of everyone that they all granted peace together and that it was their wish that I should make known this resolution to other bishops. I am sending to you a copy of that letter.

2.2 To be sure they added the proviso "to those whose conduct since their fault shall be found, upon examination, to be satisfactory." But this procedure fans even greater animosity against us; when we start hearing and sifting cases one by one, we may be looked upon as denying to many what all are now boastfully claiming they have received from the martyrs and confessors.

3.1 As a direct consequence the beginnings of this rebellion have already started. In several towns in our province[14] church leaders have been attacked and mobbed; and they have been compelled to put into execution[15] on the spot that peace which the martyrs and confessors, so they kept clamouring, had granted once and for all[16] to everyone. They have intimidated into submission their leaders who were without sufficient force of courage and strength of faith to resist them.

3.2 In our own case, too, certain rebels who in the past were only with difficulty kept by us in check and whose cases were to be deferred until we should be present, have become inflamed by this firebrand of a letter with even hotter ardour in their efforts to extort the peace so granted to them. I am sending you a copy of the letter I wrote to the clergy about them.[17]

Also I am sending for your perusal two letters, one which my colleague Caldonius wrote to me out of his characteristic integrity and faith, the other being my reply to him.[18] I am sending to you also copies of a letter addressed to this same confessor Lucianus by Celerinus, an upright and stalwart confessor, together with Lucianus' reply to Celerinus.[19] You will see that nothing escapes our watchful zeal and you will learn from the actual documents[20] of the restraint and prudence of Celerinus— he shows a modesty founded on the humility and awe proper to our religion.[21] Lucianus, on the other hand, who is, as I have mentioned, but poorly trained in an understanding of the Lord's Scriptures,[22] shows no restraint in his readiness to bequeath a legacy of ill-will directed against our own modest person.[23]

3.3 For the Lord has said that the nations are to be baptized in the name of the Father and of the Son and of the Holy Spirit and that in baptism past sins are to be remitted.[24] Notwithstanding this, Lucianus, in his ignorance of this precept and of the law, issues instructions that peace is to be granted and sins remitted in the name of Paulus, and this, he claims, was an instruction given to him by Paulus, as you will observe from the letter of this same Lucianus to Celerinus. He has paid scant regard to the fact that it is not martyrs who make the gospel but that martyrs are made through the gospel.

As Paul the Apostle, whom the Lord called a vessel of His election,[25] put it in his epistle: *I am astonished that in this way you are so quickly turning away to another gospel from Him who has called you to grace. But there is in fact no other gospel; all that there is, are some people who are confusing you and whose aim is to pervert the gospel of Christ. But should we or should an angel from heaven preach a different message from what we have preached to you, let him be accursed. We have already declared it—and now I say it a second time: should anyone preach to you a different message from what you have received, let him be accursed.*[26]

4. Your letter addressed to the clergy, which I have received, arrived most opportunely,[27] as did also the letter sent by the blessed confessors Moyses, Maximus, Nicostratus and the others to Saturninus and Aurelius and the others.[28] In them are to be found the full vigor of the gospel and the unshakeable discipline of the law of the Lord: your words have greatly assisted us as here we use every ounce of our spiritual strength in our struggle to resist this malevolent onslaught. By them our task has been, providentially, cut short and by them, even before our last letter to you actually reached you,[29] you have made known to us that your views and ours stand, in conformity with the law of the gospel, firmly and unitedly together.

I wish that you, my most dear and cherished brothers, may ever fare well.

NOTES

The typescript of this volume was submitted for publication in 1976 and I very much regret that it has not proved possible to make full note of material that has appeared in print, or which has come to my attention, since that date. An asterisk in the margin refers to one of the few additional notes.

LIST OF ABBREVIATIONS

AA.SS.	Acta Sanctorum
AB	Analecta Bollandiana
AC	Antike und Christentum
ACW	Ancient Christian Writers
AE	L'année épigraphique
AJP	American Journal of Philology
ANRW	Aufstieg und Niedergang der römischen Welt
BICS	Bulletin of the Institute of Classical Studies
CAH	Cambridge Ancient History
CCL	Corpus christianorum, series latina
CIL	Corpus inscriptionum latinarum
CNRS	Centre national de la recherche scientifique
CP	Classical Philology
CR	Classical Review
CRAI	Comptes rendus de l'Académie des inscriptions et belles-lettres
CSEL	Corpus scriptorum ecclesiasticorum latinorum
DACL	Dictionnaire d'archéologie chrétienne et de liturgie
DHGE	Dictionnaire d'histoire et de géographie ecclésiastique
Fahey	M. A. Fahey, *Cyprian and the Bible: A Study in Third-Century Exegesis* (Tübingen 1971)

GRBS	Greek, Roman and Byzantine Studies
Hefele-Leclercq	C. J. Hefele and H. Leclercq, *Histoire des Conciles* (Paris vol. 1 1907, vol. 2 1908)
HSCP	Harvard Studies in Classical Philology
HTR	Harvard Theological Review
IKZ	Internationale kirchliche Zeitschrift
ILCV	Inscriptiones latinae christianae veteres
ILS	Inscriptiones latinae selectae
JAC	Jahrbuch für Antike und Christentum
JEA	Journal of Egyptian Archaeology
JEH	Journal of Ecclesiastical History
JJP	Journal of Juristic Papyrology
JRS	Journal of Roman Studies
JTS	Journal of Theological Studies
MG	Patrologia graeca, ed. J. P. Migne
MGH	Monumenta Germaniae Historica
ML	Patrologia latina, ed. J. P. Migne
Monceaux, *Histoire*	P. Monceaux, *Histoire littéraire de l'Afrique chrétienne* . . . , vol. 2: *Saint Cyprien et son temps* (Paris 1902)
Musurillo	H. Musurillo, *The Acts of the Christian Martyrs* (Oxford 1972)
Nelke	L. Nelke, *Die Chronologie der Korrespondenz Cyprians und der pseudocyprianischen Schriften ad Novatianum und Liber de Rebaptismate* (diss. Thorn 1902)
Oxy. Pap.	The Oxyrhynchus Papyri
PBSR	Papers of the British School at Rome
PhW	Philologische Wochenschrift
PIR²	Prosopographia imperii romani (2nd ed.)
PSI	Papyri greci e latini
PWK	A. Pauly-G. Wissowa-W. Kroll, *Realencyclopädie der classischen Altertumswissenschaft*
RAC	Reallexikon für Antike und Christentum
REA	Revue des études anciennes
REL	Revue des études latines
Ritschl, *Cyprian*	O. Ritschl, *Cyprian von Karthago und die Verfassung der Kirche* (Göttingen 1885)

Ritschl, *De epist.*	O. Ritschl, *De epistulis Cyprianicis* (diss. Halle a. S. 1885)
RSR	Recherches de science religieuse
SC	Sources chrétiennes
SCA	Studies in Christian Antiquity
TAPA	Transactions and Proceedings of the American Philological Association
TLL	Thesaurus linguae latinae
TU	Texte und Untersuchungen zur Geschichte der altchristlichen Literatur
VC	Vigiliae christianae
Watson	E. W. Watson, "The style and language of St. Cyprian," *Studia biblica* 4 (1896) 189 ff.
ZKG	Zeitschrift für Kirchengeschichte
ZKT	Zeitschrift für katholische Theologie
ZNTW	Zeitschrift für die neutestamentliche Wissenschaft und die Kunde der älteren Kirche
ZSS	Zeitschrift der Savigny-Stiftung für Rechtsgeschichte

INTRODUCTION

1. H. Mattingly in HTR 39 (1946) 214 f., surmises that the gap is due to the later suppression of anti-Christian material which these lives contained (for the good press which Valerian enjoys in the *Historia Augusta,* see also A. Cameron in JRS 55 (1965) 247; for the favourable old-style-Roman image of Decius in the *Historia Augusta,* see n. 115 below); A. R. Birley in *Latin Biography* ed. Dorey 125 f., surmises that the lacuna was deliberately contrived by the writer in order to avoid offending Christian sensibilities too blatantly in the accounts of Philip, Decius, and Valerian (further elaborated in *Bonner Historia-Augusta Colloquium 1972/1974* [1976] 55 ff.). Neither thesis is altogether compelling.

2. See especially A. T. Olmstead in CP 37 (1942) 241 ff. and esp. 398 ff.

3. Consult J. Quasten, *Patrology* 2.367 ff., for description and bibliography. A. d'Alès in RSR 8 (1918) 319 ff. speculatively attempts to father a good number of the pseudo-Cyprianic works onto Cyprian's biographer, Pontius.

4. Notably *Epp.* 1–4 (where see introductory notes).

5. CSEL 3.3.272 ff. (two attributed to Cyprian, one each to Donatus and Cornelius). The forgers of the third of these letters were Donatists who cherished Cyprian's works; cf. Augustine, *Contra Cresconium* 2.32: *vos qui scripta Cypriani nobis tamquam firmamenta cononicae auctoritatis opponitis.* The fourth letter (to Turasius) appears to be Pelagian. The second letter (the spurious letter of Cornelius) may possibly have its origins as late as the eleventh century; see P. Petitmengin in REA 20 (1974) 15 ff. See also H. K. Mengis, *Ein donatistisches Corpus cyprianischer Briefe* (diss. Freiburg 1916); W. Speyer, *Die literarische Fälschung im heidnischen und christlichen Altertum* (Munich 1971) 207, 267 ff.; G. Mercati in *Studi e Testi* 77 (1937) 268 ff. (on the third letter). The first (fragmentary) letter, attributed to Donatus, may indeed be genuine; see C. G. Goetz in TU 19.1 (1899) 1 ff.; A. von Harnack, *Geschichte der altchristlichen Literatur bis Eusebius* (Leipzig 1904) 2.2.368.

6. *Ep.* 67.

7. Referred to in *Ep.* 68.

8. Referred to in *Ep.* 75. Does *Ep.* 75.2.3 hint that there had not been communication before the baptismal controversy—*nos gratiam referre Stephano in isto possumus quod per illius inhumanitatem nunc effectum sit ut fidei et sapientiae vestrae experimentum caperemus?*

Dionysius of Alexandria *ap.* Eusebius, *H.E.* 7.7.5, suggests that Cyprianic material has reached him in Alexandria ("I have learnt this also that the Africans did not introduce this practice now for the first time . . ."), and observe the Cyprianic document (proceedings of the African Synod of 251?) which Eusebius found along with letters written by Pope Cornelius to Fabius, bishop of Antioch (*H.E.* 6.43.3). Was this communication sent direct from Carthage to Antioch or did Cornelius append it with the other documents mentioned in *H.E.* 6.43.4?

9. *Epp.* 9, 20, 27, etc.

10. According to the Chronicle of 395 (MGH 9.738 ed. Mommsen) Cyprian wrote a hortatory letter during the persecution of Decius to Capua; it does not survive. Cyprian was honoured there in mosaics (now lost); cf. H. Delehaye, *Les origines du culte des martyrs* (2nd ed., Brussels 1933) 302. See further n. 230 below.

11. *Ep.* 59.9.3.

12. E.g., he refers in *Ep.* 55.4.2 to *Ep.* 19.2.3.

13. *Ep.* 55.5.2 referring to *Ep.* 30 written by Novatian. Note also the universal decree which Pope Cornelius made *nobiscum et cum omnibus omnino episcopis in toto mundo constitutis* (*Ep.* 67.6.3). That implies very wide links in communications.

14. Especially *Epp.* 8, 21, 22, 23.

15. *Ep.* 48.3.2: *sed quoniam latius fusa est nostra provincia, habet etiam Numidiam et Mauritaniam sibi cohaerentes.* The Latin translation of *Ep.* 75 (Firmilian), it could be conjectured, derives more from Cyprian's secretariat than from Cyprian's own pen; perhaps the compilation of the *Testimonia (ad Quirinum)* had a similar origin?

16. For a full discussion and catalogue, see A. von Harnack in TU 23.2a (1902). There is a useful survey of questions connected with the corpus of Cyprian's letters (including omissions) in DACL 8 (1929) *s.v.* Lettres Chrétiennes 2754 ff.

17. Thus a congratulatory letter on Stephen's election to the Roman bishopric and, likewise, on Xystus' is to be expected (cf. *Ep.* 61.1.1, referring to a lost letter of felicitation to Lucius on a similar occasion). Did Cyprian send to the African bishops an annual Paschal Letter, declaring the date of Easter and that of any Council meeting which might follow? Compare the practice of the contemporary Dionysius of Alexandria; and for the Roman custom, see the Council of Arles, canon 1: *iuxta consuetudinem litteras ad omnes tu dirigas* (Hefele-Leclercq 1.1.280 f.).

18. See M. Bévenot in *Bulletin of the John Rylands Library* 28 (1944) 76 ff. (= ML Suppl. 1, 40 f.).

19. Pontius, *Vita Cyp.* 7. He appears to be citing the works from their published order; see C. H. Turner in CR 6 (1892) 205 ff. Some confirmation may also come from the manuscript tradition of the *Sent. Episc. LXXXVII:* biographical annotations suggest a transmission dating from well before the close of the third century, before some of the participating bishops were dead. See C. H. Turner in JTS 29 (1927–1928) 117 ff.; H. Delehaye, *Les origines du culte des martyrs* (2nd ed., Brussels 1933) 318 f.; G. Mercati in *Studi e Testi* 77 (1937) 180; H. von Soden in *Nachrichten . . . Göttingen. Phil.-hist. Klasse* (1909) 3.300 ff.

20. See T. Mommsen in *Hermes* 21 (1886) 142 ff. and 25 (1890) 636 ff.; W. Sanday in *Studia biblica et ecclesiastica* 3 (1891) 274 ff.; H. K. Mengis in PhW 38 (1918) 326 ff.

21. G. Morin in *Bulletin d'ancienne littérature et d'archéologie chrétienne* 4 (1914) 16 ff.; most accessibly found in ML Suppl. 2, 610 ff.

22. Cf. J. Chapman in JTS 4 (1902) 107 on the order of the treatises: "The order of Pontius is clearly the parent of all of our existing MSS."

23. See H. von Soden in TU 25 (1904).

24. Turin, Bibl. Naz., E1115 (1459 A.D.). See H. von Soden, *op. cit.* 151 f.

25. See n. 18 above; it is exploited by M. Bévenot, *The Tradition of MSS. A Study in the Transmission of St. Cyprian's Treatises* (Oxford 1961), which see for the unravelling of MS traditions, in particular of Cyprian's *De unitate.*

26. See H. L. Ramsay in JTS 3 (1901–1902) 592.

27. E.g., *Ep.* 45.4.2: *melius autem, frater, facies si etiam exempla litterarum . . . legi illic fratribus iubeas; Ep.* 59.19.1: *Et quanquam sciam . . . plebi legere te semper litteras nostras, tamen nunc et admoneo et peto . . . ut hac epistula mea lecta. . . .* And Cornelius, *Ep.* 49.3.3, writes: *Has litteras puto te debere, frater carissime, et ad ceteras ecclesias mittere . . .*

28. *Ep.* 59.2.1; cf. *Ep.* 59.14.1, 16.1.

29. *Ep.* 45.2; this letter (cf. *Ep.* 55.2.1) was written *discordioso stilo,* it was packed *acerbationibus criminosis* by those who are slaves *vel furori suo vel libidini.* Regrettably it does not survive.

30. *Ep.* 32.1.2 (where see n.).

31. *Ep.* 45.4.3: *exemplaria autem eadem nunc quoque . . . transmisi.*

32. Compare R. P. Evaristo Arns, *La technique du livre d'après saint Jérôme* (Paris 1953) 188 ff., on copykeeping in Jerome's correspondence.

33. See *Ep.* 20.2 ff. (and nn. *ad loc.*).

34. *Epp.* 27, 25, 32, 73. For a full list of references to enclosures, see Turner, appendix to Sanday, *op. cit.* in n. 20 above, 323 n. 1.

35. E.g., *Epp.* 30 (Novatian), 59 (Cornelius), 73 (Iubaianus).

36. The only verbatim report which we have of Stephen's text occurs in the quotation in *Ep.* 74.1.2. Zonaras' note on this letter of Stephen's appears to be studiously vague (12.22, 3.139 ed. Dindorf): οὖ καὶ ἐπιστολῇ περὶ τούτου πρὸς Κυπριανὸν τὸν ἱερομάρτυρα ἀναγράφεται.

37. *Ep.* 55.

38. Polycarp, *Ad Philip.* 13.2.

39. Eusebius, *H.E.* 6.36.3: "As many of these letters as we have been able to collect, preserved here and there by various people, we arranged in separate roll-cases so that they might no longer be dispersed." The collection, like Cyprian's, appears to have included decrees of synods which concerned Origen; see H. J. Lawlor and J. E. L. Oulton's commentary on Eusebius *ad loc.* On letter collections in the early Church generally, see J. de Ghellinck, *Patristique et moyen âge* (3 vols., Louvain 1946–1948) 2.202 ff.

40. Cf. A. von Harnack, *op. cit.* in n. 16 above, 45.

41. Cf. H. K. Mengis, *op. cit.* in n. 5 above, editing a dossier consisting of *Epp.* 67, 6, 4, and 10.

42. Augustine, *De baptismo* 6.15.24 f.

43. *Saint Cyprien Correspondance*, vol. 1, xlviii; cf. H.–I. Marrou in VC 3 (1949) 216.

44. *De adult. lib. Origenis* 41 ff. This passage and Jerome's comments on it, especially *Adv. Rufinum* 2.19, are conveniently collected in A. von Harnack, *Geschichte der altchristlichen Literatur bis Eusebius* (Leipzig 1896) 1.2.694 f., 706.

45. Rufinus wrongly attributes the tract to Tertullian (refuted by Jerome loc. cit.: *nam nec Tertulliani liber est nec Cypriani*

*dicitur sed Novatiani cuius et inscribitur titulo et auctoris eloquium
styli proprietas demonstrat;* cf. Jerome, *De vir. illust.* 70: [*Nova-
tianus*] *scripsit . . . De Trinitate . . . quod plerique nescientes Cypriani existimant*). See W. Speyer, *Die literarische Fälschung im
heidnischen und christlichen Altertum* (Munich 1971) 265; H. L. M.
van der Valk in VC 2 (1957) 8; and esp. C. H. Roberts in *Proceed.
Brit. Acad.* 40 (1954) 176, 200 f. on the interpolation into *codices* of
pseudonymous material.

46. So E. Dekkers in *Sacris erudiri* 5 (1953) 197 f., and compare Augustine, *Serm.* 310.4: Cyprian while residing in Africa
has travelled *ad alia loca per alienas linguas, ad alia vero per suas
litteras venit.* Some of the letters appear to have been known to
Basil and just possibly Gregory Nazianzen—who were unfamil-
iar with Latin. See H. von Soden in TU 25 (1904) 181 f.

47. Note, e.g., Pacian, *Ep. ad Sympron.* 3.24: *lege totam de
lapsis epistolam* (referring to Cyprian's treatise). Cf. Jerome, *In
Jeremiam commentarii* 5.29.1: *haec epistula immo libellus Jeremiae
prophetae;* and his *Ep.* 112.1: *Tres simul epistulas immo libellos per
diaconum Cyprianum tuae dignationis accepi;* and see K. Goetz,
Geschichte der cyprianischen Literatur . . . (diss. Marburg 1891) 108
f.

48. Much major work was achieved in the late seventeenth
century by Pearson in his *Annales Cypriani*, the introduction to
the Oxford edition of Cyprian's works by Pearson and Fell
(1682). The late nineteenth century witnessed a thriving revival
of the problems. The dissertation of O. Ritschl, *De epistulis
Cyprianicis*, appeared in 1885 and in the same year his *Cyprian
von Karthago*, 238 ff., dealt with the chronology of his works. H.
von Soden in TU 25 (1904) 22 ff.; L. Nelke in his dissertation at
Thorn (1902); A. von Harnack in his *Geschichte . . .*, 2.2.339 ff.; P.
Monceaux in *Rev. de phil. de litt. et d'hist. anc.* 24 (1900) 333 ff.;
Bayard in the introduction to vol. 1 of his Budé edition; these
among others all made significant contributions to the question.
Recently (1972) the chronology of particularly *Epp.* 5–20 has
been thoroughly reviewed by L. Duquenne, *Chronologie des lettres de s. Cyprien.*

49. For a recent general survey on the level of development

achieved, see A. Deman (with J.-H. Michel) in ANRW 2.3 (1975) 3 ff. (with extensive bibliographical references).

50. So Herodian 7.6.1 (cf. 4.3.7), who was a contemporary of Cyprian's. On the size of Carthage, see also, inconclusively, A. Lézine in *Antiquités africaines* 3 (1969) 69 ff.

51. There is much generous literature available for the North African background; among others see M. Albertini, *L'Afrique romaine* (5th ed., Algiers 1950); A. Audollent, *Carthage romaine (146 av. J-Ch.-698 ap. J-Ch.)* (Paris 1901); E. S. Bourchier, *Life and Letters in Roman Africa* (Oxford 1913); T. R. S. Broughton, *The Romanisation of Africa Proconsularis* (Baltimore-London 1929); G. Charles-Picard, *La civilisation de l'Afrique romaine* (Paris 1959); E. F. Gautier, *Le passé de l'Afrique du nord: les siècles obscurs* (Paris 1937); S. Gsell, *Histoire ancienne de l'Afrique du nord* (8 vols., Paris 1913–1928); R. M. Haywood in vol. 4.1 of T. Frank, *An Economic Survey of Ancient Rome* (Paterson 1959); Ch.-A. Julien, *Histoire de l'Afrique du nord (Tunisie, Algérie, Maroc) des origines à la conquête arabe (647 ap. J.-C.)* (2nd ed., Paris 1961); M. Rostovtzeff, *The Social and Economic History of the Roman Empire* (2nd ed., rev. by P. M. Frazer, 2 vols., Oxford 1957) 311 ff.; A. N. Sherwin-White in JRS 34 (1944) 1 ff; B. H. Warmington, *The North African Provinces from Diocletian to the Vandal Conquest* (Cambridge 1954); and for a bibliographical survey of recent inquiries and research (since 1962), see M. LeGlay in *Chiron* 4 (1974) 629 ff. Note also the export trade in Red African Slip Ware, manufactured in Proconsularis; see J. W. Hayes, *Late Roman Pottery* (1972) esp. 296 ff., 423.

52. Herodian 7.4 ff.; *H.A.* Gord. 15, 23.6, Max. 19 (the revolts of the Gordians in 238 and of Sabinianus in 240). See also T. Kotula in *Eos* 50 (1959–1960) 197 ff.; and his article in *Travaux de la Societé des sciences et des lettres de Wroclaw*, ser. A, no. 74 (1961) 1 ff.; and for bibliography on the revolt of the Gordians, see Deman, *art. cit.* in n. 49 above, 44 n. 102. The epitaph ILS 8499 (Theveste) tellingly reveals the intensity of local divisions: . . . *pro amore Romano quievit ab hoc Capeliano captus.* . . .

53. Archaeology appears to reveal signs of growing economic regression; monumental edifices and public buildings are not

being constructed, and public inscriptions, whereas once multi-tudinous, are now rare phenomena. See A. Bourgarel-Musso in *Revue africaine* 75 (1934) 354 ff., 491 ff.; R. P. Duncan-Jones in PBSR 30 (1962) 53 f. and his *The Economy of the Roman Empire. Quantitative Studies* (Cambridge 1974) 360 ff. For a parallel dis-cussion of similar third-century evidence from the city of Nar-bonne, see M. Gayraud in ANRW 2.3 (1975) 853 ff.

54. Legio III Augusta was cashiered for the period 238–253; see PWK 12.2 (1925) *s.v.* Legio 1336 for *damnatio*, 1339 for *restauratio*.

55. Cf. R. M. Haywood, *op. cit.* in n. 51 above, 4.115: "The rest of the Third Century after the Gordian revolt saw frequent raids of the Moorish tribes. The proconsular province seems to have been free from this constant danger. . . ." For the consider-able border unrest, see my article in *Antichthon* 4 (1970) 78 ff.

56. See W. Thieling, *Der Hellenismus in Kleinafrica* (Leipzig 1911; repr. Rome 1964).

57. Some would want African Christianity to have percepti-ble Jewish origins; see, e.g., G. Quispel in VC 22 (1968) 93; cf. J. Daniélou in VC 25 (1971) 171 ff.; L. J. van der Lof in *Nederlands archiefs voor Kerkesgeschiedenis* 56 (1975–1976) 385 ff.; W. H. C. Frend, *Martyrdom and Persecution in the Early Church* (Oxford 1965) 361 f. On Jews in Carthage, see T. D. Barnes, *Tertullian. A Historical and Literary Study* (Oxford 1971) 284 f., and for recent bibliography of studies of foreign groups in North Africa gener-ally, see M. LeGlay in *Chiron* 4 (1974) 643 n. 61. For a recent discussion of the material evidence of the Jewish diaspora in North Africa, see E. Frézouls, *Acta of Fifth Epigraphic Congress 1967* (1971) 287 ff.

58. On local languages, see R. MacMullen in AJP 87 (1966) 12 f., and F. Millar in JRS 58 (1968) 126 ff.

59. See recently on the process of Romanisation H.-G. Pflaum in *Vestigia* 17 (1973) 55 ff.

60. See Appian 8.96; most recently discussed by H. Hurst in *Antiquaries Journal* 55 (1975) 11 ff.; R. A. Yorke and J. H. Little in *Intern. Journal of Naut. Arch. and Underwater Exploration* 4 (1975) 85 ff. (with general survey of harbor installations). See

also P. A. Février in *Corsi di cultura sull'arte ravennate e bizantina* 19 (1972) 141 ff.

61. See n. 11 to *Ep.* 5, n. 32 to *Ep.* 6, n. 3 to *Ep.* 7.

62. Pontius, *Vit. Cyp.* 2: *studia et bonae artes; distractis rebus suis ad indigentium multorum pacem sustinendam tota prope pretia dispensans* (there are some uncertain readings here, but compare the reading in 15: *hortos . . . quos inter initia fidei suae venditos et de Dei indulgentia restitutos pro certo iterum in usus pauperum vendidisset . . .*, and Jerome, *De viris illust.* 67: *omnem substantiam suam pauperibus erogavit*). The variant reading *praedia* in Pontius, *Vit. Cyp.* 2, could suggest landed estates.

63. Note especially Pontius, *Vit. Cyp.* 14: *conveniebant interim plures egregii et clarissimi ordinis et sanguinis, sed et saeculi nobilitate generosi qui propter amicitiam eius antiquam. . . .*

64. *Acta Cypriani* 5.4.—On the preceding, see P. Garnsey, *Social Status and Legal Privilege in the Roman Empire* (Oxford 1970) 103 ff., and his article in *Past and Present* 41 (1968) 13 f., on both the penalty of decapitation and the pre-trial treatment; and cf. Ulpian, *Dig.* 48.3.1; the proconsul decides (for an accused awaiting trial) on imprisonment, committal to guarantors or soldiers, or "to themselves" *pro criminis quod obicitur qualitate vel propter honorem aut propter amplissimas facultates vel pro innocentia personae vel pro dignitate eius qui accusatur.* It goes beyond the evidence, however, to claim senatorial class for Cyprian (against E. Sauser, *Bekenner seiner Herrlichkeit* [Innsbruck 1964] 87), but curial rank seems a reasonable hypothesis.

65. Derived from a combination of the incipit of *Ep.* 66 (*Cyprianus qui et Thascius*), the quotation by Cyprian of the wording of the proscription issued against him, in *Ep.* 66.4.1 (*de bonis Caecili Cypriani episcopi*), and compare the question put to him by the proconsul Aspasius Paternus in *Acta Cyp.* 3.3: *Tu es Thascius qui et Cyprianus?*

66. *Ep.* 81.1.1: *de hortis nostris interim secederem;* cf. *Acta Cyp.* 2.1: *in hortis suis manebat.*

67. Jerome, *De viris illust.* 67: *Cyprianus Afer, primum gloriose rhetoricam docuit; exinde suadente presbytero Caecilio . . . Christianus factus. . . .* Jerome received information about Cyprian from a

certain Paulus of Concordia who, as a very young man in Rome, had made the acquaintance of Cyprian's secretary, then a very old man; Jerome, *loc. cit.* 53: *ego quemdam Paulum Concordiae, quod oppidum Italiae est, senem qui se beati Cypriani iam grandis aetatis notarium cum ipse admodum esset adulescens Romae vidisse diceret referreque* . . . I take it that the phrase *iam grandis aetatis* describes the secretary and not Cyprian.

68. M. L. Clarke, *Rhetoric at Rome: A Historical Survey* (London 1953) 145.

69. Pontius, *Vit. Cyp.* 5; cf. *Ep.* 43.1.2 f. (addressed to his *plebs*): *antiqua illa contra episcopatum meum, immo contra suffragium vestrum et Dei iudicium, venena,* etc. On the date of Cyprian's elevation to the bishopric of Carthage, see n. 78 below.

70. Precision is not possible, as it was not for Augustine (*Sermo* 310: *quando natus sit ignoramus*). Cyprian could not have been unusually young in years—Pontius had no need to defend his bishop against that charge at least—and within a few years of his being bishop Cyprian could clearly include himself without discomfort in a class of bishops variously described in *Ep.* 55.24.2 as *in aetate antiqui, in fide integri, in pressura probati, in persecutione proscripti.*

71. That is to say, on the (doubtful) assumption that the *Ad Donatum* provides secure autobiographical data. This is discussed in my article, "The Secular Profession of St. Cyprian of Carthage," *Latomus* 24 (1965) 633 f.; and see further M. M. Sage, *Cyprian* (Cambridge 1975) 110 ff. for an able analysis.

72. The evidence is marshalled and analysed in my *art. cit.* in n. 71, to which might be added A. Quacquarelli, *La retorica antica al bivio* (Rome 1956) 99 ff. (arguing independently for the same conclusion, on different lines), and Y.-M Duval in *Epektasis. Mélanges patristiques offerts au cardinal Jean Daniélou* (Paris 1972) 551 ff. (though I find it hard to conclude, with Duval, that Cyprian must have once been a *grammaticus* and that he had "occupé . . . la chaire de rhétorique de Carthage"). The various *testimonia* on Cyprian are collected in A. von Harnack, *Geschichte.* . . . 1.2.701 ff.

73. But these are conjectural and go beyond the strict con-

trols of our sparse evidence. On public oratory and *encomia* at this period, see S. G. MacCormack in R.E. Aug. 22 (1976) 1 ff. Some have attempted to detect further pagan activity for Cyprian from Jerome's remarks in his *Comment. in Jonam* 3: *prius idolatriae assertor fuit, et in tantam gloriam venit eloquentiae ut oratoriam quoque doceret Carthagini.* Against such misuse of this passage, see my *art. cit.* in n. 71, 637; P. Antin in *Revue biblique* 68 (1961) 412 ff.; and Duval's *art. cit.* in n. 72.

74. A wife has been mistakenly provided for Cyprian by E. W. Watson in JTS 22 (1921) 366 f. (misinterpreting Pontius, *Vit. Cyp.* 2, and Cyprian's *De habitu virginum* 22); by G. Osborn in *Studies in honor of S. J. Case* (Chicago 1939) 133 (misinterpreting Pontius, *Vit. Cyp.* 2); and by G. C. Brauer, *The Age of the Soldier Emperors. Imperial Rome, A.D. 244–284* (Park Ridge 1975) 39, 102 (misinterpreting perhaps the Cyprianic fragment in Pontius, *Vit. Cyp.* 3: *non uxoris suadela deflexit*).

75. Pontius, *Vit. Cyp.* 2: *fuerint licet studia et bonae artes devotum pectus imbuerint.*

76. Pontius, *Vit. Cyp.* 4: *viri iusti et laudabilis memoriae Caeciliani et aetate tunc et honore presbyteri.* Jerome appears to have got the name wrong (*Caecilius*) and to have made a false deduction about the derivation of Cyprian's own name as a result. See Jerome, *De viris illust.* 67: *suadente presbytero Caecilio a quo et cognomentum sortitus est.*

77. See discussion and references in n. 21 to *Ep.* 1.

78. The date can be roughly fixed by Cyprian's remark about himself in *Ep.* 59.6.1 (written in the summer of 252, and certainly after May 15 of that year): *plebi suae in episcopatu quadriennio iam probatus.* That should make the possible period between summer 248 and the first half of 249. Moreover, there is *Ep.* 29.1.2 (written after Easter in 250): *Saturum et . . . Optatum . . . quos iam pridem communi consilio clero proximos feceramus quando aut Saturo die Paschae semel atque iterum lectionem dedimus aut modo cum presbyteris doctoribus lectores diligenter probaremus. . . .* The description of Cyprian's actions in the past, *iam pridem . . . modo* (but both still before the outbreak of the persecution) and possibly the phrase *semel atque iterum* in connexion

with reading the lesson at Easter suggest that Cyprian was perhaps bishop by the time of the Easter ceremonies of 249. See also Monceaux, *Histoire* 2.208.

79. See Pontius, *Vit. Cyp.* 5, and also n. 32 to *Ep.* 14. For Cyprian's action *antiquioribus cedens,* compare the confessor Felix who stood down (for the bishopric of Nola) in deference to a presbyter Quintus, seven days his senior in the presbyterate; see Paulinus, *Carm.* 16.237 ff. (= ACW 40.103). For parallels to the theme of the reluctant elevation to bishopric, see P. Courcelle, *Recherches sur saint Ambroise* (Paris 1973) 10 nn. 1–3; and for popular pressure to accept consecration, see J. Fontaine's commentary on Sulpicius Severus, *Vita Martini* 9.

80. The story is reported by Gregory of Nyssa in his *Vita Gregorii Thaumaturgi* (MG 46.933).

81. Ambrose, Basil, and Augustine provide later and notorious examples of "irregular" clerical advancement (see H. Hess, *The Canons of the Council of Sardica, A.D. 343. A Landmark in the Early Development of Canon Law* [Oxford 1958] 105 n. 3; F. H. Dudden, *The Life and Times of St. Ambrose,* vol. 1 [Oxford 1933] 66 ff., esp. 70 ff. for sources and commentary), but observe the story of the election of Cornelius' predecessor in Rome, Fabian, apparently from the ranks of the laity; see Eusebius, *H.E.* 6.29.2 f. For other examples, see J. Gaudemet, *L'église dans l'empire romain (IVe-Ve siècles)* (Paris 1958) 108 ff.

82. See n. 1 to *Ep.* 24.

83. See Jerome, *De viris illust.* 68: *cum ipso exsilium sustinens;* cf. Pontius, *Vit. Cyp.* 12: *me inter domesticos comites dignatio caritatis eius delegerat exulem voluntarium.*

84. See Introduction to ACW 39.10 ff.

85. See ACW 39.5 ff. for discussion.

86. See evidence quoted in n. 62 above.

87. As Pontius puts it, by selling his patrimony he was avoiding *ambitionem saeculi* (*Vit. Cyp.* 2).

88. Pontius, *Vit. Cyp.* 2: *postquam et sacras litteras didicit et . . . in lucem sapientiae spiritalis emersit. . . .*

89. For discussion, see Fahey 51 f. Cyprian was even less critical or defensive of the biblical style than many of his successors in the Latin apologetic tradition. See E. Gallicet in *Forma*

Futuri. Studi in onore del cardinale Michele Pellegrino (Turin 1975) 43 ff.

90. *Sent. Episc. LXXXVII* 31.

91. *Act. Scill.* 12.

92. See, e.g., W. H. C. Frend, *The Donatist Church* (Oxford 1952) 4 ff.

93. For discussion, see L. Wohleb in ZNTW 25 (1926) 270 ff.

94. So argued by Ritschl, *De epist.* 7 ff.; E. W. Watson in *Studia biblica* 4 (1896) 199, 310; further discussion in Nelke 154 ff., and H. von Soden, *art. cit.* in n. 23, 32 f.

95. *Ep.* 55.8.2.

96. Pontius, *Vit. Cyp.* 9.

97. Already the three letters, *Epp.* 15–17, repay close scrutiny for this theme.

98. Cf. *Ep.* 74.7.2: *ut habere quis possit Deum patrem, habeat ante ecclesiam matrem; De unitate 6: habere iam non potest Deum patrem qui ecclesiam non habet matrem.*

99. E.g., Celerinus; cf. *Ep.* 39.1.1. For general discussion and bibliography, see nn. 27, 29, and 30 to *Ep.* 16, and also nn. 21 and 32 to *Ep.* 11. It is no wonder that in later tradition Cyprian came to be hopelessly confused with the *magus* Cyprian of Antioch. On the confusion, see T. Sinko, *De Cypriano martyre a Gregorio Nazianzeno laudato* (Krakau 1916); A. D. Nock in JTS 28 (1926–1927) 411 ff.; H. Delehaye, *Les origines du culte des martyrs* (2nd ed., Brussels 1933) 91 ff.; J. Coman in *Stud. Patrist.* 4 (1961) 363 ff.; RAC 3 (1957) *s.v.* Cyprianus II 467 ff.; T. A. Sabattini in *Rivista di studi classici* 21 (1973) 181 ff.

100. *Ep.* 16.4.1 (and n. 30 thereto). On the following sentence, see *Epp.* 14.2.1, 20.1.2.

101. But note also Cyprian on Novatianists in *Ep.* 55.16 ff.

102. See my article, "Persecution under Gallus," to appear in ANRW for further explication of the general context of these attacks.

103. *Decline and Fall of the Roman Empire*, vol. 1, Everyman edition, London, 1960, 248; echoed by many modern authorities, e.g., G. Alföldy, *Römische Sozialgeschichte* (Wiesbaden 1975) 140: "Die Krise war total."

104. Note the studies of G. Alföldy in *Hermes* 99 (1971) 429 ff.; in *Historia* 22 (1973) 479 ff.; in GRBS 15 (1974) 89 ff.; in *Krisen in der Antike* (1975) 112 ff. on the attitudes of contemporary writers.

105. On the crisis consult, among others, A. Alföldi, *Studien zur Geschichte der Weltkrise des 3. Jahrhunderts nach Christus* (Darmstadt 1967); G. Alföldy, *Römische Sozialgeschichte* (Wiesbaden (1975) 139 ff.; G. Walser and T. Pekáry, *Die Krise des römischen Reiches* (Berlin 1962). Fo a mild corrective to exaggerated descriptions of the chaos of this period, see my article in *Antichthon* 4 (1970) 78 ff.

106. For financial aspects of the third century, along with bibliographical survey, see M. Crawford and J.-P. Callu in ANRW 2.2 (1975) 560 ff., 595 ff., adding P. Tyler, *The Persian Wars of the 3rd Century A.D. and Roman Imperial Monetary Policy, A.D. 253–68* (Wiesbaden 1975). For an account of the invasions, see A. T. Olmstead in CP 37 (1942) 241 ff., 398 ff.

107. For the evidence, see J. Gagé in REL 11 (1933) 412 ff.; A. T. Olmstead in *art. cit.* in n. 106, 260 f.; T. Kotula in *Meander* 16 (1961) 69 ff., 116 ff.

108. Note the study of J. Gagé in *Transactions of the International Numismatic Congress, London 1936* (London 1938) 179 ff. We must recall this contrasting backdrop to the composition of Cyprian's treatise *Ad Demetrianum* (in which the proposition that the world is in decline figures as a dominant theme).

109. On the emperor Decius generally and his career, see PWK 15 (1932) 1244 ff.; B. Gerov in *Klio* 39 (1961) 222 ff.; on questions of the chronology of the reign, see A. Stein in *Archiv für Papyrusforschung* 7 (1924) 30 ff.; H. Mattingly in JEA 13 (1927) 14 ff.; T. Pekáry in *Historia* 11 (1962) 123 ff.; X. Loriot in *Bulletin de la Société française de numismatique* 27 (1972) 249 f.; J. Lafaurie in *Bulletin de la Société nationale des Antiquaires de France* (1965) 139 ff. Decius' *adventus* into Rome was celebrated on the coinage; cf. H. Mattingly, E. A. Sydenham, and C. H. V. Sutherland, *Roman Imperial Coinage*, vol. 4.3 (London 1949) 111 f. (the legend *Adventus Augusti*).

110. See H. Mattingly and F. S. Salisbury in *Numismatic Chronicle* 4 (1924) 235 ff.; H. Mattingly in *Numismatic Chronicle* 9

(1949) 75 ff.; H. Mattingly *et al.*, *op. cit.* in n. 109, 117 f. and 130 ff.; K. J. J. Elks in *Numismatic Chronicle* 12 (1972) 111 ff., and *The Coinage of Trajan Decius* (Canterbury 1971); and the monograph of S. K. Eddy, *The Minting of Antoniniani A. D. 238–49 and the Smyrna Hoard* (New York 1967). The series may possibly date from late in the reign.

111. On Decius' *patria*, see R. Syme in *Historia* 22 (1973) 310 ff.

112. On the posthumous fame of Trajan, see R. Syme, *Emperors and Biography. Studies in the Historia Augusta* (Oxford 1971) 89 ff.; K. H. Waters in *Polis and Imperium. Studies in Honour of Edward Togo Salmon* (Toronto 1974) 233 ff.

113. Many examples are to be found in the pages of Livy. Unusually, the whole community was involved in such *supplicationes*, whereas in most Roman religious festivals a limited number (priests, magistrates, and attendants) normally participated. See Livy 3.7.7 f., 7.28.8, 22.10.8, 34.55.3 f., etc.

114. On the timing, see below.

115. E.g., see *H.A.* Aurelian 42.6: *Decios . . . quorum et vita et mors veteribus comparanda est;* cf. *H.A.* Valeriani duo 5.4 ff. (the story of Valerian and the censorship, on which see M. Besnier in *Mélanges Glotz* (Paris 1932) 485 ff.; L. Fronza in *Annali Triestini* 23 (1953) 315 ff. On the lacuna in our tradition of the *Historia Augusta*, see n. 1 above.

116. See Cassius Dio 52.36.1 f. (speech of Maecenas). Compare the saying of Tertullian, *Apol.* 24.9: *nec Romani habemur qui non Romanorum deum colimus* (and see R. MacMullen in JTS 26 [1975] 405 ff.).

117 See A. D. Nock in HTR 45 (1952) 219 n. 125. I. Baer, *Scripta hierosolymitana* 7 (1961) 118 ff. unconvincingly argues for the contrary view. Compare E. M. Smallwood, *The Jews under Roman Rule* (Leiden 1976) 540: "The persecutions of the Church in the third century left Judaism unscathed, though logically the Jews then came under the same condemnation as the Christians . . . silence here would seem to be strong evidence that even on this occasion [the persecution of Decius] their long-standing exemption from compulsory participation in pagan religious rites was respected." Note that in the martyrdom of Pionius

(see below n. 218 on the dating) Jews are regarded not as attacked but rather as among the attackers; cf. *Acta Pionii* 3.6, 4.2 ff. This may or may not preserve authentic tradition, but it indicates at least a memory in which Jews could not have been obviously molested in the same way as were Christians. On Jewish attitudes to Rome generally in the third century A.D., see also N. N. Glatzer in *Festgabe für Erich Vogelin zum 60 Geburtstag* (Munich 1962) 243 ff.

118. It is noticeable that the Decian *libelli* from Egypt required no specific renunciation of Christianity or abjuration of Christ, though prominent apostates might emphasize their new religious loyalties by such acts of blasphemy, e.g., the renegade bishops Basilides and Martialis. See *Ep.* 67.6.2; *Acta Pionii* 18.14. Observe that the imprisoned Christians in *Ep.* 5.2 have not been forbidden to hold their own religious rites.

119. See January 19 in *Lib. Pontif.* 21; January 20 in *Mart. Hiero.*, xiii Kal. Feb. (ML 30.440).

120. See *Epp.* 59.6.1 and 66.4.1, and n. 2 to *Ep.* 5.

121. Cf. Dionysius of Alexandria *ap.* Eusebius, *H.E.* 6.40.2. On Appius Sabinus, see PIR[2] A 1455; A. Stein, *Die Präfekten von Ägypten in der römischen Kaiserzeit* (Berne 1950) 140 ff.; O. W. Reinmuth in *Bulletin of American Society of Papyrologists* 4 (1967) 117; H.-G. Pflaum, *Les carrières procuratoriennes équestres sous le Haut-Empire romain* (4 vols., Paris 1960) 864 ff.

122. For the argument, see my article in *Antichthon* 3 (1969) 63 ff., and n. 5 to *Ep.* 22.

123. Cf. Eusebius, *H.E.* 6.39.1; also Jerome, *De viris illust.* 54; Orosius, 7.21.2; and for an assembly of other late evidence, J. M. York in *Historia* 21 (1972) 329 f. The Sibylline Oracle 13.87 f. may refer to this construing of events, a sudden wave of plundering and death suffered by the faithful "on account of the previous king" (= Philip?); that might serve to confirm Eusebius' testimony as a popularly held belief, but not necessarily as historical truth (against A. T. Olmstead in CP 37 [1942] 395).

124. Note, however, that the contemporary Dionysius of Alexandria describes the reign of Philip as having been "more kindly to us"—but that is from the view of hindsight, by way of contrast with Decius' principate. See Eusebius, *H.E.* 6.41.9.

125. Among modern discussions of Decius' motivations are A. Alföldi in *Klio* 31 (1938) 323 ff.; W. H. C. Frend, *Martyrdom and Persecution in the Early Church* (Oxford 1965) 389 ff.; J. Molthagen, *Die römische Staat und die Christen im zweiten und dritten Jahrhundert* (Göttingen 1970) 70 ff.

126. *Testimonia* are collected in E. Liesering, *Untersuchungen zur Christenverfolgung des Kaisers Decius* (diss. Würzburg 1933) 14 ff.; DACL 4 (1920) 2185 ff.; RAC 3 (1957) 624 ff.; and for the evidence for the formal status of Decius' orders ("edict"), see J. Modrzejewski in JJP 5 (1951) 202 n. 57.

127. See Pliny, *Ep.* 10.35, 100, for official ceremonies and A. N. Sherwin-White, *The Letters of Pliny. A Historical and Social Commentary* (Oxford 1966) 611 f.; M. Meslin, *La fête des Kalendes de janvier dans l'empire romain* (Brussels 1970) 30 f.; S. Weinstock, *Divus Julius* (Oxford 1971) 171 ff., 217 ff.; A. Alföldy in JAC 8/9 (1965) 54 ff.; H. Mattingly in *Proceedings of the British Academy* 36 (1950) 155 ff. and 37 (1951) 219 ff. For a list of inscriptions dated to January 3, see W. F. Snyder in *Yale Classical Studies* 7 (1940) 266. The evidence suggests public, civic ceremonies held in the town centre rather than exclusively military or official *vota*. Christians would be observably absent (cf. the charges reported earlier by Tertullian, *Apol.* 10.1: *pro imperatoribus sacrificia non penditis*, or later in *Acta Cyp.* 1.1: *eos qui Romanam religionem non colunt, debere Romanas caerimonias recognoscere*).

128. On these gods, see W. H. C. Frend, *op. cit.* in n. 57 above, 405 ff. Throughout the literature there is no sign that emperor-worship played any focal part in this persecution, though worship of the emperor's image could be introduced by way of testing a suspect's attitude. See, e.g., *Acta Pionii* 8.4. Also see A. Andreotti in *Studi in onore di Aristide Calderini e Roberto Paribeni*, vol 1 (Milan 1956) 369 ff.; A. D. Nock in HTR 45 (1952) 219; and, in general, F. Millar in *Le culte des souverains dans l'empire romain* (Geneva 1973) 145 ff.

129. *Ep.* 39.2.1.

130. On these, see commentary on *Ep.* 28.

131. *Ep.* 37.2.1.

132. So A. Bludau in *Römische Quartalschrift* 27 Supplemen-

theft (1931) 29; also L. Faulhaber in ZfKT 43 (1919) 449 f., n. 3.

133. So J. Moreau, *Lactance. De la mort des persécuteurs* (2 vols., Paris 1954) 2.214 f.

134. Lactantius, *De mort. persecut.* 4.2: *furere protinus contra deum coepit ut protinus caderet* cannot be pressed for data. At least the second *protinus* is clearly tendentious, Decius' reign lasting from c. October 249 to June 251. Decius was *divus* by June 24, 251 (CIL 6. 36760, cf. 31130, Rome), but not on the ninth of the same month (CIL 6. 31129, Rome).

135. For a list, see J. R. Knipfing in HTR 16 (1923) 358 nn. 86 f.; adding, for example, P. Roasenda in *Didaskaleion* 5 (1927) 34; L. de Regibus in *Didaskaleion* 3 (1925) 6; L. Fronza in *Annali Triestini* 23 (1953) 315 ff.; H. Grégoire et al., *Les persécutions dans l'empire romaine* (Brussels 1950) 43.

136. See, e.g., W. H. C. Frend, *op. cit.* in n. 57 above, 407.

137. For exceptions to this rule, see E. Condurachi in *Dacia* 2 (1958) 281 ff.; A. N. Sherwin-White, *The Roman Citizenship* (2nd ed., Oxford 1973) 380 ff.

138. Forty-one are edited and discussed by J. R. Knipfing in HTR 16 (1923) 345 ff. For subsequent corrections and improvements, see H. Grégoire et al., *op. cit.* in n. 135 above, 114; the further three *libelli* are published in PSI 778; J. Schwartz in *Revue biblique* 54 (1947) 365 ff.; Oxy. Pap. 2990.

139. Knipfing no. 35; see also J. G. Winter, *Life and Letters in the Papyri* (Ann Arbor 1933) 141 f.

140. See, e.g., Knipfing nos. 32, 33, 36. On the omission of the *gentilicium*, see J. F. Gilliam in *Historia* 14 (1965) 84 ff., and Z. Rubin in *Latomus* 34 (1975) 430 ff.

141. Knipfing 358.

142. See *Pap. Michigan* 3 (1936) 132 f.; H. C. Youtie in BICS Suppl. 6 (1958) 16 f.

143. On the exemption of Jews, see above. The only Christian soldiers who figure as victims are voluntary martyrs. See Eusebius, *H.E.* 6.41.22 ff. Religious adherence would be readily detected in barrack life; the authorities may have asked no questions. See A. D. Nock in HTR 45 (1952) 225; N. H. Baynes in CAH 12 (1934) 659 f. Christian soldiers were not expendable,

neither were they singled out in the subsequent rescript of Valerian, at the end of the decade.

144. *Ep*. 15.4.

145. *Ep*. 55.13.2. Knipfing no. 33 may illustrate such a sacrifice on behalf of a wife, two sons and a daughter. Compare *Oxy. Pap*. 31 (1966) no. 2601, a Christian letter where a litigant discovers that those who approach the legal court must offer sacrifice. He uses a "brother" as his proxy. Note other similar evasions in the Great Persecution; see Peter of Alexandria, *Ep. can*. 5–7 (MG 18.473 ff.). Christians might get pagans to impersonate them or send slaves, some of them Christians, in their stead.

146. See n. 33 to *Ep*. 15, tentatively adducing the *nutrix* of *De lapsis* 25. The later terms imposed by Maximinus Daia in 308 might, therefore, be parallel; see Eusebius, *Mart. Pal*. 9.2 (sacrifice, libation, and tasting of the holy victims enjoined on "the whole population, men, women, household servants and even babes in arms"); and there could be some reflection in the later fourth-century composition *Vita Abercii* I, on which see T. D. Barnes in JRS 58 (1968) 39. At any rate, babies were certainly included in Decius' orders; see, e.g., *De lapsis* 9: *infantes . . . parentum manibus inpositi*.

147. *Ep*. 19.2.1 (where see n. 10). Firmilian, writing in late 256, describes persecution in his local area of Cappadocia and Pontus "about 22 years" earlier under Maximinus Thrax thus: *persecutio illa non per totum mundum sed localis fuisset* (*Ep*. 75.10.2). That wording strongly suggests contrast with a more recent persecution which was in fact universal (*per totum mundum*), viz., that of Decius. Over in the East Firmilian had the same perception of the persecution as had Cyprian in the West. If this is a true inference, then we can also add incidentally Cappadocia to the areas in which we have evidence that the edict of Decius was applied.

148. The standard formula in the Egyptian *libelli* (see n. 138 above): the writings of Cyprian would have allowed us safely to deduce these actions as basic requirements.

149. *thurificati*, *Ep*. 55.2.1. Cyprian uses the term adroitly to draw some distinction between Trofimus and his flock (readmit-

ted to communion; see *Ep.* 55.11.1 ff.) and *sacrificati* generally (not readmitted to communion; see *Ep.* 55.12.1). For what it is worth, the pseudo-Cyprianic tractate, *De duplici martyrio,* employs the term *thurificatus* freely, e.g., in paragraph 26: *horres abominandum thurificati aut libellati cognomen* (but this *opusculum* may well be of Erasmian composition). And note the lengthy attack by Arnobius 7.26 ff. (= ACW 8.507 ff.) against the pagan use of incense.

150. So P. Keresztes in *Latomus* 34 (1975) 778.

151. See *Ep.* 21.3.2 (and n. 25 thereto).

152. See *Ep.* 15.3.1 (with n. 25) and *Ep.* 20.2.2 (with n. 16).

153. On this question, see my article, "Two Measures," in BICS 20 (1973) 118 ff.

154. See M. P. Charlesworth, *Trade-Routes and Commerce of the Roman Empire* (Cambridge 1924; repr. Hildesheim 1962) 23. In the winter of 40/41, bearers of threatening messages from Caligula in Rome sent to Petronius in Antioch were "detained three months at sea by tempestuous weather" (Josephus, *Bell. Jud.* 2.10.203). News of the accession of Pertinax in Rome (January 1, 193 A.D.) took 67 days of winter travel to reach Alexandria.

155. See the evidence set out by U. Wilcken, *Griechische Ostraka aus Aegypten und Nubien,* vol. 1 (Leipzig-Berlin 1899) 799 ff.; R. Rémondon in *Chronique d'Egypte* 26 (1951) 369 ff.

156. So Wessely in PO 4.2 (1906) 123, and P. Franchi de'Cavalieri in *Studi e Testi* 22 (1909) 83 f.

157. It took, for example, five and a half months for laws issued at Trier on November 3, 313, to reach African Hadrumetum. Diocletian's first edict against the Christians was published at Nicomedia on February 23, 303 (Lactantius, *De mort. persecut.* 12), but it was not promulgated at a town near Carthage until June 5; see R. P. Duncan-Jones in JTS 25 (1974) 106 ff. For other examples, see A. H. M. Jones, *The Later Roman Empire 284–602* (Oxford 1964) 1.403, 3.92 f.

158. In Alexandria itself rumour of the coming persecution had preceded the actual arrival of Decius' edict; see Dionysius of Alexandria *ap.* Eusebius, *H.E.* 6.41.10.

159. At least there appear to have been more than one altar set up in the Carthaginian forum supervised by these officials.

See *De lapsis* 8: *ipse ad aras . . . venisti.*

160. *Ep.* 43.3.1.

161. *Ep.* 56.1.1. The plural *magistratus* in *Ep.* 56.2.1 appears to be generalizing.

162. See my article, "Prosopographical Notes—I," in *Latomus* 30 (1971) 1141 ff.

163. *Ep.* 67.6.2.

164. *Acta Pionii* 3.1.

165. Knipfing in HTR 16 (1923) 350 ff.

166. The standard phraseology of the *libelli.*

167. See *Epp.* 11.1.2 (and n. 3 thereto), 13.1, 14.1.1.

168. It was certainly within the sphere of an emperor's *imperium* to shorten the court-lists by dropping the arrears or to exercise the imperial virtue of *clementia,* providing casual releases; see A. N. Sherwin-White, *Roman Society and Roman Law in the New Testament* (Oxford 1963) 118 f. Can we imagine a series of imperial *epistulae,* graciously commending *clementia,* despatched to the individual provinces and slowly being implemented as the orders filtered to the various localities? Such amnesties were a frequent feature of a new reign, and governors themselves might exercise their discretionary powers and have periodic gaol clearances. In any case, the end of the persecution was not hailed as sudden, unexpected, joyful news. Contrast, e.g., the clear and definite end to Maxentius' persecution as noted by Optatus 1.18: *tempestas persecutionis peracta et definita est. iubente deo indulgentiam mittente Maxentio christians libertas est restituta.*

169. See *De lapsis* 8, 25.

170. See Dionysius of Alexandria *ap.* Eusebius, *H.E.* 6.41.11.

171. See n. 20 to *Ep.* 8.

172. See *De lapsis* 8: *quid hostiam tecum, miser, quid victimam supplicaturus inponis?* On *thurificati,* see n. 149 above. See further the sacrificial scene in Rome, in *Ep.* 21.3.2.

173. Two identical *libelli* have survived for one Aurelia Charis (Knipfing nos. 11, 26). Were the officials to retain one copy for the municipal archives? For an application in duplicate, with both copies officially signed, see Oxy. Pap. 38 no. 2855. There are possible traces on one *libellus* of archive numbering. But the

condition of the extant *libelli* generally suggests that they were thrown out before being numbered and glued together for the municipal files; certainly the finds at Theadelphia, in number and at the same spot, suggest that we are dealing with official copies. See J. Schwartz in *Revue biblique* 54 (1947) 368. They were promptly rendered redundant by the end to the persecution, and discarded. On the archive and filing systems in Egypt, see, among others, O. W. Reinmuth in *Klio* 34 (1935) 42 ff.

174. For the use of scribes in preparing documents, see R. Calderini in *Aegyptus* 30 (1950) 14 ff.; E. G. Turner, *Greek Papyri: An Introduction* (Oxford 1968) 82 f.; H. C. Youtie in HSCP 75 (1971) 161 ff.

175. Perhaps the significance of *publice legitur* in *Ep.* 30.3.1. For discussion, see L. Faulhaber in ZfKT 43 (1919) 636.

176. Note the turn of phrase in *Ep.* 30.3.1 (*qui accepta fecissent*), on which see H. von Soden in TU 23 (1909) 269 f., n. 3; A. Beck, *Römisches Recht bei Tertullian und Cyprian* (Halle 1930) 141 ff.; and compare *Ep.* 55.14.1: *cui libellus acceptus est.*

177. Tertullian may be envisaging some such legal scene in *Adv. Marcionem* 5.1.3: *plane profiteri potest semetipsum quis, verum professio eius alterius auctoritate conficitur. Alius scribit, alius subscribit, alius obsignat, alius actis refert. Nemo sibi et professor et testis est.*

178. See, e.g., P. A. Brunt in *Historia* 10 (1961) 222 f.; R. MacMullen, *Roman Social Relations 50 B.C. to A.D. 284* (New Haven-London 1974) 113 f., 197 f., nn. 77–79.

179. See A. H. M. Jones in JRS 39 (1949) 51.

180. The case for the *libellatici* is put by Cyprian in *Ep.* 55.14. Christians were used to bribing their way into prisons; see, e.g., *Acts of Paul and Thecla* 18. Bribery is not condemned as a means of evasion in the Great Persecution by Peter of Alexandria, *Ep. can.* 12.

181. See *De fuga* 5.3, 12–14.

182. Cf. n. 180 above; and for the deputies, see *Epp.* 30.3.1 and 55.14.1.

183. For discussion on the attitude in the Eastern churches, see G. E. M. de Ste Croix in HTR 47 (1954) 87 f., and in *Past and Present* 26 (November 1963) 17; also my article, "Some Observa-

tions," in *Antichthon* 3 (1969) 74 ff.

There is, however, one hint in Dionysius of Alexandria which could suggest that he recognized two grades of apostates, one of which had not entirely lost the Holy Spirit: ". . . he [Novatian] entirely banishes the Holy Spirit from them, even though there was some hope of His remaining or even of returning to them" (*apud* Eusebius, *H.E.* 7.8). Are those with whom the Holy Spirit may remain to be identified as *libellatici?* Compare Eusebius, *H.E.* 6.46.1, where we are told Dionysius wrote to the Egyptians a work On Repentance in which he discerned degrees of failure among the fallen.

184. So, firmly, Cyprian, *De lapsis* 27 f.

185. E.g., W. H. C. Frend, *op. cit.* in n. 57 above, 408: "Census and tax rolls provided by local officials in each district controlled the number and identity of those who presented themselves to sacrifice."

186. But note the ideal in Ulpian, *Dig.* 50.15.4.4 (*de censibus*): *in servis deferendis observandum est ut et nationes eorum et aetates et officia et artificia specialiter deferantur.*

187. See, e.g., Ulpian, *Dig.* 50.15.3. See further A. H. M. Jones in JRS 43 (1953) 50 f., and in *The Roman Economy. Studies in Ancient Economic and Administrative History* (Oxford 1974) 164 ff.; R. P. Duncan-Jones in JRS 53 (1963) 87, and in *Historia* 13 (1964) 201 f.; F. F. Abbott and A. C. Johnson, *Municipal Administration in the Roman Empire* (Princeton 1926) 117 ff.; etc. The Egyptian poll tax (imposed upon non-citizens) seems to have disappeared by this date; see H. I. Bell in JRS 37 (1947) 17 ff.; G. E. M. de Ste Croix in HTR 47 (1954) 112 f.; S. L. Wallace, *Taxation in Egypt* (Princeton 1938) 133 f.

188. In Egypt, at any rate, it is unlikely that non-privileged classes would have registered new children since the last census taken in 244 A.D. (cf. Wallace, *op. cit.* in n. 187 above, 105) and children were included in Decius' orders. On the registration of births, see F. Schulz in JRS 32 (1942) 69 ff. and in JRS 33 (1943) 55 ff.; O. Montevecchi in *Aegyptus* 27 (1947) 3 ff.; J. A. Crook, *Law and Life of Rome* (London 1967) 46 ff.

189. In Palestine during the Great Persecution, it is clear that no accurate rolls of all citizens were available and special regis-

ters had to be drawn up. See Eusebius, *Mart. Pal.* 4.8; G. E. M. de Ste Croix in HTR 47 (1954) 98 f.

190. Knipfing nos. 5, 10, 18, 20, 21, 28, 35.

191. *Apud* Eusebius, *H.E.* 6.41.11.

192. For similar crowds at Carthage, see *De lapsis* 8: *Quot illic (i.e., forum) a magistratibus vespera urgente dilati sunt,* and 25: *aput idolum quo populus confluebat.*

193. Cf. G. E. M. de Ste Croix in HTR 47 (1954) 54, 97.

194. Cyprian can assume a mass scattering of the flock before the coming persecution of Gallus; in the time of the Diocletianic persecution Christians even fled to the harbouring safety of barbarian captivity outside the Empire; see N. H. Baynes, *Constantine the Great and the Christian Church* (London 1934; repr. 1972) 28 f. On attitudes to *fuga* in time of persecution, see n. 4 to *Ep.* 8.

195. See *Ep.* 30.8.1 (Novatian); cf. *Ep.* 8.2.2 (and n. 18). Compare the crowds in Alexandria; they were a favourite resort for those seeking to escape the rigours of governmental liturgies in the country, and hence there were periodic commands for ξένοι to return εἰς γῆν ἰδίαν. See O. W. Reinmuth in *Klio* 34 (1935) 69 ff.

196. *Ep.* 21.4.1. On Christian Africans in Rome, see further G. Bardy in *Irénikon* 14 (1937) 113 ff.

197. *Ep.* 7.2 (*peregrini*), where see n. 10.

198. *Ep.* 55.13.2.

199. Gregory Nyssa, MG 46.945; flight was general among his flock.

200. Dionysius of Alexandria *ap.* Eusebius, *H.E.* 6.42.2 ff. The outline of the story of Paul, the first anchorite, has the ring of the persecution of Decius. To escape from danger he retired first to a remote village. But when his brother-in-law sought to betray him to the authorities (to obtain the reversion of his considerable estate), he fled *ad montium deserta.* There he lived for the remainder of his life. Jerome dates this, unhelpfully, *sub Decio et Valeriano persecutoribus* (ML 23.19).

201. See G. E. M. de Ste Croix in HTR 47 (1954) 96 f. on the *stantes;* note the evidence for *stantes* in Numidia in the Valerianic *Acta Mariani et Iacobi* 2.5—there are attacked now Chris-

tians *qui superioribus persecutionibus inconcussi libere deo viverent.*

202. *Ep.* 8.1.1 (with nn. 4 and 5).

203. Cf., e.g., *Epp.* 5.2.1, 13.4.2, 14.2.1.

204. Cf. *Ep.* 80.1.2 ("Second Rescript").

205. Unless they broke the regulations against holding assemblies or visiting the cemeteries ("First Rescript"). See my article, "Prosopographical Notes—III," in *Latomus* 34 (1975) 437 ff.

206. Observe the treatment of Pionius and his companions; see *Acta Pionii* 15 ff.

207. Polemon and Theophilus, backed by soldiers and an angry crowd, attempted to usurp the proconsul's prerogatives in Smyrna (see *Acta Pionii* 15); note the death of Ischyrion at the hands of the outraged Egyptian official (see Dionysius of Alexandria *ap.* Eusebius, *H.E.* 6.42.1); and observe in *Ep.* 40.1.1 what appears to be the mob lynching of companions of Numidicus.

208. Although Cyprian at least speaks as if the death penalty has not been primarily envisaged; see, e.g., *De lapsis* 2: *non praescripta exsilia, non destinata tormenta, non rei familiaris et corporis supplicia terruerunt,* and 10: *relinquenda erat patria et patrimonii facienda iactura.* See n. 5 to *Ep.* 10 for a collection of examples of exile and confiscation; a general discussion of this form of punishment is in P. Garnsey, *Social Status and Legal Privilege in the Roman Empire* (Oxford 1970) 116 f. Known deaths are listed below. On the legal arrangements, see my article, "Double-Trials," in *Historia* 22 (1973) 650 ff.

209. Thus the cases of Celerinus (discussed in my article, "Some Observations," in *Antichthon* 3 [1969] 63 ff.), Optatus (*Ep.* 29.1.1), Dioscorus (Dionysius of Alexandria *ap.* Eusebius, *H.E.* 6.41.15 f.), Aurelius (*Ep.* 38.1.2), Saturninus (*Ep.* 21.4.2), Caldonius (nn. 1 and 5 to *Ep.* 24), etc. On the *arbitrium iudicantis,* note Dig. 29.5.1.32 (Ulpian), 29.5.14 (Maecianus), 48.13.7(6) pr. (Ulpian), 48.19.16.3 (Claudius Saturninus), 50.17.108 (Paulus), especially in cases such as some of these in which youthful culprits were involved; on the topic in general, see F. M. de Robertis in ZSS 59 (1939) 219 ff.

210. Evidence is collected under n. 8 to *Ep.* 5, n. 5 to *Ep.* 10, and n. 19 to *Ep.* 12.

211. See, e.g., *Ep.* 22.2.2.

212. Compare Ulpian, *Dig.* 48.13.7(6) pr.: *sacrilegii poenam debebit proconsul pro qualitate personae, proque rei conditione et temporis et aetatis et sexus vel severius vel clementius statuere,* and 48.19.13: . . . *quam vult sententiam ferre, vel graviorem vel leviorem, ita tamen ut in utroque modo rationem non excedat.* See further P. Garnsey in *Past and Present* 41 (1968) 11 ff.

213. Discussion is confined to secure evidence. For the accounts of more or less legendary Decian martyrs, see, for example, B. Aubé, *L'église et l'état dans la seconde moitié du IIIe siècle (249–284)* (Paris 1886) 154 ff.; on Acacius, see further H. Delehaye, *Les passions des martyrs et les genres littéraires* (Brussels 1921) 344 ff.; on Carpus, Papylus, and Agathonice, see H. Delehaye, *op. cit.*, 413 ff., and AB 58 (1940) 142 ff.; on the *Acta Tryphonis*, P. Franchi de'Cavalieri in *Studi e Testi* 19 (1908) 29 ff.

214. See Eusebius, *H.E.* 6.39.5 ff. We do not know for certain that they were "martyred in the very beginning of the persecution," as H. F. von Campenhausen states in *The Fathers of the Latin Church* (London 1964; repr. 1972) 41. For example, Babylas' anniversary has a confused tradition—January 24 was the usual date (though September 4 also occurs): see AASS Nov. 2.2 (1931) 59 f.; P. Peeters in AB 48 (1930) 302 ff. The year could well be 251 (the date of his successor Fabius being uncertain); see A. von Harnack, *Geschichte der altchristlichen Literatur bis Eusebius* 2.1 (Leipzig 1897) 215; H. Delehaye, *Les origines du culte des martyrs* (2nd ed., Brussels 1933) 225 ff.; G. Bardy, *Paul de Samosate. Étude historique* (2nd ed., Louvain 1929) 139 n. 5. In other words, on this evidence (such as it is), Babylas might well have languished up to a year in prison before attaining his crown. The data on Alexander are presented in DACL 9 (1930) 1239. He was tried at Caesarea. See Eusebius, *H.E.* 6.39.2.

215. The variant material on Origen's sufferings and death is collected and discussed by H. Delehaye in AB 40 (1922) 10. F. S. Salisbury and H. Mattingly in JRS 14 (1924) 11, 21, by a slip assign the martyrdom of Procopius, the reader of Palestinian Caesarea, to this persecution (see Eusebius, *Mart. Pal.* proem and 1, for the Diocletianic date and details).

216. The contents of Origen's letters from prison are sugges-

tive of fellow sufferers—after his tortures he left behind "sayings full of help for those who needed uplifting" (Eusebius, *H.E.* 6.39.5).

217. Possibly suggested by the phraseology of *Acta Pionii* 2.3: ἐν τῳ οἴκῳ.

218. *Acta Pionii* 2.1. Another Limnos and a Macedonian woman turn up, already in prison, in *Acta Pionii* 11.2. Some conflation and confusion is to be suspected. On the dating of the *Acta* to the period of Decius, see T. D. Barnes in JTS 19 (1968) 529 ff.; to the contrary, see H. Grégoire, P. Orgels, and J. Moreau in *Bulletin de la classe des lettres de l'Académie Royale de Belgique* 47 (1961) 72 ff.

219. *Acta Pionii* 15 ff.

220. *Acta Pionii* 7.6.

221. *Acta Pionii* 19.10 ff.

222. MG 46.944 ff.

223. MG 46.949. In his mountainous retreat Gregory Thaumaturgus had a vision of the young man's trials as they took place—just as Irenaeus in Rome knew of Polycarp's martyrdom as it took place in Smyrna (Moscow MS end to *Mart. Polyc.* 22.4) or as Apollonius of Tyana in Ephesus knew by telepathic magic of Domitian's murder as it took place in Rome (Cassius Dio 67.18.1; Philostratus, *Vita Apoll.* 8.26 f.). On this very common motif of important events being made known by clairvoyance at the time of their occurrence at points far distant, see Pease's commentary on Cicero, *De natura deorum* 2.6 (*illo die*) for a rich collection of examples.

224. See Eusebius, *H.E.* 6.40.1 ff., 7.11.20 ff. Eusebius mistakenly attributes this second extract to the persecution of Valerian; see H. Delehaye in AB 40 (1922) 11.

225. For an analysis, see H. Delehaye in AB 40 (1922) 10 ff.; A. Rousselle in *Revue historique de droit français et étranger* 52 (1974) 237 ff. (though his thesis is probable, that the varieties of punishment correspond to different social categories of Egyptians, the evidence does not supply the control over the sample that is required for proof). The anniversary dates of the victims appear to range between February 27 (Julian and Eunus [Cronion]) and

December 22 (Ischyrion). That could mean that the persecution continued actively here at least right up to the end of 250, if any reliance is to be placed on such data.

226. *H.E.* 6.42.1.

227. Just six years later (February 28, 256) it was felt natural by a local official to identify a certain Petosorapis in Mermertha as "Petosorapis, son of Horus, the Christian." In these communities adherence to Christianity was clearly a socially distinguishing feature in a way that adherence to most other cults was not; it marked a man out and the local people could be expected to know who were the Christians in their township. See *Oxy. Pap.* 3035 (11.3–5).

228. For Spain, see *Ep.* 67 (two renegade bishops, *libellatici*); for Gaul, see *Ep.* 68 (*lapsi*, manifestly a problem there).

229. For Sicily, see *Ep.* 30.6.2 (Novatian). Communication is received from Rome dealing with questions raised by the lapsed.

230. Chronicle 395, MGH 9.738 ed. Mommsen: *hac persecutione Cyprianus hortatus est per epistolas suas Augustinum et Felicitatem, qui passi sunt apud civitatem Capuensem, metropolim Campaniae.* See also H. Delehaye, *Les origines du culte des martyrs* (2nd ed., Brussels 1933) 303 f., and note *Mart. Hiero.* for *xv Kal. Decemb.*, which reads: *In Capua civitate, natalis sanctorum Augustini, Eusurii, Felicitatis* (ML 30.482). It makes sense to see Felix of Nola as initially a Decian confessor (his bishop Maximus having gone into hiding). See Paulinus of Nola, *Carm.* 15.114 ff. After a period of restored peace, Felix underwent further (? Valerianic) trials (*Carm.* 16.52 ff.); his property was confiscated, but later might be recovered. Certainty is not, of course, possible. For discussion, see P. G. Walsh in ACW 40.10; D. Gorce in DHGE 16 (1967) 906 f.

231. On the date, see n. 119 above.

232. We have lost the *testimonium* which was composed by the Roman clergy shortly after his death. C. Saumagne, *Saint Cyprien. Évêque de Carthage. "Pape" d'Afrique (248–258)* (Paris 1975) 91, describes Fabian as "mort en exil"; we do not know that.

233. See *Ep.* 28.1.1 f.; and on the dating, see introductory note to *Ep.* 27.

234. *Lib. Pontif.* ed. Mommsen 27; cf. Eusebius, *H.E.* 6.43.20 and *Ep.* 55.5.2.

235. They have clearly been at large some time before *Ep.* 49 (? summer 251); cf. *Ep.* 54.2.2: *posteaquam vos de carcere prodeuntes schismaticus et haereticus error excepit.*

236. See *Ep.* 40.1.1 (Numidicus and company).

237. See Cyprian, *De lapsis* 13: *hic Casto et Aemilio aliquando Dominus ignovit.* Cyprian's language and the context make a Decian date most probable (but for the contrary view, see C. Lambot in AB 67 [1949] 259; P. Keresztes in *Historia* 19 [1970] 576; B. de Gaiffier, *Études critiques d'hagiographie et d'iconologie* [Brussels 1967] 378); they died under torture (by fire). Their *natalis* was May 22—note Augustine, *Sermo* 285 on their anniversary, and see further my article in *Historia* 22 (1973) 656 f. Our reliance on this casual reference in Cyprian leaves us seriously in doubts about the likelihood of our having any commanding view of even the well-documented Carthaginian scene.

238. The fullest, but not always the most satisfactory, study on this question is X. S. Thaninayagam, *The Carthaginian Clergy during the Episcopate of Saint Cyprian* (Colombo 1947).

239. The duties and functions of deacons and subdeacons are discussed, with bibliography, in n. 17 to *Ep.* 3, and n. 1 to *Ep.* 8.

240. On these clerical offices, see n. 13 to *Ep.* 7 and n. 6 to *Ep.* 23. Remarks on the grade of *fossor* are to be found in n. 29 to *Ep.* 8 and n. 13 to *Ep.* 12.

241. For discussion, see n. 13 to *Ep.* 12.

242. A thirteenth possibility ought perhaps to be recorded. In the Valerianic *Acta Montani* 23.4 the martyr Flavianus urges with his dying words his last will and testament: *Lucianum presbyterum commendatione plenissima prosecutus, quantum in illo fuit, sacerdotio destinavit.* Some have seen the reoccurrence of this presbyter Lucianus in a remark of Optatus of Milevis, *De schis. Donat.* 1.19: *erat altare loco suo in quo pacifici episcopi retro temporis obtulerant, Cyprianus, (Carpophorius), Lucianus et ceteri.* The conclusion has been drawn that the *Lucianus presbyter* destined so prophetically for a bishopric in 259 and the Lucianus bishop of Carthage sometime after Cyprian are to be identified.

Lucianus, it is concluded, would therefore have figured among the Carthaginian presbyters under Cyprian (and be, in fact, Cyprian's immediate successor as bishop of Carthage). Obviously there are many vulnerable assumptions in this line of argumentation, not least the uncertain text of Optatus and the location of the diocese of the presbyter Lucianus of *Acta Montani* 23.4, and indeed of the other clergy mentioned there. They appear to have been arrested out of Carthage; see *Acta Montani* 3.

243. The three are named at the beginning of *Ep.* 43: *Virtius fidelissimus atque integerrimus presbyter, item Rogatianus et Numidicus presbyteri confessores et gloria divinae dignationis inlustres.*

244. On Sergius, see n. 1 to *Ep.* 6.

245. Cyprian implies (what we would expect) that the Church in Rome took precedence in size over the church in Carthage. See *Ep.* 52.2.3: *plane quoniam pro magnitudine sua debeat Carthaginem Roma praecedere, illic maiora et graviora commisit. qui istic adversus ecclesiam diaconum fecerat, illic episopum fecit* (of Novatus).

In this section my attention has been focussed on the clergy that appear to be ministering in Carthage itself; it is possible, however, that Cyprian served as bishop over an area wider than the actual city. For the likelihood of some local churches outside Carthage, see nn. to *Ep.* 34.1.

246. For the 90 bishops, see *Ep.* 59.10.1. On the attendance at Councils, see n. 3 to *Ep.* 1. It will be noted that in Rome the synod convened by Cornelius against Novatianism (251) consisted of sixty bishops "and a still greater number of presbyters and deacons" (Eusebius, *H.E.* 6.43.2). Might we not assume for Africa a corresponding proportion of attending clergy?

247. I give, with no overwhelming conviction, the so-called "Alexandrian" computation which, it was claimed, had coincided with the Roman Paschal calculation before Nicaea confirmed that custom. See Hefele-Leclercq 1.1.450 ff.; cf. 1.1.133 ff. It is a (totally unconfirmed) assumption that such unity in calculation goes as far back as 248 for the Western Church. It is worth noting at any rate that the Council of Arles, canon 1, suggests that considerable uniformity had been claimed as customary for

the date of Easter in the West: *de observatione Paschae Domini, ut uno die et uno tempore per omnem orbem a nobis observetur et iuxta consuetudinem litteras ad omnes tu* [Pope Silvester] *dirigas.* See Hefele-Leclercq 1.1.280 f. And at all events, whatever the basis for calculation, Firmilian does not suggest that he has any awareness of the slightest difference between Carthage and Rome over the date as currently calculated for the Easter observance (see *Ep.* 75.6.1), a difference he would have surely exploited with alacrity.

Should by any chance the Hippolytan calculation have been in fact in vogue over this period, it would have resulted in the following minor variations:

Year	Easter Sunday
250	March 31
253	March 27
254	April 16
256	March 23
257	April 12
258	April 4

The adjustments suggested by the author of the tractate *De pascha computus* (A.D. 243) would have resulted in two variations from the "Alexandrian" dates over our period (in 254, March 19; in 258, April 4).

On the computation of Easter dates, note DACL 13 (1938) 1521 ff. Further details and bibliography on this large question will be found in the commentary on *Ep.* 75.6.1.

LETTER 1

Contents: Cyprian, in Carthage, has clearly been approached by the Christian community at Furnos about the case of one of their brethren, Geminius Victor. Victor, now deceased, had nominated in his will a presbyter to be guardian of his dependants and that was against established Church discipline for this area. Cyprian, in characteristic fashion, upholds the current Church regulations and advises the imposition of the sanctions, as previously laid down, on the memory of Geminius Victor: the community is not to pray for his repose (*pro dormitione eius*), in order to ensure the observance of this rule in the future.

Date and circumstances: Indications for the date are scanty. The grounds advanced for placing this letter firmly in the pre-Decian period are spurious (against, for example, the frequently accepted argument of Pearson's: such a lax attitude towards Church discipline at Furnos would not have been countenanced after the Decian debacle). This unsound dating is still generally accepted; see R. Gryson in *Revue d'histoire ecclésiastique* 68 (1973) 361.

Cyprian, as effectively "primate" of the North African churches (see C. H. Turner, *Studies in early Church History* [Oxford 1912] 71 ff.) and as "metropolitan" of the proconsular dioceses, was the natural person to consult on the execution of a North African synodal regulation, whether he was newly appointed to his Carthaginian *cathedra* or not. Cyprian might decide to reserve the question so raised for a subsequent synodal gathering (e.g. *Ep.* 56.3), but on this occasion he is in no doubt about the course of action to be pursued.

A distinction needs to be drawn here between full African Council meetings and more local synodal (proconsular) gatherings. We have no real way of telling whether we are here dealing with merely an informal *ad hoc* Carthaginian meeting (cf. *Ep.* 4) or a proconsular episcopal gathering at Carthage (see n. 8 below), though the former sounds the more likely.

The terms of address heading the letter should imply that Furnos is without a bishop. The year 256 ought, therefore, to be ruled out; Furnos had a bishop by September of that year (*Sententiae Episcoporum* 59: *Geminius a Furnis*). And, of course, the period cannot be that of Cyprian's exile (early 250-March 251); Cyprian is free to consult his *conpresbyteri* of Carthage in *consessu* (1.1). There is perhaps one suggestion that might push the letter back a few years before 256. The bishop of Furnos produced in 256 his *sententia* as fifty-ninth (out of a list of 85) and these *sententiae* appear to be given in order of the seniority of the bishops present, with some marginal derangements. It was the long-established Roman custom to hear *sententiae* in debate, as in the Senate, and to record officers, as the patrons and decurions on the *alba* of town councils, in descending order of seniority. Hence, we might speculate, Furnos ought to have had its bishop some little time before 256 so that he can rank as fifty-ninth in order of precedence at that gathering. That is as far as one can go, and it is not very far.

In *Ep.* 67 Geminius votes thirty-second in a list of thirty-seven bishops. The date of the letter is quite uncertain; it could not properly be used in the argument here.

1. *presbyteris et diaconibus et plebi Furnis consistentibus.* Furnos is to be located at no great distance from Carthage, either at 40 km. WSW of Carthage (Furnos Minus = Henchir el Msâadine) or, more probably, at 105 km. SW of Carthage (Furnos Maius = Henchir Aïn Fourna). See PWK 7.1 (1910) 375; J. Schmidt CIL 8 *supp.* 1241, 1435; E. W. Benson, *Cyprian, his life, his times, his work* (London 1897) 580; J. Gascou, *La politique municipale de l'empire romain en Afrique proconsulaire, de Trajan à Septime-Sévère* (Rome 1972) 201; J. Mesnage, *L'Afrique chrétienne* (Paris 1912) 122. Bishops of Furnos are listed in J.-L. Maier, *L'épiscopat de l'afrique romaine, vandale et byzantine* (Neuchâtel 1973) 143 f.

Note the semi-technical usages in the introduction. (i) *plebs* = laity (for which *fraternitas, populus* are possible variants). This usage occurs already in *Clemens Latinus,* perhaps to be placed among the earliest pieces of ecclesiastical Latin surviving, e.g., 54.5 (*plebs*), 40.5 (*plebeius homo*). Cf. E. Lanne in *Verbum Caro* 18 (1964) 109 f. (ii) *consistens.* This may be taken in the Christian sense of "sojourning" (παροικῶν), but it may merely be a variant for "constitutus" (favoured by Cyprian), acting as a present participle of *esse*—See for further discussion E. W. Watson in *Studia Biblica* 4 (1896) 311; L. Bayard, *Le latin de saint Cyprien* (Paris 1902) 100 f.; A. A. R. Bastiaensen, *Le cérémonial épistolaire des chrétiens latins* (Nijmegen 1964) 154; C. Mohrmann in VC 3 (1949) 102; A. Audin *et al.* in REA 56 (1954) 331 ff.

2. *collegae mei qui praesentes aderant.* By clear Cyprianic usage

these *collegae* must be bishops (for whom Cyprian reserves almost exclusively the term *collegae;* see n. 2 to *Ep.* 9. These colleagues would be *peregrini,* visiting prelates (local, or even possibly overseas); compare the language in *Ep.* 32.1.2: *si qui de peregrinis episcopi collegae mei . . . praesentes fuerint.* To use them for consultation and advice, as occasion arose, was standard Cyprianic procedure; see *Epp.* 3.1.1, 4 *init.*, 38.2.2, etc. and note the select committee of nine colleagues in *Ep.* 59.10.2 and the presence of visiting bishops at Carthage in *Ep.* 62.4. Similarly for Cyprian's contemporary, Cornelius, in Rome—he brought in five outside bishops to join the assembled *presbyterium* to witness the reconciliation of the formerly pro-Novatian *confessores;* see *Ep.* 49.2.1. The Roman presbyterate during its *interregnum* brought in for consultation as a matter of course both local bishops and overseas bishops who were refugees in Rome at the time; see *Ep.* 30.8. *Ep.* 49.2.1 reveals that the working rules of such local councils were the same as for full synods.

3. *conpresbyteri nostri qui nobis adsidebant:* Cyprian confines the word *conpresbyter* to presbyters only. Note the verb *adsidebant.* The bishop and his presbyters characteristically sat together (see *Epp.* 39.5.2, 40.1.2, 45.2, 59.19.1), whereas the *plebs* and minor clergy remained standing, in deference. Compare *Gesta apud Zenophilum,* CSEL 26.186 f.: *sedente Paulo episcopo, Montano et Victore Deusatelio et Memorio presbyteris, adstante Marte cum Helio diaconis . . . subdiaconis . . . fossoribus. . . .* At major African synods, though presbyters continued to assist they did not cast votes (Hefele-Leclercq 1.1.27 f.); even here their role is clearly secondary to that of the outside *collegae.* The language of *Ep.* 32.1.2 (*si qui de peregrinis episcopi collegae mei vel presbyteri vel diacones praesentes fuerint*) raises the possibility that the Carthaginian *presbyterium* might be joined on these occasions by visiting *presbyteri* as well as bishops (cf. at a full synodal meeting: *episcopi plurimi ex provincia Africa Numidia Mauretania cum presbyteris et diaconibus* [*Sententiae Episcoporum praef.*]; [*episcoporum*] *numerus cum presbyteris et diaconis* [Ep. 59.15.1]; *in concilio plurimi episcopi cum presbyteris qui aderant* [*Ep.* 71.1.1 referring to *Ep.* 70, a gathering of proconsular clerics]). Note also that Firmilian, in *Ep.* 75.4.3, describes their annual synods as meetings of *seniores et*

praepositi, that is to say, of *presbyteri et episcopi*. *Ep.* 45.2.1 f. shows that at Carthage the *plebs* could be present as well. So, too, Heraclides, being interrogated by Origen, appears before "the whole church" (1), before bishops, presbyters, and laity (4); see SC 67.54, 62. Likewise, Cornelius is careful to solicit the *voluntas* of his *populus* before the return of the once pro-Novatian confessors; see *Ep.* 49.2.3.

The process of consultation is noteworthy, but quite typical of the Roman administrative mind. Such *ad hoc* councils were a feature of Roman familial as well as of public life; and many, with time, acquired quasi-legal status and great *de facto* power (e.g., a judge's *consilium*, the emperor's *consilium*).

4. Was Victor a cleric or not? Cyprian's language leaves this unclear. The ecclesiastical canon crisply stated (§2.1): *ne quis frater excedens . . .* , and Cyprian, by his language here, is rhetorically demonstrating the applicability of the canon in the case of Geminius Victor. It would, however, make very good sense (but this is surmise only) were Victor the recently deceased bishop of Furnos; his leaderless flock is facing an important issue—are they to pray, as was clearly customary, for the repose of their former *praepositus?* They turn to Carthage for guidance. (For bishops addressed simply as 'frater,' cf. *Epp.* 2 *init.*, 3 *init.*, etc.).

Note the double name Geminius Victor; this is rare in Cyprian, but is here used, doubtlessly, to distinguish the two Geminii involved in the case. (For another exception, note the *titulus* of *Ep.* 66, where, again, special reasons apply.) *Geminius Victor* is a combination of names not uncommon in Africa; examples are to be found in CIL 8.9142, 2482, 24772. See V. Saxer in *Riv. di arch. crist.* 44 (1968) 214 f.

5. *de saeculo excedens.* Note the clearly Christian overtones acquired by *saeculum*. On the word consult A. P. Orbán, *Les dénominations du monde chez les premiers auteurs chrétiens* (Nijmegen 1970) 187 ff.

6. *Geminium Faustinum presbyterum tutorem testamento suo nominaverit.* Does one guess (from the nomenclature) that Geminius Faustinus was a relative of Geminius Victor? That sounds probable enough, in the context. It would also not surpass credence (and it would diminish coincidence) if this Ge-

minius Faustinus, presbyter, was subsequently consecrated the *Geminius (episcopus) a Furnis* of *Sententiae Episcoporum* 59—if this letter happens to be dated before 256.

By Roman law it was extremely difficult for a person nominated by will as guardian to be exempted from the duties of that office. Clearly the office would involve the *tutor* in a great deal of secular *molestiae*, for in the developed law a *tutor* was concerned specifically with the management of the patrimony bequeathed to the dependants of the deceased. For further details on the rights and duties of guardians, see *Digesta* 26 and 27; *Codex Justinianeus* 5.28 ff.; H. F. Jolowicz, in JRS 37 (1947) 82 ff.; J. A. Crook, *Law and Life of Rome* (London 1967) 113 ff.; M. Lauria, 'Periculum tutoris,' in *Studi in onore di Salvatore Riccobono* (Palermo 1936; repr. Darmstadt 1974) 3.285 ff.

Tutor suggests that Geminius Victor was married (though he may have had dependent agnate relatives over whom he possessed familial rights); were he bishop this could provide a (by no means unusual) example of a non-celibate ecclesiastical minister: other contemporary examples are to be found in *Epp.* 40 (Numidicus), 52.2.5 (Novatus), 67.6.3 (Martialis); Pontius, *Vita Cypriani* 4 (Caecilianus); *Passio Mariani et Iacobi* 3.1 (Secundinus), etc.; and see in general DACL 2 (1925) 2802 ff.; R. Gryson, *Les origines du célibat ecclésiastique* (Gembloux 1970), esp. 32 ff.

Is the dying Carthaginian presbyter Caecilianus formally nominating (in a Christ-like gesture) the neophyte Cyprian as guardian, in Pontius, *Vita Cypriani* 4: *de saeculo excedens accersitione iam proxima commendaret illi coniugem ac liberos suos?* If so, what happened when Cyprian was advanced to clerical office? (Benson 18 f., not very convincingly, claims Cyprian was already a deacon by this stage.)

To so nominate a person as guardian could be interpreted as a gesture of the highest esteem and deepest trust. Compare Porphyry, *Vita Plotini* 9: "Many men and women of the noblest rank, being about to die, brought to him their children, both boys and girls, and entrusted them to him along with all their property, considering that he would be a holy and god-like guardian." Porphyry goes on to describe the business cares, account-keeping, and estate management involved in this task, distractions anticipated by the African bishops.

7. *iam pridem.* It is extremely difficult to divine quite what order of time may be implied by this turn of phrase. In *Ep.* 67.6.3, for example, it is used to refer to no more than 5 years previously, whilst in *Epp.* 11.3.2 and 13.1 it cannot be used to refer to an interval of more than a few months' duration. It is worth observing that it is glossed in §2.2 by *nuper*, a word again of somewhat elastic temporal connotations (see n. 27 below and n. 35 to *Ep.* 13). The impression given is that Cyprian uses *iam pridem* here with the overtone that this regulation was a well-established one (and ought not, therefore, to have been over-looked), whereas in §2.2 he uses *nuper* with the overtone that this regulation was enacted not so very long ago (and ought not, therefore, to have been forgotten). This would be consonant with Cyprian's instinctive rhetorical manner.

The *nuper* of §2.2 suggests we should not place the council meeting here involved too remotely in the past. (But observe that Cyprian even refers to Adam's fall as *nuper*; see *De mortalitate* 2: *possessio paradisi nuper amissa.*) Hence the anabaptist council presided over by Agrippinus is an unlikely candidate; it is described by Cyprian as having occurred deep in time past. See *Ep.* 73.3.1: *anni sint iam multi et longa aetas;* cf. *Ep.* 71.4.1, where see n.; *testimonia* on Agrippinus are conveniently collected in DHGE 1 (1912) 1039 ff. *s.v.* Agrippinus. Despite this description, many have confidently advocated identification of Agrippinus' council with the meeting here referred to. More likely is the much more recent council presided over by Donatus, Cyprian's predecessor. This was concerned with irregularities practised by Privatus, bishop of Lambaesis, and these appear to have been disciplinary in character rather than doctrinal (see n. on *Ep.* 36.4.1). The question of *clerici* and *negotia* may thus have been raised, and a context provided accordingly for the formulation of the present decree.

On the other hand, *contra* Ritschl, *De epist.* 3, *nuper* ought not to force us to place the council in Cyprian's own episcopacy.

Cyprian plainly makes (§2.1) his episcopal predecessors responsible for the regulation.

8. *in concilio episcoporum statutum sit.* We happen to know only of two synods before Cyprian's time—that of Agrippinus, attended by about seventy bishops (see Augustine, *De unico baptismo* 13.22 and *Contra Cresconium* 3.3.3; this seems a suspiciously biblical number; cf. W. H. C. Frend in *Studia Patristica* 10 [1970] 292) and that of Donatus, attended by ninety bishops (see *Ep.* 59.10.1). But they were clearly an established feature of Church life in North Africa by the time of Cyprian's episcopate—but apparently not at the time Tertullian wrote *De ieiunio* 13.6. Regulations from such earlier synods appear to be implied in *Epp.* 15.1.2, 16.1.2, 55.21, 70.1, 71.2, etc., and in *Sententiae Episcoporum* 4.

For such synods the bishops could be drawn from all over North Africa, from Mauretania to Tripolitania, but more local gatherings of bishops are suggested in our sources (e.g., Numidia, *titulus* of *Ep.* 70; *Ep.* 72.1.3: *coepiscopos in Numidia praesidentes;* in the course of the next half-century Numidia officially established its own independent synodal gathering, P. Batiffol, in *Revue des sciences religieuses* 3 [1923] 425 ff.); and the councils of *Epp.* 57 (42 present), 67 (37 present), 70 (31 present) do not seem to have been plenary (see V. Saxer, *Vie liturgique et quotidienne à Carthage vers le milieu du IIIe siècle* [Vatican 1969] 16). We cannot tell whether here Cyprian is referring to a proconsular or to a pan-African assembly.

This incident is for us a significant landmark in the history of Church discipline. As it happens, it is our first recorded instance of a *disciplinary* canon being invoked for a case other than for the incident which originally gave rise to it. We have an incipient canon law. Notice that the original canon spelt out the penalties for infringement which Cyprian merely invokes for execution. This kind of normative regulation is clearly by now established ecclesiastical usage.

9. *ne quis de clericis et Dei ministris.* This is glossed by *singuli divino sacerdotio honorati et in clerico ministerio constituti* in this same section, and later, in the next section, by *sacerdotes et ministros* (twice). There can be little doubt that the canon was

intended to cover both higher (episcopal) and lower clergy. See further n. 11 below.

10. *tutorem vel curatorem*. A *curator* was technically an administrator of an estate with a specific sphere of duty (*cura*) e.g., he might act as an assistant to a *tutor* (guardian) assigned to looking after the ward or to managing a certain part of the estate, or he might act as a business advisor to a 'minor' (aged between puberty and twenty-five) who had nevertheless taken up his patrimony. See *Digesta* 27.10 on *curatores* and n. 6 above, as well as J. A. Crook, *Law and Life of Rome*, 116 ff.

11. *divino sacerdotio honorati et in clerico ministerio constituti.* Though the question has been much debated, there seems little ground for disallowing *sacerdotium* here from carrying its normal Cyprianic connotation of *high*-priesthood, that is to say, episcopal rank, especially in view of the subsequent glossing of this phrase by *sacerdotes et ministros*. Cyprian's use of *sacerdos* and *sacerdotium* is further discussed on *Ep.* 40.1.2.

12. *altari et sacrificiis deservire*. Note the assumption, made naturally by Cyprian, that the central Christian liturgy is in some undefined sense of a sacrificial nature. It is a notion already implicit in the language of Paul but it does not receive any great prominence during the second century (but observe Ignatius of Antioch, *Ad Ephesios* 5.2, *Ad Philadelphenos* 4, *Ad Magnesios* 7.2; Irenaeus, *Adversus Haereses* 4.18 ff.; and Polycarp's sacrificial prayer, *Martyrium Polycarpi* 14, seems strongly eucharistic in character). Cyprian's general assumption must imply development of the notion (under revived O.T. influence?) before his time (see H. B. Swete, in JTS 3 (1902) 164 ff.; Watson 194 ff., 265 ff.; see also J. A. Jungmann, in ZkTh 92 (1970) 342 ff., especially for the later history of the notion). Note the language already in the past in Tertullian, *De exhortatione castitatis* 7.3: *et offers et tinguis et sacerdos es tibi solus; scilicet ubi tres, ecclesia est.* And the contemporary expressions of Firmilian over in Cappadocia in *Ep.* 75.10.5 are striking: *sanctificare se panem et eucharistiam facere simularet et sacrificium Domino non sine sacramento solitae praedicationis offerret.* Observe also the choice of the word *altare* (versus *ara*); the word *ara* for Christians was associated especially with pagan sacrifices; cf. *Epp.* 65.1.2: *quasi post aras*

diaboli accedere ad altare Dei fas sit, and 59.18.1: *Domini altare . . . simulacra adque idola cum aris suis.* Further discussion and references are in ACW 39.225 f. and in Watson 268.

13. *precibus atque orationibus.* Included, of course, would be the elaborate system of hours for prayer, by now long established. Cf. *De dominica oratione* 34 ff. and Tertullian, *De ieiunio* 10.

14. 2 Tim. 2.4. For the other uses to which Cyprian puts this text, see Fahey 511 f. Note the quotation used for similar purpose in Council of Carthage, 348, canon 6 (*clerici* not to be involved in *actus seu administrationem vel procurationem domorum*) and again in Council of Carthage, 397, canon 15 (clergy not to be *conductores neque ullo turpi vel inhonesto negotio victum quaerant*).

15. An attitude of mind which would tend to strengthen a growing inclination towards celibacy among the clergy. Note the pseudo-Cyprianic tractate *De singularitate clericorum* (of this date?); and the celebrated canon 33 of Elvira (on which see E. Griffe in *Bull. de litt. ecclés.* 74 [1973] 142 ff.) and the debate on celibacy at Nicaea (Hefele-Leclercq 1.620 ff. and 2.1321 ff.) are not too far away. It is noteworthy that in all the talk in Cyprian of stipends and provisions for the *clerici* there is no mention of their dependent wives and children.

16. Observe how Cyprian is prepared to read off present-day regulative practices from norms of the Old Law. It is a good example of his general reverential attitude towards the Old Testament; he can see there material which is not merely of illustrative significance but which may be translated into immediate terms of institutional practice. For the attitude towards Scripture, cf. *Sententiae Episcoporum* 31: *sancta et adorabilia scripturarum verba,* and for discussion of this use by Cyprian, see R. P. C. Hanson, *Tradition in the Early Church* (Philadelphia–London 1962) 115, and M. F. Wiles, *The Making of Christian Doctrine* (Cambridge 1967) 51.

Note that Cyprian's argument here requires that Levite apply to all ranks of the clergy, not just to that of deacon for which *levita* may be specifically used. On that usage, see, for example, D. L. Powell in *Stud. Patr.* 12 (1975) 451 f.

17. For the allusion see Num. 18.20 ff.

18. *qui in ecclesia Domini ordinatione clerica promoventur.* *Ordinatio* properly means appointment to an *ordo* or rank; it is not necessarily implied, in Cyprian's usage, that special liturgical rites of 'ordination' are involved. See Saxer, *op. cit.* 90 ff.; A. Vilela, *La condition collégiale des prêtres au IIIe siècle* (Paris 1971) 268 f.; A. Coppo in *Ephemerides Liturgicae* 85 (1971) 73 ff.; P. van Beneden in *Spicilegium sacrum Lovaniense* 38 (Louvain 1974) passim, esp. 121 ff. (on this passage).

19. *in honore sportulantium fratrum.* *Honos* appears to be used in its concrete sense of 'offering,' 'gift.' Cf. Tertullian, *De ieiunio* 17.4; Watson 274. (Does *presbyterii honorem* in *Ep.* 39.5.2 play on this meaning?)

The curious phrase here has been much discussed, and Cyprian appears to be using deliberately vague terms in which to describe the contributions of the brethren so that the parallelism with the tithes (in kind) of the Old Testament will not be lost. *Sportulantium*(ά.λ), from *sportula*, which originally meant a small basket (for gifts in kind), must mean in the context "giving *sportulae*," against Lewis and Short *s.v.* ('to take the dole of a patron'). *

20. *tamquam decimas ex fructibus accipientes.* The *tamquam* must imply that a strict system of tithing did not operate at the time in this area. Cf. *De unitate* 26: *at nunc de patrimonio nec decimas damus* and Tertullian, *Apologeticum* 39.5 f.: *nemo compelitur sed sponte confert.* See on the subject DACL 4 (1920) *s.v.* Dîme 995 ff.; M. Réveillaud in *Études théol. et relig.* 41 (1966) 27 ff.

21. It is clearly implied that Cyprian regards clerical office, ideally, as full-time employment; clerics were, accordingly, regularly salaried. See on *Ep.* 39.5.2. The run of Cornelius' language in Eusebius, *H. E.* 6.43.11, suggests likewise that in Rome the clergy got their livelihood from ecclesiastical stipend. Not much earlier salaried clerics figure as scandalous innovations (stipends being regarded as enticement to heresy). But elsewhere, in Egypt, the famous papyrus reveals that the near contemporary *papas* of Alexandria, Maximus, along with a lector and other clerical staff, freely involved themselves in corn transactions between Upper Egypt and Rome (see A. Deissmann, *Light from*

the Ancient East (London 1910) 192 ff.). Whereas, by contrast, Origen, *Hom. in Genes.* 16.5, is insistent that priests must give up all property. And later regulations show that Cyprian's ideal was still slow to obtain in other areas, e.g., early in the next century the Council of Elvira, canon 19, merely forbids *episcopi, presbyteri et diacones* to engage in trade outside their province. Cyprian, of course, found that not all his contemporaries lived up to his ideal. Cf., e.g., *De lapsis* 6 (on the reading there—*rerum*, not *regum*—see M. Bévenot in *Stud. Patrist.* 10 [1970], 8).

Despite Cyprian's *language* here (influenced by his supporting text), he manifestly anticipates that his clergy would have other ecclesiastical duties besides exclusively *liturgical* offices.

The payment and secular employment of clergy in the Early Church has been much discussed. Discussions relevant for Cyprian include O. Ritschl, *Cyprian von Karthago* (Göttingen 1885) 203 ff.; H. H. Janssen, *Kultur und Sprache, Zur Geschichte . . . von Tertullian bis Cyprian* (Nijmegen 1938) 104 ff., 228 ff.; C. Andresen, *Die Kirchen der alten Christenheit* (Stuttgart 1971) 210 f., 304 f.; A. Hamman, *Vie liturgique et vie sociale* (Paris 1968) 231 ff.; T. Klauser in JAC 14 (1971) 140 ff. esp. 145 ff.; S. L. Greenslade, *Shepherding the Flock* (London 1967) 44 f.

22. *episcopi antecessores nostri.* Note the deeply embedded legalistic appeal for precedent to be found in the past. For the appeal cf. *Epp.* 15.1.2, 16.1.2, 55.21.1, 63.17.2, 68.5.1, 70.1.2, 71.4.1, and Cyprian was acutely aware that rulings of his might become *in posterum . . . exemplum* (*Ep.* 34.4.1). This attitude towards past decisions, sanctioned by *antecessores,* no doubt contributed to the collision between Cyprian and his opponents over the baptismal controversy; Cyprian was committed to the tradition which he had inherited from the past. Very few of Cyprian's *antecessores* are known by name. Their list might include Optatus (203, of Thuburbo?), Agrippinus and Donatus of Carthage (see n. 7 above), ?Decimus in *Ep.* 24, ?Cyrus of Carthage (Possidius in ML 46.16 reports an oration of Augustine *de depositione Cyri episcopi Carthaginis*). Pontius, *Vita Cypriani* 19, implies a well-established succession list for the Carthaginian *cathedra.* On this use of *antecessor,* see R. F. Evans, *One and Holy* (London 1972) 28 f.

23. *religiose considerantes.* Cyprian apparently does not feel the

need to hint at the guiding presence of the Holy Spirit at this conciliar gathering; he reserves that as a telling weapon for other, less certain, situations, e.g., *Ep.* 57.5.1: *placuit nobis Sancto Spiritu suggerente* (profoundly modifying a previous conciliar regulation). See in general J. H. Crehan in *Stud. Patrist.* 9 (1966) 210 ff. on the patristic evidence for the inspiration of councils, the most direct early piece of evidence being from the Council of Arles (314), Letter to Pope Silvester, Letter A 11.33 f., Letter B 11.7 f. (*praesente spiritu sancto et angelis eius*); see I. Mazzini, in VC 27 (1973) 286 f.

24. *non offerretur pro eo.* For analysis of the locution *offerre pro*, see R. Berger, *Die Wendung 'offerre pro' in der römischen Liturgie* (Münster 1964) esp. 60 ff. (usage in Cyprian), and compare, for the commemoration of the faithful in the offering, *Ep.* 16.2.3 (and other examples cited at *Ep.* 15 n. 14). In view of the explanatory clause which follows (*neque enim apud altare Dei meretur nominari in sacerdotum prece*) I do not see why we are not permitted to associate this present phrase with the Eucharistic liturgy (but only with special memorial services at the graveside), *contra* J. H. Strawley, *The Early History of the Liturgy* (Cambridge 1913; 2nd ed. 1947) 134.

We hear first of such general memorial *oblationes pro defunctis* for the faithful departed (to be distinguished from commemorative occasions for the *martyred* dead, whether held *in ecclesia* or *in mensa*, at the graveside) in Tertullian, but already in Tertullian they figure as hallowed and established customs; cf. *De monog.* 10.4, *De exhort. cast.* 11.1, *De cor. milit.* 3.3, etc.

There seems to be a natural translation into Christian terms of the anniversary ceremonies celebrated *manibus et memoriae* in Roman cult practice. On these occasions *inferiae* were customarily offered, that is to say, *sacrificia quae dis Manibus inferebant* (Servius *ap.* Vergil, *Aen.* 10.519).

See generally H. Delehaye, *Les origines du culte des martyrs* (2nd ed. Brussels 1933) 31 ff.; DACL 4 (1920) 427 ff. esp. 441 ff.; J. A. Jungmann, *The Mass of the Roman Rite* (New York 1959) 2.202 f.

25. *nec sacrificium pro dormitione eius celebraretur.* Cyprian seems to imply some objective efficacy for the *sacrificium* which

is therefore to be denied to the deceased. For such propitiatory value, explicitly acknowledged, for the eucharistic sacrifice, see Augustine, *Serm.* 172.2 and *Enchirid.* 110.

The image of sleeping (*dormitio*) is of course common in Christian epitaphs (see ILCV index vii *s.v.* dormit), but the notion goes back both to Old Testament expression ("sleep with their fathers") and to New Testament phrases ("only sleeping," Luke 8.52, John 11.11, 13). Cyprian leaves us unclear what precisely he understands by "celebrating the sacrifice *pro dormitione,*" but it may at least be worth noting that any notion of purgatory is difficult to discover in Cyprian (see on *Ep.* 55.20.3).

26. *apud altare Dei . . . nominari in sacerdotum prece.* Note the specialized use of *prex,* used technically for the solemn eucharistic canon, in which the petition would be included, Cf. S. Salaville, *Échos d'Orient* 39 (1941–42), 269 f.; V. Saxer, *op. cit.* 200 f., 301 f.; W. C. Bishop in JTS 13 (1911–12) 257 f.; J. A. Jungmann, *op. cit.* 2.129. Examples of this usage are in *De lapsis* 25, *De unitate* 17, *Ep.* 37.1.2, etc. The clause here ought not to be taken as evidence that the bishop (*sacerdos*) alone was the celebrant of the Eucharist (though he was typically so); elsewhere, Cyprian implies presbyters (assisted by deacons) unexceptionably celebrated without their bishop (see n. 13 on *Ep.* 5.2). This was only to be expected in an unusually large city such as Carthage; there are also glimpses of an incipient parish arrangement (seen in *Ep.* 41.1.2).

27. *nuper.* See n. 7 above and the discussion in H. Koch, *Cyprianische Untersuchungen* (Bonn 1926) 144 f., on this word in Cyprian. (In *Ep.* 10.1.1 the word must refer back to a month or two at the most; in *Ep.* 44.1.2 the interval must be a matter of weeks only, whereas in *Ep.* 58.8.2 it is two years, *Ep.* 59.14.2 one year, *Ep.* 68.2.2 at least three years.)

28. *aut deprecatio aliqua nomine eius in ecclesia frequentetur.* The choice of verb (*frequento*) suggests we may have here an example of congregational praying (continuing for some time after the decease?), although Cyprian's language leaves it regrettably obscure whether the *aut* is properly disjunctive (which would thereby render the 'prayers of supplication' separable from the 'offering'). For discussion, cf. Watson 285 and A. Vilela, *op. cit.*

322. For such *deprecatio* for the dead cf. *A.E.* 1968.622 (Henchir Touta, in Numidia): . . . *ita peto (f)ratres et sorores legis, petitionibus et orationibus vestris pro spirito meo incumbatis in nomine Cristi.*

LETTER 2

Contents: Cyprian has been approached by a fellow bishop, Eucratius, for advice on a domestic problem. A former actor in the congregation of Eucratius, whilst no longer practising his profession, nevertheless continues to earn his livelihood by teaching the art of acting to others. Cyprian's advice is firm; he must stop and if the Church there cannot support him, let him come to Carthage to receive subsistence from the Church's supplies.

Date and circumstances: There is no real indication which makes it possible to posit an early or a late date. Just one (very insecure) hint to suggest a post-Decian setting: can Cyprian have been himself but recently installed as bishop in Carthage if he is prepared to address a fellow bishop, in his farewell, as *fili carissime?* See n. 13 below.

1. Eucratius is clearly a bishop; there was one so named in September 256 from Thenae (= Henchir Thina) (*Sent. Episc.* 29), a city some 345 km. southeast of Carthage, along the coast from Hadrumetum (PWK 5.A.2 (1934) 1700 ff.). Only one African bishop of that name is known for the 250's. Are the two, economically, to be identified?

For the episcopal *fasti* of Thenae, see DACL 9.1 (1930) 1286; J.-L. Maier, *L'épiscopat de l'afrique romaine, vandale et byzantine* (Neuchâtel 1973) 215; and for the Christian antiquities of the site, DACL 15.2 (1953) 2251 f.

I am ignorant of the source for an *episcopus Tenitanus* dated to 258 in K. Miller, *Itineraria Romana* (Stuttgart 1961) 903, as well as in PWK 5.A.2 1702.)

2. *de histrione quodam.* Church hostility to the contemporary stage was strident and vehement (as it was to *spectacula*

generally). Cyprian gives lengthy rhetorical voice to the by-now standard apologetic *topos* on the viciousness of the theatre in *Ad Donat.* 8 and for roughly contemporary tirades see Novatian, *De spect.*, Minucius Felix, *Oct.* 37.12, and compare earlier, Tertullian, *De spect.* The acting profession accordingly figures among those banned to Christians. Subsequent Church councils indicate that actors of various kinds continued to be a problem, e.g., Council of Elvira, can. 62, Council of Arles, can. 5, Council of Carthage in 397, can. 35, etc.

This condemnation of the immorality of actors and dancers was, of course, shared by many pagans: evidence in J. Bayet, in *Libyca* 3 (1955), 115ff.; and for further discussion on Cyprian's attitude, G. Niemer in *Deutsche Evang. Enziehung* 49 (1939) 103 ff.; G. L. Ellspermann, *The Attitude of the Early Christian Writers towards Pagan Literature and Learning* (Washington, D.C. 1949) 48 ff.; and more generally DACL 11 (1933) 1203 ff.

Cyprian does not consult colleagues on this issue; he has no hesitations as to the proper principles involved—no compromise in connection with the stage is to be tolerated (contrast n. 7 below).

3. *apud vos constitutus.* The run of the sentence suggests that this phrase could be interpreted, more narrowly, as 'being a member of your congregation.' See *Ep.* 1 n. 1.

4. Not only was the subject-matter of the theatre often licentious but also homosexuality was a charge commonly and notoriously laid against actors in antiquity; and one must bear in mind also that women's parts were normally acted by boys. Hence, in particular, the charges of training in degeneracy and effeminacy that follow here.

5. An allusion to Deut. 22.5.

6. *gestu quoque turpes et molles et muliebres . . . exprimere.* The variant manuscript reading *gestus* is attractive here.

7. *frugalioribus et innocentibus cibis.* At first glance 'et innocentibus' seems an odd touch. But Cyprian is merely anticipating, with rhetorical *variatio,* his later and more obvious phrase in §2.3, *ecclesiae sumptibus parcioribus quidem sed salutaribus.* The actor's food is being tainted by the ill-gotten source by which it is obtained.

8. *quando hoc non nobis sed sibi praestet.* A somewhat obscure clause caused basically by the uncertain reference and case of *hoc* (refers to abandoning sin?).

9. A seeming allusion to Matt. 8.11.

10. The acting-teacher is to be called back (*revoca*) to the true life, remaining content (*contentus*) with ecclesiastical sustenance. This suggests that the teacher has become dissatisfied with the arrangement once agreed to (perhaps a condition laid down at baptism? The man appears to be more than a catechumen; cf. §1.1: *an talis debeat communicare nobiscum*).

11. *si illic ecclesia non sufficit ut laborantibus praestet alimenta.* Is there more than a hint that the Christian community (at Thenae?) might be very small? If true, that would provide some brake against the easy temptation to deduce the size of the North African Church at this period merely from the known or surmised total of bishoprics established. Cyprian's language can, however, be simply diplomatic, allowing for the possibility that the Church involved may be unusually pressed with claimants upon its charity.

12. In Cyprian we have practical evidence of the Church constituting a society within a society, a regular *tertium genus,* with an elaborate alimentary system (under the bishop's control) for supporting widows and those in need (orphans, sick, prisoners, visitors, etc.), "bridging finance" for tradesmen (*Ep.* 41), and so on. For further details see *Ep.* 5 nn. 8 ff. and cf. Culcianus to bishop Phileas, *Acts of Phileas* 11.13 ff.: "you possess such abundant resources that you can nourish and sustain not only yourself but an entire city . . ." (Greek version).

13. The implications of the terms of address *fili carissime* are obscure. Ought Cyprian to be notably older than Eucratius (so A. von Harnack in TU 23 (1902) 27), or at least be well-established in his authoritative *cathedra* of Carthage? A form of address used elsewhere in Cyprian only in *Ep.* 69 (to Magnus, a layman?). Could Eucratius perhaps have been one of Cyprian's clergy at Carthage first? Discussion in Bastiaensen, *op. cit.* 21 f.

LETTER 3

Contents: An aged bishop, Rogatianus, seeks the advice of Cyprian as to how he should deal with an unruly deacon. Cyprian's reply is blunt, but revealing. Deacons are merely subordinate assistants appointed by bishops (unlike bishops, who are themselves appointed by God). The deacon can, therefore, be legitimately stripped of his office or excommunicated, unless he repents and makes amends for his disrespectful conduct.

Date and circumstances: The controls are not tight, but the outburst in §3.2 on the theme that the origins of heresy, schism, and disunity are to be found in disobedience and disloyalty is our clearest indicator. That could well mean that Cyprian has suffered the painful and personal experience of the rebellions of Felicissimus, Novatus, etc., against his own episcopal authority (251 +), and those certainly involved deacons, e.g., Augendus (*Ep.* 44.1.1) if not Felicissimus himself (*Ep.* 52.2.3). That consideration, if valid, would push the letter into the post-Decian period at the least. (In his pre-Decian days Cyprian endured opposition, e.g., *Ep.* 43.5.4, Pontius, *Vita Cypriani* 5.6, but not to the point of the establishment *foris* of an *altare profanum*). Further, in *Ep.* 59.4 and *Ep.* 66.3 we meet *catenae* of texts similar to those cited in §1 of this letter used for similar purposes, to assert the *sacerdotalis auctoritas* against unruly, and, indeed, schismatic, opposition. That strongly suggests (but does not of course establish) *rapprochement* with those "post-schism" letters (to be dated to 252/255); cf. M. Bévenot in *Recherches de science religieuse* 39 (1951) 403 n. 3.

Some have attempted to go further. There is an aged Carthaginian presbyter and confessor in 250/1, by name Rogatianus (*Epp.* 6.4, 43.1.1, etc.). We have here an aged bishop, by name Rogatianus. Therefore, the letter must be post-251, after the aged Rogatianus was raised from presbyterate to episcopate (so Ritschl *de epistulis Cyprianicis* [diss. Halle 1885] 6; further discussed by L. Nelke, *Die Chronologie der Korrespondenz Cyprians* ... [diss. Thorn 1902] 151 ff.; O. Ritschl, *Cyprian von Karthago*. ... [Göttingen 1885] 239 f.). This is not a compelling deduction. The identification of presbyter and bishop is frankly hypothetical. There are two people named Rogatianus among the bishops in the *titulus* of *Ep.* 70, and the *cognomen* is characteristically African; cf. M. G. Jarrett in *Historia* 12 (1963) 210 f.

The epistle is uncircumspectly described *tout court* by Fahey 418 as a 'pre-exile' letter.

1. The identity of this Rogatianus is further discussed by Ritschl, *Cyprian von Karthago* ..., 151 ff. and G. Niemer in *Deutsche evang. Enziehung* 49 (1939) 110 ff., and see *Ep.* 6 n. 1.

If he is to be identified with the Rogatianus of *Sent. Episc.* 60, 'Rogatianus a Nova,' and it would be sheer chance if the identity were right, that would place him in the only known see for our episcopal Rogatiani, in Numidia (=? Nova Petra or Nova Sparsa, both on the Lambaesis-Sitifis route). If there is anything in the identification, it is worth noting that both places were small towns and could be expected to have, therefore, very few clergy. That would make disobedience by one deacon all the more important an affair.

2. *ego et collegae [mei] qui praesentes aderant.* Cf. *Ep.* 1 n. 2 for this type of consultative council and *Ep.* 1, intro. n., for the referring of such ecclesiastical problems to the 'metropolitan' in Carthage for guidance and advice. There may be significance in the fact that Cyprian mentions here bishops only (*collegae*); there are no *conpresbyteri* as well, as in, for example, *Epp.* 1 and 4. The latter were not called in for their opinion as this was an issue involving essentially the subordinate role of the lower ranks of the clergy?

3. *immemor sacerdotalis loci tui et officii ac ministerii sui oblitus.* For Cyprian's heavy and frequent emphasis on the malice of forgetfulness as a source of sin, see M. Réveillaud in *Études d'hist. et de philos. relig.* 58 (1964) 160 ff.; and for Cyprian's favoured use of *locus* (= station), consult A. Vilela, *op. cit.* 286 f. Cf. *Ep.* 16.1.2 (of priests): *nec evangelii nec loci sui memores* and further parallels in *Epp.* 12.1.1, 15.1.1, 40.1.3, 41.2.1, 55.8.3, 63.19, etc. Cyprian explains more fully later what he sees as the essential *ministerium* of the deacon; the word retains some of its subservient connotation.

4. *pro episcopatus vigore et cathedrae auctoritate.* Cyprian leaves no doubt that an individual bishop might himself degrade his clerics and excommunicate his subjects. He gives no indication that the community at large need be consulted, or that a subsequent synod need confirm such decisions. Cf. the deacon and laymen excommunicated by Bishop Pomponius alone in *Ep.* 4.4.1. Contrast the case of Felicissimus: he is *abstentum et non tantum mea sed et plurimorum coepiscoporum sententia condemnatum* (*Ep.* 59.1.1). That ought to mean that the initial excommunication was wisely backed by some form of subsequent synodal confirmation (so, too, the synod of 251 endorsed the condemnation issued by a select committee of nine bishops, *Ep.* 59.10.2). Similarly, in *Ep.* 52.3, Cyprian anticipates Novatus would have been excluded by the *iudicium sacerdotum.* The community's rejection of an unworthy bishop was fraught with greater difficulties: see *Epp.* 67 and 68. On excommunication generally in Cyprian, see K. Hein, *Eucharist and Excommunication,* (Bern/Frankfurt a. M. 1973) 366 ff. and S. Hübner in ZfKT 84 (1962) 191 ff.

For analysis of the concept *auctoritas episcopatus,* see U. Gmelin, *Auctoritas. Römischer Princeps und päpstlicher Primat* (Stuttgart 1937) esp. 91 ff. Cyprian's and Rogatianus' *cathedrae* would have been characteristically *velatae, linteatae,* etc. Note Pontius, *Vita Cypriani* 16: *sedile . . . linteo tectum ut et sub ictu passionis episcopatus honore frueretur,* and see further E. Stommel in *Münch. Theol. Zeit.* 3 (1952) 19 (with references to parallel illustrations), DACL 3 (1913) 19 ff., and on Cyprian's use of *cathedra,* A. Coppo in *Eph. liturg.* 85 (1971) 71 ff.

5. Deut. 17.12f. See Fahey 92 f. for the four other occasions when Cyprian employs this text (*Epp.* 4.4.2, 43.7.1, 59.4.1, 66.3.2).

6. *tres de ministeriis.* Note Cyprian's careful choice of description to make the diaconate fit in with his Old Testament illustration. Similarly in *Ep.* 69.8.1 these three are described as *loci sui ministerium transgressi.* For Cyprian the rhetorician, such parallelisms (as with *sacerdotes* = OT priest/NT bishop) have more argumentative weight than merely superficial verbal linkage.

7. *sacerdoti praeposito.* Again Cyprian prepares his illustra-

tion carefully. These are both words which Cyprian applies freely to bishops and will do so pointedly at the conclusion to this letter. In *Ep.* 59.7.2 Cyprian even attempts the oxymoron *praepositum servum*. On *praepositus* in Cyprian, see Watson 259.

8. The allusion is to Num. 16.1 ff. This is a chapter exploited at length by Cyprian on the theme of sacerdotal authority in *De unitate* 18 and in *Epp.* 67.3.2, 69.8f., 73.8.1. See Fahey 84 f., 574 f.

9. *ut probaretur sacerdotes Dei ab eo qui sacerdotes facit vindicari.* For Cyprian there was no doubt that the *ordinatio* of *sacerdotes* (bishops) was *divina*. For this notion that the bishops (but not the *clerus* generally) are the elect of God, see *Epp.* 48.4.2, 49.2.4, 55.8.1, 59.4.1ff., 66.1.1, 66.9.1, etc, and see the study by J. Speigl in *Römische Quartalschrift* 69 (1974) 30 ff. For the notion that the bishops are also the elect of God's people, see esp. *Ep.* 67.4 f. (There is warrant for emending Hartel to *probarentur*.)

10. The allusion is to 1 Sam 8 ff. (and the quotation from 1 Sam. 8.7).

11. Sir. 7.31 and 33.

12. Acts 23.4 f.

13. *usque ad passionis diem.* Note the technical Christian usage clearly acquired by now for *passio.* For discussion of the word in Cyprian, see H. A. M. Hoppenbrouwers, *Recherches sur la terminologie du martyre de Tertulien à Lactance* (Nijmegen 1961) 116 ff.

14. Matt. 8.4.

15. John 18.22 and 23. It is worth observing that Cyprian, without hesitation, finds in the Jewish *sacerdotes* of the old dispensation types of the bishops of the Christian church, and is prepared to read off practical disciplinary rules accordingly. The New Testament thus tends to figure less prominently than the Old when Cyprian comes to discuss the ministry and the episcopate. See S. L. Greenslade in JTS 44 (1943) 162 ff.; H. E. W. Turner, *The Pattern of Christian Truth* (London 1954) 276 f.

16. *apostolos id est episcopos et praepositos.* The casual but unequivocal way in which Cyprian identifies the apostles as the first bishops themselves (as opposed to being those who appointed the first bishops) is noteworthy (implied again in *Ep.* 67.4.2 concerning Matthias: *de ordinando in locum Iudae episcopo).* By contrast, see Tertullian, *De praesc. haeret.* 32.1 ff. (the apostles

themselves appointed the first bishops). Did the two different views contribute to some of the confusion in the highly controversial numbering of the episcopal *fasti* of Rome (see on *Ep.* 74.2.4: for Cyprian, Hyginus is uncompromisingly the ninth, not the eighth, bishop of Rome)?

Cyprian's viewpoint is, of course, not novel. It is already Irenaean, *Adv. Haer.* 3.2.2 ff.; it occurs also in Pontius, *Vita Cypriani* 5; and it became the unquestioned fourth-century attitude (see e.g., Ambrosiaster, *Quaest.* 97.20: *nemo ignorat episcopos Salvatorem ecclesiis instituisse; ipse enim . . . inponens manum apostolis ordinavit eos episcopos*).

17. Acts 6.1 ff. for the appointment of the seven apostolic deacons. Cyprian's schema leaves undetermined whether in his view the first presbyters were to be considered as chosen by Christ or by the apostles; he never clarifies the question.

The general duties of the deacon at this period still retain for Cyprian this significant feature that the deacon is a servant of the bishop, not of the presbyter (with whom in fact he might be very closely associated: see *Ep.* 5 n. 13). Hippolytus, *Trad. Apost.* 8, likewise specifically makes deacons servants to their bishop.

By this time deacons acted as the bishop's deputy especially in the sphere of practical charity, visiting the sick, the imprisoned, assisting the impoverished, and generally handling the church finances, and hence they were notably vulnerable to embezzlement, or at least to the charge of it. Cf., e.g., *Ep.* 52. And they had deputed to them various liturgical functions, e.g., assisting at the baptismal ceremony, distributing the *calix* to the *plebs*, (*De lapsis* 25), and see *Ep.* 18 n. 7 for an unusual extension of delegation to emergency *exomologesis*. They strove, in vain, to acquire the power to "offer": cf. Council of Arles, can. 15; First Council of Nicaea, can. 18. Cyprian has no word of deaconesses.

The powers, functions, numbers of deacons have been generously discussed. See the lengthy study in RAC 3 (1957) 888 ff., with bibliography 909; Brightman in H. B. Swete (ed.), *Essays on the Early History of the Church and the Ministry* (London 1918) 387 f.; J. Colson, *La fonction diaconale aux origines de l'église* (Bruges 1960); A. Hamman, *Vie liturgique et vie sociale* (Paris 1968) 67 ff.,

106 ff. on Cyprian's deacons; DACL 4 (1920) 738 ff.; V. Saxer, *op. cit.* 80 f.; O. Bârlea, *Die Weihe der Bischöfe, Presbyter und Diakone in vornicänischer Zeit* (Munich 1969) 252 ff.; L. Vischer in *Verbum Caro* 18 (1964) 30 ff.

18. *haec sunt enim initia haereticorum et ortus adque conatus schismaticorum male cogitantium.* Though the classic distinction between heresy and schism was not unknown by this stage (see e.g., Irenaeus, *Adv. Haer.* 4.40.2 and Cyprian, *Test.* 3.86), in practice Cyprian tends to use the two words and their derivates quite interchangeably (with *haeresis, haereticus,* appearing to be the more pejorative), for, to his mind, both unquestionably cast their adherents *foris* (outside the Church), and that was the significant issue. See S. L. Greenslade, *Schism in the Early Church* (London 1953) 21; E. Moutsoulas in *Stud. Patr.* 7 (1966) 362 ff.; H. H. Janssen, *op. cit.* 110 ff. Cyprian proceeds in the expression *ut sibi placeant* to allude to 2 Tim. 3.2, where his text read *erunt homines sibi placentes.*

19. *contra . . . ordinationem adque unitatem Dei.* Oughtn't this to be a little more than a mere periphrasis for 'the unity appointed by God,' for Cyprian is regarding the appointed place of bishops as being of the essence of Church unity? On *ordinatio,* cf. n. 18 to *Ep.* 1.

20. 1 Tim. 4.12.

21. A re-writing of the Biblical text for dramatic effectiveness, unusual in Cyprian with his strong sense of the divine character of Scripture. There are two other examples, in *Epp.* 13.2.2 and 62.3.1, and see Fahey 51 f.

22. *vel coercere poteris vel abstinere.* What precise sanctions 'coercere' implies are left unclear. In the case of a cleric, deposition from office, or the threat to depose, was certainly possible: elsewhere Cyprian indicates that charges of ecclesiastical misbehaviour might give rise to an *interim* suspension pending a formal inquiry (*cognitio*) with the appropriate *sententia* to follow (cf., e.g., *Epp.* 34.4.1 and 52.3). In Cyprian, a cleric under formal penalty of ecclesiastical *paenitentia* is normally laicised; the *paenitentia* (undefined) to which the cleric is invited here to submit himself for his rebellious act of *audacia* is, therefore, more likely

than not to be metaphorical—humble acknowledgement of error, lowly submission to and gracious acceptance by his *praepositus*. On *abstinere*, "to excommunicate," see n. 4 above.

LETTER 4

Contents: Once more Cyprian has been approached for advice, this time concerning the proper discipline to be applied in the case of dedicated virgins who have been found sharing the same sleeping quarters with men. After an introductory sermon on one's duty to ensure that one's brothers and sisters adhere rigorously to the *ecclesiastica disciplina*, and on the need of exemplary discipline to prevent similar scandals, Cyprian, in council, states his disciplinary advice crisply.

There are four categories discerned: (1) The men involved, habitual offenders, have already been dealt with summarily; they have been excommunicated. Cyprian approves. (2) If the virgins have been doing penance and are found to be still virgin, they are to be admitted to communion (with dire warnings for any repetition of their conduct in the future). (3) Those who are found in fact to have broken their vows are to perform full penance for the appropriate period and only then are they to be readmitted. (4) The perverse and unrepentant are left in no doubt about the hopelessness of their ever gaining salvation.

Date and circumstances: The indications are but slight. The arguments for an early date (*presbyteri* appearing in a unique way in the *titulus*, such cases of indiscipline being typical of the more lax pre-Decian period) are scarcely persuasive: indeed the lengthy and insistent talk of *disciplina* is strongly suggestive rather of Cyprian's post-Decian mood after his bitter experiences of outright indiscipline during and subsequent upon the persecution of Decius.—So, e.g., O. Ritschl, *De epistulis Cyprianicis* 6; A. von Harnack in TU 23.2a (1902) 28. Many disagree, e.g., Monceaux, *Histoire* 2.68. This is further discussed by G. Niemer in *Deutsche Evang. Enziehung* 49 (1939) 108 ff.

Some attempt to be more precise. Tertullus (Cyprian's trusted confidant in *Ep.* 12.2.1 and cf. *Ep.* 14.1.2) is now a bishop, but he certainly was not in the first few months of 250 (*Ep.* 12), and doubtfully even a cleric at that time. This letter must be placed, accordingly, in the whereabouts of the mid-250's (Tertullus coming last in the *titulus* as being only recently made a bishop). This is not convincing. The identification of the two men named Tertullus is sheer guesswork.

The letter is found in a Donatist collection of Cyprianic writings and has been edited by H. K. Mengis, *Ein donatistisches Corpus cyprianischer Briefe* (diss. Freiburg 1916) 17 ff.

1. It is not unreasonable to suggest that the sees of these bishops, available for consultation, are most likely to be found not too far distant from Carthage, but prelates on a visit from more distant dioceses are still possible (cf. *Ep.* 30.8).

(a) *Caecilius:* A Caecilius from Proconsular Biltha (site insecurely identified, but possibly Sidi Salah el Balti, in Tunisia; see Benson, *op cit.* 608; J. Mesnage, *op. cit.* 137; J.-L. Maier, *op cit.* 115, with further references) gives his *sententia* first in Sept. 256 (*Sent. Episc.* 1) and apparently reappears in the *titulus* of *Epp.* 57 (fourth place after Cyprian), 67 (first place after Cyprian), 70 (fifth place after Cyprian, in a list of bishops drawn from Africa Proconsularis only?). His placing here suggests we are dealing with the same senior episcopal colleague (as again in *Ep.* 63?). He is described (imaginatively) by Battifol as 'le plus âgé des évêques de l'Afrique proconsulaire et l'un des plus dévoués à saint Cyprien dans la réforme du clergé'; see DACL 1 (1924) *s.v.* Aquariens 2650.

(b) *Victor:* Three Victors appear in *Sent. Episc.* (40 [a Gorduba], 68 [ab Assuras], 78 [ab Octavu]), three likewise in the *titulus* of *Ep.* 70 (two being Numidian), and there may well be more (episcopal Victors in the *incipit* of *Epp.* 42, 57, 62, 67, 70, 76, 77). See H. von Soden, *Die Prosopographie des afrikanischen Episkopats zur Zeit Cyprians* (Rome 1909) 255 ff. Of the three sees known Gorduba (= Draa el Gambra; see DACL 9.1 (1930) 1269; Maier 149; Benson 580; Mesnage 62) is closest to Carthage (some 60 km to the south) and is, therefore, inherently the most likely candidate. But likelihood is not certainty. If the order of names in this letter is strictly in descending order of seniority and the Sedatus who next follows is correctly identified with the bishop who gave his *sententia* in the eighteenth place in *Sent. Episc.*, the Victor here cannot be identified with any of three Victors of *Sent. Episc.* All three appear well after the eighteenth place of Sedatus.

(c) *Sedatus:* This sounds like the Sedatus *a Thuburbo* of *Sent. Episc.* 18 and of the *titulus* of *Epp.* 67 and 70. That is to say, from Thuburbo (? Maius = Henchir Kasbat, c. 60 km SSW from Carthage); Maier 218 f; Benson 579 f.; Mesnage 90; PWK 6.A (1936) 619 f. and 7.A (1939) 759 f.

(d) *Tertullus:* A Tertullus *episcopus* appears in *Ep.* 57 (fifteenth after Cyprian, with a Caecilius fourth and a Victor eleventh, but no Sedatus present) and in *Ep.* 70 (twenty-seventh after Cyprian, with a Caecilius fifth, a Victor fourteenth, and a Sedatus twenty-sixth, the precise order as in this epistle); not in *Sent. Episc.* See further discussion in n. 13 to *Ep.* 12.

2. It is unique in the correspondence of Cyprian for the *presbyteri* to appear in the *titulus* quite in this way (contrast *Ep.* 1). There may be little significance in the *variatio*. The effect would be to add to the authority, weight, and solemnity of the document when, as Cyprian would anticipate, it was read out by Pomponius to his assembled *ecclesia* before Pomponius went on to pronounce his own final *sententia*.

For the role of *presbyteri* in such councils, compare *Ep.* 1 n. 3.

3. A Pomponius *a Dionysiana* (precise site in Africa Proconsularis [Byzacena] unknown; see Benson 608; Mesnage 194; Maier 137; PWK 5 [1905] 881) occurs in *Sent. Episc.* 48, and a Pomponiusis in the *titulus* of *Epp.* 57, 67, 70. Nothing positively prevents the economy of identifying all five occurrences, but caution is still appropriate. The concluding valediction ('frater carissime ac desiderantissime') is unusually warm and may possibly suggest some degree of friendship with Cyprian.

4. *cum semel ... decreverint:* the effect of the *semel* here is rather 'once (for all)'—cf. *se semel castraverunt* in §5.1 below—than 'once (upon a time),' which is also a possible usage. Exam-

ples of this 'strong' use of *semel* in Cyprian are collected in H. Koch, *Cyp. Unter.* (Bonn 1926) 227 f. n. 2.

5. *statum suum continenter et firmiter tenere:* is any play on words (a frequent feature of Cyprian's latinity) intended in this context by *continenter* (= 'with continence' as well as 'with constancy')? For the former, and rather rare, sense, cf. Cicero, *Mur.* 12, 27; *De off.* 1.106; Augustine, *Ep.* 140.83; etc. See, in general, C. Mohrmann in *Tijdschrift voor Taal en Letteren* 27 (1939) 163 ff. (The text is somewhat uncertain, however.)

Formally dedicated virgins in Cyprian's time appear to have been not uncommon. Note, of course, his tractate *De hab. virg.* 3, 4, 9, 17, 18, 20, and *passim;* the Christian prisoners from Numidia, held for ransom, are described in *Ep.* 62.2.3 as including *membra Christo dicata et ad aeternum continentiae honorem . . . devota;* equally there are virgins to be found among the confessors in the Numidian mines in *Ep.* 76.6.2: *cuius numero nec virgines desunt* and among the triumphantly returning confessors of Carthage in *De lapsis* 2: *veniunt et geminata militiae suae gloria virgines.* Cf. *Ep.* 55.20.2: *floret ecclesia tot virginibus coronata.*

On consecrated virginity in the early Church, note J. Mayer, in *Florilegium Patristicum* 42 (1938); H. Koch in TU 31.2 (1907) 59 ff.; and, more generally, J. Leipoldt, *Die Frau in der antiken Welt und im Urchristentum* (2nd ed. Leipzig 1955) 147 ff.

6. This is a subject (*virgines subintroductae*) which will recur in the canons of Church councils and probably reflects some of the problems of consecrated sisterhood before the birth of formal monasticism and conventual organization. One glimpses the more innocent side of the picture presented here in the pseudo-Cyprianic tractate *De cleric. sing.* where women dedicated to God and spoken of with respect are found living under the same roof with clerics. Contrast, for example, Council of Elvira, can. 27, which allows only *aut sororem aut filiam virginem dicatam Deo* to live with clerics, and compare in similar vein First Council of Nicaea, can. 3, Counc. of Ancy., can. 19, Counc. of Carthage 397, can. 17, Justinian, *Nov.* 123c.29, forbidding females to dwell with unmarried clergy *citra matrem aut sororem*

aut filiam et alias personas quae omnem suspicionem effugiunt. The need for repeating the canon would suggest continued violations of it (see, e.g., Jerome, *Epp.* 22.14 and 117; Basil, *Ep.* 55).

For earlier traces of such cohabitation, see Hermas, *Sim.* 9.10 f. and Irenaeus, *Adv. haer.* 1.6.3; for Carthaginian offenders (amongst the confessors) in 250, see *Epp.* 13.5.1 and 14.3.2; and slightly later, the charges made against Paul of Samosata *ap.* Eusebius, *H. E.* 7.30.12 ff., are noteworthy and closely parallel (*subintroductae* of Paul himself, his presbyters, and his deacons). The Apostle Paul, of course, bears witness to platonic partnerships between Christians, and their difficulties, in his own day in 1 Cor. 7.36 ff.

On the whole topic note the studies of H. Dodwell, *Dissertationes Cyprianicae III* (Oxford 1684); H. Achelis, *Virgines subintroductae* (Leipzig 1902) esp. 7 ff.; A. Jülicher in *Archiv. für Religionsw.* 7 (1904), 373 ff.; P. de Labriolle in *Rev. hist.* 137 (1921) 204 ff.; H. Koch, in TU 31.2 (1907) esp. 76 ff. (on this letter) and *Cyp. Unter.* (Bonn 1926) 457 ff.; E. A. Clark, in *Church History* 46 (1977) 171 ff.

7. *ab evangelicis et apostolicis traditionibus.* For Cyprian this turn of phrase need not imply a belief in an apostolic *traditio* independent of gospel-based *traditio.* For discussion, see R. P. C. Hanson, *Tradition in the Early Church* (Philadelphia-London 1962) 99, 115.

8. *ecclesiastica disciplina:* a somewhat vague, but frequently employed, phrase (with a number of rhetorical variations), implying a mélange of Church teaching, approved institutional practice, disciplined and orderly behaviour, *et al.* For discussion on *disciplina* and its significance, see H.-I. Marrou in *Bull. du Cange* 19 (1934) 1 ff.; V. Morel in *Rev. d'hist. ecclés.* 40 (1944–45) 5 ff. and in RAC 3 (1957) 1213 ff.; W. Dürig in *Sacr. Erud.* 4 (1952) 245 ff.; S. Hübner in ZfKT 84 (1962) 58 ff.

On the text of the following phrase in the translation, where Hartel reads *per omnes utilitatis et salutis vias* note the discussion in J. Wordsworth *et al., Old-Latin Biblical Texts* (Oxford 1886) 2.130.

9. Jer. 3.15.

10. Sap. 3.11. Cyprian's text is abbreviated, omitting the ini-

tial words *sapientiam enim et* ... of the Vulgate (thereby avoiding possible overtones of suspect pagan philosophy?).

11. Ps. 2.12.

12. *et praepositis et plebi: praepositi* ought to be wider here than bishops only and include the clergy generally (versus *plebs,* laity). For this generalized sense in Tertullian, cf. *De fuga* 11.3. (referring to *diaconi et presbyteri et episcopi,* 11.1) and *De monog.* 12.2 (referring to *episcopi et clerus,* 12.1). Cf. *Ep.* 15 n. 16 for another example.

13. *pro arbitrio et ructu suo vivere:* the reading here is discussed by L. Bayard, *Le latin de saint Cyprien* (Paris 1902) 70 f.

14. *fideliter consulere:* from the run of the argument I take *fideliter* to refer back to the precepts on discipline which have been pointedly enunciated, but the adverb may possibly be used in a more general sense.

15. *ad vitam singulis ... consulere:* this is glossed later in the letter, at §5.1, as *singulis ad salutem suam consulas,* thereby clarifying the phrase (*vita* = eternal life).

16. *sexus infirmus:* a standard Roman attitude to women (cf. A. Otto, *Die Sprichwörter der Römer* [Leipzig 1890; repr. Hildesheim 1965] 231), reinforced in the Christian tradition by Eve's role in the Fall (cf. G. M. Lukken, *Original Sin in the Roman Liturgy* [Leiden 1973] 76 ff.).

17. *aetas adhuc lubrica:* does this perhaps suggest that the offenders were comparatively young?

18. Ephes. 4.27. As so often, Cyprian verbally binds his quotation into the context (*nolite locum dare ...; liberanda ... de periculosis locis navis*) habitually exploiting verbal ambiguity.

18a. *nemo diu tutus est periculo proximus.* This appears to be a line of verse (iambic senarius) with its last two words transposed to avoid (in prose) a completely metrical line. It is of unknown authorship. For the thought, see Seneca, *Her. Fur.* 326 f.: *nemo se tuto diu/periculis offerre tam crebris potest,* and Jerome quotes the adage from Cyprian here (*Ep.* 30.14: *nemo, ut beatus Cyprianus ait, satis tutus periculo proximus,* and again in *Comm. in Amos 11, prol.*). For these observations cf. Watson 204. (Both K. Goetz, *Geschichte der cyprianischen Literatur bis zu der Zeit der ersten ... Handscriften* [diss. Marburg, Basel, 1891] 79 ff. and H. von Soden in TU 25.3 [1904] 178 f. overlook this evidence for Jerome's acquaintance with *Ep.* 4).

19. The text is somewhat uncertain, but the sense is clear enough. Does Cyprian imply a view that the women concerned may be basically innocent (so Benson 54), or is he rather speaking in general terms?

20. The cementing bond of complicity in crime is a commonplace, found also in the context of the *subintroductae* of Paul of Samosata *ap.* Eusebius, *H. E.* 7.30.12. Further examples are in ACW 39.220 f.

21. For Cyprian the *praemium virginitatis* was the sixty-fold of Matt. 13.8, 13.23 (with one hundred-fold reserved for martyrdom); cf. *De hab. virg.* 21 and discussed more fully on *Ep.* 76.6.

22. A clear allusion to 1 Cor. 7.9. The implication would seem to be from this text that vows of virginity made at this time were of an uncomplicated nature that could be rescinded without much formality. There is no mention in Tertullian or Cyprian of any public, official ceremony of consecration; indeed their language suggests rather a more private (but nonetheless formal) pledge of self-dedication. For discussion on the nature of the *votum* or *pactum* involved, see Réveillaud, *op. cit.* 207 ff.; H. Koch in TU 31.2 (1907) 76 ff.; also RAC 3 (1957) 849 ff.

23. 1 Cor. 8.13.

24. For such *inspectio virginum* cf. Ambrose, *Ep.* 5 to bishop Syagrius (with strong disapproval).

25. *gladium in manus sumit: manus* is Hartel's (unnecessary) correction for the more idiomatic *manu* (on the turn of phrase *in manu*, see C. Mohrmann, *Études sur le latin des chrétiens* 1 (Rome 1961) 48 f.

It ought to be borne in mind here that the Romans (legally) were strongly sympathetic to self-help justice in cases of 'crimes passionnels'. In early Roman law an outraged husband in fact formally enjoyed such *ius necandi* that it could be said by, e.g., Cato *ap.* Aulus Gellius, *N.A.* 10.23.5: 'if you take your wife in adultery, you may slaughter with impunity and without trial'; even under the Empire, outraged fathers under certain circumstances retained this right (see *Digesta* 48.5.21, 24.1), and husbands might enjoy mitigation of their sentences for understandable inability to restrain their *iustum dolorem* (see *Digesta* 48.5.39.8). See in general P. E. Corbett, *The Roman Law of Marriage* (Oxford 1930) 127 ff.

Compare the elaborate parallel drawn by Venantius a Thinisa in *Sent. Episc.* 49.

26. *Dominus* retains here some of its marital and judicial connotations.

27. *sanctitati suae destinatam.* Is *sanctitas* used here semipersonally (His Holiness)? Probably not.

28. Cf. Cyp. *de hab. virg.* 20 on failed virgins as *Christi adulterae*.

29. On this excommunication, see *Ep.* 3 n. 4; a clear example of unilateral episcopal action. It remains a trifle obscure in what follows whether Cyprian has in mind at times that there may be other men, not habitual offenders, who have not been thus summarily excommunicated. If, indeed, men were found to have been involved in chaste *concubinatus,* they might be expected to be allowed back under the conditions of §5. For after proceeding to talk in this section about the treatment of the *virgines* in particular, from §4.2 onwards Cyprian consistently couches his language in the more generalized masculine gender (*superbi, indisciplinati, quidam de perversis*), and this seems to imply that he has a wider object in mind than the *virgines* alone. The simple explanation may be, however, that he is assuming that the excommunication of the men may prove to be temporary only, under the appropriate circumstances.

30. *inspiciantur interim virgines.* Much dispute centres around the precise meaning of the forty examples of *interim* in Cyprian, where, at times, the temporal notion of 'at once' can possibly be discerned. Here, though that significance has been advocated (cf., e.g., Watson 313 n. 3), the interpretation seems unwarranted. The repentant virgins should, before final sentence is pronounced [= *interim*], be submitted to examination. Further discussion on *Ep.* 55.17, 19, and in H. Koch, *Cyp. Unters.*, 213, 264 ff., and S. Hübner in ZfKT 84 (1962) 210 ff.

31. This passage has been discussed by most writers on penitential discipline in the early church. Cyprian is clearly distinguishing between those who have not in fact violated their vows

of virginity and those who have, the conduct of both groups being nevertheless reprehensible, though clearly not equally so.

The first group have displayed regret and repentance for their behaviour. They have been performing *paenitentia* for their improprieties (charitable *opera*, fasting, and other spiritual exercises, etc.). It would appear that they have been (temporarily) suspended from Communion pending a final verdict on their case. Cyprian's recommendation is for that suspension now to be terminated for those who are found still to be virgin. They do not appear to have to undergo any formal ceremony of *exomologesis*, and I cannot see how G. H. Joyce in JTS 42 (1941–42) 40, can conclude from this passage that they received (private) absolution from their bishop ("It would be hardly possible to have clearer evidence that it was open to the bishop to absolve without imposing public penance: in other words that private penance was in use in the Church"). Theirs had not been a formal *paenitentia* at all and they were simply acquitted of the gravamen of the *prima facie* charge against them.

Full discussion in R. C. Mortimer, *The Origins of Private Penance in the Western Church* (Oxford 1939) 35 ff.; see also P. Galtier, *L'église et la rémission des péchés aux premiers siècles* (Paris 1932) 290 f., and B. Poschmann, *Paenitentia secunda. Die kirchliche Busse in ältesten Christentum bis Cyprian und Origenes* (Bonn 1940) 416 f., etc.

32. If it is true that this group of virgins has undergone formal, but curtailed, *paenitenia*, this minatory phrase becomes a very grim understatement (*nec . . . facile recipiantur*); second *paenitentia* in these rigorous times was not in fact countenanced. Earlier Cyprian has been describing past conduct where virgins have slept with men *in eodem lecto;* now for the future they are to avoid, under threat of far worse penalties, even dwelling with men *sub eodem tecto.*

33. *agat paenitentiam plenam:* a phrase intended to stand in contrast with the terms appropriate for the previous group; it occurs elsewhere in Cyprian (e.g., *De laps.* 16, 32; *Epp.* 55.18.1, 57.1.1, 64.1.1). Quite what was involved in "full penance," however, is not altogether clear—basically achieving adequate *satisfactio* for delicts, by prayer, almsgiving, and other *opera*, and

displaying an attitude of sorrow (fasting, sackcloth, ashes, humble entreaty for readmission at the Church vestibule, etc.). It would seem that the length of the *paenitentia* might not be precisely laid down, but at the least it was certainly envisaged in this case that it should end before death-bed (contrast, for example, Counc. of Elvir., can. 13, on repentant, once-offending, fallen virgins: *placuit eas in finem communionem accipere debere*): similarly with the *sacrificati*—they are to perform (vaguely) *diu paenitentiam plenam* (*Ep.* 57.1.1), but, again, that was not basically intended to last until death-bed, for penitents *sub ictu mortis* formed a separate category. Observe that in *Ep.* 15.4 Cyprian can envisage that by the beginning of the summer of 250 (*Ep.* 18.1.2) there are lapsed whose *paenitentia* can be considered to be *satisfactioni proximam.*

34. *aestimato iusto tempore:* for the turn of phrase, in penitential contexts, cf. *Ep.* 16.2.3 (*iusto tempore*), *Ep.* 64.1.1 (*legitimum et plenum tempus*). The suggestions of this phrase (and other contemporary evidence) are that the bishop (who controlled terms of penitence; see *De laps.* 29 and *Epp.* 43.3.2 and 66.9.1) might be importuned, petitioned, etc., and after examining the particular circumstances, the penitent's attitudes, his *opera,* etc., could relent and readmit the penitent; thus the special case for readmission of those who lapsed after severe torture in *Ep.* 56.1.1 (following a *triennium* of penitence). A Roman magistrate cancelling or curtailing sentences previously imposed followed similar practice. Does Cyprian's language suggest that there was still inquiry into individual cases even after a general *pax* had been granted for the *paenitentiam facientes* in *Ep.* 57.5.1 (*examinatis singulorum causis pacem lapsis dare*)? And cf. the curtailment of the period of penitence for good faith and a reformed way of life (ἡ δὲ ἀναστροφὴ καὶ ἡ πίστις) in Counc. of Neocaes., can. 3. See generally B. Poschmann, *Penance and the Anointing of the Sick* (London 1964) 53 ff., and on the length of penance *idem* in ZfKT 37 (1913) 44 ff.

35. *exomologesi facta.* Although *exomologesis* may have a range of meanings, the liturgical act of public abasement before the assembled congregation (with imposition of the hand by the clergy collectively following) is doubtless intended here. On the

word, see, for example, Brightman in H. B. Swete (ed.), *Essays on the Early History of the Church and the Ministry* (London 1918) 372 ff., and H. Koch, *Cyp. Unters.*, 280 f.

36. Deut. 17.12 f. The text in the following sentence is shaky.

37. *nemini salus esse nisi in ecclesia possit.* Cyprian is notorious for the classic formulation of this idea (cf. *De unit.* 6 and *Epp.* 55.24.1, 69.3.1, 73.21.2, etc.) but it was certainly not novel (cf., e.g., Irenaeus, *Adv. haer,* 3.24.1 f. and Origen, *Comm. in Matt. Comm. Ser.* 46 and 47); and it is worth observing the run of the context here—*salus* clearly retains for Cyprian much of its metaphorical sense of "the healthy (spiritual) life" and is less technical and restricted in overtones than our "salvation". Nevertheless, the notion played an essential part in Cyprian's reactions to disunity, schism, heresy and Church discipline generally; not surprisingly it is crucial in understanding Cyprian's views on the baptismal dispute.

38. A conflation of Prov. 15.12 and 15.10. 'It is not clear why Cyprian reverses the order of these two verses' (Fahey 164). Surely Cyprian could not resist the rhetorical effectiveness of placing the threat *consumentur turpiter* in the final and emphatic position.

39. An allusion to Matt. 7.14.

40. Matt. 19.12.

41. *nec sacerdotes * * .* The text has a lacuna. L. Bayard, in his Budé edition *ad loc.*, suggests *non exaudiant,* an allusion back to Deut. 17.12 f. appropriate to the context and in Cyprian's manner, exploiting an earlier Biblical quotation. Discussed also by Bayard, *Le latin de saint Cyprien* (Paris 1902) 349 (*despiciant*). Hartel suggests *offendant.* The mss RV*v* (H. xlixff.) appear to yield the immediately intelligible reading: *nec sacerdotes dei aut ecclesiam Domini scandalo suae pravitatis offendant.*

42. Gal. 4.16.

43. The text is very uncertain here; discussion in Bayard, *Le latin de saint Cyprien,* 349 f. Major revision appears required.

44. Gal. 1.10.

45. *opto te, frater carissime ac desiderantissime, in Domino....* See A. A. R. Bastiaensen, *Le cérémonial épistolaire des chrétiens latins* (Nijmegen 1964) 18, 25 f. on this form of full and warm

valediction. Throughout the rest of this letter Cyprian has used consistently the first person plural; this is a joint letter. The variant reading in R, *optamus*, is therefore attractive.

LETTER 5

Contents: Cyprian is writing from a place of hiding to his presbyters and deacons urging them on two main issues.

Firstly, whilst he is away, they must continue the duties of his office and in particular maintain the Church's charitable programme. Money has already been disbursed among the *clerici* to make funds more widely accessible.

And, secondly, they must make every effort not to stir up trouble for the Christian community. In particular, prison-visiting should be done cautiously and not in provocatively large groups. The presbyters should discreetly take it in turns to make visits with different deacons.

Date and circumstances: There are several very important indications as to dating. We must be at a relatively early stage of the Decian persecution; generally speaking there is still *quies* for the Christians in Carthage and they are urged not to make any moves that might spoil those circumstances. The confessors can still be visited in prison in relative freedom (along with the celebration of the eucharist there), though Cyprian senses danger in it.

On the other hand, some troubles have already clearly begun. There are already confessors, now in prison. There appear to be people suffering from want as a result of their steadfast faith—*pauperes et indigentes laborant et tamen in Domino perseverant* (1.2). Cyprian and his clergy generally have so far managed to escape danger, but the situation is potentially explosive. As yet, however, there are no tortures, no martyrs.

We must be, therefore, later than *Ep.* 7, where there are no confessors, where the poor are simply poor, where the clergy themselves do not yet appear threatened with danger, and where the situation to Cyprian appears altogether more hopeful and less perilous.

This letter seems to follow naturally on *Ep.* 7, after Cyprian has had word of the circumstances of his clergy and the existence of the *confessores* (to whom he proceeds to write *Ep.* 6 at the same time as this letter).

This letter is referred to in *Ep.* 14.1, when he next addresses his presbyters and deacons.

For discussion, see L. Nelke, *Die Chronologie der Korrespondenz Cyprians* ... (diss. Thorn 1902) 12; O. Ritschl, *De epistulis Cyprianicis* (diss. Halle 1885) 9 f.; L. Duquenne, *Chronologie des Lettres de s. Cyprien* (Brussels 1972) 60 ff.

1. *fratribus carissimis.* The presbyters and deacons are so addressed in the earlier *Ep.* 7, but the affectionate epithet is dropped from the *incipit* by the time Cyprian next addresses his presbyters and deacons in *Ep.* 14; there are already troublesome characters amongst their ranks. It continues to be missing in the *tituli* of all the subsequent letters so addressed (they are generally sterner in tone) until *Ep.* 40 (where the *plebs* is included).

2. Cyprian has gone into hiding. From the analogy of what happened in this persecution in Rome and in Alexandria, it is attractive to conjecture that orders went out to secure compliance from the bishops in the first instance (Pope Fabian is the first known victim in Rome, and Dionysius is searched for in Alexandria promptly on receipt of the imperial orders [Eusebius, *H.E.* 6.40.2], and the words of *Ep.* 55.9.1: *cum tyrannus infestus sacerdotibus Dei fanda atque infanda comminaretur,* could possibly suggest a special clause directed against bishops). No doubt the hope was that the bishop would provide a lead in compliance to his flock. The lapsed Trofimus did precisely that, according to *Ep.* 55.11. And in the Valerianic persecution Cyprian is told by the proconsul, *eris ipse documentum his quos scelere tuo aggregasti,* (*Act. Cyp.* 4.2). As Cyprian himself remarks in *Ep.* 9.1.2, there is great danger that the collapse of a bishop may lead to the downfall of his followers, a sentiment echoed in *Ep.* 59.6.2 and cf. on this theme also *Ep.* 65.1.2, 3.3. Note, too, in the Acts of Phileas (Greek version) 11.5–7, bishop Phileas is told by the

prefect: "You have killed many men by not sacrificing. Pierius
[a presbyter] saved many by submitting."

Cyprian accordingly has made himself scarce. He was formally proscribed and a public notice went out against those who
held in their possession any of his *bona* (cf. *EP.* 66.4; would that
include the Carthaginian Church funds mentioned in this letter?). Cyprian recovered his sequestered property when the persecution came to an end; cf. Pontius, *Vit. Cyp.* 7.1, 15.1.

Cyprian clearly came under criticism for his decision to flee,
but I do not detect much note of defensiveness in this letter on
that decision (though others have). He does, however, insist
firmly on non-provocative behaviour—and he interpreted that
as the basic justification for his own flight (cf. *Epp.* 7.1 and
14.1.2, etc.). Cyprian was, of course, not alone among contemporary bishops in thus seeking refuge. Gregory Thaumaturgus
and Dionysius of Alexandria behaved similarly; so, too, bishops
fled from distant provinces to the sheltering crowds of Rome
(*Ep.* 30.8). They do not all appear to have been subject to
criticism, but Dionysius is manifestly on the defensive in writing his apologia to bishop Germanus *ap.* Eusebius, *H.E.* 6.40.1
ff., cf. 7.11.1 ff.

We do not know the whereabouts of Cyprian's *latebra.* The
apparent ease of his communications with his flock suggests that
he was at no great distance from Carthage, but the appearances
may be deceptive. At all events we find no word of lengthy and
laborious journeying to reach him. Eight years later, in the
persecution of Valerian, he was offered places to which he
might secretly retire by *plures egregii et clarissimi ordinis et
sanguinis sed et saeculi nobilitate generosi* (Pontius, *Vit. Cyp.* 14.3),
that is to say, estates owned by old friends in the Carthaginian
aristocracy. He declined the offers.

3. *circa incolumitatem quoque vestram omnia integra esse cognoverim.* A slightly opaque phrase, for in the manifestly contemporaneous letter, *Ep.* 6, he in fact addresses two *presbyters* Sergius
and Rogatianus who were in prison following their confession.
The ambiguities are illuminated by the opening of *Ep.* 14, his
next letter to these same presbyters and deacons. There, Cypri-

an says, picking up these words, that he had hoped to be able to address *universum clerum nostrum integrum et incolumem* but unfortunately some of the clergy have in fact fallen. Cyprian is, therefore, basically talking not so much about physical safety as unimpaired integrity of faith. The twofold meaning appears also in the very last epistolary words (*Ep.* 81.1.5) which we have from Cyprian: *incolumes vos, fratres carissimi, Dominus Iesus in ecclesia sua permanere faciat et conservare dignetur.* (U. Wickert, *Sacramentum unitatis. Ein Beitrag zum Verständnis der Kirche bei Cyprian* (Berlin and New York 1971) 139 n. 18, missing this point, dates *Ep.* 6 after *Ep.* 5.

4. Carthage = *illic*, as so often in Cyprian's exile letters; generally he uses *istinc* (= here) when he refers to Carthage whilst resident there. On *illic* (the equivalent of *ibi*) as an "Africanism" see F. C. Burkitt, *The Old Latin and the Itala* (Cambridge 1896) 14.

5. *ut nihil vel ad disciplinam vel ad diligentiam desit.* The next paragraph (§1.2) chiastically refers to details of maintaining *diligentia*, and the one following (§2.1) is generally devoted to the question of *disciplina* (clearly from the context in the sense of the appropriate, and disciplined, behaviour). A nice example of Cyprian's rhetorical instincts even in so brief a document as this.

6. *gloriosa voce.* For the notion of *gloria* in Cyprian, see A. J. Vermeulen, *The Semantic Development of Gloria in Early-Christian Latin* (Nijmegen 1956) 39, 64 ff., 96 ff., 109 ff., and H. U. Instinsky, *Bischofsstuhl und Kaiserthron* (Munich 1955) 83 ff.

7. *in carcere sunt constituti:* from §2.1 (*gloriosis initiis*) and from the next letter, *Ep.* 6, addressed to these confessors, it is clear that they have been put in prison only very recently. Their numbers include women and children (*Ep.* 6.3.1).

Devotion to the needs of Christians in prison is a common motif (cf., e.g., Eusebius, *H.E.* 6.3.3 f. and Dionysius *ap.* Eusebius, *H. E.* 7.11.24 f.; Tertullian, *Ad mart.* 1.1, 2.7; Athanasius, *Vit. Ant.* 46) and it is a special feature in martyr *Acta* (cf., e.g., *Act. Perp. et Fel.* 3, 9.1, 16.4; *Mont. et Luc.* 4.7, 9.2) and failure to perform this *operatio* could accordingly provide ground for criticism (cf., e.g., Cornelius *ap.* Eusebius, *H.E.* 6.43.16 against Novatian). Communal funds might be collected with this purpose specifically in mind; cf. Justin, *1 Apol.* 67.6, and Tertullian, *Apol.* 39.6. Deacons are specifically charged with this corporal work of mercy in *Didasc.* 18. For a second-century parody, note Lucian, *De mort. Pereg.* 13: Christians from the cities of Asia journey to Syria to visit the imprisoned Peregrinus, assisting him from their common funds (ἀπὸ τοῦ κοινοῦ).

But the rigorous might disparage such enervating attentions: cf. Tertullian, *De ieiun.* 12.2 f. (*martyres incerti* were thus given enticement to gluttony; he cites the case of the besodden Pristinus who was unable orally to confess, only to belch and hiccough) and *De pudic.* 22.1 f. Compare the ministrations, and the abuse, pilloried by Lucian, *De mort. Pereg.* 11 ff.; likewise, *Brev. coll. cum Donat.* 3.25: *facinerosi* and *fisci debitores* get themselves into the safety of prison, with the intention *vel certe adquirere pecuniam et in custodia deliciis perfrui de obsequio christianorum.*

For further on this topic, see M. M. Baney, *Some reflections of life in North Africa in the writings of Tertullian* (Washington 1948) 83 ff.; J. G. Davies in the *Birm. Univ. Hist. Journ.* 6 (1958) 99 ff.; F. de' Cavalieri, *Studi e Testi* 175 (1953) 3 ff.

8. *his qui pauperes et indigentes laborant et tamen in Domino perseverant.* By contrast, in *Ep.* 7.2, Cyprian urges his clergy: *viduarum et infirmorum et omnium pauperum curam peto diligenter habeatis.* The change from care of *all* the poor (unqualified), in that letter, to the care of those who suffer want but who are still loyal to their Lord, in this letter, would appear to be significant: there are some who have lapsed between times. The poor who are now to be assisted must be the meritorious poor.

The turn of phrase might imply something further: can it suggest some are suffering need *because* they have remained steadfast in their faith? That is to say, some have already been driven from their homes (whether as refugees, or, officially, as exiles), had their property forfeit, or the like, sufferings which we have evidenced in later letters of the Decian period; see, e.g., *Epp.* 8.3.1: *exclusi de sedibus suis,* and 24.1.1: *extorres facti reliquerunt possessiones quas nunc fiscus tenet.* See notes on these passages, and see n. 5 to *Ep.* 10 and n. 19 to *Ep.* 12.

For insistence on helping the deserving poor only, cf. *Epp.*
12.2.2: *pauperibus. . . . his tamen qui in fide stantes* . . . , and 14.2.1:
pauperum cura si qui tamen inconcussa fide stantes. . . .

9. *summula omnis quae redacta est illic sit apud clericos distri-
buta.* In the earlier *Ep.* 7.2 we find funds of Cyprian's own have
been left in Carthage in charge of the presbyter Rogatianus for
charitable purposes and a further subvention was sent at that
time by Cyprian. We need not necessarily be dealing here with
other monies, though a special collection is a possibility; cf. n. 40
to *Ep.* 13. The funds have now been more widely dispersed
(before Rogatianus' arrest? Cf. *Ep.* 6.4).—*Summula* is a regular
(popular) diminutive (cf. *Ep.* 62.4.2, Bayard, *Le latin de saint
Cyprien* [Paris 1902] 129). I doubt, therefore, whether it ought to
be interpreted as deprecatory ('small sum,' against D. D. Sullivan, *The Life of the North Africans as Revealed in the Works of St.
Cyprian* [Washington 1933] 69).

10. Note the implications: the Church funds are firmly at the
disposal of the bishop and charitable distribution is ultimately
directed by him and at his discretion. Cf. *Epp.* 41.2.1: *episcopo
dispensante* and 34.4.2 (suspending the monthly salary of two
subdeacons and an acolyte); Hermas, *Sim.* 9.27.2; Justin, 1 *Apol.*
67.6 (collections for charitable purposes given to the one who
presides). The presbyters and deacons are last addressed on the
charitable distribution of these funds in *Ep.* 12.2.2; sometime
thereafter the special commission seems to take over supervision
of the funds (cf. *Ep.* 41). This indicates, if indication is needed,
the breakdown of trust between Cyprian and some of his *clerici.*

On the theme of bishop and charity in Cyprian, consult J.
Colson, *L'évêque lien d'unité et de charité chez saint Cyprien de
Carthage* (Paris 1961).

The Church's resources would not necessarily be in cash only.
Half a century later, at least, in 303, the basilica of Abthugni is
found to have supplies of oil and corn (cf. *Act. purg. Felicis,*
CSEL 26.200.5) and at Cirta there are church stocks of tunics
and shoes (men's and women's), veils and capes (cf. *Gest. ap.
Zenoph.,* CSEL 187.8 ff.). We might conjecture there were similar resources at this time in Carthage (at a season of rampant
inflation).

11. *ad procurandam quietem.* Cyprian is anxious to avoid rioting and violent outcry against the Christian community; cf. *Ep.* 7.1 (where see n. 4). The situation is tense, but Cyprian does not consider it beyond control.

12. *inlustravit iam gloriosis initiis divina dignatio.* There are no privations, tortures, deaths as yet.

13. Under Valerian's persecution, with a ban on assemblies, circumstances for Christians were much more stringent; contrast the inability to celebrate in *Ep.* 76.3 (the Christians there are not in prison but *in metallo,* however).

Cyprian appears to imply that his presbyters enjoy faculties of celebrating the Eucharist as a matter of course and not as a special privilege conferred on them by their bishop under emergency conditions. That is what we might by now expect amongst a Christian community in a sprawling urban complex such as Carthage: it was not only the bishop who offered the *sacrificium* at any one time. Note the celebration, elsewhere in Carthage, mentioned in *Epp.* 15.1.2, 16.4.2, 17.2.1 (during Cyprian's absence).

There are indeed some suggestions that we have already the beginnings of regional parishes. Some Carthaginian presbyters later readmit *lapsi* to Communion, while others do not (cf. *Epp.* 15.1.2, 16.3.2, 17.2.1). Individual presbyters may be closely associated with a particular deacon-assistant (cf. *Epp.* 34.1 [Gaius Didensis and his deacon] and 52.2.3? [Novatus and Felicissimus]). Is this in different areas? And one breakaway Church seems to be associated with a particular district (cf. *Ep.* 41.1.2, 2.1, reading *in monte*). Compare in contemporary Alexandria, there were "sectional assemblies"; cf. Dionysius of Alex. *ap.* Eusebius, *H.E.* 7.11.17.

On the delegated power to offer, cf. Ignatius of Antioch, *Ad Smyrn.* 8 (ᾧ ἂν αὐτὸς ἐπιτρέψῃ); it became a formally recognized presbyteral power in the next century (Counc. of Nicaea 1, can. 18; Counc. of Neocaes, can. 9; Counc. of Ancy, can. 1). And on the growth of "parishes," see DACL 12 (1936) 2602 ff.

For the regional divisions of the church in Carthage in the later fourth century, see Monceaux, *Histoire* 3.69; N. Duval in *Karthago* 7 (1956) 191 ff; W. H. C. Frend in *Excavations at*

Carthage 1976 Conducted by the University of Michigan 3 (Ann Arbor 1977) 29. And Cyprian's "collegial" role with his presbyters in liturgical matters is further discussed by G. H. Luttenberger in *Rech. théol. anc. médiév.* 43 (1976) 52 ff.

Note, too, that Cyprian automatically supposes the presbyters will be accompanied by a deacon in their eucharistic service. Cyprian, too, in his present exile is accompanied by a deacon (see below n. 16), as he was later by the deacon Pontius at Curubis under Valerian (cf. Pontius, *Vit. Cyp.* 12.3). Similarly Gregory Thaumaturgus now goes into flight, accompanied by a deacon; cf. Gregory of Nyssa, *Vit. Greg. Thaum.* MG 46.947. Is this why Ambrose could make the deacon Lawrence poignantly ask his pope Xystus: *Quo, sacerdos sancte, sine diacono properas?* (*De off.* 1.44)

For further discussion on *missa cum diacono*, see R. Hombach, *Liturgie und Mönchtum* 14 (1954) 62 ff. And on the functions of deacons generally, see *Ep.* 3 n. 17.

14. *vicissitudo convenientium.* There may possibly be some overtones of religious gathering in the use of the verb *convenio;* it is frequently employed by Cyprian in connection with eucharistic assemblies. Cf., e.g., *De orat. dom.* 4: *quando in unum cum fratribus convenimus et sacrificia divina cum Dei sacerdote celebramus, Ep.* 75.17.3: *cum eis conveniat et orationes pariter cum eisdem misceat et altare ac sacrificium commune constituat.* Note also *Act. Perp.* 13.6: *ad te conveniunt* (of the *plebs* and Bishop Optatus).

15. *temporibus servire:* probably an allusion to Rom. 12.11, with a text based on the reading καίρῳ δουλεύοντες, instead of κυρίῳ δουλεύοντες. See Fahey 435.

16. *salutat vos diaconus.* The turn of phrase suggests that there is only one and that it is only to be expected that Cyprian should be so accompanied. Hence identification with Victor, the deacon and former *lector* of *Ep.* 13.7—with Cyprian in hiding—is likely. Observe that the *codex Remigianus* reads at the conclusion of *Ep.* 6: *Victor diaconus et qui mecum sunt vos salutant;* that is strong support for the identification.

17. It is difficult to ascertain how large a group Cyprian's *comites* formed. A cleric is recorded earlier in *Ep.* 7.2. Other clerics at later stages are seen to be with him, Saturus and the

confessor Optatus (*Ep.* 29), the confessors Celerinus and Aurelius (*Epp.* 37 & 38), possibly the confessor Numidicus (*Ep.* 40), and some bishops (*collegae*) at least visited him (*Epp.* 38.2.2, 39.1.1). No doubt the episcopal visitors included Caldonius and Herculanus (*Ep.* 41). When he wrote *Ep.* 37, he could celebrate the sacrifice *cum pluribus*. We could possibly conjecture some personal servants (cf. the *domestici comites* of the formal exile at Curubis; see Pontius *Vit. Cyp.* 12.3). And then there was the *puerorum innocens aetas* of *Ep.* 16.4.1 Cf. Dionysius of Alexandria, in flight under Decius, is accompanied by οἱ παῖδες καὶ πολλοὶ τῶν ἀδελφῶν (see Eusebius *H.E.* 6.40.3); there are two παῖδες with Polycarp when he is finally arrested (see Eusebius, *H.E.* 4.15.11)—are these servants?

The formula used here by Cyprian for sending greetings (*qui mecum sunt salutant*) is Pauline. Cf., e.g., Gal. 1.2: *et qui mecum sunt omnes fratres.*

LETTER 6

Contents: From his place of hiding Cyprian felicitates certain confessors in prison in Carthage; he exhorts them by means of a variety of texts to be both humble and steadfast in their faith, and prays that their aspirations to martyrdom may eventually be fulfilled.

Date and circumstances: There can be little doubt that this letter was composed about the same time as *Ep.* 5; Cyprian in his place of concealment has heard some details of the confessors whom he mentions in that letter (*Ep.* 5.1.2) and whose needs, spiritual and material, he there urges his clergy to meet. He names specifically among their numbers Sergius, Rogatianus, and Felicissimus; he knows that their ranks include women and children (§3.1), and he is informed that Rogatianus and Felicissimus were the first to be so imprisoned, accompanied by popular agitation (§4). The fears of public outcry against the community, which Cyprian voiced in *Ep.* 5.2.1, are real enough.

It is, further, clear that these confessors have only just recently entered upon the path that leads to martyrdom: *ingressi viam dominicae dignationis* (§1.2); *initiis ad summa pergentibus* (§4). There are no actual martyrs: indeed there are no actual, only anticipated, tortures (§2.1).

There are a few close verbal coincidences which strengthen the link with *Ep.* 5: *Ep.* 5.1.1: *permittit loci condicio*, and *Ep.* 6.1.1: *loci condicio permitteret; Ep.* 5.1.2: *qui gloriosa voce Dominum confessi*, and *Ep.* 6.1.1: *quae gloriosa voce Dominum confessa sunt.* And the confessors in *Ep.* 6 are at the same initial stage of their process as we have found them to be in *Ep.* 5.2.1: *confessores bonos quos inlustravit iam gloriosis initiis divina dignatio.*

At the very least we can set *Epp.* 5 and 6, now paired, before about April 250. For by the middle of that month tortures have been introduced for recalcitrant confessors (see *Ep.* 10.1 and nn. 5 and 6 thereto). Indeed we must be not a little time before that date, because (1) obstinate confessors, before then, were in fact exiled (*extorres, Ep.* 10.1.1) and even that has not yet happened to any of these, the initial Carthaginian confessors, and (2) the tone of this letter unmistakably suggests that the general collapse of the Carthaginian *plebs* has yet to occur (cf. *Epp.* 13.1, 14.1.1) and that debacle occurred demonstrably before mid-April also. But there is already popular outcry against some Christians (§4) and they are under pressure to conform to pagan religious demands in which their hands might be defiled (§1.1). That is to say, Decius' orders have already arrived, but it is a fair guess, all the same, that the *dies praestitutus* established for Carthage, the last possible date by which certificates generally have to be obtained, is still some time in the future. For further discussion see in BICS 20 (1973) 118 ff. esp. 121, and Introduction, pp. 25 ff.

The letter is found, from §2 to the end, in a Donatist collection of Cyprian's writings, edited by H. K. Mengis, *Ein donatistisches Corpus cyprianischer Briefe* (diss. Freiburg 1916) 12 ff., and was imitated in the fourth century by Lucifer of Calaris (ed. Hartel, 288).

1. *Sergius* is otherwise unknown. Rogatianus is a presbyter. By the rules of precedence in epistolary address we must infer

that Sergius was at least of that clerical rank also. And as this is Carthage, and there was but one bishop there, he ought, accordingly, to be a fellow *presbyter* and probably senior to Rogatianus in that class. When these confessors are next addressed (*Ep.* 13), Sergius is not included in the *incipit*—though there are still no actual martyrs (and he does not figure in Lucian's catalogue of those who have died in *Ep.* 22.2.2). Is there a possibility that he joined opposition ranks (in which troublesome *confessores* and *compresbyteri* already figure in *Epp.* 13.3.2 f., 14.3.1 ff.) and he is, therefore, quietly but deliberately overlooked? Discussed by X. S. Thaninayagam, *The Carthaginian Clergy During the Episcopate of Saint Cyprian* (Colombo 1947) 25 n. 5. His name does not appear in all mss.

Rogatianus is described as elderly (*senem*) and as a presbyter in §4: the trusted Carthaginian presbyter of the same name in *Ep.* 7 would sensibly be identified (he is still at liberty in that earlier letter). By the time Cyprian wrote *Ep.* 13 (before mid-April 250) Rogatianus, named in the *titulus*, appears to have been released (*Ep.* 13.7: *nuper cum adhuc essetis in carcere constituti*); his imprisonment cannot, therefore, have been longer than a few months' duration. When Cyprian addresses the imprisoned confessors thereafter, he is not named among their ranks (cf., e.g., *Ep.* 10). Later (in *Epp.* 41–43), Rogatianus reappears as an illustrious *presbyter confessor* (*Ep.* 43.1.1), acting as a member of an ecclesiastical commission before Cyprian's return from hiding (which was after March 23, 251).

The question is somewhat obscured by the presence of the modifier *iunior* after Rogatianus in a number of mss. That suggests an interpretation which excludes at least the otherwise natural identification with the Rogatianus described in §4.

So far as our knowledge goes, Sergius, Rogatianus, and Numidicus (see on *Ep.* 40) are the only three *presbyteri confessores* of this persecution in Carthage. Other known clerical confessors in Carthage are equally scanty—Optatus (on probation as *lector doctorum audientium,* see on *Ep.* 29.1.2), and possibly the exorcist and lector of *Ep.* 23. (The confessor Puppianus of *Ep.* 66 must surely be a layman; see n. *ad loc.*).

2. *optans ipse quoque conspectu vestro frui.* The turn of phrase

might suggest that Cyprian has received some message from the confessors in which they voiced the desire of seeing for themselves Cyprian in person.

3. *si ... loci condicio permitteret.* That is to say, Cyprian is writing from his place of concealment. It is worth observing that the fugitive Cyprian appears here to write to these imprisoned confessors without any detectable note of embarrassment or apology for his own *fuga.* See n. 2 to *Ep.* 5.

4. *manibus illis quae purae et innocentes ... sacrilega obsequia respuerunt.* It has been suggested by M. Réveillaud, *op. cit.* 32 ff., and the suggestion has been greeted with approval (e.g., L. Duquenne, *Chronologie des lettres de s. Cyprien* [Brussels 1972] 49 n. 3), that bishops alone were singled out for the performance of pagan rites at the opening stages of Decius' persecution. It was only the intransigent zeal of Sergius, Rogatianus, and company that made them into confessors.

However, the phrase *sacrilega obsequia* is difficult to interpret otherwise than implying general obligation on the part of these confessors to perform pagan rites. For an unequivocal use of *obsequium* referring to these general orders of Decius, observe *De laps.* 8: *nonne quando ad Capitolium sponte ventum est, quando ultro ad obsequium diri facinoris accessum est ...* And defiled hands, which these confessors have avoided by their refusal, are standard ingredients in the description of the fallen *sacrificati* of Decius' persecution (cf., e.g., *Ep.* 20.2.2: *sacrilegis contactibus manus suas ... maculassent,* and *Ep.* 31.7.1: *impio sacrificio manus inquinatae*) as are unspotted hands of Decian confessors (cf., e.g., *De laps.* 2: *inlustres manus quae ... sacrificiis sacrilegis restituerunt,* and *Ep.* 55.14.2: *etsi manus pura sit.*

It seems perverse, therefore, not to conclude that there exists in fact already a general obligation to perform pagan rites and in the manner required by Decius' orders. We are already at a time when Decius' requirements are generally operative. This is not to deny, however, that there may have been a very early stage when bishops were singled out for attack, but we are now clearly beyond such a period. Further discussion in BICS 20 (1973) 120 f., and Intro. pp. 25 ff.

5. *gloriosa voce Dominum confessa:* closely parallel to *Ep.* 5.1.2: *gloriosa voce Dominum confessi.*

6. These are standard epistolary flourishes of politesse in the despatch of *vicariae litterae;* see K. Thraede, *Grundzüge griechisch-römischer Brieftopik* (Munich 1970) 121, 149 ff., 192 for themes in this and other similar epistles of Cyprian.

7. Matt. 28.20. Cyprian's version has *consummationem mundi,* where *mundus* is used to translate the Greek αἰών. On Cyprian's use of this passage, see Fahey 328 ff.

8. *carcerem quem inlustravit vestra praesentia.* The terrifying darkness of Roman prisons was notorious. A good illustration is in *Act. Perp.* 3.5: *post paucos dies recipimur in carcerem: et expavi quia numquam experta eram tales tenebras.* Cf. also *Epp.* 22.2.1 and 37.2.1.

9. *ubi modo constituta sunt Dei templa.* Cyprian insists frequently on the baptized Christian being a *templum Dei* (traceable, of course, to 1 Cor. 3.16 f., 2 Cor. 6.16). Some of the numerous passages in Cyprian are listed by Fahey 445.

10. *ad tolerantiam passionis.* On *passio* (with some of its technical overtones of "suffering under persecution") see n. 13 to *Ep.* 3.

11. Ps. 115.6.

12. Ps. 50.19. Cyprian's use of the verse here is somewhat strained; he is talking about the rewards for physical sufferings.

13. Wisd. 3.4–8, omitting verse 7.

14. Note the characteristic way in which Cyprian binds his quotation into his text by picking up its key words. That martyrs would sit on the judgment tribunal with Christ was a widely distributed notion by this time (martyrs achieving immediate glory; cf. *Ep.* 12.2.1; *Ad Fort.* praef. 4: *(aliud) baptisma ... quod statim Deo copulat; Ad Fort.* 13, *ut cum Christo statim gaudeat; Ep.* 31.3 *caeleste regnum sine ulla cunctatione retinere; Ep.* 58.3.1: *martyribus patent caeli).* It is a notion based on the charismatic gifts implied by the very act of confession (with the Holy Spirit speaking in the witness) supported by such texts as Matt. 10.19 f., 19.28; Luke 22.30. For a scatter of parallels, earlier than or near contemporary with Cyprian, see *Mart. Polycarp.* 19.2; *Mart.*

Just. 5.6; Hippolytus of Rome, *In Dan.* 2.37, *De ant.* 59; Tertullian, *Ad mart.* 2.4; Origen, *Exhort. ad mart.* 14, 28; Dionysius of Alex. *ap.* Eusebius, *H.E.* 6.42.5; *Pass. Mar. et Jacob.* 6.10. And for the iconographic tradition of enthroned martyrs, see A. Grabar in *Cah. arch.* 6 (1952) 31 ff. See also nn. 19 and 31 to *Ep.* 10 and n. 1 to *Ep.* 15.

Certain corollaries might follow for confessors with their privileged access to the Spirit—they might enjoy special powers of intercession, they might lay claim to special powers of forgiveness and reconciliation, they might expect special 'clerical' status and ecclesiastical preferment, etc. When the numbers of confessors become unprecedentedly large as a result of this persecution, such traditionally sanctioned prerogatives are to pose major disciplinary and institutional problems. The acute tension between the need for practical modification of some of these ideas and the high premium placed on martyrdom becomes palpable in Cyprian's subsequent correspondence. Further discussion and bibliography are in nn. 7 and 8 to *Ep.* 15.

15. *praesentia supplicia calcetis.* The context makes it clear that Cyprian is continuing to expatiate on themes drawn from his biblical quotation; the *supplicia* are a rhetorical anticipation rather than an actuality. On the advent of tortures in the trial of Christian recusants, see n. 6 to *Ep.* 10.

16. *iusti quique et prophetae et apostoli missi.* On the theme of the martyrdom of the prophets, see H. A. Fischel in *Jew. Quart. Rev.* 37 (1946–47) 265 ff.; T. W. Manson in *Bull. John. Ryl.* 39 (1956–57) 463 ff.; H. J. Schoeps, *Aus frühchristlicher Zeit. Religionsgeschichtliche Untersuchungen* (Tübingen 1950) 126 ff.; U. Wickert, *Sacramentum unitatis. Ein Beitrag zum Verständnis der Kirche bei Cyprian* (Berlin and New York 1971) 90 f; and the texts Matt. 23.29 ff., Luke 11.47 ff. Note the assumption that the apostles died as martyrs (also apparently made by the Roman clergy in *Ep.* 8.1.2 and by Cyprian again in *Ep.* 10.4.3).

On this general theme of the slaying, in the past, of the exemplary *iusti praecedentes,* cf. *Ep.* 58.2.2, 5 f.; *De bono pat.* 10: *invenimus denique et patriarchas et prophetas et iustos omnes . . . sic Abel originem martyrii et passionem iusti initians . . .* ; *Test.* 1.2; *Ad Fort.* 11; etc.

17. John 12.25.

18. Matt. 10.28, a text (with a minor variant) found also in three other passages in Cyprian with the previous quotation. See Fahey 298 f. Observe that for Cyprian it is Christ who can kill both body and soul.

19. Rom. 8.16 f.

20. Rom. 8.18.

21. *multae pressurae iustorum, ex omnibus tamen liberantur qui in Deum fidunt*. A modification of Ps. 33.20 which is quoted in *Test*. 3.6 as *multae praessurae iustorum sed ex omnibus illis liberabit eos*, an allusion overlooked by Fahey 135.

22. A clear indication that these initial Decian confessors in Carthage include other than "Christian leaders" (against the suggestion made by W. H. C. Frend in *CR* 22 [1972] 394); see further BICS 20 (1973) 118 ff. For *feminae* and *virgines* among the confessors, cf. *De laps*. 2.

23. On Cyprian's (standard) Roman attitude towards the feminine sex, cf. n. 16 to *Ep*. 4.

24. *pueros etiam*. That the terms of Decius' edict included children emerges both from Cyprian (cf. *Ep*. 55.13.2 *uxorem et liberos et domum totam; De laps*. 9, 25; Gregory of Nyssa, MG 46.945; one of the extant *libelli*, Knipfing no. 33 (two sons and a daughter). We may be dealing here with some family groups.

At the beginning of this sentence, "the glory of your company" translates *gloriam numeri vestri*. Can H. Leclercq be right in citing this use of *numerus* here as an example of the word bearing the significance of "les fidèles," in DACL 8 (1928) 1064 *s.v.* Laïques?

Observe the close parallel to the idea here (*ut omnis vobiscum et sexus et aetas esset in honore*) in *Ep*. 76.6.2: *ut martyrii vestri beatum gregem et sexus et aetas omnis ornaret*.

25. An illustration much favoured by Cyprian (from Dan. 3) and one which clearly figured generally as a model of suffering (illustrated generously in the Roman catacombs). For Cyprian's varied exploitation of the trio, cf. Fahey 592 ff.

26. *refrigerii locum. Refrigerium* is a markedly Christian-Latin word, rather rare in pagan usage. See C. Mohrmann, *Études sur le latin des chrétiens* 2 (Rome 1961) 81 ff.; H. Pétré, *Caritas, Étude*

sur le vocabulaire latin de la charité chrétienne (Louvain 1948) Note E, 269 f.; P. de Labriolle in *Bull. d'anc. litt. et d'arch. chrét.* 2 (1912) 214 ff.; H. H. Janssen, *op. cit.* 235 ff.

27. Dan. 3.16 ff. On Cyprian's text here, consult F. C. Burkitt, *The Old Latin and the Itala* (Cambridge 1896) 25 ff.

28. Cyprian appears already sensitive to the temptations of arrogance and pride which can beset successful confessors, but there is no ground for believing that we have here a hint that these particular confessors are beginning to be in any way unruly. It is worth observing that the motif of praise for humility, self-effacement, modesty, diffidence, even shyness on the part of the martyr appears in Martyr *Acta* to be dated after the persecution of Decius, e.g., *Pass. Marian. et Jacob.* 1 and *Pass. Montan.* 13.

29. *in hoc fidere ut liberari in praesentia vellent.* The turn of phrase seems designed basically to express the future passive: discussion in L. Bayard, *Le latin de saint Cyprien* (Paris 1902) 257 ff.; Watson 139; J. Schrijnen and C. Mohrmann, *Studien zur Syntax der Briefe des hl. Cyprian* 1 (Nijmegen 1936) 26 f.

30. *complexum et osculum Domini.* Compare Perpetua's celestial vision, *Act. Perp.* 12.5: *osculati sumus illum.*

31. *cum Felicissimo fratre nostro quieto semper et sobrio.* It is not a watertight inference but it would seem likely from this description that Felicissimus is a layman. There is the Felicissimus, of course, of *Ep.* 41 ff.; he seems to be a deacon, and the remarks made in *Ep.* 41 (before April 251) that Cyprian has been aware for some time of the criminal activities of Felicissimus suggest that Cyprian's awareness of these crimes dates back to the period before the outbreak of this persecution. The description here (*quieto semper et sobrio*) must mean that in *Ep.* 41 we meet with a different Felicissimus. By his choice of description Cyprian seems at pains to underline that the savage violence was uninvited, undeserved, and unprovoked; Felicissimus was acting in the manner which Cyprian approved.

32. *excipiens ferocientis populi impetum primum.* To construe *primum* with the following *hospitium*—so Bayard—seems to weaken the clear emphasis in the passage on the precursor role played throughout by Rogatianus; *hospitium*, as it is, is depen-

dent on *praeparavit;* and construed as here, each of the three successive clauses pointedly ends with *primum, praeparavit, antecedit.*—It is somewhat uncertain what precisely this present clause may imply. In *Ep.* 40 we have a picture of mob violence (Numidicus), but here the victims end up neither dead nor left for dead in the streets, but unscathed, in prison. Already Cyprian had experienced the angry mood of the Carthaginian crowd (cf. *Ep.* 20.1.2: *cum me clamore violento frequenter populus flagitasset*), so that (he avers) he withdrew into hiding (cf. *Ep.* 7.1); he is fearful of any action by Christians which may agitate the people further (*Epp.* 7.1, 5.2); he delayed his eventual return from hiding for fear of creating a *tumultus . . . maior* (*Ep.* 43.4.2). In the present case all we need suppose are scenes similar to those described in contemporary Alexandria, with hostile pagans jostling Christians already arrested or challenging well-known Christians to commit themselves, one way or the other, over Decius' regulations (Dionysius Alex. *ap.* Eusebius, *H.E.* 6.41.10 ff., 15 f.). *Ep.* 56.1.1 suggests a similar situation about this same time in or near Capsa (*violentiam magistratus et populi frementis impetum vicerant*). Rogatianus and Felicissimus are the first to suffer similar harassment in Carthage.

33. *metator quodammodo vester nunc quoque vos antecedit.* Cyprian leaves it tantalizingly unclear in what way Rogatianus can be said to be continuing to lead the advance party. The metaphorical language appears to be, as so often, military: the *metator castrorum* preceded the army and marked out the encampment site. A likely conjecture is that Cyprian is picturing him advancing first to the proconsul's tribunal to undergo his trial.

It was clearly considered a very special honour to lead the way to confession and martyrdom. Compare the description of Celerinus in Rome (*Ep.* 39.2.1) and of the Roman confessors generally (*Ep.* 28.1.1f.). Later Cyprian was graced with that signal privilege in the Valerianic persecution, both in its first stage (*Ep.* 78.1.2: *a te sumus ad gloriam provocati qui prior nobis ducatum ad confessionem nominis Christi praebuisti . . . nam qui prior est in cursu, prior est et ad praemium,* and *Ep.* 77.2.2) and in its second (*Act. Cyp.* 4.2). Cf. Numidicus in *Ep.* 40.1.1, where see n. 5.

LETTER 7

Contents: Cyprian is in hiding and he regrets that he cannot satisfy his longing to be present in Carthage with his brethren; but he has an over-riding duty to ensure conditions of peace within the community, and his presence in Carthage may well stir up popular outcry and violence among the heathen. He urges that the practical work of charity should continue undiminished and sends a sum of money additional to the resources which he left in Carthage for this purpose.

Date and circumstances: There are several signs which should converge to pin-point this letter as the earliest of the surviving Decian letters. Cyprian is, indeed, already safely in hiding; fear of popular attack is real but no such attack has yet occurred. We are, therefore, before the *impetum primum* of *Ep.* 6 and its companion letter, *Ep.* 5.

Further, Cyprian still entertains expectations of a prompt return. Subsequent events are soon to dispel those hopes for a year at least. In addition, when he exhorts in this letter his clergy to works of charity, Cyprian urges care for *pauperes omnes*, whereas in *Ep.* 5, in a parallel context, the works are restricted to the persevering poor. Some Christians have fallen meantime. The lapse of Christians generally has not as yet started and, as a corollary, there are no imprisoned confessors to visit (again, in contrast with *Ep.* 5).

Rogatianus, the *presbyter* and *metator* of the Carthaginian confessors in *Ep.* 6, is still at liberty in *Ep.* 7. There are, to be sure, *peregrini* in Carthage needing charitable assistance; they may possibly be early refugees but they are not described as such and need only be the usual strangers and visitors who have come to the large city of Carthage. In contrast with *Ep.* 5.1.1 Cyprian does not appear to be as yet entertaining any fears for the safety of his clergy.

We should, therefore, conclude that if *Epp.* 5 and 6 are quite some time before mid-April 250, this letter is to be placed even earlier still, after Cyprian became endangered but before any serious effects of Decius' orders had been felt by the Christian community generally. Indeed, Cyprian's lack of apprehension for his Carthaginian brothers, apart from potential eruption of popular *invidia*, might even suggest that the details of Decius' orders proper are still not generally known or the implications of them appreciated. Ill-informed rumours, and Cyprian's flight, may have preceded their formal promulgation: compare the *multa varia et incerta opinionibus*, and the retirement of the *universi clerici*, that preceded the arrival of Valerian's second rescript (*Ep.* 80.1.2). As on that occasion (*Ep.* 80.1.3), the church in Rome provided the prelude to the experiences of the church in Carthage (*Ep.* 28.1).

For discussion, see L. Nelke, *Die Chronologie der Korrespondenz Cyprians* ... (diss. Thorn 1902) 11; O. Ritschl, *De epistulis Cyprianicis* (diss. Halle 1885) 9; L. Duquenne, *Chronologie des lettres de s. Cyprien* (Brussels 1972) 62 ff. (Bayard, in ed., xvi inexplicably places *Ep.* 7 after *Epp.* 5 and 6).

1. *per Dei gratiam incolumis.* On Cyprian's *fuga* and *latebra*, see n. 2 to *Ep.* 5.

2. Is there a hint of a (lost) message from the clergy to Cyprian in hiding which evinced *desiderium* for Cyprian's presence in Carthage? Or is Cyprian simply assuming that the *desiderium* which he feels himself is shared by his clergy and his flock? If Cyprian felt particularly defensive or embarrassed about his flight, this is certainly a bold front to assume.

3. *invidiam et violentiam gentilium provocat.* See n. 11 to *Ep.* 5 and n. 32 to *Ep.* 6. Cyprian was certainly the object of popular outcry among the Carthaginian *gentiles*. On the *invidia* Pontius (unclearly) states (*Vit. Cyp.* 15.1) that the *horti* of Cyprian, so curiously restored to him after sale (*de Dei indulgentia restitutos*), Cyprian would have sold again *nisi invidiam de persecutione vitaret.* Is this an oblique way of referring to this flight? In *Ep.* 20.1.2 we get the fullest description of the circumstances of which Cyprian is speaking: Cyprian was a well-known figure, and a marked man.

4. *simus auctores rumpendae pacis.* The turn of phrase suggests that in Cyprian's view there was still *pax* for the community generally.

5. *rebus compositis.* Cyprian seems still to be thinking in terms of the *invidia* of the Carthaginian crowd as eventually simmering down; the storm can blow over.

6. *si ante dignatus fuerit Dominus ostendere.* Cyprian could (later) attribute his flight itself to divine inspiration, cf. *Ep.* 16.4.1: *Dominus qui ut secederem iussit,* and see n. 30 to *Ep.* 16 on Cyprian's personal *ostensiones.* In fact, when it came to the point of returning, Cyprian displayed a prudent caution consistent with his desire to secure *quies* for his brethren (*Ep.* 43).

7. *illic ubi me Deus et credere voluit et crescere. Credere:* for Cyprian's conversion under the influence of the aged (Carthaginian) presbyter Caecilianus, cf. Pontius *Vit. Cyp.* 4 and note the description of the process in *Ad Donat.* 3 ff. *Crescere:* the context and run of the sentence should make this refer not to Cyprian's upbringing (not, therefore, evidence for Carthage being Cyprian's *patria*) but to his spiritual growth in his new life as a believer; this growth was signalled by rapid ecclesiastical advancement in Carthage (cf. *Vit. Cyp.* 5: *quamvis in primis fidei suae adhuc diebus et rudi vitae spiritalis aetate*). For the sentiment expressed here *Ep.* 81 is noteworthy; Cyprian contrives to undergo his martyrdom not in Utica but, as is fitting, in Carthage, in the city where he is *praepositus* of his *plebs.*

8. The chances of widowhood were high in a world of malnutrition (among the poor) and high mortality generally; and the strong Christian pressure against re-marriage would have reinforced the natural numbers in this class. They were grouped, by this time, as a formal Christian *ordo* in Carthage (cf. Tertullian, *De virg. vel.* 9.2; *De praesc. haer.* 3.5; *Trad. Apost.* 10), and were singled out for ecclesiastical charity (cf., e.g., Acts 6.1; Hermas, *Sim.* 9.27.2; Justin, 1 *Apol.* 67, Cornelius *ap.* Eusebius, *H.E.* 6.43.11). Note DACL 15 (1953) 3007 ff., esp. 3017 ff. on the third century evidence; *Didasc.* 3.1–11. (I do not know by what warrant X. S. Thaninayagam, *The Carthaginian Clergy* . . . [Colombo 1947] 98, can claim: "Under the name of *viduae* [in Cyprian] came mostly the deaconesses who assisted the priests in the instruction and baptism of female catechumens.")

9. *omnium pauperum curam.* On the chronological indications

suggested by this phrase, see introductory note and n. 8 to *Ep.* 5 and introductory note to this letter.

10. *peregrinis si qui indigentes fuerint.* There is considerable evidence for a widespread refugee movement among Christians endeavouring to escape the consequences of Decius' orders to sacrifice (cf., e.g., *Epp.* 21.4.1, 30.8.1, 55.13.2, 66.7.2; Dionysius Alex. *ap.* Eusebius, *H.E.* 6.42.2 ff.; Gregory of Nyssa, MG 46.945), but it cannot be asserted with any confidence that the *peregrini* here must be such fugitives.

It was the bishop's role to dispense hospitality to strangers and support their needs (cf. Hermas, *Sim.* 9.27.2); it was a role that the bishop might guard jealously against usurpation by wealthy laymen (cf. Jerome, *In ep. ad Titum.* 1.8–9) and which he might not abandon with impunity (cf. Firmilian's loud indignation at Stephen's denying *tectum et hospitium* to *legati episcopi, Ep.* 75.25). See generally RAC 8 (1972) 1061 ff. at 1107 ff. Cyprian may here simply be ensuring—as in *Ep.* 5.1.1—that his own *partes* continue to be fulfilled.

11. *de quantitate mea propria.* The emphatic *mea propria* suggests we are dealing with privately owned funds rather than with Cyprian's official portion of the Church's income (as D. D. Sullivan, *The Life of the North Africans . . .* [Washington 1933] 70 f., seems to take it). The language of the Roman confessors (who had read this letter among the enclosures of *Ep.* 20) is unhelpfully vague (*Ep.* 31.6.1). There is much obscurity over the sale of Cyprian's worldly goods and property after his conversion (cf. Pontius, *Vit. Cyp.* 2.7, 15.1; Jerome, *De vir. illust.* 67; see on *Ep.* 81). At all events, at some stage in this persecution Cyprian's *bona* were officially forfeit (*Ep.* 66.4.1)—as were those of *tot episcopi* (*Ep.* 66.7.2)—with some (unrecorded) penalty threatened against those who harboured them. The evidence converges to suggest that Cyprian belonged to the wealthy and propertied local aristocracy of Carthage. See Intro., pp. 14 ff.

12. On Rogatianus, see n. 1 to *Ep.* 6. Rogatianus must be free at the time Cyprian wrote this letter. In the later *Ep.* 5 we find that the Church funds generally have been more widely distributed. The verb which Cyprian uses here (*dimisi*) could bear the

technical overtone—but it need not necessarily do so—that Cyprian has renounced all ownership or control of the money.

13. *per Naricum acoluthum.* Naricus is otherwise unknown. This chances to be the earliest recorded reference to the office of acolyte. Acolytes do not occur in Hippolytus but are attested in 251 in Rome as being 42 in number (Cornelius *ap.* Eusebius, *H.E.* 6.43.11): as there were 46 presbyters at that time in the City, it does sound as if (allowing for vacancies) they acted primarily as servants of presbyters. Arguing from silence we might deduce that the office was perhaps instituted c. 220–240 A.D., though *Lib. Pontif.* seems to accredit Victor (186–197 A.D.)—ed. Duchesne 1.137—with the institution: *hic fecit sequentes cleros = acoluthos?*

We meet acolytes in Cyprian especially as letter-carriers (*Epp.* 45.4.3, 52.1, 59.1), as distributors of alms (directly to prisoners in *Epp.* 77.3.2, 78.1), etc. In other words, they act, as their name implies, as Church 'orderlies.'

See further on the office and its duties in DACL 1 (1924) 348 ff.; J. G. Davies in JEH 14 (1963), 7f.—*Ep.* 13.7 may refer to the sum now sent.

LETTER 8

Contents: Word has reached Rome that Cyprian has retired from Carthage. The Roman clergy are acting as good (and not as hireling) shepherds, just as Christ and Peter both acted, for, being leaderless, they must act as *praepositi* themselves. They have exhorted and continue to exhort their own brethren to be steadfast, both by word and by action, and even if any fall they do not abandon them but encourage them to do penance. The Carthaginian clergy (also leaderless) must act likewise, especially encouraging the lapsed and reconciling them, if they fall ill and are repentant, with the Church. Other works of mercy concerning the widowed, the sick, the homeless, the unburied must continue in spite of perils. And they are urged to disseminate as widely as they can copies of this letter.

Date and Circumstances: This letter, emanating from Rome, was delivered to Carthage by the hands of the subdeacon Crementius and was (apparently) given to Crementius to deliver at the same time as a *testimonium* the Roman Clergy had composed on martyred Pope Fabian, which was addressed to Cyprian specifically. Its nature as an enclosure, perhaps accompanying a copy of the eulogy on Fabian for the Carthaginian clergy, could possibly account for its being without a formal *titulus* (cf. *Ep.* 9.2.1: *nec ad quos scriptum sit significanter expressum est*); but it was clearly intended primarily not for Cyprian but for the Carthaginian clergy (as Cyprian plainly notes in *Ep.* 20.3.2: *vestra scripta . . . quae ad clerum nostrum . . . nuper feceratis*). *Contra* Fahey 232, it is not "addressed to Cyprian." We do not know whether loyalty, or malice, ensured that Cyprian received the letter; it is equally intriguing to speculate by what means the strange exchange of letters in *Epp.* 8 and 9 was preserved.

The mood in which the Roman clergy address the Carthaginians is notably imperative, authoritative, indeed episcopal, e.g., in §3: *vos hoc facere debere, alia quae incumbunt vobis, subveniri eis debet*, etc. They refer proudly to the martyrdom of Peter (§1.2) and to their own courageous record. I do not see how it can be described as a letter "from the distracted, frightened, confused, hysterical clergy at Rome"—G. C. Brauer, *The Age of the Soldier Emperors. Imperial Rome, A.D. 244–284*, (Park Ridge 1975) 41.

The value of making a steadfast stand is highly stressed. Indeed the confessors (*fratres qui sunt in vinculis*) take pride of place before the presbyters in the concluding salutation (§3.3). By corollary, their attitude to *fuga* (and that includes Cyprian's), with their sermonizing on the good and the hireling shepherd (§1) and their frequent references to desertion (e.g., §2 *deserentes, dereliquimus, relicti*) is plainly critical and scarcely veiled by the decency of innuendo. The repetition of the expression *insignis persona* (Cyprian's own?) as an explanation for flight (§1.1)—or apostasy (§2.3)—seems pointedly wilful.

On the other hand, the Roman clergy here stress with noticeable firmness that hope of forgiveness should be held out to the fallen and that reconciliation should in fact be granted to repentant lapsed *in articulo*. They give the appearance of reacting against more rigorist attitudes which, they are aware, are to be found amongst their intended audience (so M.-C. Chartier in *Antonianum* 14 (1939) 38). It may not be legitimate, however, on these grounds alone to dissociate from those who were responsible for this letter those Roman clergy who later became more purist as Novatianists or Novatianist sympathizers (see on *Ep.* 30).

The language of the letter is poor in quality, the expressions awkwardly turned, the train of thought halting and uncertain. The contrast on these counts with the next letters which we have from Rome (*Epp.* 30, 31, and 36—with 30 [and 36?] having Novatian as *scriptor*) is marked. The letter, from this point of view, provides valuable social documentation on the level of education and sophistication attained at this time by some of the Roman *clerus;* it was not high. On the language of the letter,
* consult C. Mohrmann in VC 3 (1949) 178 ff.

As to the precise date, we are clearly at a developed stage of the persecution. Pope Fabian has died (mart. January 20, 250), but a successor has not been appointed (§1.1); sacrifices on the Capitol have occurred (§2.3); there are lapsed (§2.3), confessors in prison (§§3.1, 3.3), homeless refugees (§3.1), and possibly martyred dead (§3.2). But the perils are by no means passed; the brethren continue to need exhortation to prevent their plunging into idolatry (§2.1), and it is dangerous work (§2.2); to bury the Christian dead also involves grave dangers (§3.2); and even the fallen may be subject to a second arrest (§3.1).

In *Ep.* 20.3.1 Cyprian refers to this letter as being 'recently written' (*nuper feceratis:* on *nuper,* see n. 27 to *Ep.* 1), and *Ep.* 20 enclosed, *inter alia,* a copy of *Ep.* 18 which was itself written at the beginning of the summer of 250 (*Ep.* 18.1.2 *iam aestatem coepisse*), that is to say, in the whereabouts of early June. *Ep.* 18 was despatched to Cyprian's presbyters and deacons; then Cyprian received a reply to it and he sent subsequently *Ep.* 19. A copy of *Ep.* 19 was also enclosed with *Ep.* 20. *Ep.* 20 cannot therefore be dated much before the end of June 250, and is more probably to be assigned to the course of July.

In the two letters *Epp.* 18 and 19 Cyprian maintains that the repentant lapsed may be reconciled to the Church *in articulo,* provided they have received a *libellus* of forgiveness from the "martyrs" (*Epp.* 18.1.2, 19.2.1). In *Ep.* 20, on the other hand, Cyprian drops that limiting proviso, having decided (he claims) on reading *Ep.* 8 (where there is no mention of *libelli martyrum*) that in the interests of unity *standum. . . . et cum vestra sententia.* That is to say, Cyprian, it would appear, has received *Ep.* 8 *after* writing *Ep.* 19 but *before* writing *Ep.* 20. (Cf. M. Bévenot in VC 28 [1974], 157 f.)

On this evidence, a copy of *Ep.* 8 appears, therefore, to have reached Cyprian in the vicinity of, say, late June/early July 250. It still remains a trifle doubtful how much earlier the letter was composed in Rome. Perhaps not much?

For further reading on *Ep.* 8, see L. Nelke, *Die Chronologie der Korrespondenz Cyprians . . .* (diss. Thorn 1902) 22 ff.; H. Koch in IKZ 10 (1920) 229 ff.; L. Duquenne, *Chronologie des Lettres de s. Cyprien* (Brussels 1972) 119; S. L. Greenslade in JTS 12 (1961) 217 ff.; H. J. Vogt, *Coetus sanctorum*, (Bonn 1968) 37 f.; H. Gülzow, *Cyprian und Novatian: der Briefwechsel zwischen den Gemeinden in Rom und Karthago zur Zeit der Verfolgung des Kaisers Decius* (Tübingen 1975) 27 ff.

1. *a Crementio subdiacono.* This is the only use in the correspondence of the hybrid *subdiaconus* and the earliest recorded occurrence of the word (Watson 261). Cyprian's term is regularly *hypodiaconus* (so, too, in the more elegantly composed *Ep.* 36.1, from Rome).

Subdeacons, or assistants to deacons, were required, we may surmise, partly as the deacon's work tended to become more spiritual and liturgical, and partly as it was a frequent (but not universal) practice to limit the number of deacons in a bishopric to the increasingly inadequate but New Testament figure of seven (Acts 6). See, on the restricted number, Counc. of Neocaes., can. 15, but contrast *Didas.* (Syriac) 3.13 in R. H. Connolly, *Didascalia Apostolorum* (Oxford 1929; repr. 1969) 148 ("in proportion to the number of the congregation of the Church, so let the deacons be"). Subdeacons are first recorded in Hippolytus, *Trad. Apost.* 13.

In the Cyprianic correspondence we meet subdeacons (along

with acolytes) as letter carriers (eg. *Epp.* 20, 36, 45, 77, 79); by contrast, in earlier times, we find deacons in Ignatius, *Ad Smyr.* 11 and *Ad Phil.* 10, acting as messengers. See further J. G. Davies in JEH 14 (1963) 6 ff.; DACL 15 (1953) 1619 ff.

We do not know whether Crementius belonged to the Carthaginian or to the Roman clergy, nor do we know for sure if his journeying marks the first formal exchange between the Carthaginian and the Roman clergy since the persecution began (see n. 32 below). It does sound as if it perhaps may. *Ep.* 20.1.1 refers indignantly to the report made by this Crementius, or to some similar report made by hostile Carthaginian clergy, concerning Cyprian's conduct.

In view of the ease and frequency of later correspondence between Carthage and Rome, a hiatus in communications in the first half of 250 would underline the deep confusion into which Decius' persecution threw the churches.

2. . . . *venit certa ex causa quod.* . . . It is quite obscure whether, in the ungainly style of the letter, we are to take *certa ex causa* with the preceding *secessisse benedictum Papatem Cyprianum* and the following *quod* clause ("of explanation"), producing "Cyprian had sound reasons for his retirement, namely . . . ," or whether *certa ex causa* is to be construed (a little more naturally) with *venit* (so translated here). In the latter case, it may contain an arch reference to clandestine complaints on Cyprian's actions reported *minus simpliciter et minus fideliter* (*Ep.* 20.1.1) by Cyprian's ecclesiastical opponents in Carthage (cf., for the opponents, Pontius, *Vit. Cyp.* 5: *quidam illi restituerunt*); in this case Crementius is more likely to be a Carthaginian cleric. The construing and interpretation is discussed by H. Koch in IKZ 10 (1920) 235 f.

3. *benedictum Papatem Cyprianum. Benedictus* is not used by Cyprian himself as an epithet, except possibly in "*Ep.* 82," but there it appears to be a marginal gloss; cf. M. Bévenot, *Bull. of J. Ryl. Library* 28 (1944) 78, text reproduced in Migne *Supp.* 1.41 ff.: *sanctissimas sorores nostras benedictas Metucosam et Valeriam.* The present phrase occurs already in Tertullian, with irony, *De pudic.* 13.7: *bonus pastor et benedictus papa;* cf., without irony, *De praesc. haer.* 30.2: *sub episcopatu Eleutheri benedicti.* Does the con-

ventional phraseology here harbour any irony? On the epithet (generally used with reference to witnesses of faith) see A. A. R. Bastiaensen *Le cérémonial épistolaire des chrétiens latins* (Nijmegen 1964) 32; H. A. M. Hoppenbrouwers, *Recherches sur la terminologie du martyre de Tertullien à Lactance* (Nijmegen 1961) 67 f., 83 f.; cf. *Ep.* 22.2.1 (by Lucianus): *benedictus martyr Paulus.*

Papa: Cyprian is so titled in letters addressed to him by the Roman clergy (*Epp.* 30, 31 and 36) and by Carthaginian confessors (*Ep.* 23). This leads Bastiaensen (23, 38f.) to conclude (rashly) that the word is used "toujours par des inférieurs vis-à-vis de l'évêque."

By this time *papa(s)* was a widely used form of address. In origin it is a familiar variant of πατήρ—see *Odyssea* 6.57 (Nausicaa to her father) and Aristophanes, *Pax* 120—a term by which clerics might themselves be formally addressed. Among the examples of the use of *papa(s)* in the third century are *Act. Perp. et Fel.* 13.3; Dionysius Alex. *ap.* Eusebius, *H.E.* 7.7.4; Gregory Thaumaturgos, *Epist. Can.*, can. 1; Origen, *Hom. 1. in 1 Samuel.* Cf. A. Deissmann, *Light from the Ancient East* (London 1910) 194 f.; J. G. Winter, *Life and Letters in the Papyri* (Ann Arbor 1933) 144 f.; and ILCV 3458 1.2, of bishop Marcellinus of Rome 296–304, the first attested use for the bishop of Rome. It was not until the eleventh century that the title was formally confined to the bishop of Rome. For further reading, see DACL 13 (1937) 1097 ff., P. de Labriolle in *Bull. d'anc. litt.* 1 (1911) 215 ff., and *idem*, in *Bull. du Cange* 4 (1928) 65 ff.; H. H. Janssen, *Kultur und Sprache. Zur Geschichte . . . bis Cyprian* (Nijmegen 1938) 93 ff.; E. W. Benson, *Cyprian, His Life, His Times, His Work* (London 1897) 29 f.; C. Pietri, *Roma christiana* (Rome 1976) 1609 ff.

4. *secessisse.* Cyprian himself uses this same word (in self-defence) in *Ep.* 20.1.2 (*interim secessi*), cf. *Ep.* 16.4.1 (*Dominus qui ut secederem iussit*), and regularly in *De lapsis.* A variant is *recedo.* Pontius is at pains to defend Cyprian against the charge of *fuga* and, naturally enough, he chooses non-pejorative terms, notably *secedo*, in his panegyric. See H. A. M. Hoppenbrouwers, *Recherches . . . 145* f. on the word.

One wonders whether the Roman clergy are using the euphemism with some irony (are they quoting Cyprian's choice of verb?), for their talk in the remainder of the letter is not in terms of "retreating", "retiring," or "withdrawing" but, bluntly, of "fleeing", "abandoning," and "deserting" (*relinquit et fugit, deserentes, relicti*, etc.).

Initially (in *Epp.* 7, 5 and 6), we have seen, Cyprian seems to be scarcely, if at all, on the defensive about his *fuga* (see n. 2 to *Ep.* 5, n. 2 to *Ep.* 7); but he undoubtedly soon comes under fire for this action (*Ep.* 14.1.2 f.) and the criticism rankled (*Ep.* 16.4.1). We see here that complaints got as far as Rome (§1), but Cyprian promptly scotched them in that quarter (*Ep.* 20.1 ff.), probably not long after getting hold of this letter, and effectively. He can subsequently get a fulsome eulogy precisely for this conduct of his from the Roman clerical confessors in their prison in *Ep.* 31.6.1. Cyprian is firmly confident about his own conscience, even to the point of suspending clerics of minor grade who "withdrew" without episcopal authorization (*Ep.* 34.4.1) and later, of actually condemning, without hesitation, those who lapsed only after tortures and sufferings (*De laps.* 7, 8); he speaks in praise of prudent retreat (*cauta secessio*) in *De laps.* 3, indeed of flight being divinely mandatory in *De laps.* 10: *et ideo Dominus in persecutione secedere et fugere mandavit*, and he can stress the rigours that especially beset voluntary exiles in *De laps.* 25 cf. *Ep.* 58.4 and Dionys. Alex. *ap.* Euseb. *H.E.* 6.42.2 ff. But the criticism continued and smarted (*Ep.* 66), and even after his death as the proto-episcopal martyr of Africa, his biographer still felt constrained to defend at some length this conduct of his (Pontius, *Vit. Cyp.* 7, 8, 12, 14).

Fuga, in time of persecution, was of course a controversial issue in the Roman West. Note Tertullian, *Ad uxorem* 1.3.4, *De fuga* esp. 1 ff., and *De pat.* 13.6; and see T. D. Barnes, *Tertullian* (Oxford 1971) 170 f., 176 ff.; *idem* in JTS 20 (1969) 117 ff. For further reading, see DACL 5 (1923) 2660 ff. esp. 2670 ff. and on the case of Cyprian, C. Favez in REL 19 (1941) 191 ff.; E. L. Hummel in SCA 9 (1946) 51 ff.

5. *propterea cum sit persona insignis*. The phrase is repeated when the Roman clergy are explaining why some have fallen as apostates, *sive quod essent insignes personae* (§2). Dionysius of Alexandria in fact emphasizes (without hint of reproach) that

some of his presbyters have gone into voluntary retirement in
this persecution, being "better known in the world" (τῷ
κόςμῳ προφανέτεροι) *ap.* Eusebius, *H.E.* 7.11.24 and he describes elsewhere (*ap.* Eusebius, *H.E.* 6.41.11) how Christians of
prominent status came under particular pressure in this persecution: "And of many of the more eminent persons (τῶν
περιφανεστέρων), some came forward immediately through fear,
others in public positions were compelled to do so by their
business, and others were dragged by those around them"
(trans. J. E. L. Oulton).

Likewise, in an earlier period, at Lyons, two particular Christians were singled out by the hostile crowd because they were
prominent and well-known figures, Vettius Epagathus
(ἐπίσημος) and Attalus (ὀνομαστός). Cf. *ap.* Eusebius, *H.E.*
5.1.10, 43.

Cyprian, however, is consistently at pains to point out that in
taking to flight his concern was not so much for his own self-
preservation (the effect of the bald phraseology here), but for the
prevention of anti-Christian rioting and violence which might
explode should his well-known and antagonistic figure be seen
in Carthage (cf., e.g., *Epp.* 14.1.2, 20.1.2). And he can emphasize
that the lower ranks of the Carthaginian clergy could be expected to carry on the good work in Carthage, being lost under the
cover of anonymity (cf. *Ep.* 14.2.1); they are not *insignes personae.*
See also n. 9 to *Ep.* 14.

6. *colluctandi causa adversarium simul cum servis suis.* The text
and the interpretation of it are uncertain. Can this text (Hartel's) possibly mean "so that He may cooperate with His servants in combatting the adversary" (cf. *Ep.* 10.4.4: *non sic est ut
servos suos tantum spectet, sed ipse luctatur in nobis*)? If, with
Bayard, we read *cum servo suo,* the meaning ought perhaps to be
something like "in order to wrestle with the adversary and his
minion," and the reference of *servus* would be to the *metator
antichristi* (*Ep.* 22.1.1), the emperor Decius, *servus* of the devil. In
any case, the *servi* (plural) here can equally well refer to the
devil's agents. Cf. *ministri diaboli,* 'devil's henchmen' who crucified the martyr Papylus in *Act. Carp. Papyl. Agath.* 4.2.

7. Cf. 2 Tim. 2.5.

8. It would appear that we are to find the *sententia* in the texts which follow, viz., incurring the censure and judgment of God reserved for negligent shepherds.

9. *nobis qui videmur praepositi esse.* The shape of the letter, §2 turning directly to address the Carthaginian clergy after talk by the Roman clergy of themselves in §1, leaves it doubtful that the first person plural here is intended to include the (now neglected) Carthaginian clergy.

The Roman clergy use the word *praepositi* which Cyprian normally associates with bishops (see nn. 7 and 16 to *Ep.* 3 and n. 6 to *Ep.* 9). In the Latin version of Firmilian's letter (*Ep.* 75) *seniores et praepositi* means *presbyteri et episcopi*. They are alluding to their *interregnum*, between the martyrdom of Fabian (January 20, 250) and the election of his successor (which did not occur until March 251). Other allusions to the Roman vacancy occur in *Epp.* 21.3.2, 30.5, and on the interval see L. Duchesne, *Le Liber Pontificalis* 1 (Paris 1955²) CLX f. Note that in *Ep.* 21.3.2 Celerinus, writing from Rome, refers to these Roman clergy simply as *praepositi (praeceperunt . . . praepositi . . . donec episcopus constituatur)*, and cf. n. 30 to *Ep.* 20.

10. *quod et antecessoribus nostris dictum est.* A. von Harnack, *Theologische Abhandlungen: Carl von Weizsäcker zu seinem siebzigsten Geburtstage* (Freiburg 1892) 22 takes *antecessores* as referring to preceding Roman bishops, but it would be much more natural to interpret them as the Pastors of Israel. For Ezekiel's shepherds (here alluded to) commonly figure as prototypes of neglectful and wicked Church leaders, cf., e.g., Tertullian, *De pudic.* 7.18, and *De fuga* 11.2; *Didasc.* 7, 8; and compare Cyprian's use of the same passage in *Epp.* 57.4.4, 68.4.1 and, allusively, in 55.15.1. Characteristically Cyprian would see the parallelism to be directly between the pastors of Israel and Christian bishops, whereas the Roman clergy, presbyters and deacons, in their caretaker role, here seem to link themselves with the pastors.

11. An allusion to Ezek. 34.3–4. It is worth remembering on this passage of pastoral analogy that this document comes from the Church of the Shepherd of Hermas (cf. *Simil.* 9.31.5f. on negligent pastors); see also n. 31 below.

12. John 10.11–12.

13. Adapted from John 21.17.

14. *hoc verbum factum ex actu (acto) ipso quo cessit.* "This is a very obscure passage, and is variously understood. . . . There seems no meaning in interpreting the passage as a reference to Peter's death" (R. E. Wallis in Ante-Nicene Christian Library, vol. 8, 1868, 15 n. 3). On the contrary, the simplest interpretation is to see here an allusion to the way in which Peter laid down his life (*cessit;* see Watson 284 n. 1 for this meaning) for his sheep (jumping back one biblical text, to John 10.11) in the role assigned to him by Christ as Shepherd (in the adjacent biblical text, John 21.17).

By tradition Peter was, like Christ, crucified (cf. Tertullian, *De praesc. haer.* 36.3 and *Scorp.* 15.3; Eusebius, *H.E.* 3.1.2; Acts of Peter 37), but hanging head downwards. For a full analysis of the evidence see D. W. O'Connor, *Peter in Rome* . . . (New York and London 1969) esp. 53 ff.; H. Lietzmann in TU 67 (1958) 100 f.; J. T. Shotwell and L. R. Loomis, *The Sea of Peter* (Columbia 1927; repr. 1965) 82 ff.; M. Smith, *The Secret Gospel* (London 1974) 15, and *idem, Clement of Alexandria and a secret gospel of Mark* (Cambridge 1973) 26 f. It was especially appropriate that the Church of Rome should here allude to Peter's death as martyr, for she derived particular pride and prestige from her possession of the site of the martyrdom of Peter (and Paul)—the famous τρόπαια, see Gaius *ap.* Eusebius, *H.E.* 2.25.7, cf. 3.31.1; see, too, the Roman pride in the witness of Paul to their ancient faith, *Ep.* 30.2.2.

15. *ceteri discipuli similiter fecerunt.* Is this simply an assertion that the disciples acted as good shepherds, like Peter, or is this more a claim that the disciples laid down their lives for their flocks, like Peter? On the latter compare *Ep.* 6.2 (and n. 16) and *Ep.* 10.4.3: *hunc. . . . agonem. . . . per apostolos gestum.* Origen *Contra Celsum* 2.45, also emphasizes the sufferings of Peter and the other apostles.

16. Compare 1 Cor. 16.13.

17. *praeceps euntes ad idolatriam . . . fraternitas.* Compare the scenes painted in *De laps.* 8 f., 25. Clearly the persecution is by no means over. There are *stantes* who have not complied with Decius' orders to "make sacrifice, pour a libation and partake of

the sacred victims" (though, it should be noted, there is no mention of *libelli* in this letter) and they are in constant peril of discovery, or of collapse in their resolve.

18. *a pluribus a nobis ad vos venientibus.* Is this a reference to refugees from Rome to Africa (cf. the reverse traffic in *Ep.* 21.4.1)? Not necessarily. Observe, in any case, that Christian *stantes* could still manage to travel about, in numbers, undetected.

19. *paratos esse debere ire cum Domino.* That is to say, to follow the example of the Lord and lay down their lives, like Him. Is there any allusion to John 14.6 or to 1 John 2.6? Even more appropriate for these Roman clergy would be an allusion to 1 Peter 2.21: *Christus passus est pro vobis relinquens vobis exemplum, ut sequamini vestigia eius.*

20. *sed et ascendentes ad hoc quod compellebantur revocavimus.* An unmistakable reference to mounting the Sacred Way in Rome in order to perform the compulsory rites up on the Capitol. Another such allusion to the Roman Capitol under Decius in *Ep.* 21.3.2 (*ascendisse. . . . usque ad Tria Fata*), and the *Acta Tryphonis* may possibly preserve such a Decian scene in Rome ἐν τῷ Καπετωλίῳ (see F. de'Cavalieri, *Studi e Testi* 22 [1909] 80 f.). Other Romanized cities, of course, possessed their Capitols and there, too, before the traditional temple (of Jupiter, Juno, and Minerva), the Decian sacrifices would chiefly be held; see *De laps.* 8, 24; *Ep.* 59.13.3 for Carthage. Novatianists thus came to call apostates *Capitolini* (cf. Pacian, *Ep.* 2: *apostaticum nomen . . . Capitolinum*); and note, for parallels, the wording of the general regulation against idolatry in Counc. Elvir., can. 59: *prohibendum ne quis Christianus ut gentilis ad idolum Capitolii causa sacrificandi ascendat et videat.*

See also H. A. M. Hoppenbrouwers, *Recherches . . .* (Nijmegen 1961) 144 f. on *ascendo;* DACL 2 (1925) 2043 ff.; PWK 3.2 (1899) 1538 ff.; RAC 2 (1954) 847 ff., 852 f. on provincial cult centres.

There is uncertainty over the reading: *compellebantur* (as translated) or *compellabantur* ("summoned").

21. *ruerunt:* Cyprian's favoured expression is rather *lapsi sunt* (occasionally *ceciderunt*), although *ruina* he readily admits. But

note the (Roman) parallel in *Ep.* 30.5.4: *qui ruerunt hoc ruerunt quod.* . . . See Hoppenbrouwers, *Recherches* . . . , 140.

22. *quod essent insignes personae.* See n. 5 above: the Carthaginian clergy are expected to understand the special factors which compel the prominent (unusual vulnerability and ease of detection, desire to protect position and business interests, to preserve patrimony and property, etc.).

23. An important passage. It should be observed that these Roman clergy do not react in the face of apostasy by imposing automatically a total ban on readmittance to communion for cases of idolatry. That suggests that their tradition (in recent years) on this issue may have been more lenient than, for example, the hard-line attitude which Cyprian reflects in *Test.* 3.28: *non posse in ecclesia remitti ei qui in deum deliquerit.* Or can it simply be that they are showing pragmatic charity in the face of (unprecedently large) numbers of apostates; hence the cautious vagueness of their mitigation *si quo modo indulgentiam poterint recipere?* From *Ep.* 30.8 we see that the Roman clergy claim that no innovations have been made in penitential discipline and certainly no detailed promises have been made to the lapsed on the question of their readmission (save in the case of the repentant dying—see n. 25 below). In similar circumstances of mass apostasy, Cyprian's reaction is equally careful so as not rigorously to exclude all hope for the fallen (see *Epp.* 15 ff.).

24. *si adprehensi fuerint iterato confiteantur.* . . . If a Christian, seized once, has apostatized, and thereby complied with Decius' demands, how can it come about that that Christian may be arrested a second time?

The repentant lapsed are urged to "do penance" and that would include, besides prayers, sackcloth, and fasting, works of practical charity, visiting the imprisoned, burying the Christian dead, sheltering the homeless refugees, etc. All such works of mercy put the repentant *lapsi* in danger of being detected or denounced as Christians; and when so arrested they would cancel their former lapse by a courageous "confession." Cyprian also emphasizes that a previous fall may be cancelled by subsequent confession (cf. e.g., *Epp.* 19.2.3, 55.4.1f., 55.7.1, 55.16.3, 25).

24a. *qui in hanc temptationem inciderunt . . . desiderent commun-*
ionem. Is there possibly an allusion to 1 Tim. 6.9, where Cyprian's text read *qui autem volunt divites fieri incidunt in*
temptationem?

desiderent communionem: Cyprian would normally have used
communicationem or *ius communicationis,* see Watson 268 f. He
uses *communio* only in its general senses. Cf. *Ep.* 20 n. 28. On
communicatio generally in Cyprian, see the study of A. Matel-
lanes Crespo *El terma de la "communicatio" en los escritos peniten-*
ciales y bautismales de san Cipriano de Cartago (Granada 1965) esp.
39 ff.

25. *utique subveniri eis debet.* If the Roman clergy are not
innovating in their penitential discipline concerning the apostates, then the reconciliation *in articulo mortis* of those who had
committed this "irremissible" sin of apostasy would appear to
have been already an established mitigation (in Rome). A council of local clergy and visiting bishops confirmed the policy; see
Ep. 30.8, where there is a fuller statement of the policy and of
the conditions for reconciliation. There the same technical verb
is used as here, viz., *subveniri.* Cf. also *Epp.* 20.3.2., 21.2.1,
31.6.2, 55.13.1, 68.3.1, 68.3.2, and see on the word H. Koch,
Cyprianische Untersuchungen (Bonn 1926) 236 ff. Dionysius of
Alexandria himself issued similar, and characteristically lenient,
instructions (*ap.* Euseb. *H.E.* 6.42.2 ff., the case of Serapion: note
esp. §4, ". . . . since I had given an order that those who were
departing this life, if they besought it, and especially if they had
made supplication before, should be absolved, that they might
depart in hope. . . ." (trans. J. E. L. Oulton). Such reconciliation,
possibly after only a brief attempt at *opera,* indicates the value
given to ecclesiastical absolution for winning forgiveness (but
observe the saving clause in *Ep.* 30.8: *Deo ipso sciente quid de*
talibus faciat). On this point see the discussion of B. Capelle in
Rech. de théol. anc. et méd. 7 (1935) 221 ff.

On the other hand, Cyprian's reaction to the problem is
noticeably more cautious, reserved, and rigorist (cf. *Epp.* 18.1.2,
19.2.1, where see nn., and n. 12 to *Ep.* 15); his clergy are undecid-
ed and want guidance (cf. *Ep.* 19.2.1); and it was not until he had
received this letter that, not without some embarrassment, he

brought his advice to his clergy into line with the Roman policy (cf. *Ep.* 20.3).

The curiously emphatic language here (*utique. . . . debet*) suggests reaction against a more unyielding position.

Further discussed by, *inter alios*, B. Poschmann, *Paenitentia Secunda*, (Bonn 1940) 372 ff.; O. D. Watkins, *A History of Penance* (London 1920; repr. New York 1961) 1.182 ff.; H. J. Vogt, *Coetus sanctorum* (Bonn 1968) 165 ff.

It is worth noting that Council of Nicaea 1, can. 13, requires that "the ancient custom and rule" (ὁ παλαιὸς καὶ κανονικὸς νόμος) of giving the *viaticum* to dying penitents should be observed. This is as far back as it can in fact be traced. See Hefele-Leclercq 1.1.593 ff.; DACL 3 (1948) 2446 f.; A.C. Rush, SCA 1 (1941) 92 ff.

26. *sive viduae sive thlibomeni qui se exhibere non possunt.* On *viduae* see n. 8 to *Ep.* 7. *Thlibomeni* is clearly a local Roman usage arising from the Greek elements of the Roman church. Pope Cornelius so uses the word (in Greek) when writing the following year; cf. Eusebius, *H.E.* 6.43.11. These widows and *thlibomeni* supported by the Roman church then numbered "above 1500."

27. *exclusi de sedibus suis.* These homeless do not sound like formal *relegati* or *deportati*. Carthage would be a most unlikely legal venue for such; cf. *Digesta* 48.22.7.9 (Ulpian). We have rather to do with refugees (*profugi, extorres*) forced, through loyalty to their faith, to abandon their homes in order to avoid detection and arrest. They would be safely lost amid the crowds of Carthage. On such refugee movements, cf. n. 8 to *Ep.* 5, and n. 18 above. A picture of such flight is preserved in *De laps.* 25. The Roman clergy would be experiencing similar refugee problems (cf. *Epp.* 21.4.1, 30.8, etc.).

28. *catecumini . . . ut eis subveniatur.* That is to say, catechumens are to be received fully into the church *necessitate urgente.*

Why should this group be specifically mentioned? Are these Roman clergy declaring their own approval of such (controversial) "clinical" rites and are they reacting against the known reluctance of some African (Carthaginian) clergy to perform such ceremonies *in extremis?* Cyprian's own attitude (of approval) is revealed in the (later) *Ep.* 69.12 ff., but there he prefaces his own view cautiously as a personal one. Clearly others continued to believe such *clinici* were not *legitimi christiani*. Note that Firmilian seems to suggest that baptism of dying catechumens was not a usual procedure in his area (*Ep.* 75.21.1). Half a century later it was felt necessary that the Council of Elvira should lay it down that sickness and danger of death allowed immediate baptism of a catechumen (can. 42), and such regulations and controversies continued (Counc. of Ancy., can. 12, Council of Neocaes., can. 12, etc.).

Or are these Roman clerics simply urging that the Carthaginian presbyters and deacons, in the absence of their bishop, who would be the ordinary minister, have a duty to perform *themselves* these ceremonies of charity for *catecumini adprehensi infirmitate?* This latter alternative seems the more likely in this context of the duties incumbent upon the bishopless shepherds of Carthage.

Catecumenus is a term employed only infrequently by Cyprian (*Test.* 3.98; *Ep.* 73.22.1 f.); he regularly prefers *audiens* (e.g., *Epp.* 18.2.2, 29.1.2). See Janssen 41 ff.

By the time of Hippolytus there was already a well-developed and fully regulated catechumenate (lasting generally about three years; two to three years, according to Counc. of Elvira, can. 42). See in particular *Trad. Apost.* 15–20. In Cyprian we catch glimpses of the Carthaginian organization, with special readers (*lectores*) and catechists (*doctores*)—see nn. on *Ep.* 29—and exorcists (*Ep.* 69.15.2), but we get little in the way of detail. The Roman clergy clearly anticipate that conditions similar to their own prevail in Carthage.

On the catechumenate in the Early Church, there are many generous studies. Some are W. Robinson in JTS 42 (1941–42) 45 ff.; J. Lebreton in *Recherches de science religieuse* 24 (1934) 129 ff.; B. Capelle in *Rech. de théologie anc. et méd.* 5 (1933) 129 ff.; T. Maertens, *Histoire et pastorale rituel du catéchuménat et du baptême* (Bruges 1962) esp. 63 ff., 88 ff.; M. Dujarier, *Le parrainage des adultes aux trois premiers siècles de l'église* (Paris 1962); DACL 2 (1925) 2579 ff.; A. Turck, *Revue des sc. phil. et théol.* 47 (1963) 361 ff.

29. *corpora martyrum aut ceterorum ... grande periculum immenet eis quibus incumbit hoc opus.*—Are we to infer that in addition to the known martyrdom of Pope Fabian there are already other Roman martyrs whose bodies needed Christian burial? That does not follow and the later (?August 250) *Ep.* 28.1 acts strongly against such an inference: the Romans took the lead in making their confessional stand but, unlike their Carthaginian brethren, they are yet to be graced with actual martyrs. (There are actual Roman martyrs, however, by the time of the even later *Ep.* 37.) The Roman clergy are here laying down principles of action rather than reflecting immediate experience.

grande periculum. There is ambiguity here. The danger that threatens may well refer to spiritual perils for those who neglect their duty. But for physical risks under these circumstances, cf. Dionysius of Alex. *ap.* Eusebius, *H.E.* 7.11.24: "[Eusebius] at no small risk performed the task of laying out the corpses of the blessed and perfect martyrs." So far as we know Christians in this persecution were not actually denied access to their *areae* (where, they insisted, Christians should be buried; see on *Ep.* 67.6.2). But doubtless, the occasion of a Christian burial, especially if it was in a known Christian burial-ground, exposed the participants to the severe danger of detection and arrest as Christian loyalists. (On Carthaginian cemeteries, see nn. on *Ep.* 12; on Roman cemeteries, see nn. on *Ep.* 80).

quibus incumbit hoc opus. There is attested later a minor clerical grade of *fossor* (they do not figure in Cornelius' list of contemporary Roman clerics *ap.* Eusebius, *H.E.* 6.43.11); our first recorded instance (several in number) is for 303 at Cirta, *Gest. ap. Zenoph.* CSEL 26.187; cf. Jerome *Ep.* 1.12; etc. See DACL 5 (1923) 2065 ff., esp. 2069 ff. P. Testini, *Le catacombe e gli antichi cimiteri cristiani in Roma* (Bologna, 1966) 221 ff.; J. Guyon in *Mel. de l'école franç. de Rom.* 86 (1974) 549 ff.; and for a list of recorded Roman *fossores,* Ch. Pietri in *Mel. de l'école franç. de Rom.* 89 (1977) 398 ff. For a wall-painting of a *fossor* in the Roman catacomb of Sts. Peter and Marcellinus (digging at a wall-face by the light of a lamp), M. Simon, *La civilisation de l'antiquité et le christianisme* (Paris 1972) illus. 136.

The turn of phrase here might suggest that there were already such *fossores* in Rome and Carthage (normally under the direction of the bishop; see *Trad. Apost.* 40) but that they were not yet admitted to the ranks of the *clerici*. But the phrase might concern, more simply, the immediate family of the deceased, etc.; thus, in this persecution, Numidicus' daughter followed her duty—*sollicito pietatis obsequio*—and searched for her father's lynched corpse (*Ep.* 40.1.1) and Tertullus was notably dutiful in *omni obsequio operationis*, especially *circa curam corporum* (*Ep.* 12.2.1); and, for comparison, when Justin and his companions were martyred in Rome almost a century earlier, "some of the faithful took their bodies by stealth and laid them in a convenient place, the grace of our Lord Jesus Christ working with them" (*Mart. Just.* 6.2 [Recension B, Musurillo 52]).

30. An adaptation of Luke 19.17.

31. *fratres qui sunt in vinculis et presbyteri et tota ecclesia.* The word order is significant; the position of precedence is given to the imprisoned confessors, even before the presbyters. Cf. Hermas, *Vis.* 3.1.8f., 3.2.1 (confessors and martyrs are given the seat of precedence, on the right, over all others). Contrast the order put by the Roman clergy writing later in *Ep.* 30.5.3—bishops, presbyters, deacons, confessors, and faithful laity—or by Cyprian in *Ep.* 43.3.2 (in ascending order), confessors, *clerici urbici*, *universi episcopi*.

32. *sciatis autem Bassianum pervenisse ad nos.* In *Ep.* 22.3.2 Lucian, writing from prison in Carthage to Celerinus in Rome, sends greetings to *Saturum, Bassianum et universum clerum.* If the Bassianus here is to be identified with his namesake in *Ep.* 22 that would make him one of the Roman *clerus.* And the passage here would therefore suggest that Bassianus has already been an emissary to Carthage and is now reported as having arrived safely back in Rome. That in turn would imply communications between the Carthaginian and Roman churches prior to (or at least simultaneous with) Crementius' journey to Rome.

I do not find this reconstruction completely plausible, especially in view of the fact that at the time Cyprian receives his copy of *Ep.* 8 he has heard only *incertus rumor* and *opinio dubia* of Fabian's death (*Ep.* 9.1.1) unless he is being, as is quite possible, deliberately disingenuous; messages from Rome have not, hitherto, come to him. But the absence of talk about Fabian's martyrdom in this letter certainly implies other communications between Rome and the Carthaginian clergy, be they earlier than or simultaneous with this *Ep.* 8; see introductory note and n. 1 above.

33. *petimus ... harum litterarum exemplum ... transmittere per idoneas occasiones, vel vestras faciatis, sive nuntium mittatis.* The interpretation of the text, as it stands, must remain somewhat uncertain (emendations have been suggested, e.g., K. Müller in ZfKG 16 (1896) 208 n. 5, would excise, not very attractively, 'vel' and construe *faciatis* with *transmittere*). Others, e.g., B. Aubé, *L'église et l'état dans la seconde moitié du IIIe siècle (249–284)* (Paris 1886) 47, understand *occasiones* with *vestras*, resulting in "... as suitable opportunities occur or contrive opportunities yourselves...."

Note that Cyprian does not appear to receive one of these copies; the *original* (*epistulam authenticam, Ep.* 9.2.1, where see n. 12) is delivered to him by Crementius.

LETTER 9

Contents: Cyprian has received two letters by the subdeacon Crementius. One, addressed to him, contains an account of the martyrdom of Pope Fabian and Cyprian congratulates the Roman clergy on its composition. The other, acephalous and anonymous, Cyprian suggests may be spurious or have been fraudulently tampered with. This one he is returning to Rome for identification and authentication.

Date and Circumstances: Undoubtedly the second document refers to the inscription-less *Ep.* 8, and *Ep.* 9 will, therefore, be composed after the receipt of that letter. Hence L. Duchesne, *Le Liber Pontificalis* (Paris 1955²) 1.148 n. 2 is wide of the mark: "une lettre de saint Cyprien (*Ep.* ix) écrite quelques semaines après l'évènement" (death of Fabian). See further L. Nelke, *Die*

Chronologie der Korrespondenz Cyprians . . . (diss. Thorn 1902) 35; L. Duquenne, *Chronologie des lettres de s. Cyprien* (Brussels 1972) 115.

If Cyprian, as he claims, has heard hitherto only *incertus rumor* of Fabian's death (January 20), then the *celebre et inlustre testimonium* which he has now received concerning Fabian appears to be his first formal communication from Rome since the outbreak of the persecution. This hiatus in communications, of approximately six months' duration, is a good indicator of the seriousness of the débâcle in which the persecution left the churches.

Cyprian clearly approves of the loyal *testimonium* on Fabian; he speaks of it in terms of intricate and glowing rhetoric. Can it possibly have been composed by Novatian, the (flowery) *scriptor* of *Ep.* 30 (and *Ep.* 36?) who had been warmly supported in ecclesiastical preferment, despite widespread opposition, by Fabian? Cf. Cornelius *ap.* Eusebius, *H.E.* 6.43.17.

The rejection of *Ep.* 8 is a celebrated example of spirited diplomacy. The withering but indirect attack which that letter contained on Cyprian's conduct has not failed to register, and in contrast with §1, Cyprian's language, in §2, in returning the document, is studiously curt, crisp, and controlled. The impression he puts forward is that his concern is not a personal one, but for the truth and authenticity of the letter (*ex vero . . . veritas . . . in vero*). *Ep.* 9 is hardly, therefore, to be characterized as "a familiar and friendly epistle" (R. E. Wallis in Ante-Nicene Christian Library, vol. 8, 17).

We do not know of any sequel. Cyprian next communicates with Rome in *Ep.* 20 with a defence against dishonest and misleading reports of his conduct. Can that letter (*Ep.* 20) have been written simply after more mature reflection on the implications of *Ep.* 8, together with the knowledge of the activities of *quidam immoderati* (*Ep.* 19.2.1) in opposition to his policies in Carthage? The way in which Cyprian refers to and quotes from *Ep.* 8 in *Ep.* 20.3.2 certainly does not suggest he has got any reply from Rome to this letter, *Ep.* 9. In this round Cyprian, it would appear, has outmanoeuvred his opponents.

Cornelius belonged to the Roman clergy. In the following

year can there be any element of *quid pro quo* in Cyprian's scrupulous insistence that all correspondence with Rome should be circumspectly addressed *ad presbyteros et ad diaconos* (*Ep.* 48.1.1) until the validity of Cornelius' election had been duly verified? Probably not.

For further reading on *Ep.* 9, see H. Gülzow, *Cyprian und Novatian* ... (Tübingen 1975) 20 ff., 46 ff.

1. *Romae consistentibus.* On the language, see n. 1 to *Ep.* 1.

2. *collegae mei.* Note that Cyprian carefully does not say *collegae nostri.* *Collega,* in Cyprian's usage, is reserved for bishops; he excludes the Roman presbyters and deacons from the level of collegiality. See n. 2 to *Ep.* 1.

3. *per Crementium hypodiaconum.* On Crementius and the subdiaconate, see n. 1 to *Ep.* 8.

4. *de glorioso eius exitu.* Cyprian uses language which implies martyrdom (on *gloriosus* see n. 6 to *Ep.* 5). When friendly relations with Rome had been restored, this epithet enabled Cyprian to be flattered with confessional language. Cf. *Epp.* 30.8 and 31.5.2, and in *Ep.* 48.4.1 Cyprian has been assured of Cornelius' *gloriosa* ... *innocentia,* that is to say, he is not *libelli* ... *labe maculatus* as had been alleged (*Ep.* 55.10.2).

We do not have surviving authentic details of Fabian's death; such an account might well have thrown valuable light on the opening stages of the persecution of Decius, for Fabian's is the first recorded death of the persecution. The earliest calendars referring to his death confirm the fact of his martyrdom and provide a date. Cf., e.g., *Chronog.* 354, *Depositio Martirum* (ed. H. Mommsen, MGH 9, p. 71): *xiii Kal. Feb. Fabiani in Callisti,* and (p. 75): *Fabius* (sic) ... *passus xii Kal. Feb.* On the date, see further n. 119 to Introduction. On the celebrated sepulchral inscription of Fabian *in Callisti,* where the indication of martyrdom (N̄P) seems to be added in a different hand, see H. Delehaye, *Sanctus. Essai sur le culte des saints dans l'antiquité* (Brussels 1927) 174 f.; L. Hertling and E. Kirschbaum, *The Roman Catacombs and Their Martyrs* (London 1960) 52; DACL 5 (1922) 938 ff. and 1058 ff.

Note the recording of details of martyrdom not too long after the actual events; in fact Fabian is accredited with having initiated himself the proper organisation for keeping such faithful records (see next n.). Court transcripts might well form the original basis of such *Acta*. See nn. on *Ep*. 77.2 (*Acta* of Cyprian's first trial in general circulation well within twelve months of the event) and on *Ep*. 12.2.1 (Carthaginian calendar of martyrs kept up to date even under persecution conditions).

Are we to assume that copies of the *testimonium* were circulated generally throughout the Church, in the same way that copies of the Roman *Ep*. 30 were disseminated *per totum mundum* (*Ep*. 55.5.2)?

5. *pro integritate administrationis*. It so happens that the meagre details we have registered for Fabian's pontificate do record (puzzling) measures of an administrative character: *Hic regiones dividit diaconibus et fecit vii subdiaconos qui vii notariis imminerent ut gestas martyrum in integro fideliter colligerent, et multas fabricas per cymiteria fieri praecepit* (*Liber Pontificalis* 21). But observe the parallel passages under Clemens I and Anteros and, later, under Marcellus (*Lib. Pontif.* 4, 20, 31). Also note his role in the Privatus affair (cf. *Epp.* 59.10 and 36.4.2) which seems to be basically a disciplinary problem.

6. Cf. n. 2 to *Ep*. 5, citing examples from this persecution. The sentence provides a good example of *praepositus* and *episcopus* used strictly synonymously. See n. 9 to *Ep*. 8.

7. Is this a soft-gloved rebuff by Cyprian of the criticisms (whether direct or indirect) levelled against his own line of conduct, or is he showing himself blandly self-assured as to the justice of his own behaviour? The impression certainly is that he is not in the least embarrassed; so also P. Hinchliff, *Cyprian of Carthage* (London 1974) 50.

Note for parallel sentiment *Ep*. 60.1.2, where Cyprian dilates on the glorious effects of a bishop acting as *dux confessionis*, and *Ep*. 72.2.3, on the reverse, *perditionis. . . . duces.*

8. *legi etiam litteras* (*varia lectio: legi alias litteras*). The letter is, of course, *Ep*. 8. By contrast with §1, Cyprian does not say *accepi. . . . litteras;* the document was not addressed to him. The first word of §2 is effectively distancing.

9. By the time Cyprian wrote *Ep*. 20.3.2 (addressed to the

Roman presbyters and deacons) he was prepared to identify the writers (*vestra scripta*) and the addressees (*clerum nostrum*).

10. *Ep.* 8 appears to have been written by a different hand from that of the *testimonium* on Fabian. Cyprian professes hesitation as to the authenticity of *Ep.* 8, accordingly. Hence, too, Cicero could voice suspicion of a letter purported to be Caesar's partly because of the cramped hand-writing in *Ad Att.* 11.16.1. Similarly, Synesius can express doubt to Olympius about the authenticity of a postscript appended to his letter because he recognizes "neither your hand nor the precision of your script" (*Ep.* 122 [132], MG 66.1521). St. Paul authenticates his letters by adding the concluding salutation and remarks in his own highly characteristic, large hand: "You see these big letters? I am now writing to you in my own hand" (Gal. 6.11); "The greeting is in my own hand, signed with my name, Paul: this authenticates all my letters; this is how I write" (2 Thess. 3.17). Cf. 1 Cor. 16.21; Col. 4.18; and see H. C. Youtie, *Scriptiunculae II* (Amsterdam 1973) 970, and note the detailed comments by Jerome, *In Gal.* 3.6.

It is possible that *scriptura* here may bear a more abstract significance ("composition," a regular usage) and that Cyprian is referring to the *style* of the document. See next n. for parallels to this notion.

11. *sensus et chartae ipsae.*—With superlative nonchalance Cyprian is rejecting ideas contained in *Ep.* 8. For this use of *sensus,* cf. Jerome, *De viris ill.* 15. Cf. also *Ep.* 77.1.1 (Numidian martyrs): *cum semper magnis sensibus pro temporis condicione litteris tuis locutus es; Test. 1 praef.: intellectum legentis et sensum.*

Is there some chance that *sensus* signifies here not so much "sense" or "sentiments" as "sentences" (cf. for this meaning Quintilian, 9.4.26: *verbo sensum cludere multo. . . . optimum est)* and that Cyprian is referring the disparate *styles* of the *testimonium* and *Ep.* 8? Though attractive, the run of the sentence is rather against this interpretation, but compare, for doubts on the authenticity of an epistolary note, by reason of divergent style, Synesius, *Ep.* 133 (132): "I do not recognize a style resembling your own. . . ." Jerome, though reluctant to admit the possibility that a letter was genuinely Augustine's, had to confess that the *stylus et* ἐπιχειρήματα appeared to be his (*Ep.* 102.1).

chartae: Does Cyprian imply that the *testimonium* was written on different quality paper (on the various types of paper available in antiquity note Pliny, *N.H.* 13.11 ff. and see the commentary of N. Lewis, *Papyrus in Classical Antiquity* [Oxford 1974] 42 ff.), or is he referring to the suspicious condition of *Ep.* 8 as he received it (torn, smudged, unsealed, with writing scored out, visible rewriting, etc.)? For the state of *membranae* used as proof of authenticity, cf. Optatus Milev. 1.14: *vetustas membranarum testimonium perhibet quas dubitantibus proferre poterimus*, and, conversely, for erasures and rewriting as presumption of deliberate corruption, Rufinus, *Liber de adul. lib. Orig.*, MG 17.630: *litura illa corruptionis ac falsitatis videretur indicium.* See further H. U. Instinsky, *Bischofsstuhl und Kaiserthron* (Munich 1955) 51 ff.

12. Compare the complaints of Dionysius of Corinth *ap.* Eusebius, *H.E.* 4.23.12, on the contemporary corruption of his own letters: "When Christians asked me to write letters I wrote them, and the apostles of the devil have filled them with tares, by leaving out some things and putting in others" (trans. Kirsopp Lake). Symmachus affects fear of forged imitations and corruption of his letters in his *Ep.* 2.12; does Flavianus receive them still sealed (*cupio cognoscere an omnes obsignatas epistulas meas sumpseris eo anulo quo . . .*)? Instructive for this subject are Jerome's accusation against Rufinus of forging a letter over his name and his defence against a similar accusation directed at him by Rufinus; cf. *Adv. Rufin.* 3.20, 3.25; and Rufinus, *Liber de adulteratione librorum Origenis*, MG 17.615 ff. esp. 627C ff. (stories of forgery and corruption connected with Hilary Pictaviensis, Cyprian's *epistolarum corpus*, Athanasius, Origen, etc.). See also Athanasius, *Ep. ad monachos* 1.3. He sends monks a work on the Arians with instructions that they should read it but not copy it, returning the original lest the document fall into Arian hands.

13. *eandem ad vos epistolam authenticam remisi.* Observe that Cyprian has got hold of the original (on *epistolam authenticam*, cf. *P. Oxy.* 7.1022, ll. 29 ff. [A.D. 103]: *scripsi authenticam epistulam in*

tabulario cohortis esse); he will have taken a copy, however—he can quote from it in *Ep.* 20.3.1. And compare Jerome in *Ep.* 102.1 to Augustine requesting assurance as to the authenticity of a letter: . . . *epistulae tuae vel eius qui sub tuo nomine scripserat.* . . . *si tua est epistula, aperte scribe vel mitte exemplaria veriora* and in *Ep.* 105.3, again to Augustine, demanding another copy, authentically signed.

14. This provides clear enough indication that *Ep.* 8 was delivered at the same time as the *testimonium* on Fabian. We do not know for sure whether Crementius on his return to Africa came to Cyprian in hiding direct, or *via* the Carthaginian clergy (cf. intro. note to *Ep.* 8). The latter is much the more probable, for otherwise Cyprian would now be returning the original letter to Rome before his Carthaginian clergy have seen it. Could he then conceivably refer to the document openly in a public letter as having been recently sent *ad clerum nostrum per Crementium hypodiaconum* (*Ep.* 20.3.2)?

15. *si epistulae clericae veritas mendacio aliquo et fraude corrupta est. Mendacium* and *fraus* are strong words; Cyprian is referring to deliberate deception, not just *lapsus calami.* For evidence of forged ecclesiastical letters, or accusations of such, see W. Speyer, *Die literarische Fälschung im heidnischen und christlichen Altertum* (Munich 1971) 193 ff. It was no doubt in part concern for the danger of such corruptions that led to the establishment of the system (on which Cyprian is insistent; cf. *Epp.* 29.1.1, 80.1.1) that Church correspondence should be conveyed by the hands of clerics (acolytes, subdeacons, etc.). Even so, in *Ep.* 47.1.2 Cyprian takes the precaution of having his clerical messenger read his letter (*Ep.* 46) to Pope Cornelius before delivering it to Novatianist sympathizers in Rome—for fear of misrepresentation (*ne quis me scripsisse fingeret quam quod meis litteris continetur*).

16. *subscriptionem.* That is to say, the concluding greetings. Compare the Pauline examples given in n. 10 above and Jerome in his *Ep.* 105.3 to Augustine, demanding another copy, authentically signed. Is Cyprian referring here to *Ep.* 8.3.3 f., or to lost additional greetings, signatures, and personal messages, like those of *Ep.* 79.1.2? For a lost *subscriptio,* note *Ep.* 30; our surviv-

ing version fails to record at least the *subscriptio* of the confessor, later martyr, Moyses, which was attached to the original. Cf. *Ep.* 55.5.2; on this see H. Koch in ZNTW 34 (1935) 303 ff. And note the perils of writing *subscriptiones* without carefully reading the contents of a letter, *Ep.* 49.1.4, where see n. See in general on *subscriptiones,* O. Roller, *Das Formular der paulinischen Briefe. Ein Beitrag zur Lehre vom antiken Briefe* (Stuttgart 1933) 43 ff., 73 ff.; PWK 4A (1932) 490 ff. On imperial *subscriptiones,* see U. Wilcken in *Hermes* 55 (1920) 1 ff.; W. Williams in JRS 64 (1974) 86 ff.; F. Millar, *The Emperor in the Roman World (31 B.C.-A.D. 337)* (London 1977) 221 f. And on the ὑπογραφή on records of court proceedings, see R. A. Coles in *Papyrologica Bruxellensia* 4 (1966) 53 f.

LETTER 10

Contents: Cyprian writes to the confessors in prison in Carthage; instead of exile, tortures have now become the penalty for steadfast confession. Some of their number have already thus died in a blaze of crimson glory, notably the prophetically inspired Mappalicus. Those that now remain of his companions are urged to prepare themselves for a like honour—but they must rest assured that should peace anticipate their martyrdom, their renown and rewards will remain undiminished thereby.

Date and Circumstances: Ep. 10 provides the first fixed point of the Cyprianic correspondence. Cyprian clearly composes this elaborate and highly stylized epistle after receiving details of the martyrdom of Mappalicus, and the date of Mappalicus' *natalia* happens to be preserved in the earliest calendars (April 17, 18 or 19; see n. 20 below). Cyprian was being kept scrupulously informed by the devoted Tertullus as to the *dies quibus in carcere beati fratres nostri ad immortalitatem gloriosae mortis exitu transeunt (Ep.* 12.2.1). We ought, therefore, to be somewhere in the second half of April, 250—and possibly earlier rather than later in that half. So much is non-controversial.

The place of *Ep.* 10 in the sequence of the letters is more debatable, but there ought to be little doubt, at the least, that letters earlier than *Ep.* 10 are not only *Epp.* 5, 6, and 7, but also 13 and 14. In all those letters no actual martyrs are mentioned in contexts where reference to them would be prescriptive. Furthermore, *Ep.* 13, which is palpably contemporaneous with *Ep.* 14, is directed, like this *Ep.* 10, to the confessors. In that letter, however, the presbyter Rogatianus, one of the confessors, is addressed specifically in the *titulus,* and §7 of that same letter shows that these confessors are no longer in prison. By the rules of epistolary *politesse* Cyprian ought to have mentioned *nominatim* the presbyter were he still among the ranks of the imprisoned confessors of *Ep.* 10. Contrast the correspondence of Cyprian with the Roman confessors; without exception the presbyters involved are named in the *tituli* of *Epp.* 28, 31, 37, 46, 54. Rogatianus, one of the initial confessors (*Ep.* 6), must, therefore, have been released before *Ep.* 10 was written—and perhaps according to the now outmoded policy indicated in *Ep.* 10.1.1. This should put beyond doubt the priority of *Ep.* 13 (and *Ep.* 14) over *Ep.* 10.

Cyprian undoubtedly refers to this letter in *Ep.* 20.2.2 (*init.*): *postea quam vero et tormenta venerunt. . . . ad corroborandos et confortandos eos noster sermo penetravit* (enclosing a copy of this letter with *Ep.* 20).—The more delicate question of the relationship of *Ep.* 10 with *Ep.* 11 (prior?) and *Ep.* 12 (later?) is discussed in the introductory notes to those letters.

It is worth noting that by now, the second half of April 250, the lapsed in Carthage are in very large numbers (*ruinas et funera plurimorum*), but that the *stantes* still need good example for encouragement (§4.4)—the persecution is far from over. Mappalicus has martyred companions (*quosdam iam. . . . coronatos* [§1.2], *in quaestione victores* [§4.4], *ad Dominum. . . . venerunt* [§5.1], *temporibus nostris gloriosus martyrum sanguis* [§5.2]), but they are the very first martyrs of this persecution in Carthage ([*ecclesia nostra*] *erat ante in operibus fratrum candida: nunc facta est in martyrum cruore purpurea* [§5.2]).

But, above all, the ardent and lyrical tone of the letter is remarkable; the military metaphors, lavishly exploited, highlight the fighting spirit roused in this church by the prospect of martyrdom, and the poetic images and verbal elaboration only serve to underline the high premium placed by such a church on a martyr's death. However overblown the rhetoric is to our taste, we have to remember that this a letter composed with care with the object of bringing encouragement and comfort to those enduring the harsh realities of Roman dungeons and Roman tortures; it was read in the heat and stench of dark and cramped cells by men and women literally dying from hunger and thirst (as described by one of these confessors in *Ep.* 22). At least seventeen from amongst them perished (cf. *Ep.* 22.2.2).

The theme that runs throughout the epistle for their comfort, with, in turn, the charismatic words of the martyr Mappalicus as its centerpiece, is that of *Christus in martyre:* Christ not only contends within the martyr, Christ and the martyr become as one, Christ's glory becomes the martyr's glory (see n. 31 below).

The letter is to be found, not surprisingly, in a Donatist collection of Cyprianic writings (edited by H. K. Mengis, *Ein donatistisches Corpus cyprianischer Briefe* [diss. Freiburg 1916] 23 ff.) and it is imitated by Lucifer of Calaris (ed. Hartel, 294–296). In the Codex Casinensis the letter is preceded by an extraordinary title (cf. H. L. Ramsay in JTS 3 (1901–2) 592) now known to be the *incipit* of "*Ep.* 82." L. Pauchenne, *Epistola decima et de mortalitate liber* (Liège 1930), provides a text and a brief study of the letter.

On the military language note the study of J. Capmany-Casamitjana, *"Miles Christi" en la espiritualidad de san Cipriano* (Barcelona 1956).

1. *Cyprianus martyribus et confessoribus Iesu Christi domini nostri in deo patre perpetuam s.* The *titulus* sets the tone of the epistle: Cyprian is wishing, with elaborate verbal play, "eternal greetings/good health", that is to say, "salvation for eternity in God the Father." For discussion, see C. D. Lanham, *Salutatio Formulas in Latin Letters to 1200: Syntax, Style and Theory* (Munich 1975) 24, 26 f. And he is sending his wishes "to the martyrs and confessors"—with panegyrical and encouraging prolepsis they are granted the more laudatory and honorific title of "mar-

tyr" as again in *Epp.* 15.1.1, 16.4.2, 17.3.2, 20.2.2, 25.1.2, 39.1.1, 76.7.2 (contrast *Ep.* 6 *init.*). This meaning of *martyr* has been discussed many times: H. Delehaye in AB 39 (1921) 20 ff. esp. 33; H. A. M. Hoppenbrouwers, *Recherches sur la terminologie du martyre de Tertullien à Lactance* (Nijmegen 1961) 93 ff.; K. Holl in *Hermes* 52 (1917) 301 ff.; R. Reizenstein in *Hermes* 52 (1917) 442 ff.; E. Günther in ZNTW 47 (1956) 145 ff.; H. H. Janssen, *Kultur und Sprache* . . . (Nijmegen 1938) 136 ff. esp. 163 ff.; H. F. von Campenhausen, *Die Idee des Martyriums in der alten Kirche* (Göttingen 1964²) 90 ff.; E. L. Hummel in SCA 9 (1946) 5 ff.

2. *fortissimi ac beatissimi fratres.* With contrived artifice, Cyprian concludes his letter, as he here begins it, with greetings to his *fortissimi et beatissimi fratres,* just as he opens, and closes, the epistle with remarks contrasting past circumstances with the present (*nuper. . . . praesens; ante. . . . nunc*).

Note the honorific use of *beatissimus* (as already in *Ep.* 6 *ad fin.*)—as again of Mappalicus the martyr in §4.1, §4.4—and frequently on African inscriptions (examples are given in H. Delehaye in AB 28 (1909) 177 f.). This superlative is found in Cyprian exclusively of martyrs and confessors; by curious linguistic convention the apostle Paul in §4.3 is *beatus* only (for *sanctus* used for gods, *sanctissimus* for mortals, cf. H. Delehaye, *Sanctus. Essai sur le culte des saints dans l'antiquité* [Brussels 1927] 20 ff.) For further discussion on *beatus/beatissimus,* see DACL 15 (1950) 385 ff. Note, therefore, the "confessional" flattery, addressed to Cyprian from Rome, in *Ep.* 30.8 *ad fin.: beatissime ac gloriosissime papa* (on *gloriosus,* see *Ep.* 9 n. 4).

3. *cognita fide et virtute vestra in quibus mater ecclesia gloriatur. Mater ecclesia* is a frequent image much favoured by Cyprian; among the letters cf. *Epp.* 10.4.4, 15.2.2, 16.4.2, 41.2.1, 43.6.2, 44.3.2, 45.1.2, 45.3.2, 46.1.3, 48.3.1, 59.13.2, 71.2.2, 73.19.2, 74.7.2. For a brief analysis, see J. C. Plumpe in TAPA 70 (1939) 535 ff.; there are more elaborate studies of the concept by Plumpe in SCA 5 (1943) 81 ff. (on Cyprian) and K. Delehaye, *Ecclesia Mater* (French trans., Paris 1964) esp. 103 ff., 164 f., 232 f.

The phrase *fides et virtus* is to recur in the letter (again in §1.2 and §4.1); could Cyprian have possibly been thinking of the Maccabees and their mother—in *Ep.* 58.6.1, referring to the seven Maccabees and their mother, he asks, *nonne magnae virtutis et fidei documenta testantur?* On the pervasive influence of Maccabees on Christians and martyrdom, see W. H. C. Frend, *Martyrdom and Persecution in the Early Church* (Oxford 1965) *passim*, esp. 39 ff.

4. *gloriata et nuper quidem.* Unfortunately the elasticity of *nuper* (see *Ep.* 1 nn. 7 and 27) does not permit of precise analysis. The context suggests that the very recent past is being referred to; the very outside limit is three months (back to January 250).

5. *suscepta poena est quae confessores Christi fecit extorres.* Cyprian is doubtless referring to an earlier stage in the treatment of obstinate confessors of this persecution; they were sent into exile—though of what particular variety or varieties we do not know precisely (relegation, deportation, *ad tempus, in perpetuum,* etc.), with (apparently) confiscation of their possessions. For what it is worth, Cyprian nowhere anticipates that exiled confessors will remain out of Carthage indefinitely; cf., e.g., *Ep.* 19.2. For examples of exiles in Cyprian's correspondence, see *Epp.* 13.4.1 (*alius in eam patriam unde extorris factus est . . .*), 19.2.3 (*extorres facti et patria pulsi*), 24.1.1 (*extorres sunt facti; ipsa extorris facta est*), 38.1.2, 66.7.2. And for the confiscation of property, cf. *Epp.* 19.2.3 (*boni suis omnibus spoliati*), and 24.1.1 (*possessiones quas nunc fiscus tenet*).

In some cases the language in our evidence is imprecise and *extorris* can be used of refugees, forced (not legally, but by circumstances) to flee their *patria*. Rome, as the *communis patria,* was specifically excluded as a possible place of residence for *relegati;* cf. Suetonius *Claud.* 23.2; *Digesta* 48.22.7.15 (Ulpian) and 48.22.18(19) (Callistratus). Such fugitives would have their patrimony sequestrated; cf. *Digesta* 48.27.5—likewise the proscribed bishops of *Ep.* 66.7.2 (and Cyprian himself, *Epp.* 66.4.1 and 59.6.1).

6. *confessio tamen praesens quantum in passione fortior. . . .* The turn of phrase suggests that the new treatment of recusants is in fact quite recent. *Ep.* 20.2.2, referring to this letter, reflects this change (*postea quam vero et tormenta venerunt*), as does *De laps.* 13: *sed tormenta postmodum venerant* and *Ep.* 11.1.3: *dum quosdam*

insolenter extollit confessionis suae . . . iactatio, tormenta venerunt.
Why should there be such a change in policy? The arrival of the
proconsul on his assize round, or special orders from the emper-
or (see *Ep.* 22.2.1 and n. 13 *ad loc.*), or simply outworn impa-
tience at the obstinacy of the remaining *confessores?* For
discussion, see C. Saumagne in *Bulletin de la société nationale des
antiquaires de France* 1957 (1959) 23 ff. and *Byzantion* 32 (1962) 1
ff., and in my articles in *Latomus* 31 (1972) 1053 ff., *Historia* 22
(1973) 650 ff., BICS 20 (1973) 118 ff.

I find it impossible to believe (with Saumagne) that all the
Carthaginian *extorres* have now been recalled and are being
subjected to *tormenta* in an increased effort to induce apostasy.
Under these circumstances, for Cyprian to have failed to elaborate on such two-fold sufferings, double trials, multiple tribulations, etc., on the part of these confessors in this very lavish
epistle seems quite implausible (contrast the description of the
passiones of Aurelius in *Ep.* 38.1.2).

7. *prompta devotione.* Cyprian is stressing in this martial
context (cf. again below in §2.3, *sacramento et devotione militis*)
the military overtones of *devotio*, a technical term for a formal
act of dedicating one's life in battle in return for victory. Cf.
Livy 8.9.4 ff.; Macrobius *Sat.* 3.9.9 f.; PWK 5.1 (1903) 277 ff.;
RAC 3 (1957) 849 ff.

8. In the later *Ep.* 22.2.2 we have registered the names of
seventeen such victims (including that of Mappalicus, in second
place on the list). It is worth noting that these martyrs have not
been condemned to death—they die as a result of the rigours of
imprisonment or interrogation, etc. Hence there are in *Ep.*
11.1.3 *tormenta . . . sine exitu damnationis.*

9. An adaptation of 1 John 4.4

10. *ad deiciendum. Deicere* has by now become almost a "Christianism," with the meaning "to make deny the faith." This is a
frequent usage in Cyprian.

11. *durissimam quaestionem.* Note the definition of *quaestio* in
Digesta 47.10.15.41 (Ulpian): *quaestionem intellegere debemus tormenta et corporis dolorem ad eruendam veritatem.*

12. On Cyprian's celestial chronology, see n.14 to *Ep.* 6.

13. *armis fidei credentes (varia lectio: credentis) armatos.* Cyprian exploits here ambiguities in *credo* (= "trust" as well as "believe").

14. Can Cyprian have possibly been influenced in this bizarre image by knowledge of the account of Polycarp's death, *Act. Polyc.* 16 (Musurillo 15): When the executioner stabbed him with a dagger "there came out such a quantity of blood that the flames were extinguished and all the crowd marvelled that there should be such a difference between the unbelievers and the elect"?

15. *spectaculum domini.* Cyprian is so insistent throughout this epistle on the theme of *Christus in martyre* that we are perhaps to translate this phrase quite literally. The *spectaculum was* the Lord's (not "for the Lord").

16. *sacramento ac devotione militis eius.* Sacramentum is here clearly being employed in its sense of military oath of loyalty, with profession of faith being considered the solemn oath of the soldier of Christ; cf. *De laps.* 13: *sacramenti mei memor devotionis ac fidei arma suscepi.* For this sense, and parallels, see J. de Ghellinck *et al.*, *Pour l'histoire du mot "sacramentum"* 1 (Louvain-Paris 1924) 162 f. Note on early Christian sarcophagi the theme of the *miles Christi* taking his *sacramentum* by placing his hand on the sacred book, see M. Ch. Pietri in *Mélanges d'archéologie et d'histoire* 74 (1962) 649 ff.—For ideas in Stoic literature comparable to many expressed in §2, note H. Koch, *Cyprianische Untersuchungen* (Bonn 1926) 306 f.

17. Ps. 115.6.

18. *dans credentibus tantum quantum se credit capere qui sumit.* For the notion and turn of phrase in Cyprian, cf. *Test.* 3.42 (*tantum nos posse quantum credimus*); *Ad Fortunat.* 10 *ad fin.* (*unusquisque . . . tantum accipiat de Dei ope quantum se credat accipere*); *Ad Donat.* 5 (*quantum illuc fidei capacis adferimus, tantum gratiae inundantis haurimus*). This is central to Cyprian's pneumatological viewpoint: it is the recipient who makes the Holy Spirit more or less efficacious by the manner of his reception. The Holy Spirit comes itself *non de mensura* (*Epp.* 64.3.2, 69.14.1); there is no *mensura ulla vel modus* (*Ad Donat.* 5).

19. Matt. 10.19 f. This is "one of the most frequently cited Biblical quotations in Cyprian's writings" (Fahey 294). Cyprian clearly finds it especially apposite for the public appearance on the tribunal of the Christian witness; doubly so in the present case when Mappalicus' utterance to the proconsul was veridically prophetic. Cyprian obviously interprets the passage in a very literal sense: this indicates an essential feature of the current theology of martyrdom—martyrs were in a position of privileged access to the Holy Spirit (cf. n. 14 to *Ep.* 6); hence the dominant motif in the *Acta* tradition of an *apologia* by the martyr before the magistrate on the tribunal. For abundant parallels for the theme of the inspired words or dreams of the would-be martyr, K. Holl, *Neue Jahrbuch für das klassichen Altertum* 33 (1914), 538 f.; E. L. Hummel in SCA 9 (1946) 95 f.

20. *cum Mappalicus beatissimus. . . . proconsuli diceret.* Mappalicus is clearly not a cleric; neither were any of his *comites* as listed in *Ep.* 22.2.2. It seems that, of those who have died already, Cyprian highlights the particular *exitus* of Mappalicus precisely because of the report of his inspired *dictum* which follows. We have no other details about him (save *Ep.* 27.1.1).

The martyr's *vox* is here described as *plena Spiritu Sancto.* Later Cyprian, now a confessor in exile, can be similarly said to prophesy; cf. *Ep.* 78.2.2: *prophetiam quam litteris tuis Spiritu Sancto plenus spopondisti* (from the Numidian martyrs).

The (sixth century) Carthaginian Calendar reads for April 19: XIII *K. mai martyris Mappalici* (AA.SS. nov., vol. 2, pars prior, LXX). The Hieronymian Calendar for April 17 and April 18 records: XV *K. mai. . . . in Africa. . . . Mappalici:* XIV *K. mai. . . . Mappalici* (AA.SS. nov., vol. 2, pars posterior 195, 196f.). Consult H. Delehaye, *Les origines du culte des martyrs* (Brussels 1933²) 379 f.; R. Aigrain, *L'Hagiographie: ses sources, ses methodes, son histoire* (Paris 1953) 20 ff., 32 ff. (on these calendars), and AA.SS. nov., vol. 2, pars posterior, 195 ff. for critical notes.

That is to say, we will not be far wrong in dating this utterance (and death) of Mappalicus to mid-April, 250: that is what our sources in their present state force us, methodologically, to take as a working basis—though the possibility must always remain that the tradition itself is distorted and garbled (and Mappalicus was found a place in it precisely because of this letter). See further the observations on the names in *Ep.* 22.2.2

As for the *proconsul,* there is recorded in AA.SS., April 10, p. 851, a governor of Africa, with the undistinguished name of Fortunatianus (there are variants), who is credited with being responsible for the deaths of Terentius, Africanus, and their companions (more than forty in all) under Decius. But the *Acta* are late in origin and of palpably dubious value, and the *cultus* of Terentius *et al.* is Eastern in tradition, so there is no real likelihood that we have preserved in these wretched records any shreds of genuine history (and hence further evidence for the proconsul at work in this month of April 250). This is ably discussed by T. D. Barnes in JTS 25 (1974) 110 ff. For other activities of this proconsul, see *Epp.* 22, 38, and 56, and discussion in *Latomus* 31 (1972) 1055 ff.—*Fasti* for the African provinces are now conveniently listed in PWK 13 (1973) 1 ff. (Africa Proconsularis), 307 ff. (Mauretania), 315 ff. (Numidia).

21. Isa. 7.13b, 14b. The collection of texts in this section is designed to illustrate passages (from O.T. and N.T.) which accurately prophesied an *agon,* just as Mappalicus has now prophesied his *agon* to the proconsul. Cyprian uses, for emphasizing this message, the verb *ostendo* ("reveal", "prophesy") three times, in connexion with each of the three sets of quotations.

22. 1 Cor. 9.24 f., omitting verse 25a. On Paul's agonistic imagery, see V. C. Pfitzner, *Paul and the Agon Motif* (Leiden 1967) *passim,* esp. 82 ff. on this passage.

23. 2 Tim. 4.6 ff., Fahey 516. In 4.6 Cyprian's text reads *tempus. . . . assumptionis* (Vulgate: *tempus. . . . resolutionis*): does *assumptionis* translate ἀναλήψεως?

24. Cyprian is picking out the implication of his quotations from Isaiah (representing the prophets) and from Paul (representing the apostles). On the martyrdom of the apostles see n. 16 to *Ep.* 6, n. 15 to *Ep.* 8.

25. *collegarum suorum nomine:* that is to say, Mappalicus' fellow confessors and martyrs. Thus, too, the confessor Lucian of the confessor Saturninus, *Ep.* 22.3.1: *Saturninus . . . et collega meus.*

26. *repromisit*. Though this meaning of "promise anew" is very rare (cf. Suetonius, *Otho* 4.1), the run of the argument seems to demand that Mappalicus is re-presenting the *agon* of Christ and His apostles. The use of *repromitto* in *Act. Perp.* is worth noting: §1.5: *prophetias. . . . et visiones novas pariter repromissas*, and *semper Deus operetur quae repromisit;* §4.1 (Perp.): *fidenter repromisi ei dicens: crastina die tibi renuntiabo.* And for Cyprian's general usage, compare *De dom. orat.* 10: *eis et aeternitas repromittitur;* 13: *regnum . . . a Deo nobis repromissum;* 33: *adesse se repromittit.*

27. *in quaestione victores*. These must be fellow *martyrs* of Mappalicus (see on these introductory note and n. 8 above, and on *quaestio*, n. 11.

28. Cyprian seems to have here nuptial imagery in mind (*vinculum . . . hospitium . . . iunxit iungat . . . consummatio*).

29. *ceterorum quoque stantium firmitatem*. See introductory note to this letter for the implications of this phrase for the history of this persecution.

30. For this familiar military image, cf. *Ep.* 58.4.2: *spectat militem suum Christus ubicumque pugnantem*, and *Ep.* 58.8.1: *imperatore praesente.* Cf. also E. L. Hummel in SCA 9 (1946) 56 ff., 84 ff. and Minucius Felix, *Oct.* 37.2, and n. 622 on that passage in ACW 39 (adding to that note the example of Titus, at the siege of Jerusalem, persuaded by his officers not to engage in the fall of the Temple but to watch from the Antonia, so that "under Caesar's gaze, all will be brave fighters"—Josephus, *B.J.* 6.133).

31. *et coronat pariter et coronatur*. There is a nice iconographic illustration of this notion in A. Grabar, *Martyrium—recherches sur le culte des reliques et l'art chrétien antique* (Paris 1943–1946) 1.Plate LXVI.2 and 2.56 f. (a Christ-martyr figure, standing on the four rivers of paradise, both carries a crown and is being presented with a crown, on a fifth-century African reliquary).

On this theme of *Christus in martyre* see introductory note to this letter. There are many obvious parallels to be found, and it is commonly found in Cyprian's writings (cf., e.g., *Ep.* 58.5.2: *ipse in nobis et loquitur et coronatur*). For further examples and discussion see F. J. Dölger in AC 4 (1934) 73 ff.; M. Lods, *Confesseurs et martyrs. Successeurs des prophètes dans l'église des trois premiers siècles* (Neuchâtel 1958) esp. 27; M. Pellegrino in *Revue des sciences religieuses* 35 (1961) 151 ff.; E. Lohse, *Märtyrer und Gottestnecht* (Göttingen 1955); E. L. Hummel in SCA 9 (1946) 91 ff., 104 ff.

32. *Dominus scrutator est renis et cordis.* An allusion to Apoc. 2.23. Cyprian's text here reads, *ego sum scrutator renis et cordis.* See Fahey 540 f.

33. *accepto post gloriam commeatu. Commeatus,* a military technical term ("furlough"), is found not infrequently in similar Christian contexts. Cf., e.g., *Epp.* 39.1.1 and 55.13.1; *De mort.* 19. Tertullian, *Apol.* 33.1, can even refer to the "respite" provided by the Roman Empire before the horrors of the end of the world as a *commeatus.*

34. The contrast between white and crimson is a cliché of Latin verse and, specifically, that of the lily and the rose (red, of course, in antiquity; see Pliny, *N.H.* 21.10 ff., for the varieties) has many parallels in classical iterature e.g., Vergil, *Aen.* 12.68 f.: *aut mixta rubent lilia multa/alba rosa;* Propertius 2.3.10 ff.: *lilia . . . utque rosae puro lacte natant folia;* and for many more examples, see H. Blümner in *Philologus* 48 (1889) 157 f. Cyprian concludes his tractate *De op. et eleemos.* 26 with a sentiment closely similar to that expressed here: *in pace vincentibus coronam candidam pro operibus dabit, in persecutione purpuream pro passione geminabit,* and *Ad Fort.* 13 closes with a parallel idea: *in persecutione militia, in pace conscientia coronatur.* Likewise *De zelo* 16 and *De mort.* 17. Later, Paulinus of Nola, *Carm.* 18.146 ff. (= ACW 40.119) played on the idea of the two crowns, white and roseate. In the Martyrdom of Dasius the martyr is described as "blossoming like a rose amid thorns" (*Mart. Dasii* 2) contrasting with the "lily amid thorns" of Song of Songs 2.2 which is being alluded to. The imagery would lie behind Saturus' vision of a *viridiarium arbores habens rosae* (*Act. Perp.* 11.5), James' vision of a boy, recently martyred, *corona rosea collo circumdatus* (*Act. Marian. et Jacob.* 11.5), and Jerome, *Ep.* 54.14, indicates that the imagery became standard: *inter virginum lilia et martyrum rosas.* For a survey of the later history of the *topos,* see W. Fechter, *Lateinische Dichtkunst und deutsches Mittelalter* (Berlin 1964) 48 ff.

esp. 53 ff.; S. Poque in *Revue des études augustiennes* 17 (1971) 155 ff.; P. L. Thomas in *Rheinisches Museum* 122 (1979) 310 ff.

Cyprian's classical tradition may have here been reinforced by the liturgical convention; according to *Trad. Apost.* 32 (ed. Botte), liturgical blessing is pronounced on certain fruits, and sometimes on flowers, the rose and lily being offered, but no other variety.

There is a close iconographic illustration of Cyprian's conceit in the "Crypt of the Six Saints" of the catacomb of Domitilla; there, Christ has presented in paradise the saints with crowns— of roses; they are presumably, therefore, martyrs; G. Wilpert, *Roma sotterranea. Le pitture della catacombe romano* (2 vols., Rome 1903) pl. 125; P. Testini, *Le catacombe e gli antichi cimiteri cristiani in Roma* (Bologna 1966) fig. 172; and see in general on flowered crowns DACL 5 (1923) 1693 ff.

In *Ep.* 21 Celerinus' language seems to reflect similar notions: §1.2: *tam floridam confessionem,* §3.1: *te floridiorum ministerium percepisse* (where see n.). And in *Ep.* 37.2.2 there are accruing to the Roman martyrs in their barren prison *rosae et flores de paradisi deliciis.*

LETTER 11

Contents: Cyprian writes a stinging letter to his clergy. They are to persevere in prayer and good works in order to win reconciliation with God, for the persecution has visited them as a consequence of the *mala* in their community—worldly cares and concerns, pride and self-will, and above all rivalries and dissensions. The same indiscipline has now occasioned a further visitation—the tortures have come, for some of the confessors themselves are insolent, arrogant and unruly. Cyprian adduces two visions, one recent, one in the past, to reinforce his plea for unity, *disciplina,* and repentance. The persecution continues as a time of testing of their reformed resolve. Peace will come if and when they are not found wanting.

Date and circumstances: It was Cyprian's custom, in communicating with his brethren in Carthage from his place of hiding, that he should write at least two letters, one to his presbyters and deacons (at large) and one to the confessors (confined in prison, etc.), and hence the pairs 5 and 6, 13 and 14, 15 and 16. *Ep.* 7 had no such counterpart; there were no confessors yet at the time of writing. There can be little doubt that *Ep.* 11 is to be associated in this way with *Ep.* 10: §1.3 of *Ep.* 11 indicates that *tormenta* have now started for the confessors, just as they have in §1.1 of *Ep.* 10. There is one distinct hint, however, to suggest that *Ep.* 11 may be, if anything, marginally earlier than (rather than being strictly contemporaneous with) *Ep.* 10. In §1.3 Cyprian, in a rather off-hand way, admits the possibility that some confessors may have already died under these new tortures, but his tone is markedly ungenerous. They have merely been, by God's mercy, quick at dying; the word "martyr" is not mentioned. That is in strong contrast with the lyrical exultation at the story of the edifying martyrdom, under torture, of the confessor Mappalicus and the divinely inspired words vouchsafed to him, which we find in *Ep.* 10. *Ep.* 11, we might conclude, was despatched shortly before news of Mappalicus' death reached Cyprian (though it could be argued that in this letter, which is overall one of rebuke, it was not to the point to emphasize the glories of martyrdom but rather the horrors of torments—the punishment for slackness). It thus falls, in the sequence of letters, after 7, 5 and 6, 13 and 14 (see notes there), but just before 10 and 12 (where see introductory note).

Can we place it, therefore, very roughly, in early to mid-April 250 A.D.? For discussion, see L. Nelke, *Die Chronologie der Korrespondenz Cyprians* . . . (diss. Thorn 1902) 15; and L. Duquenne, *Chronologie des lettres de s. Cyprien* . . . (Brussels 1972) 80, 104 ff.

The letter is apparently referred to in §2.1 of *Ep.* 20 which enclosed a copy of *Ep.* 11.

The epistle is preoccupied with disunity and indiscipline—for which evils, Cyprian explains, the persecution itself has befallen them, and then, in turn, the tortures have beset the turbulent confessors. The two visions, one in the past (*prius longe ostensum,*

§4.2), one recent (*non olim*, §5.1), match these two stages of the *divina censura*. Cyprian is here presenting a theme not at all common in his works—persecution figures more usually as a time of testing rather than of outright punishment—and this indicates the severity of his present reaction. For a parallel, cf. *De laps.* 6, and for discussion, see E. L. Hummel in SCA 9 (1946) 39 ff.

Cyprian's concern here is to give a sermon on the need for repentance, humility, and lamentation, and to give a theological explanation of the present *mala*, not to deal directly with the details of the indiscipline and disunity (as the *incipit* of a number of mss has it: *incipit ad clerum de deprecando Deo pro peccatis nostris*). We find, therefore, more specific information on the background to this letter in the earlier pair, *Epp.* 13 and 14, and in the later letters, *Epp.* 15 sqq. This letter, addressed to the clergy, is to be open and cyclical (§7.1), though Cyprian strikes a note of worry that attempts may be made to obstruct its dissemination. The next time he writes, he pens a separate letter to the faithful laity (*Ep.* 17), as well to the clergy (*Ep.* 16) and the martyrs and confessors (*Ep.* 15). Some later letters, which he wishes to reach both clergy and laity, he takes the precaution of addressing *presbyteris et diaconibus et plebi universae* (*Epp.* 38, 39, 40).

We might note the stage which the persecution has now reached: there has already been general devastation (§1.2, §8.1), there are confessors, now undergoing tortures, with some possible deaths (§1.3), there is a residue of *stantes* living in hiding and peril (§8) for whom danger and fear have not yet passed (§1.2, §6.1). There has already been evidence of indiscipline, insolence, and improper conduct among the confessors (§1.3) and the repentance of the lapsed stands in need of reform (§8). Despite the general atmosphere of disaster and disharmony, hopes of peace can stil be entertained (§6.1, §8).

M. Réveillaud, *Saint Cyprien. L'oraison dominicale* (Paris 1964) 39 ff., 159, 202, rightly adduces many parallels with this letter and *De dom. orat.*, but his thesis that the treatise was in fact composed during these early months of Cyprian's retirement is less than compelling.

Augustine, *De bapt.* 4.2.3, 4.10.16, 4.13.19 quotes four times the phrase of §1.2: *saeculo verbis solis et non factis renuntiantes*, and three times in paraphrase, with acknowledgment, *op. cit.* 5.15.19, 5.18.24, 6.12.19. There are further allusions to the letter in Augustine, *De bapt.* 4.3.4, 4.14.21, 4.31.60.

1. Cyprian avoids any reference in this letter to a document which he has already received from the four presbyters (*Ep.* 14.4), the issues of which he has firmly shelved, for more general consultation, until his return.

2. That is, *illic* See n. 4 to *Ep.* 5. Cyprian is still in hiding.

3. *pressurae istius tam turbidam vastitatem quae gregem nostrum maxima ex parte populata est.* For the notion and language, cf. *Epp.* 13.1 and 14.1.1; *De laps.* 4, 7, 26. Whilst we must take due account of rhetorical hyperbole, we ought still to conclude that it appeared to Cyprian that the bulk of his community had in fact lapsed. We ought also to conclude that by this date at least (c. April, 250) the *dies praestitutus* for Carthage (by which time *libelli* were to have been obtained) has well and truly come and gone. (D. D. Sullivan, *The Life of the North Africans as Revealed in the Works of St. Cyprian* (Washington 1933) 58, mistakenly interprets this passage literally and lists it as describing the plague.)

4. That is to say, the *stantes* (who have refused to obtain their apostatizing *libelli*) are still in danger of detection or delation; and the cases of *confessores* in prison are still being tried (§1.3).

5. *patrimonio et lucro studentes. Amor patrimonii* is emphasized as one of the underlying causes for defections in *De laps.* 6, 10, 11, 12, (and cf. n. 5 to *Ep.* 8) an explanation which is particularly telling, for confiscations threatened the faithful *stantes* (see n. 5 to *Ep.* 10).

6. *aemulationi et dissensioni vacantes.* Though speaking in generalizations Cyprian is addressing his own clergy primarily and his reference must extend to conditions prevailing before the persecution began only some three months or so earlier. We ought to conclude that he has, at least partly, in mind the dispute over his own election to the office of bishop which

roused the antagonism of certain older Carthaginian presbyters (cf *Ep.* 43.3f.). Pontius, *Vit. Cyp.* 5.2 ff. provides an apologetic version of the wrangle. Despite the claim of Pontius that these rivals were wooed by Cyprian's indulgent pardon, gentle patience, and kindly clemency, so that they subsequently figured among his *amicissimi,* Cyprian's own view, stated a year after this letter, was that the antagonism continued to fester; it provided the base for the clerical group who opposed his *forma* on penitential discipline (cf. *Ep.* 43). See further nn. on *Epp.* 14 and 43.

7. *saeculo verbis solis et non factis renuntiantes.* Is Cyprian alluding to a renunciation formula recited at Baptism? Cf. *Epp.* 13.5.3: *saeculo renuntiaveramus cum baptizati sumus,* and 57.3.1; *De laps.* 8; *De orat. dom.* 9, 13, 19; *Ad Fort.* 7; *De hab. virg.* 7. See further V. Saxer, *Vie liturgique et quotidienne à Carthage vers le milieu du IIIᵉ siècle* (Vatican 1969) 121 f.; J. H. Waszink in VC 1 (1947) 13 ff.; J. Capmany-Casamitjana, *"Miles Christi" en la espiritualidad de san Cipriano* (Barcelona 1956) 41 ff.

7a. *unusquisque sibi placentes et omnibus displicentes.* The rather odd phraseology is explained by an allusion to 2 Tim. 3.2, where Cyprian's text read, *erunt homines sibi placentes.* See Fahey 515 f., and cf. n. 18 to *Ep.* 3, *Ep.* 55.12.1 (*nobis displicentes*), *Ep.* 59.5.2 (*nemo sibi placens*), etc.

8. Luke 12.47.

9. *nec. . . . teneant disciplinam. Disciplina* is used here in its regulative sense. The word appears repeatedly in Cyprian's letters concerned with suppressing schism and enforcing uniform (especially penitential) regulations; it has been subject to considerable analysis: H.-I. Marrou in *Bull. du Cange* 19 (1934) 1 ff.; W. Dürig in *Sacris Erudiri* 4 (1952) 245 ff.; V. Morel in *Revue d'histoire ecclésiastique* 40 (1944–45) 5 ff. and in RAC 3 (1957), 1213 ff.; S. Hübner in ZfKT 84 (1962) 58 ff. In *Epp.* 13.4 ff. and 14.3.2 Cyprian has already been more specific about the confessors' misdemeanours (drunkenness, women, quarrelling, illicit return from exile, etc.). *Ep.* 15.3.2 adds accepting bribes; cf. *de laps.* 16. In *de unit.* 20 they are listed as *fraudes et stupra et adulteria.*

10. *confessionis suae tumida et inverecunda iactatio.* Compare

Tertullian's description of Praxeas *qua* confessor: he was *de iactatione martyrii inflatus ob solum et simplex et breve carceris taedium* (*Adv. Prax.* 1.4)

11. On the advent of tortures, see introductory note and n. 6 to *Ep.* 10.

12. *sine exitu damnationis.* Note the implication that the death penalty was not here imposed (*contra* W. H. C. Frend, *Martyrdom and Persecution in the Early Church* [Oxford 1965] 407). Cyprian's language elsewhere supports the deduction; in his catalogues of the dangers and sufferings involved in confession the risk of death is not uppermost. Cf., e.g., De laps. 2; *Ep.* 66.7.2. See further Introduction, pp. 35 ff.

13. *deiciant.* On this verb, see n. 10 to *Ep.* 10.

14. On the contrast between this grudging description of martyrdom and that of Mappalicus to be found in *Ep.* 10, see introductory note to this letter.

15. *sicut praemonuit divina censura.* On the phrase *divina censura* in Cyprian, see S. Hübner in ZfKT 84 (1962) 60 ff.; RAC 2 (1954) 968 f.

16. Ps. 88.31 ff. See Fahey 147 f. Cyprian's text here unusually omits *filii eius* after *dereliquerint.* Cyprian seldom gives partial quotations.

17. *rogemus . . . misericordiam Dei.* The argument here (ask, seek, knock—*rogemus, petamus, pulsemus*) is clearly structured on Matt. 7.7 f. (cf. Mark 11.24, Luke 11.9, John 14.13 f., etc.) and prepares the ground for the message of the vision which follows in §3.1.

18. Ps. 88.34a. In the sentence which follows (*petamus et accipimus*) there is strong ms warrant for reading more easily *petamus et accipiemus* ("let us seek, and we shall receive").

19. Imagery particularly apposite for seeking forgiveness. See n. on *Ep.* 30.6.3 for the considerable evidence for vigils kept by repentant sinners at the Church portals, begging to regain admittance, and for similar penitential ceremonies held *in vestibulo.*

20. *si sit unanimis oratio.* The appendage to this sentence is now to be turned into a dominant theme of the epistle: the need for *harmonious* prayers for forgiveness. On the use of *unanimis* in

Cyprian, see H. Pétré, *Caritas, Étude sur le vocabulaire latin de la charité chrétienne* (Louvain 1948) 326 ff.

21. *dictum esse in visione.* We learn from §4.2 that this vision was vouchsafed *prius longe,* even before this persecution ever arose. Cyprian's language about it here appears to be studiously impersonal; he does not claim specifically the vision to have been his. The vagueness matches the generality of its message. By contrast, in §5.1, Cyprian firmly ascribes the second vision to himself: *nam et hoc nobis non olim per visionem . . . exprobatum.* The particularity matches the specificity of its message (§§5.1, 6.1 f.) It is hard to resist the conclusion that the first vision was Cyprian's also (so A. d'Alès, *Revue d'ascétique et de mystique* 2 [1921] 257; cf. *idem, Théologie de s. Cyprien* [Paris 1922] 80 f.; E. L. Hummel in SCA 9 [1946] 41 f.; P. Hinchliff, *Cyprian of Carthage* [London 1974] 42, among many others, simply assume that the dream was in fact Cyprian's).

For parallel, one might compare *Epp.* 57 ff. In *Ep.* 57 a coming persecution of Gallus is sensed by many divine signs. In *Epp.* 58, 60, and 61, however, we find that Cyprian himself is at least one, if not the only, recipient of these special premonitions. For Cyprian's *visiones* generally, see nn. 27–30 to *Ep.* 16.4.

22. *plebi adsistenti.* The language has technical Christian over-tones (cf. nn. 1 and 3 to *Ep.* 1), a surmise confirmed by the use of *fratres* as a synonym for *plebs* (*nec esset fratrum consensio*) in this same sentence.

23. Ps. 67.7.

24. Acts 4.32.

25. John 15.12.

26. Matt. 18.19. See Fahey 313 ff. Note the ecclesial exegesis made by Cyprian of these last two texts.

27. Cf. John 14.27. This allusion is omitted by Fahey.

28. *iam pridem:* cf. n. 7 to *Ep.* 1.

29. A *iuvenis* (generally a Christ-figure) appears not infre-quently in martyrs' dreams and visions; cf., e.g., *Act. Perp.* 10; *Act. Marian.* 7; *Act. Montan.* 8; Pontius, *Vit. Cyp.* 12. For a good collection of evidence, see P. Courcelle, *Les Confessions de saint Augustin dans la tradition littéraire: Antécédents et postérité* (Paris 1963) 127 ff.

30. *maxillam manu tenens maesto vultu sedebat.* A classic pose, found not infrequently on grave stelai, sarcophagi, and similar monuments; the still, dejected posture is generally exploited to depict the helpless sorrow of the mourner in the face of bereavement, grief, and death. A few examples: P. E. Arias and M. Hirmer, *A History of Greek Vase Painting* (London 1962) fig. 189; D. E. Strong, *Roman Imperial Sculpture* (London 1961) fig. 125; A. W. Lawrence, *Greek and Roman Sculpture* (London 1972) plate 68c. This seated and meditative figure is in sharp contrast with the malevolently active figure who is next described. For a literary parallel, compare the portrait of Medea in Apollonius of Rhodes, *Argon.* 3.1159 ff.: She sat down on a low stool . . . leant over and rested her cheek on her left hand, with tears in her moist eyes as she pondered. . . .

31. *non olim:* another obscure temporal phrase.

32. *et hoc nobis . . . per visionem . . . exprobatum.* On Cyprian's penchant for introducing what may, perhaps unfairly, appear to be conveniently vouchsafed dreams and signs, see nn. 27–30 on *Ep.* 16.4. That Cyprian might at this season be particularly disturbed by dreams, which he would take, without question, to be veridical and portentous, is psychologically likely, given the high state of tension and anxiety occasioned by the persecution and its aftermath. The turn of phrase here seems to carry the implication that the first vision was Cyprian's own.

33. Could this be an allusion in Cyprian to Heb. 12.6? Here the Vulgate reads, *quem enim diligit Dominus castigat.* The possibility is not discussed by Fahey 41. It would be unique.

34. Col. 4.2.

35. *disciplinae magister et exempli nostri via.* On *disciplina,* see n. 9 above. On *via,* cf. n. 19 to *Ep.* 8 and the expressions that occur earlier (§1.2: *viam Domini non tenemus*) and later (§5.3: *ambulare in viis eius*) in this same letter.

36. Luke 6.12.

37. *cum . . . nostra peccata portaret.* For the idea, cf. *Ep.* 63.13.1 and *De laps.* 17, going back, of course, to Matt. 8.17, Rom. 4.25, 1 Peter 2.24. For the notion in the earlier patristic writers of Christ's mission as being essentially to free humanity from the tyranny of sin, see J. Daniélou, *Message évangélique et culture*

hellénistique au IIe et IIIe siècles (Paris 1961) 154 ff.; and on the sometimes ambiguous Christian use of *portare,* see T. P. O'Malley, *Tertullian and the Bible. Language—Imagery—Exegesis* (Utrecht 1967) 45 f.

38. *adeo autem. . . . ut legimus.* The variant reading *legamus* would lead to the translation: "so sure is it that He sought . . . that we read. . . ."

39. Luke 22.31 f.

40. *advocatum et deprecatorem.* An allusion to 1 John 2.1. See Fahey 526. Cf. *Ep.* 55.18.3.

41. *confitentes adque intellegentes.* Not used, of course, in any sacramental sense (so, rightly, S. Hübner in ZfTK 84 [1962] 186). For the verbal combination, cf. *intellegendum est enim et confitendum* (§1.2).

42. Rom. 8.35.

43. *persecutio ista examinatio est adque exploratio peccati nostri.* The variant reading *pectoris* (for *peccati*) seems preferable.

44. *excuti.* As so often, Cyprian seems to be picking up an image from a Biblical quotation cited earlier (in §5.2: Luke 22.31).

45. We are presumably being given a continuation of Cyprian's *visio* of §5.1; the mechanical vagueness (to whom is the message being entrusted to be relayed to Cyprian?) is consistent with dream descriptions.

46. Cyprian was less circumspect in his criticism in *Ep.* 13.4.1: *alius aliquis temulentus et lasciviens demoratur.*

47. Note the open and encyclical nature of the epistle; see introductory note to this letter. Cyprian's admonishments are more general than particular in accordance with this wider audience envisaged.

48. *conversationem veteris hominis exponant.* An allusion to Eph. 4.22. *Conversatio* had, of course, a rich and varied development in later Latin. Cf., e.g., C. Mohrmann, *Études sur le latin des chrétiens* 2 (Rome 1961) 341 ff.; E. Gilson, *Heloise and Abelard* (Ann Arbor 1960) 151 ff.   *

49. Luke 9.62.

50. An allusion to Luke 17.31 f. Cf. Gen. 19.17, 26.

51. *exiguam stantium firmitatem* (variant reading: *paucitatem*).

The text here is discussed by L. Bayard, *Le latin de saint Cyprien* (Paris 1902) 351.

52. Cyprian here breaks into a notable passage of euchological composition, doubtless echoing the current style of public prayer; cf. J. Chapman in JTS 4 (1902) 109. F. Cabrol in DACL 1 (1924) 615 f., collects such passages in Cyprian. For the imagery of the present passage, compare *Ep.* 31.1.2 and *De laps.* 1, and consult B. Melin, *Studia in Corpus Cyprianeum* (Uppsala 1966) 30 f., for other parallels.

53. That is to say, the blessings of the peace which will follow if the lessons of the visions are heeded.

54. *solita magnalia.* On the Christianism *magnalia* see C. Mohrmann, *op. cit.* in n. 48 above, 122 (the Christians having need of the neologism in order to avoid words, like *portenta*, tainted with pagan connotations).

55. *lapsorum paenitentia reformetur.* The only hint in the letter of the dispute already started (see *Ep.* 14.4) over the penitential discipline proper for the *lapsi.* For the expression, compare *Ep.* 25.1.2: *post lapsum paenitentes in statum pristinum reformentur, Ep.* 55.23.2: *reformatum ... et ad innocentiae disciplinam paenitentiae dolore correctum, Ep.* 73.22.3: *correctos ... ac reformatos, Ep.* 74.5.2: *in novum hominem spiritaliter reformatus.*

56. *magnalia quibus. ... fortis et stabilis perseverantium fiducia glorietur.* The rhythm of the sentence strongly suggests we are (unusually) dealing with a truly passive verb, as again in *Ep.* 66.2.2: *iudicio ac testimonio Dei non probantur tantum sed etiam gloriantur.* See TLL *s.v.* 11.2099, *sensu passivo;* Watson 223, 310. In both instances Cyprian is seeking a rhetorically emphatic rhyme (*reformetur ... glorietur; probantur ... gloriantur*).

LETTER 12

Contents: Cyprian exhorts his clergy not to be in any way deficient in their solicitude during his enforced absence, both for the imprisoned confessors and for the faithful poor. In particular, they should treat the bodies of those confessors who, without having been subjected to the tortures, die in prison, with all the special regard they would show to the bodies of the martyrs; note should be made of their deaths, so that the celebration of their anniversaries may be included in the lists of the commemoration of the martyrs.

Date and circumstances: The phrases in §1.2: *etsi torti non sunt, qui se tormentis . . . optulit,* ought to imply that *tormenta* are now possibilities for Christian recusants, though not all the confessors who are still in prison have yet been subjected to them. We must be, therefore, in the "second phase" of the persecution as noted in *Epp.* 10.1.1 (see nn. 5 and 6) and 11.1.3, after the advent of tortures. This letter is accordingly *later* than *Epp.* 13 and 14 (where see intro.), as well as 7, 5, 6. And we are, furthermore, at a stage when some of the confessors have already died of the privations of their imprisonment. We appear to have circumstances such as described by Lucian in *Ep.* 22.2.1 f. (death of Paulus *et alii*) when the traffic in *libelli pacis* arose; this we hear first mentioned in *Ep.* 15. The notably uncensorious tone here distinctly suggests that this trade is still unknown to Cyprian. So we appear to be *earlier* than *Ep.* 15.

The precise relationship of this letter with *Epp.* 11 and 10 is less easy to determine.

On the one hand, the language of *Ep.* 12 does not indubitably imply that martyrs' deaths (under torture, etc.) have already occurred. If Cyprian was so jubilant over Mappalicus' death, might he not have mentioned that fact (esp. in §2). We may, therefore, be earlier than *Ep.* 10. And the general and unqualified exhortation to lavish every care and attention on the confessors in prison—they lack nothing in glory—suggests we may possibly be earlier also than the strictures voiced in *Ep.* 11.1.3 on the reprehensible conduct of some of these imprisoned confessors. We may, therefore, be earlier than *Ep.* 11 as well.

On the other hand, the references to deaths in prison are vague and unspecific in *Ep.* 10 (§§1.2, 4.4, 5.1) and even off-hand in *Ep.* 11 (§1.3), whereas in this epistle they are firm and definite. Cyprian has been kept fully acquainted with the details (§2.1) and his estimation of them could hardly stand higher. Ought this rather to push *Ep.* 12 after *Epp.* 11 and 10?

These hints, such as they are, are so faint that either order (12, 11, 10, or 11, 10, 12)—after *Epp.* 7, 5, 6, 13, 14 and before *Epp.* 15, 16, etc.—seems not illogical. To date the letter c. April/May 250 is really, therefore, as far as one can legitimately go.

1. That is, in *Epp.* 5.1.2 and 14.2.2.

2. *gloriosa voce Dominum confessis.* Echoing, appropriately, phrases from his earlier letters, *Ep.* 5.1.2, where see n. 5, and *Ep.* 14.2.2 (*qui gloriosi voce fuerint*).

3. *loci et gradus mei condicio.* On this phrase and its interpretation, see n. 3 to *Ep.* 3. Cyprian appears to be thinking, in part, of his ecclesiastical position as bishop (in which capacity he was outlawed; see n. 2 to *Ep.* 5), and of his civil position as *persona insignis* (in which capacity he was sought both by the hostile crowd and by the authorities; see n. 5 to *Ep.* 8).

4. *cuncta . . . dilectionis obsequia.* For the phrase, cf. Pontius, *Vit. Cyp.* 6.4: *obsequium exhibendae dilectionis.*

5. *officium meum vestra diligentia repraesentet.* On the curious use here of *repraesento,* see Watson 309, L. Bayard, *Le latin de saint Cyprien* (Paris 1902) 107.

6. *glorioso exitu mortis.* Cf. §2.1: *gloriosae mortis exitu.* The language is carefully contrived to be appropriate to martyrdom: so, of the martyred Pope Fabian, *Ep.* 9.1: *de glorioso eius exitu.* On the particular premium placed on this work of mercy, see n. 29 to *Ep.* 8.

7. *ipsi quoque inter beatos martyras adgregentur.* On the epithet *beatus*—associated especially with martyrs—see n. 2 to *Ep.* 10. For a description of the gruesome circumstances in which such confessors died, and for a catalogue of their names, see *Ep.* 22.2.2. Compare the insistence in the earlier African document, the Acts of Perpetua, that the title of martyr should be conferred on those who were deceased in prison: *et Quintum qui et ipse martyr in carcere exierat* (11.9); *Secundulum vero Deus maturiore exitu de saeculo adhuc in carcere evocavit* (14). Similarly, the surviving confessors from Lyons and Vienne insist on giving

the title of martyr to "those whom Christ judged worthy to be taken up as soon as they had confessed Him" *ap.* Eusebius, *H.E.* 5.2.3, that is to say, those who died in prison. And, the catechumen Donatianus, who died after baptism in prison, is described as *ab aquae baptismo ad martyrii coronam immaculato itinere festinans* in *Act. Mont. et Luc. 2.*

Cyprian dilates on the theme that the rewards and honours of martyrdom are due also to those who resist under persecution, *etiam si passio fidelibus desit,* in *Ad Fort.* 12, 13.

8. *passus est quidquid pati voluit.* Cyprian is here emphasizing the importance of a would-be martyr's disposition (*voluntas*) as providing the essential ingredient of true martyrdom (cf. *Ep.* 10.5.1, *Ep.* 37.3.2). Hence the doctrine of "spiritual martyrdom" in *Ad Fort.* 12 f. and *De mort.* 17. Consistent with this view also is Cyprian's description of death during flight from persecution in terms of martyrdom in *Ep.* 58.4.2 (*non minor est martyrii gloria*): it is equally death *propter Christum.* And note the description of Cornelius in *Ep.* 55.9.2; Cyprian claims that he is *inter gloriosos confessores et martyras deputandus,* for he suffered whatever he was in a position to suffer (*passus est quidquid pati potuit*). The way is opening out for the cult of non-martyr saints; see H. Delehaye, *Les origines du culte des martyrs* (2nd ed., Brussels 1933) 96 ff. See also E. E. Malone, *The Monk and the Martyr. The Monk as the Successor of the Martyr* (Washington 1950) 37 ff., and S. Deléani, *Christum sequi* (Paris 1979) 40 ff.

9. There are now three texts, with remarks attached, marshalled to reinforce the argument that those confessors who have died in prison ought to be treated as martyrs. This quotation is from Matt. 10.32.

10. Matt. 10.22.

11. Apoc. 2.10.

12. *ut conmemorationes eorum inter memorias martyrum celebrare possimus.* A celebrated clause which says much about the enthusiastic *cultus* of martyrs already established in North Africa, and which was to prove to be there of such enduring popularity (the Donatists even claiming to be an *ecclesia martyrum*). Hence Augustine can describe Africa as a land filled with martyrs' corpses: *Africa sanctorum martyrum corporibus plena* (*Ep.* 78.3).

And it was a country noted for the plenitude of its martyrs' shrines (*memoriae*), arguably of considerable influence on Church architecture: see, for example, A. Grabar, in *Archaeology* 2 (1949) 95 ff.; J. B. Ward-Perkins in *JTS* 17 (1966) 20 ff. and *idem*, in *Akten des VII Internat. Kongr. für christl. Archäol.* (1969) 3 ff.; P. A. Février in *Corsi di cultura sull'arte ravennate e bizantina* 17 (1970) 191 ff.

Such annual commemorations appear as an already standard custom by the mid-second century, in *Mart. Poly.* 18.2 f. Here we can observe that even in the midst of the adverse circumstances of persecution, the Church calendars and *fasti* are being kept up-to-date; by such ecclesiastical habit Cyprian, in *Ep.* 80.1.4, again under similar pressures of persecution, still annotates place and date of martyrdom (Pope Sixtus and his four deacons). Accounts of the martyr's *acta* or *gesta* might also be registered in the church archives and read on the anniversary day (see n. on *Ep.* 77.2.1). Africa has in fact bequeathed us our richest collection of ancient hagiographic literature; see H. Delehaye, *op. cit.* in n. 8 above, 371 ff.

It is worth observing that the names of those deemed here to be martyrs (the names are preserved in *Ep.* 22.2.2) may in fact survive, in garbled form, in our received calendars and martyrologies (see nn. on *Ep.* 22.2.2). On the early evidence for the Carthaginian archives, see *DACL* 2 (1925) 2290 f. On the form which the commemoration might take, see n. 15 below.

13. *Tertullus fidelissimus ac devotissimus frater noster.* Tertullus is taken by Thaninayagam, *The Carthaginian Clergy during the Episcopate of Saint Cyprian* (Colombo 1947) 74, to be "a very zealous priest"; H. Leclercq in *DACL* 5 (1923) 2671 calls him "prêtre ou évêque du voisinage"; Monceaux, *Histoire* 2.11 says he is "peut-être un évêque du voisinage"; L. Nelke, *Die Chronologie der Korrespondenz Cyprians . . .* (diss. Thorn 1902) 12 n. 2, styles him a deacon of Cyprian's. But the language here, when Cyprian is addressing his presbyters and deacons—there is no *compresbyter*, as in the case of Rogatianus (*Ep.* 7.2), no *collega*, as in the case of Fabian (*Ep.* 9.1)—suggests rather that he may in fact be a layman, able to come and go to Cyprian in hiding (*Ep.*

14.1.2) and clearly a close confidant of his. Tertullus carries on a correspondence with Cyprian in hiding (pointedly noted by Cyprian), whereas Cyprian's clergy generally failed to respond to his letters; the epithet *fidelissimus* is not idle. Saxer, *Vie liturgique et quotidienne à Carthage vers le milieu du IIIe siècle* (Vatican 1969) 285 f., suggests that he may actually have been a *fossor* (see n. 29 to *Ep.* 8), but that is unnecessarily to convert his virtues into obligations. For Cyprian's sentiment here, compare Lactantius, *Div. inst.* 6.12: *ultimum illud et maximum pietatis officium, peregrinorum et pauperum sepultura.*

On the archetype of the *Codex Veronensis* there occurred various annotations against the names of some of the bishops participating in the *Sent. Episc.* (*in pace, confessor, martyr*, etc.). Against Successus (no. 16) is read *conf. et post. mart. positus in Tertulli.* If we are to interpret this as referring to a Carthaginian *area*, in operation by May 259 (the *terminus ante quem* of Successus' death—see n. on *Ep.* 80), then it would be attractive to consider the burial-ground as connected in some way with Tertullus— especially used by him, or donated by him (cf. CIL 8.9585 = ILCV 1583: *aream et sepulchra ... contulit et cellam struxit*), or simply appropriately named in his honour. On these *tituli gloriae*, see further G. Mercati in *Studi e Testi* 77 (1937) 179 ff.; H. von Soden, *Nachrichten von der Königlichen Gessellschaft der Wissenschaften zu Göttingen. Philologisch-historische Klasse* (1909) esp. 278 ff.; and for the final trial and burial in Carthage of a non-Carthaginian bishop (Successus was bishop of Abbir Germaniciana), compare *Passio Felicis* (303) esp. 31 ("Felix of Thibiuca").

On Tertulus, see intro. and n. 1 to *Ep.* 4 and n. 9 to *Ep.* 14.

14. *nec illic circa curam corporum deest.* On *illic* (= Carthage), see n. 4 to *Ep.* 5. Doubtless Tertullus ran grave risks of detection and arrest in collecting the dead (was bribery needed?) and burying them in a Christian burial-ground (see n. 29 to *Ep.* 8).

Contrast the thwarted attempts of the brethren at Lyons: ". . . we were greatly distressed by our inability to give the bodies [of the martyrs] burial. Darkness did not make it possible, and they refused all offers of money and were deaf to entreaty" (*ap.* Eusebius, *H.E.* 5.1.61). For Christians' apologetic defence of the special care that they take over the bodies of their dead, cf. Origen, *Contra Celsum* 8.30; Minucius Felix, *Octavius* 34.10 (with nn. 143 and 577 in ACW 39.116, 230 ff., 354)

For Christian *areae*, cf. Tertullian, *Ad Scap.* 3.1; Cyprian, *Ep.* 67.6.2; *Act. Cyp.* 1 and 5. This last registers the name and locality of one such Carthaginian cemetery: *areas Macrobii Candidiani procuratoris quae sunt in via Mappaliensi iuxta piscinas.* Another contemporary Carthaginian cemetery seems to be referred to in the *titulus gloriae* (see n. 13 above) against *Sent. Episc.* 13: Leucius is annotated as *in Fausti positus.* Likewise Felix, bishop of Thibiuca, is buried in Carthage in 303, *in via quae dicitur Scillitanorum, in Fausti* (*Passio Felicis* 31). Similarly the annotation against *Sent. Episc.* 30 has *conf. et mart. in novis areis positus:* can the Carthaginian *Basilica Novorum* be connected (cf. Augustine, *Serm.* 14; *Brev. Coll. cum Donat.* 3.25)? And the *Basilica Majorum* at Mcidfa, with its considerable *area*, was the burial-place and cult centre for Perpetua and Felicity; cf. Victor Vit. 1.3; J. Vaultrin, *Les basiliques chrétiennes de Carthage; étude d'archéologie et d'histoire* (Algiers 1933) 82, 86 ff. See further DACL 1 (1924) 2794 ff. and 2 (1925) 2283 ff.; G.-G. Lapeyre and A. Pellegrin, *Carthage latine et chrétienne* (Paris 1950) 39 ff.; J. Vaultrin, *op. cit.* 145 ff.

15. *celebrentur hic a nobis oblationes et sacrificia ob conmemorationes eorum.*—Is the subjunctive dependent on the preceding *ut* with a lengthy parenthesis, introduced by *quanquam*, intervening?— For the notion, cf. *Ep.* 39.3.1: *sacrificia pro eis semper . . . offerimus quotiens martyrum passiones et dies anniversaria conmemoratione celebramus.* On funeral *sacrificia* for the dead generally (*pro dormitione*), see nn. 24, 25 and 26 to *Ep.* 1. In this present case, concerning avowed martyrs, the "offerings and sacrifices" can hardly have had quite the same intention as the propitiatory rites for the repose of the faithful departed generally: the purpose may in fact have been vague, to include their names in annual and festal remembrance at the memorial gatherings of the faithful (*ob conmemorationes*), the Christian equivalent of the *parentalia* ceremonies. They were, after all, celebrating their birthdate as Christians, their *dies natalis.* Cf. A. C. Rush in SCA 1 (1941) 74 ff. For similar anniversary celebrations in the con-

temporary East, cf. Gregory of Nyssa, *Vit. Greg. Thaum.* PG
46.953. Augustine, later, could be more specific about the intention: it was to win the prayers of the martyred for the living; cf.,
e.g., *Serm.* 159.1 *In Johann. Evang. tract.* 84.1; *AE* 1908.17
(Thugga), recording a shrine-side prayer: *sancti et beatissimi
martyres, petimus in mente habeatis . . .;* likewise *AE* 1968.622
(Henchir Touta): . . . *ita peto [f] ratres et sorores legis, petitionibus
et orationibus vestris pro spirito meo incumbatis in nomine Cristi.*

These gatherings might take a variety of forms: commemorative services (*agapai*) at the martyr's *mensa* or graveside (such
celebrations might occasionally degenerate into riotous behaviour, e.g., Counc. Elvira, can. 35; Augustine, *Ep.* 22.3, *Serm.*
252.41, cf. *Contr. Faust.* 20; etc.) or—Cyprian's celebrations
here were of this variety—anniversary eucharistic sacrifices *in
ecclesia* (esp., in later times, if dedicated to the martyr) etc.

The topic has been richly discussed. The ample bibliography
includes: DACL 10 (1932) 2430 ff.; DACL 11 (1933) 296 ff.; J.
Quasten in HTR 33 (1940) 253 ff.; H. Delehaye, *Les origines du
culte des martyrs* (2nd ed., Brussels 1933) 24 ff., 68 f.; E.L. Hummel, in SCA 9 (1946) 14 ff., 164 ff.; J. Toynbee and J. Ward-
Perkins, *The Shrine of St. Peter and the Vatican Excavations*
(London 1956) 189 f.; RAC 1 (1950) 335 f.; P. A. Février, *art. cit.*
in n. 12 above; A. Ferrua in *Civiltà Cattolica* 2 (1941) 373 ff., 457.
ff.; W. Rordorf in *Irénikon* 55 (1972) 315. ff.

16. Cyprian was in fact to be cheated of this aspiration for
almost another twelve months.

17. That is to say, *Epp.* 7.2, 5.1.2, 14.2.1.

18. Note the insistence on aid to the deserving poor (as in *Ep.*
5.1.2). In *Ep.* 14.2.1 (dated earlier than the present epistle) Cyprian expresses himself somewhat more hesitantly about the existence of such *stantes pauperes: pauperum cura si qui tamen
inconcussa fide stantes gregem Christi non reliquerunt.* He appears
now to be more certainly informed. By Tertullus? The clergy in
Carthage have failed so far to reply to any of his letters; see *Ep.*
18.1.1.

19. *nec paupertate adacti.* Cyprian is talking of *stantes* who
have not succumbed to the temptations of apostasy under the
pressures of poverty. What does this imply? Can there be refer-

ence to the confiscation of the *bona* of the unyielding Christians
that was a concomitant of this persecution (see n. 5 to *Ep.* 10) or
to the loss of domicile, means of livelihood and trade, etc., from
which the faithful Christian refugees suffered (see n. 8 to *Ep.* 5)?

LETTER 13

Contents: Cyprian, from his place of retirement, writes to the
Carthaginian confessors a letter exhorting them to continued
perseverance in confession and model behaviour in virtue. Some
of their company, however, carried away by pride, are corrupting the reputation of their group by their behaviour and vicious
living; unseemly quarrels have broken out in their ranks. They
are told in no uncertain but rousing terms that after their
display of *in virtutibus gloria* what is now needed is *in moribus
disciplina*.
  A further subvention has been sent by Cyprian, and one from
his deacon Victor, to help meet the needs of the confessors.

Date and circumstances: In §1 Cyprian refers to an interval (*iampridem*) since his previous communication with the confessors.
That previous communication is undoubtedly *Ep.* 6. General
devastation amongst the flock had not then occurred (see note §1
of *Ep.* 5, the companion piece of *Ep.* 6), whereas losses are by
now heavy. Nevertheless, in this letter the confessors can still be
regarded as being at the beginnings of their ordeals (§2: *prima
hac congressione, haec initia, rudimentis felicibus . . . coepistis*); there
are as yet no tortures and no martyrs. We are, therefore, later
than *Ep.* 6, but before the tortures, deaths under prison conditions, and martyrs of *Epp.* 11, 10, 12, and, accordingly, before
mid-April 250.
  It is worth noting that in this letter we meet confessors who
have been sent into exile (see §4.1; §7, confessors are no longer in
prison; the scandalous cohabitation of §5.1 also suggests out-of-
prison conditions). And there is no word here of the ordeals of

imprisonment. By contrast, *Ep.* 10.1 reports exile as having been the penalty of the recent past.

There are dissensions among the ranks of these confessors (§5.2), but these do not appear as yet to have manifested themselves in disputes over theological issues (see, for contrast, the later *Ep.* 15, esp. §3). Cyprian's exhortation in this letter is couched in general terms of moral stricture, and does not enter into theological argument.

On the evidence we are to imagine that, by the time of this epistle, Rogatianus and all or most of his company of initial confessors have been released (under whatever penalty) from their Carthaginian gaol. Rogatianus does not figure in the talk of the subsequent *Epp.* 11, 10, 12, which concern, specifically, currently imprisoned confessors, constituting, in all likelihood, a later batch of prisoners and dealt with by harsher means (see nn. 5 and 6 to *Ep.* 10). Certainly contemporary or later epistles imply close and ready contact between some of these (released) confessors and the clergy of Carthage (eg. *Epp.* 14.2.2, 15.1.2 etc.). Leclercq is therefore wide of the mark when he asserts of these prisoners (in Hefele-Leclercq, 1.2.1094): "Ce ne fut que vers la fin de l'année qu'on commença de les mettre en liberté."

The dating is further discussed by L. Nelke, *Die Chronologie der Korrespondenz Cyprians* . . . (diss Thorn 1902) 13 f.; L. Duquenne, *Chronlogie des Lettres de s. Cyprien* . . . (Brussels 1972) 68 ff. M. Réveillaud, *Saint Cyprien. L'oraison dominicale* (Paris 1964) 39, discusses possible links between this epistle and the treatise *De dom orat.* Cyprian enclosed a copy of this letter with *Ep.* 20; *Ep.* 20.2.1 (*epistulae . . . in quibus . . . nec extorribus quando oportuit obiurgatio . . . defuit*) refers to §4.1 of this letter.

1. On Rogatianus, see n. 1 to *Ep.* 6 and n. 41 below. Observe that Sergius does not figure. When Cyprian next addresses the confessors as a group (in *Epp.* 10 and 15) they have become, honorifically, *martyribus et confessoribus;* tortures (and deaths) have occurred in the interval.

2. *iampridem vobis . . . litteras miseram.* On *iampridem*, see n. 7 to *Ep.* 1. The reference is, of course, to *Ep.* 6; Cyprian begins

with appropriate echoes of the opening paragraph to that letter.

3. *ecclesiae enim gloria praepositi gloria est.* For Cyprian "there could be only one Church, and it was the Church of the bishops. Of all ecclesiastical writers Cyprian attached the highest importance to the role of the bishop in his Church"—R. A. Markus, *Christianity in the Roman World* (London 1974) 110. This present expression encapsulates neatly Cyprian's centripetal model of a Church's life, pivoting about its bishop. It was a sentiment that prevailed with Cyprian to the end; he contrived to die his martyr's death in Carthage, for it was fitting *plebem universam praepositi praesentis confessione clarificare* (*Ep.* 81.1.1). This is further discussed on *Ep.* 33.1.1, with bibliography.

4. *prima hac congressione.* Confessors certainly appear to be out of prison with at least some of them in exile out of Carthage. Their cases must have come already before the proconsul's tribunal. Others, presumably, after an initial hearing, may still be in prison, awaiting sentence. That constitutes their first battle. To both these groups, it would appear, Cyprian is urging perseverance in faith and humility. That will constitute their second battle. See further on the trial procedures involved, *Historia* 22 (1973) 651 ff.

5. John 5.14. Note the rewording of scripture which follows. This is for Cyprian an unusual practice. The passage is intended to be arrestingly emphatic (cf. n. 21 to *Ep.* 3).

6. *recedente ab his disciplina dominica recessit et gratia.* There is a double edge to *disciplina* throughout this letter, signifying (moral) teachings as well as (moral and submissive) behaviour. On the word in Cyprian, see n. 8 to *Ep.* 4, n. 9 to *Ep.* 11.

7. The allusion is to Matt. 7.14.

8. The *Dei vox* referred to is Isa. 66.2.

9. The allusion is to Rom 2.24. See Fahey 426. Other passages which reveal Cyprian's (scripturally-based) attitudes towards Jews are *Ep.* 59.2.3, *De orat. dom.* 10, 13, *De mort.* 15, *Test.* esp. Book 1. For a context for these attitudes, see J. Parkes, *The Conflict of the Church and the Synagogue* (London 1934).

10. Matt. 5.16.

11. Phil 2.15.

12. 1 Pet. 2.11 f. See Fahey 520. Observe Cyprian's instinctive

rhetorical habits—the rules demanding triple illustration (again in §4.2): called by Pliny, *Ep.* 2.20.9: *scholastica lex* (cf. Quintilian 4.5.3: *tres propositiones*).

13. *numerum vestrum.* Cf. n. 24 to *Ep.* 6.

14. *quando aliquis temulentus et lasciviens demoratur.* This appears to constitute a category of offender separable from that referred to in §5.1 (scandalous cohabitation). The presumption would be that such offenders are no longer in prison?

15. *alius in eam patriam unde extorris factus est regreditur.* On the penalty of exile imposed initially on recusants in Carthage, see n. 5 to *Ep.* 10.

16. *ut deprehensus non iam quasi christianus sed quasi nocens pereat.* Note the penalties for illegal return from exile as laid down in *Digesta* 48.19.28.13: *in exulibus gradus poenarum constituti edicto divi Hadriani, ut qui ad tempus relegatus est, si redeat, in insulam relegetur, qui relegatus in insulam excesserit, in insulam deportetur, qui deportatus evaserit, capite puniatur.* It would be unsafe, however, given the rhetorical nature of the context, to press the passage for the deduction that the form of exile was that of *deportatio* (Cyprian anticipating capital punishment). Cyprian speaks here like a Roman aristocrat, insisting on the proper respect for law however misguided; disregard for a legal sentence of exile is categorized by him among instances of *prava conversatio* ("evil conduct"). There appears to be an allusion to 1 Pet. 4.15 f. This is omitted by Fahey 524.

17. Rom. 11.20 f.

18. Isa. 53.7.

19. Isa. 50.5 f.

20. *per ipsum nunc adque in ipso vivens.* Can this phrase possibly allude to Acts 17.28, *in ipso. . . . vivimus* (Vulgate), or do we have here a reflexion of an euchological formula? Note the stress on the malice of being unmindful (*immemor*) in that which follows; see M. Réveillaud, *Saint Cyprien. L'oraison dominicale* (Paris 1964) 160 ff.

21. An allusion to John 13.16 and 15.20.

22. Luke 9.48.

23. *Dei templa.* For the frequent notion that man is a temple of God, see, e.g., 1 Cor. 3.16 and 2 Cor. 6.16.

24. *post confessionem sanctificata et inlustrata plus membra.* Note the language, appropriate for baptism, martyrdom of course constituting a *secundum lavacrum* (*inlustrata* = φωτισθέντα?). There is further baptismal talk in §5.3, §6.

25. See *Ep.* 4 on the topic of *subintroductae* and Cyprian's view of the practice.

26. The disputes are described as being *inter vos.* They do not appear, at this relatively early stage (before *Ep.* 11), to be directed outside the ranks of the confessors, and we are left to speculate whether they were caused by anything other than usual sources of social contention and abrasion in highly charged circumstances.

27. *pacem suam nobis dimiserit Dominus.* An echo of John 14.27, where Cyprian's text reads *pacem vobis dimitto* in *De unit* 24.

28. Gal. 5.14 f.

29. An allusion to 1 Cor. 6.10.

30. *Christum cottidie confitetur.* As he concludes, Cyprian returns to the theme with which he began in §2.1 (*de vita nostra cottidie dimicamus*).

31. *saeculo renuntiaveramus cum baptizati sumus.* Cf. n. 24 above. It is possible, without being a necessary deduction, that Cyprian is alluding to an actual formula of renunciation recited during the ceremony of baptism: see n. 7 to *Ep.* 11.

32. *nostra omnia relinquentes.* Possibly an oblique reference to the proscriptions and sequestrations involved for the *stantes* in this persecution, but more likely to be explained by an allusion to Matt. 19.27, where the Vulgate reads, *nos relinquimus omnia et secuti sumus te.* On the confiscations, cf. n. 8 to *Ep.* 5, n. 5 to *Ep.* 10, n. 19 to *Ep.* 12.

33. *pacem . . . quam se facturum repromittit.* Cyprian seems to be exploiting John 14.27 (see n. 27 above) introducing a systematic ambiguity sliding from domestic peace towards public peace. The later *Ep.* 11, especially in §3.2, lays heavy emphasis on the correlation between harmony within the brotherhood and outward peace for the community; it seems that there is there a further allusion to John 14.27 (see n. 27 to *Ep.* 11).

34. *ut . . . novi et paene mutati ad ecclesiam revertamur.* Cyprian appears to speak as if he understands that both he and the

confessors are in similar circumstances, being, whether in hiding or in exile, out of Carthage. The whole letter is notably reticent about enduring the rigours of imprisonment. The epithets (*novi, mutati*) are, again, appropriate for baptism (see n. 24 above). On the precise meaning here of *ecclesia* (church building? used metaphorically?), see Watson 270; H. H. Janssen, *Kultur und Sprache* ... (Nijmegen 1938) 34 ff.

35. §7 appears to be by way of a *postscriptum;* its place is not strong in the manuscript tradition but there appears to be no ground for doubting its genuineness. Given the practical nature of its contents, the paragraph may have been edited out in some of the copies subsequently distributed (cf. L. Duquenne, *Chronologie des Lettres de s. Cyprien* ... (Brussels 1972) 66 f., n. 2). The words *nuper cum adhuc essetis in carcere constituti* (repeated, with change of person, in *Ep.* 14.2.2) confirm the impression drawn from the rest of the letter that Cyprian understands the initial confessors to be now out of prison.

In §1 Cyprian referred to *Ep.* 6 using the expression *iampridem;* he now refers to the companion letter of *Ep.* 6, viz. *Ep.* 5, using *nuper,* whereas in the contemporary *Ep.* 14.2.2 he refers to *Ep.* 5 using *pridem.* Compare nn. 7 and 27 to *Ep.* 1 (for a similar case of *iampridem* glossed by *nuper*), and *Ep.* 59.9.1 (where *iam pridem ... nuper ... pridem ... nuper* are to be found in the one sentence, all referring to events of the same year, 251).

36. A reference to *Ep.* 14, which Cyprian, on this evidence, appears to have composed first of this pair of letters (*Epp.* 13 and 14).

37. *de sumpticulis propriis quos mecum ferebam.* See n. 11 to *Ep.* 7, nn. 9 and 10 to *Ep.* 5, on Cyprian's financial arrangements during this persecution. As in *Ep.* 7.2, he appears to be speaking here of his own funds (*de quantitate mea propria*).

38. *sed et alia CCL. proxime miseram.* Can this be the *alia portio* which Cyprian sent to Rogatianus *de quantitate mea propria* by the acolyte Naricus in *Ep.* 7.2 destined for general charitable purposes (*circa laborantes*)? It is difficult to provide a clear idea of the purchasing power of Cyprian's donation. Pliny the Younger's (generous) pensions for his freedmen appear to have been between 70 and 85 sesterces per person per month (and this

was intended to cover housing as well as food and clothing). Of the alimentary schemes—intended to provide all the necessities of life for male and female children—the one which we have for Africa, given in the late 170's at Sicca Veneria (*ILS* 6818), provided monthly amounts of 10 and 8 sesterces per head for the two sexes. For discussion and further evidence on subsistence costs and allowances, see R. P. Duncan-Jones, *The Economy of the Roman Empire. Quantitative Studies* (Cambridge 1974) 30 f. (Pliny the Younger), 144 ff. with tables, 207 ff. (alimentary schemes).

39. *Victor quoque ex lectore diaconus qui mecum est.* Is the description of Victor merely to identify this particular cleric from his many homonyms (see, for example, H. von Soden, *Die Prosopographie des afrikanischen Episkopats zur Zeit Cyprians* (Rome 1909) 255 ff., on the African episcopal *Victores* at this season)? Cyprian seems to refer to this Victor anonymously in *Ep.* 5.2.1 (*salutat vos diaconus*), where see nn. 13, 16, 17. On lectors, see n. 6 to *Ep.* 23.

40. *certatim concurrere et ... suis conlationibus adiuvare.* Can this be a reference to special collection of Church funds (cf. *Ep.* 5.1.2: *summula omnis quae redacta est illic*) or is Cyprian speaking in more general terms of charitable endeavour? He glosses this passage in *Ep.* 14.2.2 by describing the confessors as *fratrum voto et dilectione susceptos.* Note that whilst Cyprian has not yet heard formally from his clergy by letter (cf. *Ep.* 18.1) he is still being kept informed of events in Carthage (cf. *Ep.* 12.2); *Ep.* 14.1.2 indicates that Tertullus has been on a visit to Cyprian; he is to render a personal account of Cyprian's decision to remain in hiding.

41. Observe the change to the singular. Cyprian is addressing the senior confessor and presbyter, Rogatianus, as leader of the group. The letter is sent to him and he communicates it to the others. (There is a manuscript variant, however, which does record, more naturally, the plural.)

LETTER 14

Contents: As he indicated in *Ep.* 13.7, Cyprian writes to his clergy in Carthage urging them to continue, on his behalf, the works of charity both to the poor and to the confessors; regard for the well-being of his brethren, despite his own longings and pressing questions of church government, still prevents him from returning to Carthage personally. But the confessors need more than practical charity from the clergy; the wayward among them must be explicitly counselled to reform their undisciplined lives, and by proving their worth the confessors may thus preserve their glory untarnished. Issues raised in a letter composed by four presbyters must remain unanswered until a return to Carthage makes communal discussion and agreement possible.

Date and circumstances: The contents of the letter leave it beyond doubt that this is the companion letter to *Ep.* 13. There is a similar description of the devastation of the persecution (adding, appropriately for the recipients, regret at the ruin of some of the clergy), §1.1; there are parallel lists of the faults of some of the confessors, §3.2; the request to the clergy to support the physical needs of the confessors, reported in *Ep.* 13.7, is made in §2.2. As with *Ep.* 13, we are, therefore, before mid-April 250 and this is our third letter from Cyprian to his clergy since the persecution began (after *Epp.* 7, 5; in all probability he wrote our fourth letter to them, *Ep.* 11, next).

It seems likely that Cyprian has been visited by Tertullus, who is to render an account to the clergy of Cyprian's motives for continuing in retirement; at the very least Tertullus has been in communication with him (§1.2). From the first-hand information he has thus received, Cyprian plainly understands the confessors to have been released from their prison (§2.2) and he also plainly assumes that the clergy can have direct access to these released prisoners themselves generally for both words and deeds (§2.2). It is difficult to resist the conclusion that these confessors were not all under ban of exile (though undoubtedly a number were; cf. n. 5 to *Ep.* 10). Further discussion on other examples of (unqualified) release in this persecution may be found in my article in *Antichthon* 3 (1969) 67 f.; cf. Introduction, p. 35 and n. 209.

Word has plainly also now reached Cyprian that his flight is being subject to criticism; in his previous letter there was only a hint, if that, of a defensive pose on that question (see *Ep.* 5 n. 2). Cyprian insists that his clergy can go about their clerical tasks undetected in Carthage, whereas his well-known figure (the *insignis persona* of *Ep.* 8) remains a dangerous source for outright hostility.

Cyprian is acutely aware of urgent problems that cry out (*exposcit*) for resolution (§1.2); and he has been written to by a group of his clergy about matters "that have been done or ought to be done" (§4). When he next writes to his clergy (*Ep.* 11) Cyprian dilates on disunity in the flock and God sending them punishment for their lack of spiritual unanimity; and he ends that letter with a prayer, the final crescendo of which includes the hope *lapsorum paenitentia reformetur* (*Ep.* 11.8). We must deduce that even by this stage in 250 the pressing problems of the fallen and their readmission to communion and the role of the confessors and the clergy in that readmission have arisen, along with divisions of opinion about their solution; they are to be aired more explicitly in the sequence of epistles, *Epp.* 15 ff. It won't be too long before the dissident clergy are communicating the differences in Carthage to their brethren in Rome *Epp.* 20.1.1 and 8.1.1).

1. On the form of address, see n. 1 to *Ep.* 5.

2. *ut universum clerum nostrum integrum et incolumem . . . salutarem.* There is a pointed echo of (and contrast with) the opening of the previous letter to the clergy, *Ep.* 5.1.1: *saluto vos . . . laetus quod circa incolumitatem quoque vestram omnia integra esse cognoverim.* On the meaning, note n. 3 to *Ep.* 5.

3. *plebem nostram ex maxima parte prostravit.* There is parallel language in the contemporary *Ep.* 13.1 and in the later *Ep.* 11.1.2 (where see n. 3: there are chronological implications concerning the implementation of Decius' orders for universal sacrifice).

4. *etiam cleri portionem:* named *lapsi* among the Carthaginian clergy are difficult to detect but Cyprian may well intend to include here the very many clergy (cf. *Ep.* 29.1.1) who, in Cyprian's view, improperly deserted their clerical posts without authorization and took refuge from Carthage (cf. *Ep.* 34.4.1); their cases were to be reviewed in precisely the same way as those who had lapsed. There were at least presbyters among the actual *lapsi* (cf. *Ep.* 40.1.2: *per lapsum quorundam presbyterorum nostrorum*).

5. *tractare simul et plurimorum consilio examinata limare.* Language which Cyprian is to employ throughout the dispute over the treatment of the *lapsi* (cf. previous n.). The *plurimi* would doubtless be intended to include both Carthaginian clergy and laity (cf. §4: *nihil sine consilio vestro et sine consensu plebis*) and, following normal practice, (episcopal) "colleagues" as well (see nn. 2 and 3 to *Ep.* 1, and n. 33 below).

6. *ea quae circa ecclesiae gubernacula utilitas communis exposcit.* An elusive turn of phrase, but the general description here must mean the reference is to the ecclesiastical treatment of the *maxima pars* of the Carthaginian Christian community who have fallen. It is important to remember that the problem arises so swiftly (before at least mid-April 250) and has to be left to fester for a full year before the situation which Cyprian here demands can take place (the post-Easter synod of 251).

7. *latebram et quietem tenere.* On Cyprian's place of hiding, see n. 2 to *Ep.* 5.

8. *respectu utilitatum aliarum quae ad pacem omnium nostrum pertinent et salutem.* The implied run of thought is that whereas *utilitas communis* demands Cyprian's presence and a prompt settlement of questions of church government that involve part of the church (the fallen), Cyprian, by his absence, is showing overriding regard for different and even more fundamental questions that concern their universal welfare, the peace and safety of them all. On the arguments of Cyprian for his flight, see n. 2 to *Ep.* 5, nn. 4 and 5 to *Ep.* 8, nn. 5 and 6 to *Ep.* 20; for the language here, cf. *Ep.* 20.1.2: *non tam meam salutem quam quietem fratrum publicam cogitans interim secessi.*

9. *a Tertullo fratre nostro carissimo.* Tertullus is discussed at

n. 13 to *Ep*. 12. The natural inference here is that Tertullus has been to visit Cyprian. It is attractive (but idle) to speculate that the warmth of Cyprian towards Tertullus may be due to the fact that he has been given harbour on property of Tertullus'. (There were no doubt penalties against those who sheltered the proscribed; cf. P. Oxy. 12.1408, ll.22 ff. against those who provided shelter for robbers; Livy 39.17: *ne quis reciperet, celaret ope ulla iuvaret fugientes*, of the Bacchanalians). The description here (as in *Ep*. 12.2.1) strongly suggests that he is without clerical status.

Does Tertullus now report in explanation that Cyprian was an *insignis persona*, a phrase which the Carthaginian clergy so scornfully reported in turn to Rome (*Ep*. 8.1.1)? E. W. Benson, *Cyprian, His Life, His Times, His Work* (London 1897) 86, seems to go somewhat beyond the evidence in deducing from this passage that "Tertullus ... was the prime mover and most strenuous advocate of the concealment of Cyprian."

10. *huius consilii auctor*. The advice seems to have been rather that he should remain in hiding than that he should go into hiding (the latter action, at least in *Ep*. 16.4.1, being assigned to *divine* advice—*Dominus qui ut secederem iussit*). Note how Cyprian proceeds to seek some shelter behind the counsels of the eminently virtuous Tertullus. This is unusual for Cyprian, and makes it plain that he is being somewhat defensive; he is going to uncharacteristic pains to establish that his dereliction of duties is only apparent.

11. *eius loci ubi totiens flagitatus et quaesitus fuissem*. For public hostility towards Cyprian, see *Ep*. 7.1 (and n. 3), n. 32 to *Ep*. 6, n. 5 to *Ep*. 8. In *Ep*. 59.6.1 Cyprian specifies the circus and the amphitheatre as the scenes for frequent popular outcry against himself (*totiens ad leonem petitus in circo, in amphitheatro ... honoratus*) cf. *Ep*. 20.1.2; Pontius, *Vit. Cyp*. 7. Cyprian will not have been present himself at circus or amphitheatre (cf. *Ep*. 2 n. 2); *locus* must, therefore, be more general in reference (Carthage).

12. *fretus ... et dilectione et religione vestra*. In his previous letter (*Ep*. 5.1.1) Cyprian wrote *peto vos pro fide et religione vestra* with a similar object in view.

13. *vos quorum minime illic invidiosa et non adeo periculosa praesentia est.* Cyprian continues to be of the opinion that his clergy, not prominent like himself, can go about the work of the church in Carthage unmolested; in *Ep.* 5.2.1 they had already been warned, however, of the need, in this situation, to be *mites et humiles.*

14. *circa gerenda ea quae administratio religiosa deposcit.* Cyprian proceeds to make precise what he has in mind—care for the poor and, in §2.2 ff., care for the confessors (a similar division in *Ep.* 5.1.2 ff.).

15. *si qui tamen inconcussa fide stantes gregem Christi non reliquerunt.* For similar restrictions of the Church's charity to the meritorious poor, compare *Ep.* 5.1.2 (and n. 8) and *Ep.* 12.2.2 (and n. 18). The confessors, below in §2.2, are to show themselves equally deserving.

16. *ne quod circa fidentes tempestas non fecit circa laborantes necessitas faciat.* Does Cyprian imply anything more than that despairing poverty may lead to a loss of faith and hope? There appears to be a similar line of thought in *Ep.* 12.2.2 (where see n. 19). Or does he mean, less elaborately, that penury (unlike persecution) may cause them to sin?

17. *plurimos ex his fratrum voto et dilectione susceptos.* A cross-reference to *Ep.* 13.7 (and see n. 40 there). *Voto et dilectione* appears to be (an unusual) variation on *dilectione et religione* (see n. 12 above). In a subsequent letter in a parallel context, Cyprian uses *dilectio et cura* (*Ep.* 12.2.2). On Cyprian's somewhat personal penchant for the word *votum*, see Watson 269.

18. *sicut etiam pridem vobis scripseram cum adhuc essent in carcere constituti.* The reference is to *Ep.* 5.1.2 and there is a cross-reference in *Ep.* 13.7 (where see nn. 35 and 36).

19. *humiles et modestos et quietos esse debere.* The key-note of this epistle. In what follows, until the end of §3, Cyprian dilates on these fundamental virtues required of the genuine confessor. There appears to be a remote echo of Isa. 66.2, already alluded to in *Ep.* 13.3.1 (and n. 8), where Cyprian's text read: *Et super quem aspiciam alium nisi super humilem et quietum et trementem sermones meos?*

20. *plus enim superest quam quod transactum videtur.* The theme

of *Ep.* 13, addressed to the confessors themselves, was perseverance in daily confession. For the sentiment here, note especially *Ep.* 13.2.1

21. Sir. 11.30.

22. Apoc. 2.10.

23. Matt. 10.22.

24. John 13.14 f.

25. Allusions to Paul's experiences as described in 2 Cor. 11.23 ff. and 2 Cor. 12.2 ff. See Fahey 468 ff., 609. Does Cyprian produce the rhetorically-sanctioned third member, *bestias,* after *carcerem* and *flagella,* from *in itineribus saepe . . . periculis in solitudine* of 2 Cor. 11.26? It is an extrapolation which suits effectively a context of Roman martyrdom—and Cyprian's own experience, §1.2. Note how Cyprian assumes suffering (coupled with the third heaven) to be clear indication of divine favour; see *Test.* 3.6 and, for a good illustration, *Ep.* 59.6.1 f.

26. 2 Thess. 3.8.

27. An allusion to Luke 18.14.

28. *dominus faciet ut. . . .* The variant reading *faciat* ("May the Lord make it possible. . . .") is only weakly attested.

29. *ad ineptias vel ad discordias vacare.* On these misdemeanours, see especially *Epp.* 11.1.3 and 13.3.1 ff., and nn. thereto. The preceding phrase, *quosdam improbe et insolenter discurrere,* may possibly allude to illegally returned exiles; see *Ep.* 13.4.1 and n. 16 thereto.

30. Explained more fully in *Ep.* 13.5.1

31. *nec a diaconis aut presbyteris regi posse.* Does this suggest anything more than failure to keep the moral "discipline" (e.g., involvement in the penitential problems, as evinced in the later *Ep.* 15)? At any rate Cyprian does not seem to be thinking of deacons or presbyters as figuring among these disreputable confessors.

32. *quod scripserunt mihi conpresbyteri nostri Donatus et Fortunatus et Novatus et Gordius.* Several assumptions are normally made on this passage. These presbyters formed the core of the opposition to Cyprian's election as bishop; they are the ringleaders in the opposition to Cyprian's authority in the penitential dispute, and at least two of them are prominent in

subsequent schismatic movements against Cyprian's episcopal leadership. They are writing in an endeavour to force Cyprian's hand; they are seeking agreement to their interpretation of, and a major role in, the procedures for reconciling the *lapsi* and *libellatici*.

Though all this, on the balance of evidence, is not at all an unlikely inference, it ought to be underlined that the picture is a construct from disparate pieces of evidence.

Cyprian, in *Ep.* 43, attacks the present hostility and persecution of *quinque isti presbyteri*, who are inveterate enemies of his, having opposed his election as bishop (§1; cf. Pontius, *Vit. Cyp.* 5) and having introduced a *nova traditio*, contrary to the Gospel, concerning the lapsed (§3). (The opposition to Cyprian's election as bishop continued even later; see *Ep.* 66.1.2). They have joined forces with Felicissimus (cf. *Epp.* 43.3.2 and 45.4.1). One of their number (*unus ex quinque presbyteris*) is identified as Fortunatus (cf. *Ep.* 59.9.2) who was subsequently appointed a (laxist) *pseudoepiscopus* in Carthage by a group of five lapsed or heretical bishops centred on Privatus of Lambaesis (*Ep.* 59.10). The name of Fortunatus, of course, is extremely common (two different sub-deacons of that name in *Epp.* 34.4.1 and 36.1.1), but identification with our Fortunatus here is by no means implausible; for he is found here in company with one Novatus. That appears to be the turbulent and rebellious Carthaginian presbyter whose misdemeanours receive lavish abuse in *Ep.* 52.2. He is specifically connected with Felicissimus in *Ep.* 52.2.3, and is described as the ringleader in sedition (*primum discordiae schisma et incendium seminavit*); he caused the overthrow of the souls of his brethren *in ipsa persecutione* (*Ep.* 52.2.2), (but any role he may have played in the establishment of Fortunatus as *pseudoepiscopus* remains undocumented). Donatus and Gordius are otherwise unknown. The context of this letter—and the sequel, *Ep.* 12, *Epp.* 15 ff.—makes it altogether probable that the letter which these four presbyters wrote concerned questions of penance and reconciliation for the fallen, the urgent questions to which Cyprian alluded at the beginning of this epistle. Cyprian has taken some care in this letter, first to emphasize his personal solicitude—and the laxity of some of the confessors, who became associated with these *aliqui de presbyteris* (cf., e.g., *Epp.* 15.3.2, and 43.2.1)—before he finally, and firmly, shelves their letter.

If these four presbyters constituted members of *quinque isti presbyteri*, we are uninformed as to their missing partner; a frequent guess is the Gaius Didensis, presbyter, of *Ep.* 34.1 (where see n.). Another (but highly unlikely) guess that is proffered is the Florentius of *Ep.* 66 (where see nn.). We are unfortunately in no position to tell clearly what proportion these five were of the Carthaginian *presbyterium*. Contemporary Rome had 46 presbyters (Cornelius *ap.* Eusebius, *H.E.* 6.43.11). Rome also appears to have had a parallel rebel group of five (rigorist) presbyters (Cornelius *ap.* Eusebius, *H.E.* 6.43.20: σὺν τοῖς πέντε πρεσβυτέροις).

For further reading, see E. W. Benson, *Cyprian, His Life, His Times, His Work* (London 1897) 108 ff.; X. S. Thaninayagam, *The Carthaginian Clergy During the Episcopate of Saint Cyprian* (Colombo 1947) 71 f.; Monceaux, *Histoire* 2.30 ff.; etc.

33. *nihil sine consilio vestro et sine consensu plebis.* The consultative roles of clergy and laity are distinctly different—the clergy may proffer counsel, the people may voice agreement, but the bishop decides. (Note, however, that there is no implication that the *plebs* might either veto or vote on a proposal: their assent only is solicited. See Hefele-Leclercq 1.1.27 f.). There are many similar illustrations throughout the epistles of Cyprian's endeavour to carry his flock with him in unity under his leadership: for an assembly of references, see, e.g., R. Gryson in *Revue d'histoire ecclésiastique* 68 (1973) 360 ff., and cf. n. 5 above. Cyprian varies his formulation somewhat according to mood and to audience. Thus in *Ep.* 17.3.2 (to his *plebs*), the clergy are not even mentioned but he adds, to the *sententia* of the people, the confessors and an assembly of bishops (*convocatis episcopis*); in *Ep.* 19.2.2 (to his clergy) the formula also now adds, more uncompromisingly, the bishops (*praepositi cum clero convenientes praesente etiam stantium plebe*); in *Ep.* 20.3.2 (to Rome) *plebs, confessores* and *clerus* are simply omitted, and the bishops alone are authoritatively mentioned (*plures praepositi*).

34. *de his quae vel gesta sunt vel gerenda.* This seems to suggest

(*quae . . . gesta sunt*) that some of the clergy have taken—irregularly—decisive steps already on their own in the reconciliation
of lapsed Christians. This deduction, in turn, helps to explain
the background to the austere letter on unity which Cyprian is
soon to pen to his clergy, in all probability the very next letter
he addresses to them, *Ep.* 11; and the bitterness of the dispute
becomes more explicable if it is seen to begin so early and is left
basically unresolved for so long. Cyprian can even—rhetorically—describe (in a context alluding to, *inter alios*, Novatus) that
apostates were received back into communion by these rebels *a
primo statim persecutionis die* (*Ep.* 59.12.2).

35. *fraternitatem si qua vobiscum est.* A pathetically vague and
hesitant phrase, suggestive of the dissipation and confusion
which, in Cyprian's perception, now besets his community.
When he writes later in *Ep.* 12.2.2, he appears to be more
certainly informed of a significant group of *stantes* in Carthage.

LETTER 15

Contents: A letter to the confessors and martyrs on the necessity
to maintain "discipline." Some of the clergy have not only failed
in their duty of instructing the confessors in the discipline of
the gospel; they have themselves prematurely reconciled some
of the fallen, contrary to that gospel. The confessors are showing the true discipline by directing to their bishop requests for
reconciliation. They must resist importunities and exercise
great caution and restraint in presenting such requests, and
curb those among them who derive profit, or do personal fa-
vours, in rendering this benefaction. Open certificates of reconciliation must be avoided; only named individuals, known
personally to the confessors and manifestly repentant, should
appear on such certificates.

Date and circumstances: Ep. 15 is one of a group of three letters
(*Epp.* 15–17), addressed respectively to the "martyrs and confessors," the "presbyters and deacons," and to the "faithful laity";

each letter was intended to be read to the other groups (*Epp.* 15.4, 16.4.2, 17.3.2). All three letters are manifestly referred to as a group in *Ep.* 20.2 f., after Cyprian has referred to *Ep.* 10; he proceeds to refer in *Ep.* 20.3.1 to *Epp.* 18 and 19, two letters directed to his clergy. Cyprian's way of describing all these letters in *Ep.* 20 leaves us in no doubt that he is presenting them in chronological sequence. We have seen *Ep.* 10, which comes *before* our group, to be datable to latish April (see introductory note to *Ep.* 10). And the first of the letters *after* our group, *Ep.* 18, is datable to early summer, that is to say, in the vicinity of early June 250. Our group must accordingly be assigned to the interval, to the month of May 250—and possibly some time on in that month to allow opportunity for the traffic in *libelli martyrum* to get really under way after the initial tortures and martyrdoms in about mid-April. By the time this letter, *Ep.* 15, was written, the certificates, Cyprian avers, were being issued in their thousands each day. And Cyprian was slow to come to the stand he adopts here; his decision was made *non sine librata diu et ponderata ratione* (*Ep.* 55.3.2). We ought also perhaps to allow room for *Epp.* 11 and 12: if one or both of these come after *Ep.* 10, they are still to be placed before this set of epistles—the wide-scale indiscipline over penitence hadn't yet reached Cyprian's attention when he wrote those letters.

Further on the chronology may be found in L. Nelke, *Die Chronologie der Korrespondenz Cyprians* ... (diss. Thorn 1902) 19 ff.; L. Duquenne, *Chronologie des Lettres de s. Cyprien* ... (Brussels 1972) 92 ff.

The tone is remarkable. Though firm from the start, Cyprian shows himself also anxious to keep on the right side of the confessors and martyrs, displaying considerable circumspection in getting round—eventually—to any errors on their part in the issuing of certificates of forgiveness. He is careful to assign beforehand any faults in the matter to the dereliction of duty by his clergy; they ought to have instructed them in what was customary (a refrain that runs throughout these letters) and in the gospel teachings as well as counselled them in the proper vetting of candidates for their certificates. All this implies deviations on the part of the confessors from the *dominica praecepta,* but Cyprian cautiously does not yet say so very openly. Only then, after further flattery about their future roles as celestial judges, is he prepared to note that whilst, in their ranks, *plurimi* keep to the proprieties, this is not universally so: there *are* improper dealings in issuing the certificates (including bribery and corruption). And it is only at the end that he adds, as if it were a postscript, words that are uniformly critical. These concern the "portmanteau" certificates, the effects of which on Church order must have been quite disastrous from Cyprian's point of view.

This attitude pervades the other letters—the confessors are unusually given a specific place in the deliberations planned to be held after the coming of peace (*Epp.* 16.4.1, 17.3.2) and the martyrs' deviations are charitably—and not very illuminatingly—ascribed to their "fervour for glory" in *Ep.* 16.3.2.

Cyprian's political sense may indeed have been acute and well developed, but his stance nevertheless also highlights the instinctive regard in which his church held the martyrs and confessors and their spiritual prerogatives and charismatic status: at this critical stage they could not be gainsaid (as he says in self-defence in *Ep.* 20.3.2: *videretur . . . honor martyribus habendus*); only later, the persecution over and their *libelli* discredited, could they be tacitly ignored (as at the Council of 251; see *Ep.* 55, esp. §§6, 17, 23). Dionysius of Alexandria *ap.* Eusebius, *H.E.* 6.42.5 f., showed himself equally indulgent (but, there, the fallen do not appear to have been admitted as far as *communion*). Hence Cyprian can find explanation for the presence of Novatian sympathizers among the Carthaginian brethren simply on the grounds that such people thought they would be in communion with *confessors* (*Ep.* 51.2.2). And he can insist on the value of a policy to be found in *Ep.* 30.5 largely because one of the signatories to that letter was Moyses, *tunc adhuc confessore nunc iam martyre* (*Ep.* 55.5.2). To Pope Stephen, in *Ep.* 68.5.1, he presents as the final and knock-down argument for his case: *servandus est enim antecessorum nostrorum beatorum martyrum Cornelii et Lucii honor gloriosus* (enhancing the status of Lucius from that of *confessor*, for the purposes of his argument).

Among the abundant discussion note E. W. Benson, *Cyprian,*

His Life, His Times, His Work (London 1897) 89 ff.; Monceaux, *Histoire* 2.26 ff.; DACL 10 (1932) 2464 ff.; W. P. LeSaint, ACW 28 (1959) 290 ff.; J. H. Taylor in *Theol. Stud.* 3 (1942) 27 ff.; M. Bévenot in *Theol. Studies* 16 (1955) 175 ff.; B. Poschmann, *Paenitentia secunda. Die kirchliche Busse im ältesten Christentum bis Cyprian und Origenes* (Bonn 1940) 374 ff.; etc.

The extreme turmoil prevailing amongst the Christian community in Carthage is readily discernible. After the general devastation, described in earlier letters (*Epp.* 13.1.1, 14.1.1, 11.1.2), the *lapsi*, in large numbers, are now making desperate efforts to be reinstated amongst their brethren. They are freely and busily visiting the confessors (out of prison? in Carthage?) and martyrs (still in prison?) which they could do openly with immunity, having been issued with or obtained apostatising *libelli*. Though the danger of persecution continues (*Ep.* 16.3.2: *ante extinctum persecutionis metum,* and note the later *Ep.* 19.2.3: *acies adhuc geritur et agon cotidie celebratur*), some Church services are nevertheless being held (see *Epp.* 15.1.2, 16.2.3, 17.2.1).

In spite of all his circumspection Cyprian's letter met with a disastrous reception; the reaction is described in *Ep.* 27.2.1.

1. *martyribus et confessoribus, carissimis fratribus.* On the laudatory and proleptic use of *martyr,* see n. 1 to *Ep.* 10.

Epp. 15–20 provide an interesting study for Cyprian's distinctions—and lack of them—between *martyr* and *confessor.*

At the one extreme, the certificates of peace to which Cyprian is prepared to concede some efficacy are always ascribed to martyrs, never to confessors (*Epp.* 18.1.2, 19.2.1, 20.3.1). And Cyprian is horrified that reconciliation could have been—illicitly—attempted almost before the martyrs had breathed their last, *ante ipsum paene martyrum excessum* (*Ep.* 16.3.2). That is to say, in these contexts martyrs are confessors who have died or who are expected soon to die: they issue certificates before their anticipated death; the special potency of their *libelli* may be activated when the martyrs, after death, exercise their *praerogativa . . . apud Deum* (*Ep.* 18.1.2). (Cf. Celerinus' request in *Ep.* 21.3.2: *rogo . . . ut . . . ab eis petas ut quicumque prior vestrum coronatus fuerit, istis sororibus nostris . . . talem peccatum remittant:* he and a company of confessors put this request to the *martyrs*-to-be.) The texts in Cyprian on the special intercessory powers of the martyrs are assembled by E. L. Hummel, SCA 9 (1946) 156 ff. (typical example in *Ep.* 76.7.3).

There is a good description of this activity in *Ep.* 27.1. Lucian issues droves of certificates (*gregatim*) in the names of the imprisoned and dying Paulus—he died (it would seem) eventually *a quaestione* (*Ep.* 22.2.2)—and of the tortured and illiterate Aurelius: in prison the martyr Mappalicus (see *Ep.* 10) issued two such certificates before his death (out of domestic piety), whilst Saturninus, though tortured and in prison, refrained altogether.

At the other extreme, when Cyprian envisages conciliar gatherings after the restoration of peace, it is anticipated that confessors will be present, but never martyrs: in *Ep.* 17.3.2, instructively, we observe that in the presence of the *confessors* at these gatherings will be examined the *martyrum litteras et desideria*. Ultimately, confessors are survivors, martyrs are deceased. Hence the exiles in *Ep.* 19.2.3 who are one day to return, despite their sufferings (*patria pulsi ac bonis suis omnibus spoliati*) are *confessores*, not *martyres*.

In between these extremes, Cyprian can vary—partly for flattery (hence §1.1 of this letter, the invocation to valiant *martyrs*), partly for rhetorical *variatio* (e.g., the same letter directed to Cyprian can be described as coming from martyrs and confessors [*Ep.* 16.3.2] as well as from the blessed martyrs *tout court* [*Ep.* 17.2.1]), partly for emphasis (in *Ep.* 16, with strictures for the clergy, there is a noticeable bias towards *martyres* rather than *martyres et confessores:* their exalted dignity is being stressed).

There is one corollary. We ought to deduce that there are in Carthage Christians in circumstances where death seems imminent, that is to say, in prison or undergoing trial there. In *Ep.* 22.2, a closely contemporary letter, we in fact get a vivid glimpse of Christians in the Carthaginian prison dying of hunger in suffocating conditions—and issuing wide-ranging *pax: universis pacem dimisimus* ("collective confessors"), *non tantum hae sed et quas scis ad animum nostrum pertinere* (Lucian).

2. *sollicitudo loci nostri.* On this use of *locus* (= station, rank,

etc.), see n. 3 to *Ep*. 3. S. Colombo in *Didaskaleion* 6 (1928) 1 n. 2
unwisely deduces from this phrase that Cyprian calls Carthage
'il suo luogo' and that he was therefore a native-born Carthaginian; he ought to have at least observed *Ep*. 16.1.2: *nec loci sui
memores* (of the rebellious presbyters), *Ep*. 16.3.2: *memores loci
nostri* (of the blessed martyrs).

3. *timor Dei*. A phrase that helps to sound the serious, even
minatory, note of the letter. For emphasis, Cyprian ends his
introductory paragraph, as he begins it, repeating the phrase:
the martyrs, by contrast with *Ep*. 10.1.1 (see n. 3 there) and
elsewhere, are now not models in *virtus* and *fides*, but in *virtus*
and *timor Dei*. The "certain presbyters," it is noted, are significantly failing in this *timor Dei* (§1.2). (Later, in *Ep*. 37.4.2,
Cyprian goes so far as exclaiming *ad timorem Dei ceteros provocas-
tis* at the climax of his list of the Roman confessors' achieve-
ments; so too in the case of Cornelius, now confessor, and his
colleagues in Rome, in *Ep*. 60.2.1: *docuistis granditer Deum timere*
is given pride of place.) Compare J. N. Bakhuizen van den Brink
in *Studia Patristica* 13 (1975) 105: "The fear of God is . . . one of
the main motivations in the pastoral care Cyprian exercised in
his Church. . . ."

4. *fortissimi ac beatissimi martyres*. On the epithet *beatissimus*,
see n. 2 to *Ep*. 10; on *martyr*, see n. 1 above. Cyprian concludes
his letter with a variant valediction, *fortissimi ac dilectissimi
fratres* (see n. 35 below). In *Ep*. 76.1.1. (to Numidian martyrs in
the mine) Cyprian employs a combination of the two, *beatissimi
ac dilectissimi fratres*.

5. *a quibus tam devote et fortiter servatur fides Domini ab isdem
lex quoque et disciplina Domini reservetur*. Note the careful verbal
elaboration (*servatur . . . reservetur*) along with the military overtones (*devote, fortiter, fides, disciplina*) preparing for the general
message of the need to maintain good Church order. Cyprian
has taken pains with this introduction. *Lex* and *disciplina* are
keynotes of these three letters, occurring on six occasions each.
On *disciplina* (which carries at times in these letters the distinct
colour of the virtue of *disciplina*, viz. docility), see n. 9 to *Ep*. 11.
As for *lex*, one is very much left to speculate what precise
biblical texts Cyprian might have invoked if pressed to reveal

the scriptural basis which he claims for his policy. In fact, biblical quotations are unusually infrequent in these letters, *Epp.* 15–17.

6. *qui illic praesentes sunt.* On *illic* = Carthage, see n. 4 to *Ep.* 5. Cyprian was aware of losses in their ranks and perhaps already of a serious number of absentees; see n. 4 to *Ep.* 14.

7. *sicut in praeteritis semper sub antecessoribus nostris factum est.* Cyprian is careful in these letters to underscore the fact that he is asking, reasonably, only for the observance of customary procedures (again in §3.1 §4, *Epp.* 16.1.2, 16.3.2). On Cyprian's *antecessores,* see nn. 7, 8, and 22 to *Ep.* 1. His appeal in fact affords us a glimpse, seldom provided in his works, of outbreaks of persecution in the past. There is a touch of irony in the fact that, later, Cyprian can appeal to the frequent example of *antecessores nostri* (*Ep.* 55.11.1) in justifying the anomalous reconciliation of *thurificatus* (*Ep.* 55.2.1) Trofimus and his flock.

8. *diaconi ad carcerem commeantes martyrum desideria . . . gubernarent.* On deacons and their duties, see n. 17 to *Ep.* 3. *Act. Perp.* 3.7, 6.7 (and 10.1) provide a clear picture of *diaconi ad carcerem commeantes.*

martyrum desideria: On the powers and privileges of the martyrs, see the evidence assembled in n. 14 to *Ep.* 6, nn. 19 and 31 to *Ep.* 10. We can trace back into the second century, to Lyons and Vienne (c. 177 A.D.), the ancillary notion (here referred to) of the martyrs' powers of intercession (*ap.* Eusebius, *H.E.* 5.1.45 and 5.2.5, on which see G. Jouassard in *Revue des sciences religieuses* 30 (1956) 217 ff.); cf. *ap.* Eusebius, *H.E.* 5.18.6 f. (Apollonius asks how can Montanist pseudo-martyrs forgive sins). Tertullian, likewise, in *Ad martyras* 1.6 indicates that this is no novelty: *quam pacem quidam in ecclesia non habentes a martyribus in carcere exorare consueverunt:* he provides further, not always uncritical, evidence of the practice in *De pudic.* 22, *Scorp.* 10.8, *De paenit.* 9.4 (if the emendation *caris dei* is correct). Perpetua's visions (c. 203 A.D.) concerning her deceased brother, Dinocrates, imply a belief in similar powers of intercession (*Acta Perp.* 7 f.); they are prompted by the realization that she is worthy so to petition, being now in prison and condemned to the beasts (*cognovi me statim dignam esse et pro eo petere debere*).

Cyprian insists that the past practice was for the martyrs' requests not to have absolutely independent validity; the reaction even of Lucian in *Ep.* 22.2 would help to confirm that claim, though we cannot in fact trace any great distance back in the process of institutionalization.

Note what appears to be the continuance of such *litterae confessoriae* (despite the experience of this persecution) into the early fourth century in the canons of the Councils of Elvira (*can.* 25: *omnis qui attulerit litteras confessorias. . . .*) and of Arles (*can.* 9: *de his qui confessorum litteras afferunt. . . .*). See Hefele-Leclerq 1.1.234 f., 287.

9. *nec timorem Dei nec episcopi honorem cogitantes.* On *timor Dei*, see n. 3 above. Cyprian's coupling of God and His bishop twice in the one sentence conveys some of his sense of the dignity of his office, and of the outrage that it is suffering (cf. esp. *Ep.* 33.1). On the "certain presbyters," see n. 32 to *Ep.* 14. Cyprian appears in this and the subsequent correspondence to keep the "certain presbyters" studiously anonymous—in order to ease the hoped-for process of reconciliation?

10. *cum . . . convenire in unum cum clero et recolligi coeperimus.* Cyprian is stressing throughout this section the need for all the due procedures to be observed; he intends this to be read by the hasty and the ignorant, *properantes vel ignorantes* (§2.1), as well as by these (respectful) martyrs.

11. Hartel's text reads, *illic contra. . . .* The variant reading, *illi contra . . .*, seems much to be preferred, the corruption being due to false word division. *Illic* is not an acceptable nominative plural form of *illic*, the strengthened form of *ille* (TLL 7 *s.v. illic -aec -uc*), but this seems to be the required sense.

12. *ante actam paenitentiam, ante exomologesim gravissimi atque extremi delicti factam.* On *paenitentiam agere*, see n. 33 to *Ep.* 4. And on *exomologesis*, see n. 35 to *Ep.* 4. From the context Cyprian clearly has in mind the final public acknowledgement of sinfulness before the full congregation—though necessity (sickness) could cause *exomologesis* to become a more private ceremony (see *Ep.* 18.1.2: *apud presbyterum* or even *apud diaconum*; cf. *Ep.* 19.2.1).

It is very clear from Cyprian's reaction that he does not now regard apostasy, however grievous a fault, as an absolutely irremissible sin. He has moved a little from the unyielding rigour of his earlier *Test.* 3.28: *non posse in ecclesia remitti ei qui in deum deliquerit,* submitting, as he describes it later in *Ep.* 55.7.2, to the needs of the time (*necessitati temporum succubuisse*), almost sinning on the side of leniency (*Ep.* 59.16.3: *delictis plus quam quod oportet remittendis paene ipse delinquo*); his change of stance, he insists, was not made *leviter* (*Ep.* 55.3.2,7.1) but only after prolonged and careful deliberation (*Ep.* 55.3.2: *non sine librata diu et ponderata ratione*). His words show unease. *Ad Fort.* 4 is devoted to the topic *non facile ignoscere deum idolatris:* the expression *non facile* reveals the shift from the position of *Test.* 3.28 but also reveals how reluctant and diffident was that move: cf. *De laps.* 16, 35, for fuller expressions of his attitude. See n. 25 to *Ep.* 8 for further discussion and to the bibliography there add Brightman in H. B. Swete (ed.), *Essays on the Early History of the Church and the Ministry* (London 1918) 359 ff.; DACL 7 (1926) 59 ff.; K. Rahner in ZfKT 74 (1952) 257 ff., 381 ff.; M. Bévenot, *Theol. Stud.* 16 (1955) 175 ff.; W. Telfer, *The Forgiveness of Sins* (London 1959) 67 ff.

13. *ante manum ab episcopo et clero in paenitentiam impositam.* On the imposition of the hand, see the studies of J. Coppens, *L'imposition des mains et les rites connexes dans le Nouveau Testament et dans l'église ancienne* (Louvain-Paris 1925) 374 ff., and of L. de Bruyne in *Rivista di archeologia cristiana* 20 (1943) 113 ff., esp. 247 ff.; DACL 7 (1926) 391 ff., esp. 405 ff. On the phraseology and its meaning, J. Schrijnen and C. Mohrmann, *Studien zur Syntax der Briefe des Cyprians* (2 vols.; Nijmegen 1936–37) 1.48 ff. Cyprian has listed the three regular stages in the penitential order, viz., *paenitentia, exomologesis, manus impositio in paenitentiam;* for emphasis, he repeats this listing in *Ep.* 16.2.3 and again in *Ep.* 17.2.1 (cf. *Ep.* 20.3.1). Only after their completion is the *ius communicationis* restored to the penitent in the regular procedure. Note the five stages in penance outlined in the contemporary Canonical Epistle of Gregory Thaumaturgus, *can.* xi, MG 10.1048.

14. *offerre pro illis et eucharistiam (dare).* The restoration of *dare* or *tradere* seems certain in view of the parallel passages in

Epp. 16.2.3 (*offertur nomine eorum . . . eucharistia illis datur*), 16.3.2 (*offerant et eucharistiam tradant*), 17.2.1 (*offerre pro illis et eucharistiam dare*); I know of no passage in Cyprian where he uses the expression *offerre . . . eucharistiam*. From these passages, it seems clear that the reinstated penitent was commemorated individually in the liturgical offering which followed the *exomologesis*. For a similar instance of being "named at the altar" in Cyprian see *Ep.* 62.4.2 (*eis in sacrificiis . . . repraesentetis*, of donors), *Ep.* 1.2.1 (*apud altare Dei . . . nominari in sacerdotum prece*, of the dead), cf. *Ep.* 67.2.3, *Ep.* 12 n. 15, and Counc. of Elvira, can. 29: . . . *huius nomen neque ad altare cum oblatione esse recitandum.* For the expression *offere pro*, see nn. 24 and 26 to *Ep.* 1 and further discussion by F. J. Dölger in AC 4 (1934) 110 ff.

Does the language of *Ep.* 34.1.1: *communicando cum lapsis et offerendo oblationes eorum*, suggest that on such occasions the reinstated penitent provided himself the sacred elements for the offering?

15. 1 Cor. 11.27. This is the only biblical quotation in the letter.

16. *praepositorum est.* On Cyprian's use of *praepositus*, see nn. 7 and 16 to *Ep.* 3, and n. 9 to *Ep.* 8. He appears here to be talking not only of his own duty as bishop, but also of the presbyters and deacons who are acting in his stead in Carthage (an interpretation confirmed by *Ep.* 16.3.1); cf. n. 12 to *Ep.* 4 on this wider usage.

17. *per Dei offensam.* The phrase is repeated, again not idly, in *Epp.* 16.1.2 (*de offensa Domini*) and 17.1.2 (*divinae indignationis offensa*). Cyprian here seems to imply that the *lapsi* by the objective act of pollution in being (illicitly) reconciled incur personal guilt, or judgment, even if, subjectively, they offend the *divina praecepta* only unwittingly; Cyprian recoils from the unexpiated pollution of the fallen (as he emphasizes, on this letter, in *Ep.* 20.2.2). There is an instructive illustration of this attitude in the story of the *parvula* in *De laps.* 25: Cyprian makes it very clear that the infant did not comprehend the nature of the sacrificial food she was given to taste, but he also makes it very clear that the child was *polluted* nevertheless (*de pollutis visceribus*).

18. *vel ex vobis itaque discant quando docere debuerant.* The variant reading *quod* (for *quando*) makes attractive sense in the context.

19. There is heavy play on the sense of *pax* ('freedom from persecution,' 'reconciliation') in this section. Hartel's reading, *expectent, ante est ut . . . mater prior sumat,* emending *expectant* of the mss, is awkward (on the construction, see J. Schrijnen and C. Mohrman, *op. cit.* in n. 13 above, 1.137). Bayard's emendation *expectentes, ut . . .,* has much to recommend it (though note in *Ep.* 16.3.2: *ipsa ante mater . . . prior sumpserit,* and *Ep.* 9.2.1: *expectent ante:* did the archetype have in fact *expectantes ante ut?*)

20. On the notion of *mater ecclesia,* see n. 3 to *Ep.* 10.

21. *inpudentia vos quorundam premi et verecundiam vestram vim pati.* The outrageous pressure, from the sequel, appears to be coming from importunate *lapsi.* They are called *immoderati* in *Ep.* 19.2.1; cf. *Ep.* 55.4.2, and their activities are further described in *Ep.* 20.2.2, on this letter (*exambire . . . passim . . . importuna et gratiosa deprecatione corrumpere*); cf. *De laps.* 15 f. and *Ep.* 27.3 for later developments.

22. *quae et qualia in praeteritum antecessores vestri martyres concesserint.* See nn. 7 and 8 above for this appeal to traditionally sanctioned practices and observe that Cyprian here gives the martyrs the dignity—and guidance—of *antecessores,* just as he has himself episcopal (and guiding) *antecessores* in §2.1.

23. *ut pote amici Domini et cum illo postmodum iudicaturi.* See n. 14 to *Ep.* 6. on the judgment-seat of the martyrs. Cyprian is both flattering the martyrs as heavenly judges of the future and urging them here and now to show the judicial discernment that will one day be expected of them.

24. *actum et opera et merita singulorum.* On the weight given to the dispositions (*actum*), the good works (*opera*), and the deserts (= spiritual vigils, fastings, prayers, etc.?) in assessing the readiness of a penitent for readmission, see nn. 33 and 34 *Ep.* 4.

25. *ipsorum quoque delictorum genera et qualitates.* The first hint in the correspondence of grades in apostasy, a notion reappearing more specifically in *Ep.* 20.2.2 (on this letter) where the fundamental groups—*sacrificati* and *libellatici*—are discerned; it is a distinction destined to play a vital role in the settlement of

this penitential dispute. By the time of the Council of 251 (see *Ep.* 55.13.2 ff.) and the *De laps.* (8 f., 27 f.) these basic divisions had become further refined.

26. *apud gentiles quoque ipsos.* As a convert who retained acquaintance with his pagan contemporaries (cf. Pontius, *Vit. Cyp.* 14), Cyprian appears at times anxious that the Church should be *seen* to live up to its moral standards. Cf. *Ep.* 13.6 (*sive fratres nostri sive gentiles*).

27. *visitamur.* The sense seems to be "we have frequent castigating visions," but I cannot find an exact parallel for this usage in this period. A. Blaise, *Dictionnaire Latin—Français des auteurs chrétiens* (rev. ed., Turnhout 1967) *s.v.* visito 2, interprets, "visiter (pour juger, punir)." Cyprian explains less cryptically his meaning in *Ep.* 16.4.1, where his use of the same verbs and expressions as here puts the interpretation beyond dispute (here: *visitamur ... castigamur ... admonemur ... instruat ... divina censura;* in *Ep.* 16.4.1: *castigare ... divina censura ... nocturnas visiones ... monere et instruere*). On Cyprian's visions, see n. 21 to *Ep.* 11 and n. 27 to *Ep.* 16 (where, again, Cyprian exploits supernatural illuminations to strengthen the respect due to his episcopal attitudes).

28. *plurimos quoque ex vobis instruat ad ecclesiae disciplinam divina censura.* Cyprian is carefully equating the majority of the martyrs and himself, both described as being divinely guided to preserve the *Domini mandata* (or *ecclesiae disciplina*). On the phrase *divina censura,* see n. 15 to *Ep.* 11. Cyprian is now at last coming to the crux of this letter: there are regrettable exceptions to be found in the ranks of the martyrs—*plurimos* (not *universos*) are receptive to God's instructions. *Epp.* 13, 14, 11 have already revealed reprehensible confessors, but not hitherto in the trafficking of *libelli pacis.*

29. We should deduce from this rather opaquely phrased sentence that even the requests of the (good) martyrs stood in need of some restraint, whilst there has been also on the part of the (bad) martyrs favoritism (*personas accipientes ... gratificantur*) as well as outright trading in the *libelli* (*nundinas aucupantur*). Cyprian does not repeat these charges (unlike almost everything else) in *Epp.* 16 and 17. Cyprian's remonstration here is remark-

ably restrained for the habits of his pen, given the fact that he is aware (cf. *Epp.* 20.2.2 and 27.1 f.) that (he claims) thousands of *libelli* are being issued daily with no examination made or distinctions drawn.

For these purveyors of *libelli*, see *De lapsis* 15 f.: *pacem putant esse quam quidam verbis fallentibus venditant.* Later, Cyprian was prepared to claim outright (cf. e.g., *Ep.* 43.2.1) that it was the five presbyters joined with Felicissimus (see n. 32 to *Ep.* 14) who were responsible for urging "certain confessors" to this indiscipline.

The phrase *personas accipientes* has biblical overtones; Luke 20.21 reads *non accipis personam* (cf. Mark 12.14; Matt. 22.16; Rom. 2.11; Deut. 1.17, 16.19; etc.)

30. The other two letters are, of course, *Epp.* 16 and 17. Note the instructions that the letters should be *read* to the martyrs and confessors. The words conjure up prison-scenes with the martyrs gathering round the visiting (clerical) messenger (see *Ep.* 29.1.1) or meetings of groups of (released) confessors secretly convened for the reading. This process seems to be standard practice (and there could well be illiterates amongst their number; cf. *Ep.* 27.1.2), but can it also be that Cyprian is afraid that a distribution of multiple copies (*exempla*) might give opportunity for the corruption of his message (cf. nn. 11 ff. to *Ep.* 9, and *Ep.* 32.1.1)? Most unusually, on this occasion, he is writing separately to the laity, as well as to the clergy (some of whome he plainly cannot trust); he does this on only one other occasion (*Ep.* 43), when the five presbyters are actively plotting against him.

31. *sed et illud ad diligentiam vestram redigere et emendare debetis.* Note the way in which this message, surely a most grave issue, is added as if it were an afterthought.

32. *quod numquam omnino a martyribus factum est.* See nn. 7, 8, 22 above. Cyprian is not quite laying down the guiding principle *nihil innovetur nisi quod traditum est* (Stephen *ap.* Cyprian, *Ep.* 74.1.2; cf. Cyprian, *Ep.* 43.3.2: *nihil innovetur circa lapsorum causam*); rather he is asserting that the present innovations cannot be ground on precedents set by martyrs of the past.

33. *propinqui et adfines et liberti ac domestici esse adseverentur eius qui accepit libellum.* These are people who apostatized and

are accordingly seeking readmission to communion. The phrase *liberti ac domestici* strongly suggests (but does not establish) that *entire* households were therefore involved in the Decian sacrifices, that is to say, embracing even freedmen and slaves. Cf. *Ep.* 55.13.2, a man might protectively sacrifice on behalf of his *uxorem et liberos et domum totam;* other dependants could be similarly protected (*inquilini et coloni*). It would indeed be tempting to throw responsibility on to such a patron or master. The *nutrix* of *De laps.* 25 is, as likely as not, of servile status; cf. PWK 17.2 (1937) 1495 ff. *Nutrix* in the Digest is characteristically a slave. See M. Maxey, *Occupations of the Lower Classes in Roman Society* (Chicago 1938; repr. New York 1975) 53 ff. for evidence and discussion.

If Decius' orders were conceived in the ancient manner of a *supplicatio,* then the inclusion of non-citizens would be no novelty. Cf. Livy 34.55.3 f.: *supplicatio per triduum fuit . . . edictumque est ut omnes qui ex una familia essent supplicarent pariter.* Compare the edict of Maximinus Daia, Eusebius, *Mart. Pal.* 9.2, ed. Schwartz 928; πάντας, ἄνδρας ἅμα γυναιξὶν καὶ οἰκέταις καὶ αὐτοῖς ὑπομαζίοις παισί. This likelihood would serve to underline the generous lines along which Decius envisaged his national rally around the gods of the Empire. Further discussion in my article in *Antichthon* 3 (1969) 69 f. and Introduction pp. 26 ff.—H. W. Pleket in VC 28 (1974) 65, expresses a frequently held contrary view: "It is indeed hard to believe that during the *official, nationwide* Decian persecution *the* slaves-qua-tales were officially included among those who had to pass the sacrificial test. This would have disrupted the social fabric completely." The correspondence of Cyprian does indeed witness such disruption to the social fabric. See esp. *Epp.* 21.2 and 55.13 ff. J. Scheele, *Zur Rolle der Unfreien in den römischen Christenverfolgungen* (diss. Tübingen 1970) esp. 123 ff., similarly neglects the Cyprianic evidence on this question.

One might make one other social footnote: the phrases here and in *Ep.* 55.13.2 (quoted above) suggest entirely Christian households. There was much awkwardness in having pagan *domestici*—and hence the risk of polluting *idola*—under one's roof. Such an attitude would have further encouraged the formation of (socially antagonizing) Christian ghettoes. Compare Counc. of Elvira, can. 41: (with the significant exception, *si vero vim metuunt servorum, vel se ipsos puros conservent*). Was it difficult for Christian domestics to act in a manner different from their (apostatizing) masters?

34. *quorum paenitentiam satisfactioni proximam conspicitis.* On the length of the period of penance, see nn. 33 and 34 to *Ep.* 4. At the maximum, the penitents here have been making reparation for less than six months. Cyprian appears to be surprisingly accommodating. For example, at Nicaea, 3 years was the penitential period laid down for a lapsed catechumen (can. 14), 12 years for Christians who lapsed under little pressure (can. 11)—unless we are to suppose that he is thinking of very special cases; cf. *De laps.* 28 (Christians who got only as far as considering apostasy). Note also the (very Roman) notion of paying satisfaction, with a tariff related to the nature of the offence: this juridical idea of compensation is commonly found in Tertullian (see Le Saint, ACW 28, 155 f., 158 f.) and consult further W. Telfer, *The Forgiveness of Sins* (London 1959) 71 f.; L. Landini in *American Ecclesiastical Review* 169 (1975) 133 ff.

35. *dilectissimi fratres:* note the warm and affectionate epithet, not very commonly used by Cyprian. See n. 4 above and A. A. R. Bastiaensen, *Le cérémonial épistolaire des chrétians latins* (Nijmegen 1964) 25.

LETTER 16

Contents: Cyprian's patience with his clergy is at an end. Insults were endurable in the past—but not now at the expense of people's salvation. His episcopal prerogatives have been usurped by some of the presbyters who are admitting to communion, without due regard for the regular penitential procedures, the fallen—and they are in fact guilty of the gravest of sins. By contrast, the martyrs and confessors are showing the true discipline by directing to their bishop requests for reconciliation, but the presbyters and deacons have even failed to provide them with the guidance traditionally proffered in putting such requests. Divine warnings have been vouchsafed, even including the advice to suspend persistent offenders.

Date and circumstances: c. May 250; see introductory note to *Ep.* 15. The devastating severity with which the clergy are here castigated is noteworthy: they are to be blamed for deceiving the lapsed; they are to be blamed for any offences the lapsed may cause in being readmitted to communion unworthily; they are to be blamed for rousing ill-will against the martyrs, who are circumspectly referring requests for reconciliation to their bishop, as is proper; they are to be blamed for causing conflict between the martyrs and their bishop, by failing properly to guide the martyrs in their requests, as was their duty. They are accordingly the subject of intimidating heavenly censure sent both in dreams and in waking visions, and they are threatened with suspension (sanctioned by God) from their faculties to make the offering. The whole epistle is strongly redolent of Cyprian's authoritarian interpretation of his episcopal role. There is God, then there is the bishop of God (who is in close contact with God, and is the dispenser of His Spirit; see *Ep.* 73.9.2), then there are the clergy who are ministers (servants) of the bishop of God. . . .

1. Observe the curtness of address. See n. 1 to *Ep.* 5.
2. We do not necessarily have to deduce from this that the indiscipline over the admission of the lapsed to communion has been going on for some time (*diu*), but see n. 34 to *Ep.* 14. Cyprian has also long been patient, for the general good, over such matters as the failure to receive any replies as yet from the clergy to his letters (cf. *Ep.* 18.1.1), perhaps their failure to disseminate properly his messages (cf. *Ep.* 11.7.1), certainly their criticism of his own behaviour and flight (cf. *Epp.* 14.1.2 and 20.1.1), etc.
3. That is to say, certain rebellious and turbulent presbyters and deacons. See n. 32 to *Ep.* 14 on the presbyters; the Carthaginian rebel deacons play much less significant a role. We know only of Augendus (cf. *Ep.* 41.2.2, but his clerical status is open to

some doubt; see n. 13 to *Ep.* 41), and possibly Felicissimus and the deacon of Gaius Didensis (cf. *Epp.* 52.2.3 and 34.1.1). In *Ep.* 43.1.1 Cyprian names specifically three presbyters (one recently enrolled) who are dutifully and properly guiding the *lapsi;* by contrast he refers fulsomely to the deacons, as a class, who are carrying out this work (*diaconi boni viri et ecclesiasticae adminis- trationi per omnia obsequia devoti*).

4. In *Ep.* 11 Cyprian argued that the persecution was itself a punishment for their general failure to live as true Christians, that the coming of tortures was a special heavenly visitation for the sinful behaviour of some of their confessors; he appears now to be suggesting that further sinfulness in their community may lead to even more disastrous retaliation affecting the laity (*plebis*) and clergy (*nostrum*) alike—though he may be (more simply) suggesting that to allow the people to go on being misled is spiritually perilous, equally for those people and for their spiri- tual leaders.

5. *de offensa Domini.* See n. 17 to *Ep.* 15.

6. *nec loci sui memores.* See n. 3 to *Ep.* 3 and n. 2 to *Ep.* 15.

7. *nunc sibi praepositum episcopum.* By *sibi* Cyprian effectively elicits the verbal force usually only latent in his use of *praeposi- tus* (on which word, see nn. 7 and 16 to *Ep.* 3, n. 9 to *Ep.* 8).

8. *quod numquam omnino sub antecessoribus factum est.* On this appeal, see n. 7 to *Ep.* 15.

9. *totum sibi vindicent.* On the delegated faculties of presby- ters, cf. n. 13 to *Ep.* 5. Cyprian is insisting on the essentially *subordinate* role presbyters ought to play to their bishop, just as he does concerning deacons in *Ep.* 3.

10. *non prostrata fratrum nostrorum salute.* This could mean simply "not at a time when the salvation of our brothers lies in ruins," but the rhythm of the argument which follows suggests rather the interpretation as given in the translation.

11. *sicut dissimulavi semper et pertuli.* A reference to preperse- cution *contumeliae* and, more specifically, traceable doubtlessly to *antiquiores* among the presbyters who opposed his election as bishop (see Pontius, *Vit. Cyp.* 5; n. 32 to *Ep.* 14). Pontius ex- presses wonderment at the exercise of *tam memoriosae mentis oblivio* concerning those opponents; but Cyprian shows that he

may have overlooked, but he did not forget, their affront (cf. the protestation on these inveterate enemies in *Ep.* 43.1.3: *nobis . . . ignoscentibus et tacentibus*).

12. Matt. 10.32 f. In this letter to the clergy, Cyprian appropriately lectures on the nature of the sin of apostasy in the way in which the clergy ought to have themselves instructed their community. By contrast, his actual letter to the *plebs* (*Ep.* 17) is much more homilectic in manner (esp. §3).

13. Mark 3.28 f. A text once used by Cyprian to prove that "the man who has sinned against God cannot be forgiven in the Church" (*Test.* 3.28). See n. 12 to *Ep.* 15, and on *aeterna peccata*, see n. 9 to *Ep.* 17.

14. 1 Cor. 10.20 f.

15. *precibus et operibus suis satisfacere.* See n. 34 to *Ep.* 15, and nn. 33 and 34 to *Ep.* 4.

16. *Deo qua patri et misericordi.* The reading is rather uncertain; this is Hartel's (not very satisfying) version.

17. *iusto tempore.* Cf. n. 34 to *Ep.* 4.

18. *ad communicationem admittuntur et offertur nomine eorum:* See n. 14 to *Ep.* 15 for an explication and parallels. Cyprian seems here to distinguish the right to rejoin the liturgical community (*communicatio*) from the reception of communion which follows. On *communicatio* in Cyprian (*communio* bearing only its general senses), see Watson 268 f. Cf. n. 24a to *Ep.* 8.

19. 1 Cor. 11.27. See n. 15 to *Ep.* 15.

20. *instructi a praepositis faciant omnia . . . praescripta observatione.* On *praepositis*, see n. 16 to *Ep.* 15. There seems to be a remote allusion to Matt. 28.20, where Cyprian's text read, *docentes eos observare omnia quaecumque praecepi vobis.*

21. *exponunt deinde invidiae beatos martyres, et gloriosos servos Dei cum Dei sacerdote committunt.* Two rather opaque clauses; in what follows Cyprian dilates on these two propositions, but along rather contorted lines. He is contriving, by his indirectness, not to expose the martyrs to blame. He proceeds to explain that the martyrs incur *invidia* by insisting, unlike some of the clergy, on the slow and proper processes for reconciliation, and that conflict with the bishop on this issue may have arisen with the martyrs because, carried away in the heat of their triumph,

they were not counselled in their requests by the customary instruction of the clergy. Either way the clergy are to blame.

22. *Domini lege et observatione quam ... tenendam mandant.* Cyprian is carefully enlisting to his cause the support of the martyrs and confessors; it is, however, probable that they have "enjoined that it should be kept" only indirectly, by their example in putting their requests to their bishop.

23. *ante ipsum paene martyrum excessum.* It seems a clear deduction from the insertion of this phrase that the lapsed who have been irregularly readmitted were all armed with *libelli* from martyrs. These latter had gone to sit on their celestial throne, there to exercise on behalf of their clients their special prerogatives. See nn. 1, 8, and 23 to Ep. 15.

24. *communicent cum lapsis et offerant et eucharistiam tradant.* See n. 18 above.

25. Cyprian takes care to use remote conditional subjunctives (*etiam si quando ... cuperent ... admoneri deberent*) to reduce the immediacy of any implication for the martyrs. This is as far as Cyprian goes in touching upon conflict between himself and the martyrs. It is obvious, however, as a close scrutiny of *Ep.* 15.3 also reveals, that some martyrs have in fact, and to Cyprian's embarrassment, exceeded the normal bounds in their requests (in addition to the issue of "portmanteau" certificates; see *Ep.* 15.4). For this appeal to the traditional procedures *(semper in praeteritum factum)*, see n. 7 to *Ep.* 15.

26. *divina censura:* On this favourite phrase of Cyprian's, see n. 15 to *Ep.* 11.

27. *praeter nocturnas visiones.* Cyprian seems to introduce here the standard combination of dreams (at night) and waking visions (by day). See A. D. Nock, *Conversion* (Oxford 1933; repr. 1963) 86 ff., discussing *P. Oxy.* XI. 1381 (note esp. col. v ll.107 ff. and col. vii ll.137 ff.: "Everything she saw in the vision appeared to me in dreams"). We may well be inclined to react unsympathetically to Cyprian's exploitation of what appears to be unduly convenient heavenly illumination as knock-down argument in order to assert control over his turbulent clergy. He even has at disposal a reserve power of divine *ostensio* and *admonitio* to which he can, as of right, refer: *et prius Dominum meum consulam*

an ... te ad communicationem ecclesiae suae admitti ostensione et admonitione permittat (*Ep.* 66.9.2); *Dominus ... sacerdotes ... gubernanter inspirans ac subministrans* (*Ep.* 48.4.2). But we ought at least to recall that this is written in a society where such inspiration was considered as a normal part of affairs. Cassius Dio, for example, Cyprian's consular contemporary, can report from personal experience the condemnation of the former aedile Baebius Marcellinus and the governor of Asia Apronianus, on the evidence of a dream (77[76].8.1 ff.), and observe such expressions found widely scattered on African *ex voto* inscriptions as *iussu dei, somnio iussus, somnio monitus, ex praecepto dei, ex viso monitus,* etc. (See M. Leglay, *Saturne Africain 1 Monuments* (Paris 1961) I, 64 no. 116; II, 28 no. 7, 74 nos. 3 and 4, and 2, *Histoire* (1966) 341 ff. The tradition continued; the Third Council of Carthage (397 A.D.) was constrained to deplore that "everywhere altars are being set up through the dreams and empty so-called revelations of various men." See H. Delehaye, *Sanctus. Essai sur le culte des saints dans l'antiquité* (Brussels 1927) 126.

And Cyprian's view of his episcopal position as intermediary between God on the one hand, and *clerus* and *plebs* on the other, would lead him to expect a special share in such divine communications; there is no reason to doubt that many of his contemporaries shared this same view—contemporary episcopal visions and dreams in *De mort.* 19; Eusebius, *H.E.* 7.7.2. For discussion of Cyprian and the occult see A. d'Alès in *Revue d'ascétique et de mystique* 2 (1921) 256 ff.; *idem, La théologie de s. Cyprien* (Paris 1922) 80 ff.; A. von Harnack in ZNTW 3 (1902) 177 ff; H. Koch, *Cyprianische Untersuchungen* (Bonn 1926) 243 ff., 320 ff.; O. Perler in *Unam Sanctam* 39 (1962) 51 f.; my article in *Auckland Classical Essays Presented to E. M. Blaiklock* (Auckland 1970) 211 ff. For ancient attitudes towards the supernormal generally consult, e.g., E. R. Dodds, *The Ancient Concept of Progress and Other Essays on Greek Literature and Belief* (Oxford 1973) ch. 10, 156 ff.; C. A. Behr, *Aelius Aristides and the Sacred Tales* (Amsterdam 1968) 171 ff. (on dreams). Further bibliography in ACW 39 (1974) 203, adding, on dreams among Church fathers and later paganism generally, P. Antin in REL 41 (1963) 350 ff., and, on dreams in the period of Augustine, P. Courcelle, *Les confessions de s. Augustin dans la tradition littéraire: Antécédents et postérité* (Paris 1963) 127 ff.

Curiously, on the other hand, the miraculous and wonder-working generally does not figure prominently in Cyprian's thought (by contrast with some of his contemporaries, on whom see J. Speigl in ZfKT 92 (1970) 287 ff.).

28. *apud nos.* On Cyprian's companions in hiding, see n. 17 to *Ep.* 5. We simply do not know whether these *pueri* were servants; an attractive guess is that they were youthful trainee lectors or the like. Cf. *Ep.* 29.1.2: Optatus and Saturus, who are at this time with Cyprian; in *Ep.* 38.1.2 the new lector Aurelius is *in annis adhuc novellus;* he is later with Cyprian, §2.2. The young Celerinus, who also later joined Cyprian in his place of hiding, received *per noctem* a guiding vision (*Ep.* 39.1.1).

29. *puerorum innocens aetas quae in ecstasi videt. . . .* Boys below the age of puberty (*innocens*) were highly valued for scrying by proxy. There is a good example in Apuleius, *Apol.* 42 f., citing 'Varro philosophus' (consult the rich commentary *ad loc.* by A. Abt, 232 f.). Compare Iamblichus, *De mysteriis* 3.24 (νέοι among those most suitable for possession by spirits); Olympiodorus, *In Alc.* 8 (young boys among those most apt for mediumship); and for the use of παῖς: μαθητής in magical papyri and related texts, see A.-J. Festugière, *La révélation d'Hermès Trismégiste* 1 (Paris 1950) 348 f. On the employment of *pueri innocentes* in Biblical *sortes,* P. Courcelle, in VC 7 (1953) 199 ff. And generally E. R. Dodds, *op. cit.* in n. 27 above, 190; *idem, The Greeks and the Irrational* (Berkeley and Los Angeles 1951; repr. 1964) 263 n. 70, 309 n. 115; E. Peterson in *Ephem. liturg.* 48 (1934) 439 ff.; and more generally on *pueri innocentes* H. Herter in JfAC 4 (1961) 146 ff. All this is to suggest that it would not be so bizarre as might appear at first sight for Cyprian and his audience to take seriously the witness of young boys *in ecstasi* (on this word, which had special Montanist overtones for Tertullian, see J. H. Waszink on Tertullian, *De anim.*, 481 ff. Tertullian wrote seven, now lost, books on the subject). Note for later Christian parallels the inspired *vox infantis* which cried out, *Ambrosium episco-*

pum, in the church of Milan, and the visions seen by the *infantes baptizati* (cf. Paulinus, *Vit. Ambros.* 6, 48).

There is a curious six-line funerary epitaph, dated to the fifth or sixth century A.D., related to this passage: it is in honour of a *Magus* (proper name?) *Puer Innocens;* the inscription consists largely of phrases culled from Cyprian's works, notably from *De laps.* and *Ad Donat.* See L. Saint-Paul in *Revue d'histoire et de littérature religieuses* 11 (1906) 232 ff.; L. Bayard, in CRAI (1913) 63 f.; DACL 4 (1920) 2236 ff.; text in ILCV 2500 B.

30. *audietis omnia quando me ad vos reducem fecerit Dominus qui ut secederem iussit.* This is no defensive remark about his retirement but a further assertion by Cyprian that he is under direct guidance from heaven. There is no such remark about personally vouchsafed divine orders in the fuller statement on his withdrawal in *Ep.* 20.1.2 but observe *Ep.* 7.1: *si ante dignatus fuerit Dominus ostendere, tunc ad vos veniam.* (E. W. Benson, *Cyprian, His Life, His Times, His Work* [London 1897] 85 n. 5, seems to overlook the present general context in claiming "it is not necessary to interpret *Ep.* 16.4 ... 'Dominus qui ut secederem jussit' of 'visions etc.' rather than of Scripture.") See generally on this topic of Cyprian's *fuga* n. 4 to *Ep.* 8.

Cyprian clearly belonged to a community which, generally speaking, highly prized dreams, visions, and similar signs, and felt it important to narrate them for the edification and instruction of others; the cherished autographs of Perpetua and Saturus in *Act Perp.* 4, 7 f., 10, 11 ff., composed under prison conditions, are good illustrations; in like manner Pontius is at pains to repeat in considerable detail a dream of Cyprian's as reported to him, *Vit. Cyp.* 12 (and we have met already two such visions in *Ep.* 11, where see nn. 21 and 32), and further parallels are to be found in contemporary African *Acta* e.g., *Acta Mariani et Jacobi* 6 ff. (visions of Marian, James, Aemilian), 11 (a further vision of James); *Acta Montani et Lucii* 5 (Renus), 7 (Victor), 8 (Quartillosa), 11 (Montanus), 21 (Flavian); and on such experiences before imminent martyrdom, see P. Franchi de'Cavalieri in *Studi e Testi* 175 (1953) 209 f. Such signs might be regarded as proper grounds for not avoiding arrest and martyrdom; see, e.g. *Mart. Polyc.* 5.2 ff. Cyprian intends to describe the present spiritual experiences in more impressive, telling—and intimidating—detail on his return to his community.

31. *qui hominem non cogitant, vel Deum timeant.* An allusion to the parable of the unjust judge, where in Luke 18.2 the Vulgate reads, *qui Deum non timebat et hominem non verebatur.* Note a return to the theme of the fear of God. See n. 3 to *Ep.* 15.

32. *interim:* On this word in Cyprian, see n. 30 to *Ep.* 4.

33. *prohibeantur offerre.* At this moment this is merely a (divinely-sanctioned) threat of suspension. It is later transformed into the threat of provisory *excommunication* for offending deacons and presbyters (*Ep.* 34.3.2: *a communicatione nostra arceatur*), with an actual case recorded in *Ep.* 34.1 (Gaius Didensis and his deacon). Later still (*Ep.* 55.4.3), the threat appears to have become more actual (*si quis . . . lapsis temere communicare voluisset, ipse a communicatione abstineretur*). By using here the term *offerre* Cyprian implies not only that his presbyters regularly have delegated to them the faculty to offer sacrifice independently of their bishop (see n. 13 to *Ep.* 5) but that he has troublesome presbyters particularly in mind (see n. 3 above).

34. *acturi et apud nos.* The "nos" is probably intended to include Cyprian along with his loyal clergy; he has used "me" of himself alone earlier in this sentence (*admonitione qua me uti Dominus iubet*). Compare earlier in this letter (§3.2), *memores loci nostri ad me litteras direxerint,* with perhaps similar overtones. At the beginning of *Ep.* 20 (where see n. 3) the variation between first person singular and plural is clearly deliberate and bears the same distinction as here. Compare also n. 45 to *Ep.* 4.

35. *apud confessores ipsos:* on the use of confessors (not martyrs) here, see n. 1 to *Ep.* 15.

36. Compare n. 30 to *Ep.* 15.

LETTER 17

Contents: Despite the pressing grief which Cyprian and the laity share together in compassion for their fallen brethren, they must act with all caution in the matter of their reconciliation; the martyrs themselves have shown the proper way in modestly putting their requests on behalf of fallen brethren to their bishop. But certain presbyters have disregarded their duty to lead and instruct, they have disregarded their bishop, they have disregarded the action of the martyrs, they have disregarded the natural instincts for sobriety and fear of the Lord in the fallen themselves. They have admitted them to communion, despite the heinousness of their sins and without concern for the due stages of penitence. It is accordingly up to the faithful laity to give guidance to their fallen brothers. They must patiently await their bishop's return when, together, bishops, confessors, and laity may examine each case individually.

Date and Circumstances: c. May 250, contemporaneous with *Epp.* 15 and 16; see introductory note to *Ep.* 15. This letter is most unusual in the Cyprianic collection for being addressed to the laity by themselves; the one other example is *Ep.* 43. Cyprian cannot trust all his clergy to relay his message to the people and he is manifestly anxious that his communication should reach all sections of his community. On the number of Cyprian's clergy, see Introduction pp. 39 ff.

By contrast with the other two letters Cyprian appears to be more at ease in addressing his laity. It is clear that Cyprian regarded the role of the clergy to provide instruction and to lead, and the role of the laity to receive instruction and to be led. He seems here more sure of their acceptance of his own role as leader and instructor, of the loyalty of those whom he leads; he slips easily into a homiletic mode with them, and for the first time in these letters he is prepared specifically to mention that he intends that an assembly of bishops (§3.2: *convocatis coepiscopis*) will examine the cases. It is worth noting that Cyprian is still not prepared to say all cases of the fallen, but only such cases as appear in the letter of the martyrs, that are supported by *libelli martyrum* (§3.2).

1. *fratribus in plebe consistentibus.* For the turn of phrase, see n. 1 to *Ep.* 1. Cyprian is addressing the *stantes;* these are neither fallen brethren (§3.1 demonstrates this) nor confessors who have been brought before the magistrates, nor are they refugees in hiding. They have simply managed to escape official detection remaining in their own homes in Carthage; they are clearly a significant number.

2. 2 Cor. 11.29.

3. 1 Cor. 12.26.

4. *quibus potens est divina misericordia medellam dare.* Cyprian describes this letter in *Ep.* 20.2.3 as designed in part to allay the fears of his laity (*quantum potuimus animum composuimus*); throughout he is reassuring his people that reconciliation is in fact possible, ultimately, but all in due course. See n. 12 to *Ep.* 15, n. 25 to *Ep.* 8, and n. 9 below.

5. *divinae indignationis offensa gravius provocetur.* On the theme of *divina offensa* in these letters, see n. 17 to *Ep.* 15.

6. This *martyrum litterae* is not of course the note for universal *pax, Ep.* 23; Cyprian has not yet received that communication (enclosed with his letter to Rome, *Ep.* 27). This earlier letter, or letters, named specific individuals (*de quibusdam*).

7. *praesentibus et iudicantibus vobis.* Cf. in §3.2: *secundum . . . vestram quoque sententiam.* Note the politician's instinct in Cyprian to lay emphasis on one aspect of an issue in a given situation. Compare n. 33 to *Ep.* 14, and see n. 3 to *Ep.* 1 on the composition of synods. Though it is clear that the *plebs* were present at the synod convened after Easter 251 (*Ep.* 45.2.1 f.; *Ep.* 43.7.2 for the date), they in fact play no part in Cyprian's account of that synod's proceedings (see esp. *Ep.* 55.6 ff.)—neither, by that stage, were the requests of the martyrs any longer considered.

8. *nec episcopo honorem sacerdotii sui et cathedrae reservantes.* On Cyprian's *cathedra,* see n. 4 to *Ep.* 3. Cyprian appears confident, by contrast, of receiving due honour from his *plebs.*

9. *in minoribus delictis quae non in Deum committuntur:* Cypri-

an's argument is here *a fortiori*, for even in the case of less grave sins the due penitential order is scrupulously observed (see nn. 12 ff. to *Ep.* 15 for explication: *minora delicta* are not of course for Cyprian the daily sins which he regarded as falling outside the formal penitential *disciplina*; cf. *De dom. orat.* 12 and 22). For effective contrast Cyprian describes the sin of the lapsed (*in Deum committuntur*) in language suitable for *aeterna peccata*, irremissible sins. It is notorious that such sins (e.g., idolatry, homicide, sins of the flesh)—at least for a period and for certain Christians—had formed a category of reserved sins under what appears to have been a move towards rigorism (witnessed for example in Tertullian, Hippolytus, Origen: there is a precisely parallel contemporary movement in Roman law towards harsher penalties, P. Garnsey in *Natural Law Forum* 13 [1968] 141 ff.). It is clear that much sympathy continued still for such general attitudes (hence the Novatianist movement)—and Cyprian was not uninfluenced (see n. 25 to *Ep.* 8, n. 12 to *Ep.* 15)—but pastoral compassion appears to have generally prevailed. On this topic see G. H. Joyce in JTS 42 (1941–42) 19 ff.; P. Galtier, *L'église et la rémission des péchés aux premiers siècles* (Paris 1932) 184 ff.; R. C. Mortimer, *The Origins of Private Penance in the Western Church* (Oxford 1939) 6 ff.; P. de Labriolle, *La crise montaniste* (Paris 1913) 425 ff.; DACL 7 (1926) 59 ff.; E. Langstadt, in *Stud. Patr.* 2.2 (1957) 251 ff.; Brightman in H. B. Swete (ed.), *Essays on the Early History of the Church and the Ministry* (London 1918) 374 ff.; J. N. D. Kelly, *Early Christian Doctrines* (2nd ed., London 1960) 217 ff.; M. Bévenot in *Theol. Stud.* 16 (1955) 188 f.; H. Koch, *Cyprianische Untersuchungen* (Bonn 1926) 246 ff.; A. d'Alès, *La théologie de s. Cyprien* (Paris 1922) 282 ff.; S. L. Greenslade, *Shepherding the Flock* (London 1967) 75 ff.; etc. And for the evidence of Cyprian on adultery, see n. on *Ep.* 55.20.2.

10. *nostros presbyteri et diaconi. . . . Nostros* is an unusual expression for Cyprian. The variant reading *nostri* is attractive. Hartel rightly ponders whether *nostros* might in fact harbour an original *nostri eos*.

11. *plebis nostrae et quietem novi pariter et timorem*. On *timor (Dei)* in these epistles, here in an intimidatingly emphatic position, see n. 3 to *Epp.* 15, n. 31 to *Ep.* 16.

12. *gratificantes*. Cf. *Ep*. 15.3.2 and n. 29 thereto on the (bad) martyrs.

13. Cyprian proceeds to provide a homely list of three illustrations (a rhetorically sanctioned number; cf. Pliny, *Ep*. 2.20.9). The nautical imagery is particularly favoured in such penitential contexts; cf. *Epp*. 4.2.2, 21.2.1 (where see n. 17), 59.11.2. Is it traceable to 1 Tim. 1.19? Further on the metaphor in K. Rahner in ZfKT 79 (1957) 42 f.; *idem*, *Symbole der Kirche* (Salzburg 1964) 445 f.; E. R. Curtius, *European Literature and the Latin Middle Ages* (New York and Evanston 1953) 128 ff.

14. *convocatis coepiscopis*. See introductory note to this letter. From *Ep*. 43.7.2 we learn that the synod of 251 was convened to meet after Easter even before Cyprian had returned from hiding.

15. *secundum . . . confessorum praesentiam*. Cf. *Ep*. 16.4.2 and see n. 1 to *Ep*. 15 on the use here of confessors (not martyrs).

LETTER 18

Contents: Cyprian has failed to receive any replies to his messages to his clergy; they would have been valuable for information upon which he might form policy decisions. Nevertheless the unhealthy summer season has begun. Under these emergency circumstances, lapsed who possess certificates from the martyrs may be, if in danger of death, reconciled to the Church by a presbyter or even a deacon. The fallen generally the clergy must comfort and encourage in their repentence; and catechumens *in articulo mortis* should not be denied God's mercy.

Date and circumstances: The date is fixed by internal indication. We are at the beginning of summer 250 (say, about early June or so). The letter comes after the series *Epp*. 15–17, for it includes, for the first time, a concession to the policy firmly announced in those letters, viz. that *all* reconciliation must await the reassembling of the Church in Carthage—penance must be regulated by all the due procedures. Cyprian received a (lost) reply to this letter; *Ep*. 19 manifestly answers that reply.

In *Ep.* 20.3.1 Cyprian describes the circumstances and purpose of this letter's composition. There has been violent pressure from the lapsed to receive the peace promised to them by the martyrs. He is seeking to mitigate that pressure and at the same time respect the honour due to the martyrs. Hence, Cyprian rules, the most urgent (death-bed) cases which are supported by *libelli martyrum* can now receive the Church's reconciliation with minimum ceremony; he hopes thus to take the sting out of the argument of the lapsed and gives some official acknowledgement to the intercessory powers of the martyrs, but all under restricted conditions.

Cyprian does not appeal, in this concession, to *antecessores* or to tradition; neither does he air the problem sympathetically but defer confirmation to the next synod (as in *Ep.* 56.2 f.). And he certainly does not cite as support for his decision practice elsewhere (e.g., Rome). He appears to be responding to a novel situation, with a characteristic blend of charity and politics, and on his own initiative. "This is the first recorded and certain example of a Christian bishop, acting alone in a monarchical fashion to resolve a new and significant problem" (G. Pell, *The Exercise of Authority in Early Christianity from about 170 to about 270* [diss. Oxford 1971] 324).

It has been maintained (e.g., L. Duquenne, *Chronologie des Lettres de s. Cyprien. . . .* (Brussels 1972) 116 f.) that Cyprian has received *Ep.* 8 after composing *Epp.* 15–17, and he has in fact been stimulated to follow the recommendations in §3.1 of that letter. This does not have to follow. Cyprian is reacting to his own pastoral and domestic situation, and he significantly includes in his ruling the proviso that the penitent possesses a *libellus martyrum;* this does not figure at all in *Ep.* 8. In fact *Ep.* 20.3.2 (where Cyprian refers verbally to *Ep.* 8.3) strongly suggests that he does not receive *Ep.* 8 until he has written *Epp.* 18 and 19 and has come to compose *Ep.* 20; in a somewhat embarrassed manner, after some defensive remarks (he protests *nec in hoc legem dedi aut me auctorem temere constitui,* etc.) he drops the significant proviso in urgent cases, asserting *standum putavi et cum vestra sententia.* See further M. Bévenot in VC 28 (1974) 157 f., and introductory note to *Ep.* 8.

1. On the rather curt form of address, see n. 1 to *Ep.* 5. In the *incipit* of the manuscript T occurs the word *aepuae* after *incipit ad clerum*. This seems inexplicable; perhaps a corruption of *Capuae* and the incipit has been contaminated by a rather similar incipit from a lost letter?—For a lost epistle to Capua, see Chronicle of 395, MGH 9.738 ed. Mommsen: *hac persecutione* (of Decius) *Cyprianus hortatus est per epistolas suas Augustinum et Felicitatem, qui passi sunt apud civitatem Capuensem, metropolim Campaniae*—on this, see H. Delehaye, *Les origines du culte des martyrs* (2nd ed., Brussels 1933) 303 f. For parallel cases of hybrid or contaminated titles in Cyprian's correspondence, see H. L. Ramsay in JTS 3 (1901–02) 592; M. Bévenot in *Bulletin of the John Rylands Library* 28 (1944) 76 ff.; *idem, The Tradition of MSS* (Oxford 1961) 30 f.; my article in *Antichthon* 3 (1969) 63 n. 3.

2. *multas epistulas meas quas ad vos frequenter misi nihil rescripsisse.* The combination of *multas . . . frequenter . . . nihil* gives a very emphatic effect. There are six letters in all which have been directed to the clergy (in chronological sequence, *Epp.* 7, 5, 14, 11, 12, and 16; the clergy may well have received copies of others, e.g., *Epp.* 6, 13, 10, and certainly *Epp.* 15 and 17 were to be read to them). It is only after this letter that the silence of nearly six months' duration is eventually broken. Cyprian has heard, however, from one group of four presbyters (*Ep.* 14.4) and he may perhaps have heard by now the news that there has been already communication between the Carthaginian clergy and Rome (see *Ep.* 20.1.1). The long silence underlines both the confusion in which the persecution left the Carthaginian community and the estrangement between bishop and clergy which the aftermath of the persecution exacerbated. It is quite some time later (and after the enrolment of Numidicus in the Carthaginian *presbyterium*) that Cyprian establishes the commission of two bishops and two Carthaginian presbyters virtually to manage the affairs of the Carthaginian Church (*Ep.* 41, joined by bishop Victor in *Ep.* 42), but the basic cause for its establishment is the persistence of this breakdown in relations between Cyprian and some of his clergy.

3. There is no reason to surmise an early beginning to the "plague of Gallus" (see n. on *Ep.* 59.6.1) nor to see here specifi-

cally "épidémies de malaria" (L. Duquenne, *Chronologie des Lettres de s. Cyprien*. . . . [Brussels 1972] 113). Cyprian is merely making a deduction from general observation about a notoriously unhealthy season.

4. *occurrendum*. . . . *fratribus nostris:* Cyprian appositely employs medical metaphors through the letter eg. *fovete, focillate, divino remedio*, a metaphor common in penitential contexts (cf. *Epp.* 30 §§3, 5, 7, 34.2, 55.16, 59.13, 75.4, *de laps.* 5, 14, 15, 28, 35 etc.): for an analysis of "sick" and "wounded" metaphors in Scripture, and patristic writers and early liturgy, see G. M. Lukken, *Original Sin in the Roman Liturgy* . . . (Leiden 1973) 297 ff.

5. *praerogativa eorum apud Deum adiuvari possunt. Praerogativa* would mean literally that they have the right to cast the first and guiding verdict when judgment is passed; he paraphrases in *Ep.* 19.2.1: *auxilio eorum adiuvari apud Dominum in delictis suis possunt.* For the martyrs' seat on God's tribunal, see n. 14 to *Ep.* 6; and for the efficacy of their intercession and certificates, see nn. 1 and 8 to *Ep.* 15. The best commentary on the thinking is provided by the exchange of letters, *Epp.* 21 and 22 (where see nn.).

6. *non expectata praesentia nostra.* A crucial change from *Ep.* 17.3.2: *expectent regressionem ut cum ad vos . . . venerimus . . .*, a clause firmly repeated with minor variants in *Epp.* 15.1.2 and 16.4.2.

7. Note the delegation of powers of absolution as far as deacons; despite considerable controversy, there seems little doubt from the wording of the sentence that Cyprian is intending to delegate full powers of (sacramental) reconciliation to the Church (not merely formal, external re-entry)—though Cyprian may not have been able to formulate precisely what authority in discipline he was delegating, yet he clearly regarded penitents so forgiven as reconciled, and, therefore, as absolved. Early in the next century the Council of Elvira, can. 32, reveals similar thinking: *apud presbyterum, si quis gravi lapsu in ruinam mortis inciderit, placuit agere paenitentiam non debere, sed potius apud episcopum; cogente tamen infirmitate necesse est presbyterem communionem praestare debere, et diaconem si ei iusserit sacerdos.* See V.

Saxer, *Vie liturgique et quotidienne à Carthage vers le milieu du IIIe siècle* (Vatican 1969) 174 f.; P. Laurain, *De l'intervention des laïques, des diacres et des abbesses dans l'administration de la pénitence* (Paris 1897) 68 ff., 109 ff.; P. Galtier, *De paenitentia tractatus dogmatico—historicus* (2nd ed., Rome 1957) 464 ff.; B. Poschmann, *Paenitentia secunda. Die kirchliche Busse in ältesten Christentum bis Cyprian und Origenes* (Bonn 1940) 421 f.; J. Colson, *La Fonction diaconale* (Bruges 1960) 115 f.; etc.

8. *manu eis in paenitentiam inposita.* See n. 13 to *Ep.* 15.

9. On the martyrs' requests, see n. 8 to *Ep.* 15, and n. 6 to *Ep.* 17.

10. Cyprian is aware that the ranks of the Carthaginian clergy have been depleted by some lapsed (*Ep.* 14.1.1 and n. 4 thereto); is he yet apprised of the very many (*plurimos*) clerical absentees (*Ep.* 29.1.1)?

11. *in bonis opinionibus perseveraverint.* There is a variant reading, *operibus* ("good works"), which is what we might rather expect (cf., for example, *Epp.* 16.2.3 and 19.1); it occurs in Hartel's μ (the fifteenth-century Monacensis 18203), which normally derives from T (Hartel xlvi ff.), a case of *recentiores non deteriores?*

12. *audientibus.* In *Ep.* 8.3.1 the word used by the Roman clergy is *catecumeni.* See n. 28 to *Ep.* 8 on the catechumenate and "clinical" rites.

13. *inplorantibus divinam gratiam misericordia Domini non denegetur.* Somewhat vaguely expressed (should it be translated, "If they beseech God for His grace, the Lord's mercy should not be denied them"?), but Cyprian plainly has in mind the charitable reception into the Church of dying catechumens by the administration of baptism. The phrase *misericordia Domini* may suggest that Cyprian is talking about a further category of *lapsi* (so Bayard, in ed. xix), but it could well be that Cyprian is proffering nothing other than customary pastoral counsel at this point (as in the previous paragraph, §2.1). On the Christian nuances of *misericordia*, see H. Pétré, *Caritas. Étude sur le vocabulaire latin de la charité chrétienne* (Louvain 1948) 229 ff.

LETTER 19

Contents: Cyprian responds to a letter from his clergy, encouraging them to urge restraint and perseverence in penance among the lapsed. To those who cannot be so restrained the guidelines which he provided in his previous letter still apply. Except for a dying penitent who has a certificate from the martyrs, all must await the formation of a common policy for this universal problem when peace has been restored. If they cannot wait, it is within their power to redeem their fall by seeking martyrdom.

Date and circumstances: §2.1 of this letter which paraphrases §1.2 of *Ep.* 18 (terming that epistle *proximis litteris*) makes it indisputable that this letter is next in sequence to *Ep.* 18. These are the two letters to his clergy which are referred to in *Ep.* 20.3.1 where the circumstances of composition are described. If *Ep.* 18 was composed in the whereabouts of early June (*Ep.* 18.1.2) we have to allow time for a collective response to that letter by Cyprian's clergy in Carthage—their first epistolary reply to his messages—and now we have Cyprian, after receiving their epistle, dealing with its contents. Perhaps he was writing *Ep.* 19 in or about late June 250. On the date, see L. Nelke 35 f.

In §2.3 we see that the exiled are still abroad; the battle with the enemy still rages; it is possible to go out and seek martyrdom. The persecution in Carthage is far from over, though one gets the impression that the community has rallied and reformed somewhat after an initial debacle. The turbulence it is now experiencing is more domestic than external. And danger does not threaten acutely; one needs to seek it out.

It is tempting to speculate that some of the Carthaginian clergy, dissatisfied with Cyprian's replies in *Epp.* 18 and 19, despatched Crementius to Rome after receiving *Ep.* 19 in which Cyprian manifested his refusal to shift his ground. They sent information to the discredit of their bishop (*Epp.* 8.1.1 and 20.1.1) and copies or verbal reports of the contents of *Epp.* 18 and 19, complaining of the *forma* of their now discredited leader. Some of the Roman clergy then replied with *Ep.* 8, and §3.1 of that letter with its curiously emphatic and authoritarian tone covered the main issues dealt with by Cyprian in these two letters, assuring the Carthaginian clergy of their duties in the absence of their shepherd.

1. On the form of address, see n. 1 to *Ep.* 5.

2. Now lost; Cyprian does not exclaim with joy that his clergy in Carthage have at last broken their long silence—they are now only doing what they ought to have been doing all along. We learn a little of the contents of their letter; it contained protestation that the lapsed were in fact being counselled by them and it requested rulings (*forma*) for dealing with the demands being made. The clergy may have given the impression that they did not take *Ep.* 18 to contain Cyprian's final concession on the issue of reconciliation before the advent of *publica pax.* We are left wondering how many of Cyprian's clergy agreed to the composition of this lost letter; on the numbers of the Carthaginian clergy, see Introduction, pp. 39 ff.

3. *salubre consilium vestrum non deesse.* This protestation was no doubt stimulated by such minatory and admonitory remarks addressed to them as *Epp.* 16.3.1 and 18.2.1.

4. *de omnibus speciebus secundum ecclesiasticam disciplinam.* Despite the turmoil, Cyprian will not be stampeded into abandoning the regular and traditional institutional practices (*disciplina;* see n. 9 to *Ep.* 11); the phrase *de omnibus speciebus* suggests Cyprian has in mind the discernment of types and degrees of apostasy (see n. 25 to *Ep.* 15).

5. Apoc. 2.5.

6. *mitis et patiens et sacerdotibus Dei obtemperans.* Cyprian has significantly made specific his interpretation of the general exhortation to the lapsed to be *mites et humiles* in *Ep.* 18.2.1.

7. That is, *Ep.* 18. Cyprian's firm stand here accords awkwardly with his own protestation in *Ep.* 20.3.1 (on *Epp.* 18 and 19): *nec in hoc legem dedi aut me auctorem temere constitui.*

8. For explanatory comment on this sentence, see nn. 5 ff. to *Ep.* 18. Cyprian's phraseology, *cum pace a martyribus sibi promissa ad Dominum remittantur,* might possibly give the impression

that he considered no final forgiveness was possible for the sin of apostasy from the Church; a passage such as *Ep.* 58.8.2 adequately demonstrates that such an impression would be mistaken. For discussion, see M. Bévenot in *Theol. Stud.* 16 (1955) 195 f.

9. *invidiam faciunt.* That is to say, their constant and strident demands, publicly voiced, are making the repeated refusals required of Cyprian (and his clergy) highly invidious; and they are stirring up bad blood by highlighting through their ceaseless demands the odious comparison between the prospects of possessors of certificates from the martyrs (should they fall seriously ill) and of those without such certificates.

10. The line of argument is highly characteristic of Cyprian. The churches should seek unanimity and harmony in their actions, and manifestly that cannot be achieved until there is *publica pax.* The passage provides the incidental information that Cyprian perceived the persecution—and the decimation of the Christian ranks—to be a universal phenomenon (cf. *Epp.* 30.5.4, 31.1.1, 31.6.2 [from Rome]), though one wonders how detailed was the information he could have obtained in his place of hiding.

11. *vitae ipsi omnium nostrum convenit.* That is to say, the life of brothers who love one another and dwell in harmony together. The thrust of the paragraph is on the need for a community decision.

12. *praepositi.* That is to say, bishops. See nn. 7 and 16 to *Ep.* 3, n. 9 to *Ep.* 8.

13. Observe the laudation of the *stantium plebs* (the loyal clergy are not similarly treated); cf. introductory note to *Ep.* 17. For laity present at Council meetings, see n. 3 to *Ep.* 1.

14. *consilii communis religione.* A typically compact, and elusive, Cyprianic phrase; *religio* is even made to bear some of its primitive sense of "(sacred) binding power." This phrase ("the sanctity of a common decision") need not imply that Cyprian holds any developed theory on the inspiration of conciliar decisions. See n. 23 to *Ep.* 1.

15. *extorres facti et patria pulsi ac bonis suis omnibus spoliati.* On exile and confiscation in this persecution, see n. 8 to *Ep.* 5, n. 5 to *Ep.* 10, n. 19 to *Ep.* 12. The phrases here probably do not

embrace (voluntary) refugees as well, for Cyprian would not term them, *tout court*, as he proceeds to do here, *confessores* (though note *de laps.* 3 in praise of *cauta secessio*, prudent withdrawal: it is the *secundus ad gloriam gradus*, it is *privata confessio*). Observe that there is no homecoming yet for exiles (save illegally). But Cyprian remains confident that they, and he, will one day return. Is it significant that Cyprian does not mention the imprisoned (still separated from their church), even though at this time they formed a substantial group in Carthage? He is already aware of the indiscriminate granting of *pax* by this group (cf. *Ep.* 22.2).

16. *ante ad ecclesiam introire festinent.* The imagery is probably reinforced by the actual ceremonies proper for the readmission of the penitent—vigils at the vestibule before the church threshold, knocking upon the church doors for re-entry, etc.—on which see n. on *Ep.* 30.6.3 (and cf. *Ep.* 11.2.2 and n. 19 thereto).

17. *qui differri non potest potest coronari.* Ecclesiastical authorities were emphatically opposed to "voluntary martyrdom" as a general rule—clear statements by Cyprian in *Ep.* 81.1.4: *nec quisquam vestrum ... ultro se Gentilibus offerat*, and in *Acta Proconsularia Cypriani* 1.5: *cum disciplina prohibeat nostra ne quis se ultro offerat.* For further evidence, see H. Delehaye, *Sanctus. Essai sur le culte des saints dans l'antiquité* (Brussels 1927) 166 ff., and G. E. M. de Ste Croix in HTR 47 (1954) 83; and note the care with which Athanasius, *Vit. Ant.* 46, depicts Antony in the Great Persecution avoiding offence in this way. (Of course, by no means all Christians were obedient to this general injunction; see Dionysius *ap.* Eusebius, *H.E.* 6.41.16, 22, for Decian examples in Egypt).

However, one of the rare cases for which church *praepositi* were prepared to relent this rule was that of lapsed Christians so that they might blot out their former fault by offering themselves for martyrdom (which acted as a "second baptism"; cf. E. L. Hummel in SCA 9 [1946] 110 ff.). For a good example, see Eusebius, *H.E.* 5.1.25 f., and note the cases in *Ep.* 24 and Cyprian's observations on them in *Ep.* 25.2 (*atque utinam sic et ceteri post lapsum paenitentes in statum pristinum reformentur*); compare also *Ep.* 55.4.1f., 7.1, 16.3, 25; *De laps.* 36 (*provocabit hostem et quidem factus ad proelium fortior per dolorem. . . . nec iam solam Dei veniam merebitur sed coronam*); etc. For further discussion on this point, see E. L. Hummel, *op. cit.* above, 48 ff., 114 ff., and for speculation on the means whereby a Decian *libellaticus* or *sacrificatus* might in fact redeem his fall and seek his crown, see my article in *Historia* 22 (1973) 656 ff. and cf. n. 24 to *Ep.* 8.

LETTER 20

Contents: Cyprian has heard that misleading accounts of his conduct are being reported to Rome. To correct those biased impressions he explains the circumstances which in fact induced him to flee and encloses copies of thirteen letters he has written to his flock in Carthage from his place of hiding. They bear witness to his continued concern and zeal for his charges and for his anxiety to maintain discipline in the church. His policy on the reconciliation of the lapsed is in harmony with that expressed by the Roman clergy in their recent letter to his clergy. Final resolution of the full question must await conciliar gatherings possible only when peace has come.

Date and circumstances: In the sequence of letters this must be placed after *Ep.* 19 (manifestly referred to in §3.1); and Cyprian has not yet received *Ep.* 23 (from the *universi confessores*) to which he alludes when he next writes both to his clergy (*Ep.* 26) and to Rome (*Ep.* 27). What sort of gap intervened between the composition of *Ep.* 19 and this epistle, we can only surmise. It would appear that in the interval he has received *Ep.* 8 (see introductory note to that letter and to *Epp.* 18 and 19). It may be that his first reactions to that offensive letter were promptly to send the letter back to Rome (*Ep.* 9), and it was only after further and more mature reflection on the implications of *Ep.* 8 that he decided to write this *apologia* (*Ep.* 20). It seems to have met a favourable hearing; see *Epp.* 30.1, 31.6. To place *Ep.* 20, therefore, in the course of July 250, or shortly thereafter, would not be unreasonable (later in that time-range being the more likely if the suggestion has any foundation that *Ep.* 8 came in response to messages from Carthage sent after the reception there of *Epp.* 18 and 19; see introductory note to *Ep.* 19). See also L. Duquenne, *Chronologie des Lettres de s. Cyprien ...* (Brussels 1972) 96; L. Nelke, *Die Chronologie der Korrespondenz Cyprians...*

The letter arranges the events of the first half of the 250s, as seen from Cyprian's viewpoint, in (rough) chronological blocks. First (*orto statim ... impetu primo*), there is the initial mob agitation for Cyprian—and his flight, §1.2; then, in §2.1, there come four clauses describing his epistolary solicitude, from hiding, for four categories of his flock (clergy, confessors, exiled, the full brotherhood). This is followed by a further chronological pointer, the advent of tortures (*postea quam ... et tormenta venerunt*) in §2.2. Thereafter, we have an additional category who are comforted, tortured brethren and brethren imprisoned, awaiting torture—and the word martyr occurs for the first time in the letter. It is now that Cyprian hears (*cum comperissem*) that the martyrs and confessors have been importuned by the *sacrificati* and *libellatici,* and that *libelli* are being issued by them in their thousands; three groups of his flock (martyrs and confessors, presbyters and deacons, laity) are addressed on the question of Church discipline accordingly. After another time shift (*postmodum vero cum,* §3.1), some of the lapsed persisting in their recalcitrance, a further two letters are sent to the clergy. And §3.2 concludes the letter with a defensive explanation of the policy adopted in those final two letters, and (somewhat apologetically) brings it into line with that of Rome.

The letter is of invaluable assistance in forming a realistic picture of the rhythm of the persecution in Carthage, and in sorting out the thirteen letters enclosed into their chronological groups. With rough dates available for the beginning of the troubles (c. Jan. 250; see Introduction, pp. 25 f., and my article in *Antichthon* 3 (1969), 66 f., and n. on *Ep.* 37.2.1), the advent of tortures (in April; see introductory note and n. 20 to *Ep.* 10) and for the second-to-last letter mentioned ("summer already begun," *Ep.* 18.1.2), we have a chronological framework within which we may place—approximately—the Decian correspondence so far. The most recent and generous discussion on this set of letters is to be found in L. Duquenne, *op. cit.* above, 50–113. See also H. Gülzow, *Cyprian und Novatian: der Briefwechsel zwischen den Gemeinden in Rom und Karthago zur Zeit der Verfolgung des Kaisers Decius* (Tübingen 1975) 58 ff.

It may well be that stimulated by the personal attack made on his actions and the criticism of his policies, Cyprian now proceeded also to send copies of *Epp.* 15–19 to *plurimi collegae;* they replied, with expressions of approval for his counsel (*Epp.* 25.1.2, 26.1.2). In this, to achieve unity of action was no doubt his prime goal, but was he also, in part, rounding up concerted support for his point of view, in the same way as we get the impression he did from the unwavering unanimity of *Sent. Episc.* LXXXVII? When he next writes to Rome (*Ep.* 27), he pointedly encloses copies of *Epp.* 25 and 26, in both of which letters the fact that many colleagues (= bishops) have written to him aligning themselves, *secundum catholicam fidem,* with the policy which he himself enunciated is stated with marked firmness. See also on the tone of this letter U. Wickert, *Sacramentum Unitatis. Ein Beitrag zum Verständnis der Kirche bei Cyprian* (Berlin and New York 1971) 138 f.

1. *presbyteris et diaconibus Romae consistentibus.* On the phraseology, compare n. 1 to *Ep.* 1. There has been no bishop of Rome since January 20. By a curious vagary Baluzius was insistent that this letter was written not to the Roman clergy but *ad eos e clero Carthaginiensi qui Romae tum erant.*

2. *minus simpliciter et minus fideliter vobis renuntiari quae hic a nobis et gesta sunt et geruntur.* We know of at least one communication between Carthage and Rome for which the subdeacon Crementius was the emissary. See *Ep.* 8 and n. 1 thereto. The message was from the Carthaginian clergy to whom *Ep.* 8 was addressed in reply. It is possible to believe (Cyprian writes *renuntiari,* not *renuntiavisse*) that there was more than one such hostile report (*via* Bassianus? see n. 32 to *Ep.* 8), but they are not necessarily implied by the wording here. To judge from the course of Cyprian's defence we would deduce

that Cyprian felt he had been attacked concerning his flight, his zeal for his flock (*diligentia*), and his maintenance and interpretation of *ecclesiastica disciplina;* he feels himself particularly vulnerable on the last issue. A close reading of *Ep.* 8—along with a knowledge of the sources of contention in Carthage—would be enough to reveal the grounds of the attack (e.g., *fuga* in *Ep.* 8.1.1, cf. *Ep.* 14.1.2; *diligentia* in *Ep.* 8.1.2 ff.; *disciplina* in *Ep.* 8.3.1 f.; clergy dissatisfied with his rulings on *disciplina, Ep.* 19.2.1, cf. *Ep.* 14.4; etc.).

3. *actus nostri et disciplinae et diligentiae ratio. Disciplinia* is multivalent (see literature cited in n. 9 to *Ep.* 11), but the contents of the letter suggest that Cyprian means by the term here both his advocacy of Church order (administration) and his own adherence to Church teachings and practice (orthodoxy). In Cyprian's *Acta* 4.2, the proconsul Galerius Maximus is made to declare before passing sentence, *sanguine tuo sancietur disciplina.* Cyprian would have approved of the linguistic ambiguity.

Note in the first section the significant change between first person plural (Cyprian with the clergy whom he leads) *a nobis . . . gesta, actus nostri, fratribus nostris,* and first person singular (Cyprian on his own) *me clamore violento . . ., meam salutem, monitis meis, mea mediocritate.* The distinction, though real enough, is not watertight (*praesentiam nostram*).

4. *cum me clamore violento frequenter populus flagitasset.* For public hostility against Cyprian, see *Ep.* 7.1 and n. 3 thereto; n. 11 to *Ep.* 5; n. 32 to *Ep.* 6; n. 5 to *Ep.* 8; n. 11 to *Ep.* 14. Was there a special clause against bishops as such (see n. 2 to *Ep.* 5) or, rather, did the orders of Decius merely serve to rouse latent popular hostility against the Christians, hostility which became focused naturally enough on their well-known *auctor et signifer* (*Acta Cyp.* 4.2) in Carthage? For parallel attacks by pagans in this and other persecutions on Christians of noted prominence, see n. 5 to *Ep.* 8, and Introduction, pp. 34 ff.

5. *sicut Domini mandata instruunt.* That is to say, scriptural injunctions. Perhaps Cyprian is alluding to Matt. 10.23 ('when they persecute you in one town, flee to the next'); cf. Fahey 297. In *De laps.* 10 Cyprian, after quoting Isa. 52.11 and Apoc. 18.4 in

defence of retreat, concludes, *et ideo Dominus in persecutione secedere et fugere mandavit adque ut id fieret et docuit et fecit* (*fecit* alludes to Christ's withdrawals in Matt. 4.12, John 11.54). He may therefore have these two passages (Isa. 52.11, Apoc. 18.4) in mind also. Cyprian here is not prepared to invoke personally vouchsafed signs (as he does to his own clergy in *Ep.* 16.4.1; cf. *Ep.* 7.1); did he sense the vulnerability of such an argument?

After Cyprian's eventual martyrdom his biographer was prepared to be more outspoken, Cf. Pontius, *Vit. Cyp.* 7 f. Cyprian was shackled by divine admonitions (*mens. . . . de divinis admonitionibus mancipata*); he went into hiding in obedience to God's orders (*Domino latebram tunc iubenti; secessum illum non hominis pusillitate conceptum, sed sicuti est vere fuisse divinum*); we can now see that it was all part of a providential plan (*ego sine Dei nutu necessarios reservari non admitto, non credo*).

By 252 Cyprian, in *Ep.* 59.6.1, was himself prepared to invoke his survival in time of persecution as a special mark of divine favour (*quando* [*episcopus*] *Dei auxilio in persecutione protegitur*).

6. *interim secessi.* On *interim,* see n. 30 to *Ep.* 4; on *secessi,* see n. 4 to *Ep.* 8 where the topic of *fuga* in time of persecution is discussed. Cyprian proceeds with a defence which proved highly effective. The Roman confessors in *Ep.* 31.6.1 observe in tones of approval, *licet interim a fratribus pro temporis condicione distractus es, tamen. . . ;* they repudiate the charge that he was *aliquis desertor* (contrast *Ep.* 8.2.2, *deserentes fraternitatem*).

7. *ne per inverecundam praesentiam nostram seditio . . . plus provocaretur.* Cyprian's most consistent defence of his withdrawal—he was a crowd-provoking *persona insignis.* See material collected under n. 5 to *Ep.* 8.

8. *absens tamen corpore nec spiritu . . . defui.* An allusion to 1 Cor. 5.3 (Vulgate: *ego quidem absens corpore praesens autem spiritu*) or Col. 2.5 (Vulgate: *nam et si corpore absens sum sed spiritu vobiscum sum*)? The epistolary style of this passage is analysed by K. Thraede, *Grundzüge griechisch-römischer Brieftopik* (Munich 1970) 109 ff. (esp. on the epistolary topos of *corpus-spiritus* in Cyprian and other patristic letter writers).

9. The letters in §2.1 basically come before the advent of

torture. The letters bearing *clero consilium* are, therefore, to be identified as 7, 5, 14, and possibly 11 and 12.

10. *confessoribus exhortatio*. That is to say, *Epp.* 6 and 13 (see next note).

11. *extorribus . . . obiurgatio.* §4.1 to *Ep.* 13 (to the confessors); cf. §3 of *Ep.* 14 (to the clergy).

12. *universae fraternitati ad deprecandam Dei misericordiam adlocutio.* This suits the contents of *Ep.* 11; though this epistle was sent to his clergy, §7.1 shows that Cyprian was consciously addressing his flock generally (*legendam fratribus suggeratis*) on the need to supplicate for God's mercy.

13. *Domino suggerente.* This may well allude to the visions of *Ep.* 11.3 f. So far Cyprian has described 6 (or 7 if we include *Ep.* 12) letters in all.

14. *postea quam vero et tormenta venerunt.* On this change of events, see *Ep.* 10.1.1 and nn. 5 and 6 thereto.

15. That is to say, *Ep.* 10; if we do not include *Ep.* 12 under *clero consilium*, it will need to be placed here. *Ep.* 12 is addressed to the clergy, but it does send reassurance that those who die in prison even without torture merit glory no less brilliant than the martyred dead. Cyprian would assume that this message would be passed on to the imprisoned confessors by the clergy on their visits to them.

16. Observe the firmness with which Cyprian identifies with apostasy the sin of the *libellatici* as well as of the *sacrificati*. It is his first major statement on the two basic groups of *lapsi* (but see n. 25 to *Ep.* 15, n. 4 to *Ep.* 19). From Cyprian's insistent wording it is clear that some maintained that merely to obtain a *libellus* (without sacrifice, etc.) was not sinful; Cyprian outlines the case put by such *libellatici* in *Ep.* 55.14 and gives a reasoned statement of his own position in *De laps.* 27. For further discussion, see my article in *Antichthon* 3 (1969) 73 ff.

17. *exambire ad martyras . . . confessores quoque inportuna et gratiosa deprecatione conrumpere.* Cyprian uses words suggestive of bribery and corruption (*exambire, gratiosa, conrumpere*); cf. n. 29 to *Ep.* 15 for charges of trafficking in certificates of forgiveness. Note how the flattery is given to *confessors;* they are not natural-

ly on as elevated an eminence as "martyrs" (tortured; in prison with prospects of death; etc.) and need more to be cajoled into issuing any certificates (cf. n. 1 to *Ep.* 15).

18. *darentur cotidie libellorum milia.* Cyprian prudently refrained from emphasizing the vastness of the extent of indiscipline over this question in *Epp.* 15 (and see introductory note to that letter) *et sqq.*

19. That is, *Ep.* 15.

20. That is, *Ep.* 16. *De laps.* 15 provides a good commentary on this situation (*temeritate quorundam laxatur incautis communicatio: inrita et falsa pax, periculosa dantibus et nihil accipientibus profutura,* etc.).

21. *plebi quoque ipsi quantum potuimus animum composuimus.* Cyprian is referring to *Ep.* 17. He was aware that his flock would be upset and confused especially through the failure of the clergy properly to instruct them.

22. *bis ad clerum litteras feci et legi eis mandavi.* The two are *Epp.* 18 and 19, though in the text Cyprian does not specify that they should be read out to the troublesome lapsed. Doubtless these instructions were sent with the messengers who delivered the letters.

The tally of thirteen enclosures is now complete: 6 epistles (or 7) in §2.1, 5 (or 4) in §2.2, 2 in §3.1.

23. *ut ad illorum violentiam interim quoque genere mitigandam.* Cyprian is being carefully insistent that the counsel he has given is intended to be of temporary duration only (pending general peace—and assemblies). We catch here a neat glimpse of Cyprian at work as an instinctive politician, with an ability to emphasize at any one moment one aspect of a situation to the exclusion of others. In *Ep.* 18.1.2 the onset of summer (and its attendant diseases and illnesses) is given to his own clergy as the (charitable) setting for the concessions made; Cyprian there displays the concern of a pastor. Here, to the Roman administrators, he underlines his role as practical administrator, adroitly and diplomatically conceding minimal allowances (both to the lapsed and to the martyrs) under very difficult circumstances.

24. See *Epp.* 18.1.2, 19.2.1, and nn. on these passages for explication.

25. *nec in hoc legem dedi aut me auctorem temere constitui.* To judge from the run of the rest of the letter, Cyprian has been attacked for the authoritarian nature of his guidelines. *Ep.* 19.2.1 shows that *Ep.* 18 did not meet with universal approval. In defence Cyprian avers that he has given but interim advice (not a *lex*), and (it can now be seen) he is taking his stand in the good company of the Roman clergy themselves.

26. *nuper.* On this word in Cyprian, see nn. 7 and 27 to *Ep.* 1. See also introductory note to *Ep.* 8 for the date. Cyprian is, of course, referring to *Ep.* 8.

27. See n. 1 to *Ep.* 8. This letter, *Ep.* 20, was crossed by another, sent by the Roman presbyters and deacons, also *ad clerum factas.* Cf. *Ep.* 27.4.

28. Cyprian is virtually quoting from *Ep.* 8.3.1 (where see n. 25): he changes *communionem* to *communicationem*, his preferred term (cf. n. 18 to *Ep.* 16). It should be noted that there is no word of a martyrs' certificate in the Roman letter, whereas Cyprian has hitherto specifically restricted forgiveness for the dying lapsed to holders of such certificates. Though it is put a little obscurely, Cyprian is now altering his previous stand, in the interests of unity. Others, however, have considered that Cyprian leaves us with the rather ambiguous impression that he is claiming that he came to his own views (in *Epp.* 18 and 19) only after reading *Ep.* 8; that is far from proven (see introductory notes to *Epp.* 8, 18, 19).

29. Cyprian might be accused here of being less than frank—precisely the fault of which he accuses others at the beginning of this letter! His counsel has hitherto in fact differed in one very important respect from the Roman *sententia.* Cyprian's embarrassed protestation here shows how anxious he is not to appear to be creating disunity and disharmony. This is basic to his instincts as a churchman. He now removes that offending difference. There is no trace in the correspondence that he proceeds to distribute copies of *Ep.* 20 amongst his own African colleagues or his Carthaginian clergy; indeed he can blandly say to his clergy when he next writes to them in *Ep.* 26.1.2: *instetur interim epistulis quas ad vos proximis feceram,* giving no hint at all about rescinding the necessity for the dying penitent to possess

a *libellus martyrum.* (Perhaps, given their wholesale distribution, by now most possessed such *libelli* anyhow.) That provision appears to have been dropped by the Council of 251. In his later episcopate Cyprian was more prepared to be rather less accommodating and to resort to the argument that a bishop was responsible to God alone. Cf. M. Bévenot in *Recherches de science religieuse* 39 (1951) 398 f.

30. *plures praepositi convenire in unum coeperimus.* By contrast with his letters to various members of his own flock, Cyprian here emphasizes the paramount role of bishops (= *praepositi*) at the future conciliar gathering; He loses sight of *plebs, clerus, confessores.* He is writing (with a touch of flattery) as one bishop to colleagues in clerical leadership (episcopal vicars, to be exact). See n. 33 to *Ep.* 14, and n. 9 to *Ep.* 8 (on the Roman presbyters as *praepositi*).

31. *disponere singula vel reformare possimus. Singula* could refer to individual cases rather than problems; *reformare,* carefully placed at the conclusion, leaves us in no doubt that his rulings may indeed be changed—certainly he has laid down no final *lex.* Cyprian was a trained *rhetor;* all his professional instincts were to make the very best of his case. He has done just that.

Note the stages which Cyprian requires for a satisfactory settlement: return to his own diocese, convening of an (African) episcopal synod, consultation with others (e.g., Rome) in the interests of unity, and then agreement on the rules and regulations (*disponere singula vel reformare*).

LETTER 21

Contents: From Rome Celerinus (who has himself been a confessor) writes to Carthage to his old friend Lucianus, leader of a band of imprisoned confessors now awaiting their martyrdom. With repeated appeals to the bonds of old friendship, he begs for help for his sisters Numeria and Candida, one of whom at a late stage bribed her way out of actually offering pagan sacrifice, the other of whom is manifestly guilty of having sacrificed. To atone for their sin, they have been doing penance and good works, in particular caring for refugees from Carthage. But after hearing their case the ecclesiastical authorities in Rome have deferred decision upon it until the appointment of a bishop. Celerinus urges that pardon may be won for his sisters through the heavenly influence and prayers of these witnesses of Christ, in particular by the confessor among them who is first to receive his martyr's crown. He is joined by many others in sending greetings and putting this request.

Date and circumstances: A likely dating can be sifted out by stages. Easter has already come and gone (§2.1); that fell on April 7, 250.

Montanus has come from Carthage with news of Lucianus and his companions (§1.1); it is plain that Celerinus is told that not only are they in prison (§§1.1, 3.1) after successful confession, but that they stand in clear prospect of martyrdom (§§1.3, 3.2). That means we should be, at the least, in about mid-April of 250 A.D., as outlined in *Ep.* 10.1.1 (at which date Mappalicus and others died in Carthage). Celerinus knows that there are already Carthaginian martyrs (§2.1).

In the reply (*Ep.* 22) which Lucianus wrote on receipt of this letter, we see that in fact Mappalicus and others are already dead after interrogation and that a number of others have died or are dying as a result of prolonged starvation and thirst and their suffocating prison conditions—which appear to include overwhelming heat (*Ep.* 22.2.1). Are we, therefore, up to June (or later) of 250?

It is, furthermore, clear that Cyprian did not receive copies of this exchange of letters (as well as the companion piece *Ep.* 23) until after he wrote *Ep.* 20 which he addressed to Rome, probably some time in the course of July 250. But when Cyprian writes his next letter to Rome (*Ep.* 27), he encloses copies of these epistles (*Epp.* 21–23) and makes this correspondence the main subject matter of his letter.

These considerations suggest that the composition of these letters should be brought well down into 250, at least as far as the middle months of that year. L. Duquenne, *Chronologie des*

Lettres de s. Cyprien . . . (Brussels 1972) 130; L. Nelke, *Die Chronologie der Korrespondenz Cyprians . . .* (diss. Thorn 1902) 16 ff.; H.
Gülzow, *Cyprian und Novatian . . .* (Tübingen 1975) 52 ff.

How Cyprian came to receive his copies, we do not know.
When he talks of these letters in *Ep.* 27.3.2 he speaks in strong
terms of personal approval of Celerinus (*boni et robusti confessoris; moderatus et cautus et humilitate ac timore sectae nostrae
verecundus*), and he later accorded him an enthusiastic welcome when Celerinus joined him in hiding (cf. *Ep.* 39.1.1). Did
Celerinus, with some naiveté as well as deference, send Cyprian
copies in order to inform him about the case of his sisters and, in
particular, of the prayer which the martyr-to-be had made,
secundum praeceptum Pauli, over them in *Ep.* 22.2.2 (*exposita causa
apud episcopum et facta exomologesi habeant pacem non tantum hae
. . .*)? Celerinus hasn't shown the documents to the Roman authorities; cf. *Ep..* 27.3.2.

Celerinus, with impressive reticence about his own trials
(these are found outlined in *Epp* 22.1.1 and 39.2), displays a
remarkable deference towards the status and dignity, the influence and powers of the martyrs. He is anxious to obtain their
efficacious patronage before Christ; and by martyrs he means
those who have died or who are about to die in honoured
confession. He is a confessor himself (§1.2), he has confessors
about him (§4.1f.)—but clearly they enjoy no immediate hopes
of becoming privileged martyrs themselves. And (with the exception of Fabian) Rome has yet to be graced by actual *martyria*
(there are none still in *Ep.* 28.1), and its imprisoned confessors
are strongly opposed to such *inlicitas petitiones* (*Ep.* 30.4; cf. *Epp.*
27.4.1 and 28.2.1). So Celerinus turns to his native Carthage; he
appears to be aware that he can expect there a favourable
reception for his request, addressing his rather touching plea to
Lucianus as the *antistes* of the confessors who are now facing
death, and martyrdom. He may well have heard (*via* Montanus)
of the import of *Ep.* 23, which, Cyprian claims in *Ep.* 27.2.1, was
issued by Lucianus as a reponse to his *Epp.* 15 *et seqq.* (datable to
May 250). See further introductory note and n. 1 to *Ep.* 15. In
Ep. 22.2.2 (where see n. 24) Celerinus is, in effect, given a *libellus
martyrum* in favour of his fallen sisters.

All this affords us with valuable insight into the mentality of the beleaguered Church. And we are given other important glimpses of these Christians under persecution conditions. We catch an actual picture of pressure being applied both to Church leaders (§3.2) as well as to "the confessors and martyrs" to grant reconciliation to *lapsi*, whilst the persecution still continues. We see that in Rome there was general sacrifice before early April (Easter) in 250 A.D.; and from §3.2 we can imaginatively reconstruct the sacrificial scene in Rome—a long, slowly moving procession winding along the length of the Via Sacra on its way up to the Capitol, accompanied perhaps by sacrificial animals (cf. *De laps.* 8: *ad Capitolium sponte ventum est. . . . Quid hostiam tecum, miser, quid victimam supplicaturus inponis (v.l. inportas)?*, with crowns worn and heads solemnly veiled (cf. *de laps* 2), etc. And we observe that the crowded streets and tenements of Rome provided shelter for a significant number of Christian refugees from Carthage (§4), some of whom have themselves already been released after an initial confession. The concluding greetings in this letter (§4.1)—as well as those in the reply it provoked (*Ep.* 22.3)—allow us a fleeting glimpse of what appears to be a cohesive colony of Carthaginian Christians maintaining some degree of separate identity in Rome; Lucianus has visited them in earlier days, perhaps just before the persecution broke out (§1.1), and has personal acquaintance with a number of Christians in that city (21 names are given and many more are implied in *Ep.* 22.3). It reminds us that Rome and Carthage are not far apart. Even six and a half centuries earlier the coast of Africa and Sicily could be described as being two days and one night's sail apart; cf. Thucydides 7.50.2. See also O. Perler, *Les voyages de saint Augustin* (Paris 1969) 65 ff.

In many places the precise meaning of the awkwardly turned and meandering Latin remains elusive. On aspects of the language of *Epp.* 21 and 22, see J. Schrijnen and C. Mohrmann, *Studien zur Syntax der Briefe des Cyprians* (2 vols., Nijmegen 1936/37) 1.72 f. Some of the incoherence in phraseology which the original appears to have had is necessarily lost in any interpretative translation, but the general lines of the letter's argument are left unchanged; and it would be difficult to obscure the native virtues of familial piety and naiveté combined with knowing cajolery and flattery displayed in this letter.

On the text of *Epp.* 8, 21–24 note Hartel's observations (*eas non ita edidi ut edendas esse bene intellexi; incertioribus id genus neglectis; totus hic locus sic emendandus est;* etc.); a more satisfactory text for these letters is provided by A. Miodoński (1889) 117 ff., followed by L. Bayard (revised Budé edition, vol. 1, 56 ff.)

1. Celerinus is a young man; around the end of this year (see *Ep.* 37.2 for the dating) he was too young to be appointed to anything more elevated than the lowest clerical grade, that of lector. At this time he is undoubtedly writing from Rome (for his arrival from there, see *Ep.* 37.1.1) where he has already undergone trial (*Ep.* 22.1.1), being one of the very first to face that ordeal (*Ep.* 39.2.1); his sufferings included 19 days of imprisonment *in nervo ac ferro*, exacerbated by hunger and thirst (*Ep.* 39.2.1). (By a slip, H. Delehaye, *Les passions des martyrs et les genres littéraires* [Brussels 1921] 355, places this trial in Carthage.) We are not aware of his circumstances at this present time of writing—but his behaviour at the Easter celebrations (§2.1), and the fact that in his praises of his confession Lucianus fails to entertain any hopes of actual martyrdom for him (see *Ep.* 22.1.1) and that in his description of his sufferings Cyprian fails to emphasize prolonged imprisonment (see *Ep.* 39.2.2), all these suggest that he is already out of prison, released, in all probability, as a youthful, and hopelessly obstinate, recusant (for parallels, see my article in *Antichthon* 3 (1969) 67 f.). This deduction is strongly supported by the past tense in § 1.2; *cum essem et ego in tam florida confessione.* . . . Why Celerinus was in Rome we do not know; there may be a chance that he went there to join military service (hence his ready detection as a Christian and early trial?). For Cyprian says of his two martyred uncles *in castris et ipsi quondam saecularibus militantes sed veri et spiritales Dei milites* (*Ep.* 39.3.1); but that whole letter is too heavily laden with Cyprian's favoured military metaphors for us to be able to place much weight on this phrasing. (H. Gülzow, *Cyprian und Novatian* . . . [Tübingen 1975] 53, misinterprets *Ep.* 39.3.1 to deduce a patrician family for Celerinus ["Er gehörte einer Patrizierfamilie in Karthago an"]; cf. n. 2 below.)

In Cornelius *ap.* Eusebius, *H.E.* 6.43.6, there is a (temporarily)
Novatianizing Roman confessor called Celerinus. Should he be
kept distinct? Certainly Celerinus' attitudes here hardly square
with those professed later by Novatian. *H.E.* 6.43.6 refers to
events in the course of the following year, 251, and there may
well be confusion between Cornelius' Celerinus and the Macarius who appears in his stead in the *tituli* of *Epp.* 53 and 54
(written from and to these once pro-Novatian confessors; the
person may indeed have had the two names and was known by
either; cf. P. Nautin, *Lettres et écrivains chrétiens des II*ᵉ *et III*ᵉ
siècles (Paris 1961) 162 n. 1, and cf. nn. 21 and 25 below). On the
other hand, the redactors of the *Liber Pontificalis* appear to have
had a letter addressed by Cyprian to Pope Cornelius about our
future lector Celerinus: *scriptam epistulam . . . a Cypriano accepit
. . . et de Celerino lectore* (*Lib. Pontif.* 22, p. 29 ed. Mommsen), but
it is possible that this refers to *Ep.* 39 and is simply another case
of a confused incipit (see *Ep.* 18 n. 1), or that it is but a figment
drawn from the worthless *passio Cornelii.*

For further on Celerinus, see O. Ritschl, *Cyprian von Karthago
und die Verfassung der Kirche* (Göttingen 1885) 45 f.; Monceaux
Histoire 2.69 ff.; E. W. Benson, *Cyprian, His Life, His Times, His
Work* (London 1897) 69 ff.; J. Haussleiter in *Göttingische Gelehrte
Anzeigen* (1898) 350 ff.; my article in *Antichthon* 3 (1969) 63 ff.

Lucianus describes his present circumstances in Carthage
graphically, if ungrammatically, in *Ep.* 22. There is an alternative picture of his activities, provided by Cyprian for the information of Rome, in *Ep.* 27.1 ff. There, his blundering ignorance
and misunderstanding of the Sacred Scriptures (§1.1: *bene minus
dominica lectione fundatus;* §3.2: *circa intelligentiam dominicae lectionis . . . minus peritus*), his self-appointed leadership (§ 1.1 *se auctorem constituens*) and his arrogant and wholesale distribution
of certificates of forgiveness (§§1 ff.) come in for much indignant censure. We lose sight of Lucianus after *Ep.* 27; he held no
clerical rank (observe *Ep.* 23 *ad fin.*). G. Bardy, *Recherches sur
saint Lucien d'Antioche et son école* (Paris 1936) 49 n. 51, discusses
this Lucianus and the others of that name who occur in the
Cyprianic corpus.

2. *Domine frater.* To his old friend Celerinus employs a
respectful and honourable form of address (*Domine*), often given

to nobility as a courtesy title. It can be applied, for example, by Fronto in the course of the second century A.D., not only to the Emperor, but also to the eminent Arrius Antoninus (*mi domine, fili carissime,* Naber 192), to his son-in-law, the prominent Aufidius Victorinus (*domine,* Naber 179), and to the consular Squilla Gallicanus (*domine frater,* Naber 188). The frequency (six times all told) and the method of its employment throughout this epistle indicates that by it Celerinus is consciously honouring in complimentary terms the new Christian nobility, the revered witnesses of Christ. (Thus, earlier, the address of Perpetua's brother to his confessor sister, *Domina soror* [*Act. Perp.* 4.1]; cf. Perpetua's father in his entreaty to his daughter, *me iam non filiam nominabat sed dominam* [*Act. Perp.* 5.5]). We have here, therefore, a form of title destined to have a long and rich tradition in its application to the martyred dead. Cyprian (in exile after trial) is so addressed in *Ep.* 77.3.3 (*Domine frater*), it is probably used as a more general address in *Ep.* 79.1.2 (*dominum meum Eutychianum saluto*), and he uses it himself once in the new fragment, addressing confessors (*dominis meis fratribus;* cf. M. Bévenot, *Bulletin of the John Rylands Library* 28 (1944) 77.

The word has been the subject of much discussion. See H. A. M. Hoppenbrouwers, *Recherches sur la terminologie du martyre de Tertullien à Lactance* (Nijmegen 1961) 148 f.; H. H. Janssen, *Kultur und Sprache . . .* (Nijmegen 1938) 93; A. A. R. Bastiaensen, *La cérémonial épistolaire des chrétiens latins* (Nijmegen 1964) 23 f., 31 f., 39 f.; H. Delehaye in AB 53 (1935) 81 ff.; idem, *Sanctus. Essai sur le culte des saints dans l'antiquité* (Brussels 1927) 59 ff.; F. J. Dölger in AC 5 (1936) 211 ff.; DACL 4 (1920) 1386 f.; E. L. Hummel in SCA 9 (1946) 153 ff.

This title (Lucianus returns the compliment in *Ep.* 22.1.1) leads L. Nelke, *op. cit.* above, 17 n. 1, mistakenly to deduce "Celerinus gehörte einer Patricierfamilie an" and, in 18 n. 3, that Lucianus "war gleichfalls Patricier."

Celerinus in this opening greeting, manages to establish his desired tone—reverence mingled with that touch of reproach which will stimulate Lucianus to compensatory action.

3. *te pro nomine Domini nostri Iesu Christi salvatoris nostri*

tentum. There are two words here, *tentum* [variant reading: *tenitum*] and *salvator*, that Cyprian would not normally use.

For *tentum* his favoured phrase is *in carcere constitutus* (eg. *Epp.* 5.1.2, 12.1.1, 13.7, 14.2.2, etc.); cf. *adprehensus* (*Ep.* 56.1.1). However, in *Ep.* 59.2.4 he can write: *cum videamus ipsum Dominum a fratribus esse detentum.*

In the *Testimonia* Cyprian uses *salvator* (e.g., 2.7, CCL 3.38: *Deus . . . salvator generis humani*—but there he is alluding to Ps. 24.5 where Cyprian's text read *tu es Deus salvator meus*). Thereafter Cyprian avoids *salvator* (preferring *auctor salutis* or the like): see P. de Labriolle, *Mélanges en hommage à la mémoire de Fr. Martroye* (Paris 1941) 67 ff.; cf. C. Mohrmann, *Etudes sur le latin des chrétiens* (Rome 1965) 3.134 ff., esp. 139.

Among other linguistic usages in this letter uncharacteristic of Cyprian are *testis* (for *martyr:* see n. 29 below), the form *operae* (for *opera:* see n. 19), *mundus* (with reference to the future world: see n. 12), the use of *florida* (see n. 9), the use of *ibi . . . hic* (see n. 36); and on *cecidit,* (§2.1) see n. 21 to *Ep.*8.

4. *penes magistratus huius mundi confessum.* Lucianus describes his appearance before these officials himself as *apud pusilliores* in *Ep.* 22.1.1 (as opposed to the *metator antichristi*). They ought to include, at the least, the *quinque primores illi qui edicto nuper magistratibus fuerant copulati* (*Ep.* 43.3.1), who appear to have constituted the local panel which supervised the orders to sacrifice in Carthage. But the nature of his subsequent sufferings as detailed in *Ep.* 22 suggests that he has appeared there before the proconsul also. For some of his confreres in prison die as the result of their *quaestio;* one of these is in fact Mappalicus whose *quaestio,* conducted by the proconsul in person, has been outlined in *Ep.* 10. The case of Lucianus, we might conjecture, has by now been passed on by the minor officials to the proconsul himself. Compare my article in *Historia* 22 (1973) 652.

5. *ex eo quo te deduxi.* It was a standard courtesy to escort travellers down to the harbour and there to wait with them until favourable winds blew. I interpret this elliptical expression as referring to such a scene; cf. Augustine, *Conf.* 5.8.15 ([Monica] *usque ad mare secuta est*), and see D. Gorce, *Les voyages,*

l'hospitalité et le port des lettres dans le monde chrétien des IVe et Ve siècles (Paris 1925) 106 f.; O. Nussbaum in RAC 9 (1976) 915 f., 996. It would be reasonable to deduce that Lucianus had paid a visit to Rome (this would interlock with the evidence for his wide circle of acquaintances in Rome: see *Ep.* 22.3 and introductory note above). In view of the hiatus in communications since that conjectured visit, is it to be dated shortly before the outbreak of this persecution?

6. *Montanum fratrem communem abs te de carcere ad me esse venturum.* From this description Duquenne, *Chronologie des Lettres de s. Cyprien* ... (Brussels 1972) 122, concludes that Montanus was "un exile sans doute." That conclusion is, however, doubtful. Rome was specifically excluded as a venue for the legally banished (cf. *Historia* 22 [1973] 660), and had Montanus been honoured with the grace of confession, it would be out of keeping with the tone of this letter for that dignity to go unmentioned. Montanus can readily fit into the categories of prison-visitors (cf. *Ep.* 5 n. 7) and of Christians who can still travel at large undetected (cf. *Ep.* 8.2.2 and n. 18 thereto).

C. Saumagne, *Saint Cyprien. Évêque de Carthage. "Pape" d'Afrique (248–258)* (Paris 1975) 67 n. 1, is hopelessly confused at this point: "Le messager de Rome était un certain Montanus, libéré lui aussi de la prison de Rome et qui revenait librement dans sa patrie d'Afrique."

7. *maxime eis qui in confessione Christi sunt constituti.* It is a little difficult to assess what is precisely intended by this clause. Cyprian uses a parallel expression in *Ep.* 57.4.2 in the sense here translated (*in traditis adque in confessione nominis constitutis*—"in the case of those who have been given up and are in the course of confessing the Name"). But there is no room for doubt that Lucianus has already made some confessional stand (observe §§1.3, 2.1). Can Celerinus, therefore, be wanting to convey the sentiment "those who are *confirmed* in their confession of Christ"?

8. *ut tibi quoque de infimo tuus vel frater dicar, si fuero dignus Celerinus audire.* Celerinus wishes to argue persuasively from the position that though a fellow confessor he did not himself fail to keep remembering his old friends. But in his contorted efforts to

say this both with deference and without reproach (he is, after all, about to urge a request), he has managed to pen a clause which has troubled copyists and editors alike. I translate, as usual, Hartel's text, but not with any great sense of security. The general sense is, however, put beyond doubt by Lucianus' echo in the *incipit* of his reply (*si dignus fuero vocari collega*) and by his specific reference in *Ep.* 22.1.1: *scribens mihi diceres "si dignus fuero frater nominari tuus."* Celerinus appears to have been intrigued by the potency of names (see §3.2 and n. 25). Is it possible that he may be trying, fancifully, to allude here ("if I have proved worthy of my name of Celerinus") to his own swiftness (*celer*) in becoming a confessor (cf. *Ep.* 39.2.1: *inter Christi milites antesignanus;* the *celeres* were the historical precursors of the *equites*). Or he may even be alluding to the fact that his name of Celerinus was now celebrated by the martyr's death of his grandmother Celerina (cf. *Ep.* 39.3.1); Celerinus was now a name to have to live up to.

9. *cum essem et ego in tam florida confessione.* This ought to imply that Celerinus considers himself no longer to be in a confessional situation, that is to say, he is out of prison (see n. 1 above). For *florida,* cf. §§3.1 (*floridiorum ministerium,* where see n. 21), 4.2 (*de confessione tua florida*), and *Ep.* 10.5.2 and n. 34. It sounds as if this word was current parlance amongst this group, a variant for *gloriosus,* Cyprian's favoured epithet or the like.

10. *caritatem pristinam.* With this phrase Celerinus introduces his basic argument for being accorded special favour; for good measure he repeats the phrase twice, in §2. (It might be possible to interpret the Latin as meaning: "By my letters I reminded them that their old affection was still remembered by me and mine.").

11. *cruore illo laveris.* Signifying, of course, in the blood of martyrdom. Hartel's text proceeds to excise the following clause, *si prius passus fueris,* which appears to be a gloss explaining *ante . . . quam litterae meae te in hoc mundo adprehendant.* It is not in all mss.

12. *etsi in hoc mundo nos non viderimus, in futuro tamen nos. . . .* A. P. Orbán, *Les dénominations du monde chez les premiers auteurs chrétiens* (Nijmegen 1970) 225, 234, 236, refers to this passage as

the first recorded instance of *mundus* employed in the sense of "monde futur," "monde qui vient." By a slip, he imputes the usage to Cyprian (224). The novelty depends on the assumption that *mundo* is to be understood after *futuro*.

13. The tone is that of pious aspiration for martyrdom; Celerinus is presently out of the immediate running for his crown. See nn. 1 and 9 above.

14. *in morte sororis meae*. In Christian usage it is impossible to tell whether this person and the other in §2.2 are blood-sisters of Celerinus or rather sisters-in-Christ. However, his special solicitude and the use of *meae* here (not *nostrae*) strongly suggests some family tie. On the Christian usage of *soror*, see DACL 15 (1953) 1548 ff.

15. The Easter must be that of 250—the persecution was over before Easter of 251 (*Ep.* 43.1.2); X. S. Thaninayagam, *The Carthaginian Clergy during the Episcopate of Saint Cyprian* (Colombo 1947) 86, therefore puts these events in the wrong year. The date of Easter in 250 was April 7 (on the conputation of Easter dates, note DACL 13 (1938) 1521 ff., and Intro., p. 45 and n. 247). Celerinus did not break the customary Paschal fast (for evidence of this as an early practice, see Irenaeus *ap.* Eusebius, *H.E.* 5.24.12f.) *in die laetitiae Paschae* after which even Tertullian describes, *quinquaginta exinde diebus in omni exultatione decurrimus* (*De ieiun.* 14.2, and on the evidence provided by Tertullian for Easter practices generally, see H. Koch in *Zeitschrift für wissenschaftliche Theologie* 55 (1914) 289 ff.). Even those unable by circumstances to prepare for Easter with the fast are to delay making their fast until the fifty days of celebration are over (see Hippolytus, *Trad. Apost.* 33); during this period, it was later decreed by the Council of Nicaea, can. 20, the (penitential) position of kneeling was prohibited—prayers were to be made standing (a practice already evidenced in Tertullian, *De orat.* 23; cf. *De coron.* 3.4). By sharp contrast with Church custom, Celerinus has continued *in cilicio et cinere lacrimabundus*, a description frequent in Scripture as well as in contemporary church writers, for penitential grief. See RAC 1 (1950) 725 ff.; RAC 2 (1954) 812 ff.; DACL 2 (1910) 3037 ff., and 3 (1914) 1623 ff.

16. *per te vel per eos dominos meos qui coronati fuerint, a quibus postulaturus es.* Observe the confidence placed in the intercessory influence of a confessor's prayers and the reliance placed on the efficacy of the martyrs' powers; cf. n. 14 to *Ep.* 6, and n. 1 to *Ep.* 15.

17. *auxilium Domini nostri Iesu Christi et pietas ... subvenerit tam nefando naufragio.* On *subvenio,* cf. n. 25 to *Ep.* 8, and on the (frequent) nautical imagery see n. 13 to *Ep.* 17, adding M. Guarducci in *Hommages Renard* (1969) 2.322 ff.

On *pietas,* in the developed sense of "pity" (= *misercordia*), see H. Pétré, *Caritas. Étude sur le vocabulaire latin de la charité chrétienne* (Louvain 1948) 251 ff. Though the word is occasionally to be found with this sense in secular Latin (e.g., Suetonius, *Dom.* 11.3), this usage is characteristic of "Christian Latin." For Cyprianic examples, see *De dom. orat.* 26, 30; *Ep.* 54.3.3; and compare Cyprian's parallel use of *pius* in, e.g., *Ep.* 55.29.1: *ille misericors et pius est.*

18. *pro sorore nostra (v.l. sorores nostras)***quas et tu bene nosti, id est, Numeriam et Candidam.* Hartel conjectures a lacuna, probably unnecessarily. It is clear at any rate that Lucianus was acquainted with Celerinus' "sisters" and that Celerinus wishes to exploit any obligation he can derive from that fact.

19. *operas quas penes collegas nostros fecerunt extorres qui a vobis venerunt.* For further details on these refugees, see §4.1. The word *collegae* tells us that they are confessors (*confessores* in §4.1), but we cannot deduce from the (inexplicit) *extorres* that they have been *legally* banished (cf. n. 6 above) to Rome. Texts which demonstrate that relegation specifically excluded Rome as a place of residence include Suetonius, *Claud.* 23.2; *Dig.* 48.22.7.15 (Ulpian), 48.22.18(19) (Callistratus), cf. 3.2.2.4 (Ulpian), 27.1.8.9 (Modestinus). It does not take too much imagination to visualize a Roman magistrate on giving release to these confessors also telling them to make themselves scarce.

The use of the form *operas* appears to be idiosyncratic in the sense of "charitable works"; cf. H. H. Janssen, *Kultur und Sprache* ... (Nijmegen 1938) 223 n. 5; Watson 278.

Cyprian was himself prepared to concede that such hospitality constituted mitigating circumstances, see *Ep.* 55.13.2 (*fratres etiam plurimos qui extorres et profugi recedebant, in sua tecta et hospitia recepit*) and cf. n. 3 to *Ep.* 23.

20. *Christum eis vobis martyribus suis petentibus indulturum credo.* With shrewd flattery Celerinus now includes Lucianus himself among the privileged *martyres* (contrast n. 16 above).

21. *te floridiorum ministerium percepisse.* Celerinus wishes to elicit from Lucianus agreement to put his petition before his fellow confessors. Accordingly he is described not merely as one of these hallowed *floridii*, he is actually the leader of that holy company; and for "leader," Celerinus uses, appropriately, a word (*ministerium*) by now endowed with sacral associations (cf. *antistes* in n. 24 below). Less flatteringly, Cyprian styles him as the self-appointed *auctor* of this society of confessors (*Ep.* 27.1.1). The signature to *Ep.* 23 demonstrates Lucianus' dominance of the group. Did Lucianus perhaps owe that superiority in part to his ability to read and write (cf. *Epp.* 15 n. 30, 27.1.2)?

On *floridii* cf. n. 9 above. The word appears to be used here very much in the manner of a *signum* or club-name, that is to say, an auspicious soubriquet not infrequently adopted by sodalities in this period—these confessors form a special fraternity (though this word is not attested in our evidence as a formal *signum*). No such club-name is indubitably in the comparative, so the group name *floridiores* is unlikely; formations in *-ius* are commonly found in this use, e.g., *innocentius* (on which see *Antichthon* 1 (1967), 45 ff. with other examples at 47 n. 19). For further on *signa*, see H. Wuilleumier, *Mémoires présentés par divers savants à l'Académie de l'Institut de France* 13.2 (1933) 559 ff.; I. Kajanto, *Supernomina: a Study in Latin Epigraphy* (Helsinki 1967), and *Onomastic Studies in the Early Christian Inscriptions of Rome and Carthage* (Helsinki 1963); P. R. C. Weaver in *Antichthon* 5 (1971) 77 ff.; and see n. 25 below and comment on n. 1 to *Ep.* 66.

22. *vel in terra dormiens.* This appears to be used as a proverbial phrase, otherwise *terra* is an odd way of alluding to a hard prison floor. I cannot, however, find a clear parallel; there may perhaps be some allusion to Gen. 28.13 (Jacob, sleeping on the ground, receives his heart's desire after his vision of the ladder):

terram in qua dormis tibi. ... dabo. Can the intended meaning perhaps be "the hopes which you have always yearned for, even in your dreams (= when sleeping upon the ground)"?

I suspect error in the phrase *in terra* (cf. *Ep.* 31.3.1 where some mss read *in terris,* but the correct reading is most probably *interritum*). However, a possible meaning for *in terra* is "within the ground" (= underground, in a dungeon), with *dormiens* used in the common Christian sense of "dying," yielding at last the adequate, but not immediately obvious, sense, "even though you lie dying underground."

23. Ps. 19.5, a passage not used by Cyprian.

24. *Et nunc super ipsos factus antistes Dei recognovit † idem minister.* Despite uncertainties over the reading, this appears to express a variant of the sentiment with which this section began (see n. 21 above), repeated for good measure before Celerinus actually puts his request. *Antistes* (here glossed as *minister*) is an already acceptable Christian word, being the etymological equivalent of Justin's προεστώς (1 *Apol.* 67 MG 6.429); it is much employed by Tertullian (J. H. Waszink in VC 8 [1954] 129 f.). Cyprian can use it as an equivalent of *sacerdos* (see, e.g., *Ep.* 59.18.3). Cf. V. Saxer, *Vie liturgique et quotidienne à Carthage vers le milieu du IIIe siècle* (Vatican 1969) 85; H. H. Janssen, *op cit.* in n. 19 above, 90; Watson 258 f. Like the word *minister,* *antistes* can also be used in a more general sense (= "patron," "protector," etc.); for discussion, cf. P. Testini in *Rivista di archeologia cristiana* 36 (1960) 141 ff.

On the text, see Watson 260 n. 1. *Recognovit,* rightly obelized by Hartel, has the textual variant, *recognovi*—perhaps introduced into the text from a scribe's marginal gloss? To be on the safe side I have done my best to translate *recognovi* as a parenthesis. The readings of ms T in fact render tolerable sense: *Et nunc super ipsos factus antestites [=antistes es?] Dei [recognovi], id est minister.*

The obscure text may conceal some passing allusion to the Vision of the Seven Seals and in particular Apoc. 5.10, where Cyprian's text read: *et eos regnum Deo nostro sacerdotesque fecisti et regnabunt super terram (Test.* 2.15).

25. *nam hanc ipsam Etecusam semper appellavi ... quia pro se*

dona numeravit ne sacrificaret. The *incipit* (repeated in the *explicit* of ms T) reads *Numeria ut dicit praemium dedit ne sacrificaret.* That is to say, it was understood by the composer of the *incipit* that this sentence refers to *Numeria;* Candida will be the other sister who actually sacrificed (§2.1). In this case, Celerinus appears to be alluding to the common name by which "Etecusa" was known, viz. Numeria, and he is demonstrating how the power of that name (*Numeria*) prevented her from doing worse than bribing (*numeravit*) her way out of full apostasy. One might compare the elaborate explanation of the names of the martyrs Agape, Irene, and Chione in their *Acta* (c. 2); or the grim comment on the epitaph of the person who had been given—in vain—the hopeful *signum* of Viventius: *qui et Viventi vano signo cognominatus* (CIL 13.11205 [Lyons]). Such additional names are very common in this period; to the references in n. 21 above, add J.-J. Hatt, *La tombe gallo-romaine. Recherches sur les inscriptions et les monuments funéraires gallo-romains des trois premiers siècles de notre ère* (Paris 1951) 43 ff., 251 ff.

Etecusa is otherwise unattested as a personal name. There have been accordingly many emendations and suggestions, among others being Aëcusa (= ἀεκοῦσα), Pesousa (= πεσοῦσα), Tecusa (= τεκοῦσα), etc.

The problem is rather more complicated; for in the new epistolary fragment (M. Bévenot, in *Bulletin of the John Rylands Library* 28 (1944) 78, ll. 21 ff.), Cyprian sends greetings to *sorores nostras (benedictas) Metucosam et Valeriam quas vobiscum in cursu et stadio sanctitatis deus custodiat.* The strange Metucosa may possibly be related to our Etecusa (especially with *ipsam* being the preceding word); if so, Valeria and Numeria will have to be identified (the one being an alias of the other, retaining the same scansion and ending of the original?). It would have to follow that it is Metucosa/Candida (now separated from Numeria/Valeria) who in fact paid the bribes; she shares still (μετέχουσα) in some way in the Christian communion (so suggests Bévenot, *art. cit.,* 80). This argument would bear the consequence that the new letter is post-Decian in setting. A Valerianic date is not, in fact, improbable.

At all events and whatever the reading (*se dona* is an emendation of Morelius), we are most reasonably to suppose that this second sister purchased her *libellus* and thereby became a *libellatica*. It is possible of course that in some other way she simply bought immunity from the officials but her action was such that she has incurred exclusion from communion (cf. Tertullian, *De fuga* 12 ff., on this general topic of avoiding the effects of persecution by means of bribery).

J. Haussleiter, in *Archiv für lateinische Lexikographie und Grammatik* 11 (1900) 86, suggests, not very plausibly, the reading, *quia pro se D vota numeravit,* in order to keep closer to the garbled manuscript reading, *pro sedunta.*

26. The Three Fates were statues of Clotho, Lachesis, and Nemesis that stood on the north side of the Rostra, close to the Curia (Senate House). They were, according to Pliny the Elder, among the oldest pieces of statuary erected in Rome, all three of them being subsequently restored (cf. *N.H.* 34.11.22). Several later documents allude to *Tria Fata* as that area of the forum about the Curia. See PWK 6.2 (1909) 2050 f. The *Acta Tryphonis* 4 f. purport to describe the sacrificial scene in Rome at this time (text in P. Franchi de'Cavalieri, *Studi e Testi* 19 [1908] 54 ff., and, for comment, 29 ff. and *ibid.* 22 [1909] 75 ff.).

27. *praepositi.* See n. 9 to *Ep.* 8 on the use of this word.

28. *donec episcopus constituatur.* On the *interregnum* after the death of Pope Fabian, see n. 9 to *Ep.* 8. And compare the decision taken not much later in Rome on similar cases in *Ep.* 30.8: *ante constitutionem episcopi nihil innovandum putavimus;* those whose cases can wait should remain *in suspenso, dum episcopus dari a Deo nobis sustinetur.* We are dealing manifestly with a hierarchically-minded church.

29. *estis amici sed et testes Christi qui omnia indulgeatis.* Observe *testis* for *martyr,* a usage not found in Cyprian himself though he is prepared to play on the word *martyr* (the Greek equivalent of *testis*), e.g., *Ad Fort.* 11: *martyres enim qui . . . testantur; Ep.* 58.4.2: *sufficit ad testimonium martyrii sui testis ille qui probat martyras.* Pontius appears to use *testis* in the opening words of his *Vita* for contrived verbal effects: *Cyprianus religiosus antistes et testis Dei gloriosus.*

The grammatical construing of this sentence defeats me; I can only hope that I have caught the sense.

30. Not unadroitly Celerinus slips from the second person singular (*fratribus tuis*) to the second person plural (*a vobis auxilium recipiant*), neatly working on the assumption that his request has met with success.

31. *Statium et Severianum et omnes confessores qui inde huc a vobis venerunt.* Note the presence of African confessors who have been released and have fled to Rome (cf. n. 19 above). Being no longer likely to win a martyr's crown themselves, they join the confessor Celerinus in placing his petition before these would-be *martyrs*. It is their imminent death which puts them in their special class.

32. *in urbem levaverunt:* an unusual turn of phrase ("took up to the city"), but this is what it must mean. Compare *Act. Cyp.* 2.3: *in curriculum eum levaverunt.*

33. *sunt enim penes illas omnes.* This could well mean that all sixty-five are actually staying with them in their dwelling-place. The rather haphazard train of thought doesn't allow us to deduce with any certainty that all the refugees were also all confessors. Were they perhaps one boat-load?

H. Gülzow, *Cyprian und Novatian* ... (Tübingen 1975) 55 f., interprets the text, attractively but without adequate warrant, to mean that the sisters have been ministering to the refugees for 65 days.

34. *laetatur de confessione tua florida sed et omnium fratrum.* Cf. nn. 9 and 21 above.

35. *luctatus est cum diabolo.* For abundant parallels of this very common motif in martyrdom contexts, the devil being conceived as the ultimate source and active agent of persecution, cf. *Epp.* 8 n. 6, 25.1.1, 38.1.2 (*adversarius*), 39.2.2, 60.2.2, 66.4.1, etc. See also F. J. Dölger in AC 3 (1932) 177 ff.; V. C. Pfitzner, *Paul and the Agon Motif* (Leiden 1967) 201; E. L. Hummel in SCA 9 (1946) 73 ff.; H. F. von Campenhausen, *Die Idee des Martyriums in der alten Kirche* (2nd ed., Göttingen 1964) 156 f.; M. L. Ricci, *Topica pagana e topica cristiana negli "Acta Martyrum"* (Florence 1964) 48 ff.

36. Celerinus by this (for him) unusually elaborate and carefully patterned sentence is seeking to arrest Lucianus' attention;

one of his former colleagues who went so far with him towards martyrdom is now also pressing this suit.

From this passage we deduce that Saturninus was tortured in Carthage (*ibi*) after confession (Lucianus calls him *collega meus* in *Ep.* 22.3.1) but that he is now in Rome (*hic*); and the fact that he joins in the petition should indicate that he is at large like the other confessors. He provides yet another instance of the release of an obstinate recusant. Note that in his case it is release *after torture;* not common, but Celerinus himself (in Rome) and Aurelius (in Carthage, *Ep.* 38.1.2) present not dissimilar cases. He cannot have been in Rome too long if tortures were not introduced in Carthage until the month of April (see *Ep.* 10).

There is, however, a problem of identity with the Saturninus of *Ep.* 27.1.1, 4, a Carthaginian confessor who remained in prison *post tormenta*, but who is no longer there at the time of writing; he headed the list of addressees of a letter from the Roman confessors which exhorted them to strict adherence to Church discipline in opposition to illicit petitions (*Epp.* 27.4, 28.2.1, 30.4). So far as I can detect, chronology does not prevent identification and all the relevant facts interlock, but the name Saturninus (above all in Africa, see CIL 8, suppl. 5 index, 112 f.) is extremely common. For further discussion, see my article in *Historia* 22 (1973) 659 ff. (especially against the thesis of Saumagne that he was recalled from Rome for a second trial in Carthage). See L. Nelke, *Die Chronologie der Korrespondenz Cyprians* . . . (diss. Thorn 1902) 18 f., n. 7, 42; A. Ferrua in *Civiltà Cattolica* (1939) 436 ff. (implausibly suggesting identification with the martyr Saturninus in Damasus, *Epig.* 45 and 46).

For *ibi* . . . . *hic* Cyprian would normally have written *illic* . . . .*istic* (cf., e.g., *Epp.* 45.4.2, 51.2.1, 60.1.2).

37. *fratres tui Calpurnius et Maria.* The use of the masculine (*fratres*) as a collective in a mixed set is regular; for other parallels, cf. A. A. R. Bastiaensen, *Le cérémonial épistolaire des chrétiens latins* (Nijmegen 1964) 21.

38. *quas peto illis eas legere digneris.* For parallel and comment, cf. *Ep.* 15.4 and n. 30 thereto. The clause is suggestive of Lucianus' role as *minister* and *antistes.* Hartel reports one manuscript (codex Vindobon. 798 saec. xv) as adding *valere te oro et*

mei semper memoriam facere, "I ask that you fare well and be ever mindful of me."

LETTER 22

Contents: Overjoyed as he is to receive the letter from Celerinus and the undeserved flattery it contains, Lucianus is downcast by its news about their fallen sisters. But he can assure Celerinus that he has a personal injunction from the martyr Paulus to grant peace on his behalf, and all of his fellow confessors, prompted by this behest and the emperor's directive to starve them to death, have agreed to grant universal reconciliation. And in their company there are already seventeen martyred dead, to which he will shortly be added. He asks accordingly that they and any fellow sisters dear to him may receive peace when the persecution is over, after their case is heard before a bishop and they have made confession of their sin. Greetings are returned by all his colleagues to their fellow confessors and brethren, but he is too weary to write all of their individual names.

Date and circumstances: On the date, see introductory note to *Ep.* 21.

The glimpse we catch of the prison conditions for the confessors in Carthage is indeed vividly moving; and the incoherent vagueness of Lucianus' account of what has been happening to them only serves to add a touch of poignant realism. The information certainly suggests the confessors are being put under intense pressure to comply, and the apparent stop-go technique of punishments and privations would naturally fit into such a context. They are not legal penalties; there are easier Roman ways of punishing those who have actualy been condemned (for the general legal theory—not always honoured in practice—that imprisonment was merely detentive, not punitive, see Ulpian, *Dig.* 48.19.8.9). E. W. Benson, *Cyprian, His Life, His Times, His Work* (London 1897) 75, is unlikely to be right in his claim "The edict prescribed ... imprisonment with starvation as penalties." Rather we are observers of the sequel to the decision to step up measures to induce apostasy as seen in *Ep.* 10.1.1; on this aspect, see my article in *Latomus* 31 (1972) 1053 ff. (noting the correctives of T. D. Barnes in JTS 25 (1974) 110 ff.). Their sufferings are paralleled by the experience of the Roman confessors, who endured at least twelve months of imprisonment (*Ep.* 37.2), broken by bouts of interrogation, etc. Cf. my article in *Historia* 22 (1973) 654. On the general question of imprisonment as punishment, consult RAC 9 (1976) 322 ff., 330 f., with bibliography 344 f.; PWK 8A.2 (1958) 2198 ff.

It is clear that the surviving confessors are convinced that death, and martyrdom, is for them inevitable. We now have a realistic setting for the issuing by these near-martyrs of their universal certificate of forgiveness (*Ep.* 23) in advance of any episcopal hearing. For indignant commentary on Lucianus' course of action, see *Ep.* 27.1 ff. Lucianus' justification by appeal to the dying request of the blessed martyr Paulus (§2.1) provides further incidental evidence of the prestige with which the martyr was popularly honoured. Cyprian grimly contrasts threatening monitions uttered by the blessed apostle Paul (*Ep.* 27.3.3).

Ep. 22 is further discussed by H. Gülzow, *Cyprian und Novatian . . .* (Tübingen 1975) 56 ff. A critical edition is supplied by A. Miodoński (1889) 121 ff.

1. *Celerino domino si dignus fuero vocari collega in Christo s.* On *domino,* see n. 2 to *Ep.* 21. On the clause, *si dignus fuero vocari collega* (which echoes *Ep.* 21.1.2), see n. 8 to *Ep.* 21. It is a little doubtful whether the phrase *in Christo* should be construed with *collega* or with *s(alutem mittit)*; most parallels (cf., e.g., *Epp.* 10, 77, 78, 79 *init.*) suggests the latter.

2. For the interval in communication, see *Ep.* 21.1.1 (and n.5 thereto.).

3. *si dignus fuero frater nominari tuus.* A paraphrase of *Ep.* 21.1.2.

4. *apud pusilliores.* See n. 4 to *Ep.* 21, where they are described as *magistratus huius saeculi.*

5. *ipsum anguem maiorem, metatorem antichristi . . . deterruisti.* For the apocalyptic interpretation of the persecution, cf. Diony-

sius of Alexandria *ap.* Eusebius, *H.E.* 6.41.10: "And what is more, the edict arrived, and it was almost like that which was predicted by our Lord, well nigh the most terrible of all, so as, if possible, to cause to stumble even the elect." But to what precisely does Lucianus refer? Does he imagine his own trial being held before lesser demons (*pusilliores*), whereas Celerinus' was a struggle with the Devil himself? Cyprian's language in *Ep.* 39.2.1 may be thought to be equivocal on this point, though elsewhere Cyprian firmly attributes responsibility for the persecution to the emperor Decius himself (*Ep.* 55.9.1: *cum tyrannus infestus . . . fanda adque infanda comminaretur*). But it is hard to resist the concluson that *apud pusilliores*, being a gloss on *penes magistratus huius saeculi*, most naturally refers to legal magistrates and therefore, by corollary, so does the parallel *metator antichristi*. By it Lucianus is referring to the devil's henchman, the Emperor himself, the *execrabile animal* of Lactantius, *De mort. persecut.* 4.1 (cf. n. 6 to *Ep.* 8) before whom Celerinus defiantly appeared on trial. (Prudentius, *Peristeph.* 6.23 f., makes Fructuosus refer to his persecutor, the governor Aemilianus, as *cruentus . . . coluber.*) One might compare the treatment of the persecuting (Arian) Emperor Constantius at the pen of Lucifer of Cagliari a little over a century later. He is not only a viper, a serpent (ML 13.916, 917, 930, 931), but he is also, on at least a dozen occasions, *praecursor antichristi* and there are further variations. For a full catalogue of these terms of polemic, see I. Opelt in VC 26 (1972) 205 ff. And Nero the persecutor figures already in Lactantius, *De mort. persecut.* 2.8 as *praecursor diaboli ac praevius.*

So interpret, among others, J. A. F. Gregg, *The Decian Persecution* (Edinburgh and London, 1897) 103; B. Aubé, *L'église et l'état dans la seconde moitié du IIIe siècle (249–284)* Paris (1886) 51; P. Franchi de' Cavalieri in *Studi e Testi* 19 (1908) 40, and 33 (1920) 187 n. 2; G. Alföldy in *Historia* 22 (1973) 484 f.; etc. On this question and its implications, see my article in *Antichthon* 3 (1969) 63 ff. On *metator*, see n. 33 to Ep. 6.

As a footnote one might draw attention to the Latin apocalyptic fragment (Codex Treverensis 36) on the *signa Antichristi*, published by M.R. James in *Texts and Studies* 2.3 (1893) 153 f.

The fragment concludes with the words: *haec autem omnia ante ventum antichristi erunt. Dexius erit nomen antichristi.* Can *Dexius* possibly = Decius?

By contrast with his reactions during the Principate of Gallus, when talk of the advent of Antichrist becomes obsessive and strident, there is remarkably little millennial foreboding in Cyprian's own writings under the Decian persecution. Perhaps the only exception may be *Ad Fort., praef.* 1 (*in fine adque in consummatione mundi antichristi tempus infestum adpropinquare iam coepit*) and *praef.* 2 (*sex milia annorum iam paene conplentur ex quo hominem diabolus inpugnat*), but that depends on the (controversial) dating of *Ad Fort.;* it could indeed date to the period of plague and fears under Gallus (cf., e.g., G. Alföldy, *art. cit.* above, 486 f., n. 39) or even later, but a Decian date is still not unreasonable (observe the essentially Decian detail in *Ad Fort.* 11; for further discussion, see H. Koch, *Cyprianische Untersuchungen* [Bonn 1926] 149 ff.). For the theme of Antichrist generally in Cyprian, see A. D'Alès, *La théologie de s. Cyprien* (Paris 1922) 77 ff.; E. L. Hummel in SCA 9 (1946) 75 ff.; and in his works during the principate of Gallus in particular, see my article, "Persecution under Gallus," in *Aufstieg und Niedergang der römischen Welt* 11.27.

On the symbolism of the serpent in the patristic period, note the study by A. Quacquarelli, *Il leone e il drago nella simbolica dell'età patristica* (Bari 1975).

6. *vocibus illis et verbis deificis.* On this theme, see n. 19 to *Ep.* 10. On the epithet *deificus* (rare in Cyprian), see Watson 244 f.; L. Bayard, *Le latin de saint Cyprien* (Paris 1902) 41 n. 1.

7. This is the best I can make of Hartel's (obelized) text—and Lucianus' anacoluthic style. Lucianus can vary between singular and plural for the second person throughout the letter; he appears to do so within the same sentence here (*amatores fidei . . . vicisti*) For parallels, see ACW 39.189 n. 63 on Minucius Felix, *Oct.* 6.1; L. Bayard in *Revue de philologie* 38 (1914) 207 ff. considers the text here and (not unreasonably) suggests drastic surgery (reading *te . . . versato* for Hartel's *te . . . versari,* and interpreting *novi vivacitate* as meaning "with the enthusiasm of a neophyte"). Once again a close adherence to ms T and its

derivates would produce tolerable sense without excessive strain.

8. *iam inter martyres deputande.* Observe the (consciously) honorific use of *martyr.* Cf. n. 1 to *Ep.* 15.

9. *voluisti nos litteris tuis gravare.* If there is a specific reference, it is probably to *Ep.* 21.2.1 (*peto ut . . . mecum doleas*).

10. *cum benedictus martyr Paulus adhuc in corpore esset.* Paulus is further mentioned in *Ep.* 27 (cf. *Ep.* 35.1.1) where Cyprian is careful to put blame on the (living) confessor Lucianus, leaving this martyred Paulus unassailed by any direct attack. Do we deduce from the wording in §2.2 (*Paulus a quaestione,* as opposed to *Mappalici in quaestione*) that Paulus died in prison as a consequence of his interrogation (and tortures), or rather does he die in prison of starvation (with the thirteen others) after having previously been submitted to interrogation? As it is put succinctly in the commentary of Pearson and Fell, *verisimile videtur alterum inter tormenta, alterum post tormenta mortuum.* Lucianus, not without some art, may be here alluding to words of the apostle Paul in 2 Cor. 12.2 and 4 on being caught up into paradise.

On *benedictus,* normally eschewed by Cyprian, see n. 3 to *Ep.* 8.

11. *post arcessitionem meam.* On the euphemism (used both by Cyprian, e.g., *de mort.* 3, 18, 19, 20, 24, and his biographer, Pontius, *Vit. Cyp.* 4.3) see Watson 283; H. Koch, *Cyprianische Untersuchungen* (Bonn 1926) 171, 180. Lucianus repeats the usage in the next sentence (*quos Dominus. . . . arcessire dignatus est*).

12. *universi litteras ex compacto universis pacem dimisimus.* Lucianus is endeavouring to impress emphatically that there is universal agreement among the martyrs (note the conviction that death is certain) about granting universal reconciliation. *Ep.* 23, here being referred to, repeats the emphasis (*universi confessores. . . . nos universos*). Cyprian goes to some pains in *Ep.* 27.1.1 to point out that Mappalicus issued two specific certificates only and the confessor Saturninus none at all. Has Lucianus therefore been less than candid about the unanimity among the confessors, or does the united action rather date to a period after Mappalicus' death and Saturninus' release?

13. *cum iussi sumus secundum praeceptum imperatoris fame et siti necari.* The perception of Lucianus is of some significance, whether it is accurate or not; he understood the persecution to be emanating from the emperor himself (cf. n. 5 above). If it is accurate, and they were told what was to happen to them by the proconsul after an intransigent appearance before his tribunal, it would tell us much about the personal involvement of the emperor in the success of his edict: on his orders the hopelessly obstinate are now to be starved into submission (see introductory note to this letter). This is further discussed in my article in *Latomus* 31 (1972) 1055 f.

14. *ita ut † non efficiebat fame et siti.* The translation is a sheer guess at the sense which may be intended. Despite deaths, the treatment has won no apostates. For a parallel, see *Acta Mont. et Luc.* 6.5: *diabolus . . . fame nos et siti temptare molitus et hoc suum proelium multis diebus fortissime gessit ita ut . . . aegrorum copia . . . laboraret.*

15. *sed et ignis ab opere pressurae nostrae tam intolerabilis erat. . . .* I have interpreted *pressura* literally as "overcrowding" (cf. Watson 289) and *ignis* figuratively in the sense of "burning heat" (cf., e.g., Ovid, *Met.* 7.556: *igni aspera lingua tumet;* Statius, *Theb.* 9.748: *sacri facies rubet igne veneni*). For stifling heat combined with an intolerable press of people in the airless dungeons there is an exact parallel in *Act. Perp.* 3.6: *aestus validus turbarum beneficio;* cf. Tertullian, *Apol.* 44.3: *de vestris semper aestuat carcer;* and some of the martyrs at Lyons appear to perish in their prison because of such suffocating conditions *ap.* Eusebius, *H.E.* 5.1.27: ὥστε ἀποπνιγῆναι τοὺς πλείστους ἐν τῇ εἰρκτῇ. On prison conditions generally, see also n. 7 to *Ep.* 5.

It may be possible, however, that Lucianus wishes to refer to actual tortures and that *ignis* is to be taken literally (with *pressura* meaning, as often, figuratively, "suffering"?). For fire used as a method of torturing during this persecution, note the general observation in *De laps.* 13: *nunc flamma torreret* (in a catalogue of torments), and the particular case of the martyrs Castus and Aemilius who died whilst being tortured by fire (*De laps.* 13).

Observe that in Matt. 25.46 the Greek κόλασις was translated in Cyprian's version as *ambustio* (cf. Fahey 324); other early texts read *ignis* as well. See H. von Soden, in TU 23 (1909) 341.

16. *sed nunc in ipsam claritatem sumus constituti.* One despairs of a coherent timetable for the martyrs' ordeals—for in the next section Lucianus declares that they have now been shut up again (*iterato reclusi sumus*). Can he be wanting to say here, "But after that (*nunc* = at that time, then?), we were brought up into the open air"?

The Theodosian Code 9.3.1, recording a Constantinian regulation of 320 (on holding an accused in prison pending completion of a trial), instructively illustrates the variable prison quarters available which these martyrs experience: ".... Meanwhile the man who has been produced in court shall not be put in manacles of iron that cleave to the bones, but in looser chains, so that there may be no torture and yet the custody may remain secure. When incarcerated he must not suffer the darkness of an inner prison (*sedis intimae tenebras*), but he must be kept in good health by enjoyment of light (*usurpata luce vegetari*), and when night doubles the necessity for his guard, he shall be taken back into the vestibules of the prisons and into healthful places (*salubribus locis recipi*). When day returns, at early sunrise, he shall forthwith be led out into the common light of day (*ad publicum lumen educi*) that he may not perish from the torments of prison, a fate which is considered pitiable for the innocent but not serious enough the for the guilty" (trans. C. Pharr). See also n. 7 to *Ep.* 5.

17. The text has a lacuna; the supplement appears to be the intended sense.

18. *Bassi in petrario: Petrario* ("quarry") is Rigaltius' conjecture adopted by Hartel, whereas ms T reads the ἁ.λ. *pignerario* = (?) "debtor's prison," cf. πρακτόρειον Rigaltius' conjecture would imply Bassus had been condemned thither; but as the remainder of his comrades do not appear yet to have undergone sentence (cf. introductory note), it would have been prudent to retain here the (unusual) manuscript reading. Was there an overflow of Christian prisoners into the *pignerarium* from the *carcer publicus?* If the list of martyrs is given in chronological sequence—a bit too much to anticipate under the circumstances—Bassus (and Fortunio) may constitute the martyred

companions of Mappalicus referred to in *Ep.* 10; the deaths of all the remainder appear to date to the subsequent period of prolonged hunger (cf. n. 10 above).

DACL 6 (1925) 2275–77 records the description of an intriguing underground chapel on the southeastern slopes of the "Byrsa" excavated by Dellatre in 1895 (now no longer visible). It was reached by a long narrow corridor which opened out into a room 5.50 × 3.80 metres, decorated on the back wall with a fresco which could represent a bishop in the act of benediction. Was this a *pignerarium*-type dungeon sanctified by the presence of Christians who once there awaited their trials that led to death and martyrdom? It is unlikely to have been a funerary chapel given its situation in the city; there are no traces of burials. See W. H. C. Frend in *Excavations at Carthage 1976 Conducted by the University of Michigan* (Ann Arbor 1977) 3.39; N. Duval in *Mél. école franç. de Rome* 84 (1972) 1122.

19. On Mappalicus, see introductory note and n. 20 to *Ep.* 10.

20. H. Leclercq in DACL 10 (1932) 2537 avers that here "nous lisons une série de martyrs dont on ne retrouve aucune trace dans l'hiéronymien"; cf. C. Saumagne, *Saint Cyprien. Évêque de Carthage. "Pape" d'Afrique (248–258)* (Paris 1975) 63 n. 2: "Le martyrologe d'Afrique et le *Martyrologion hieronymianum* ... n'ont gardé le souvenir que de Mappalicus." There is room to wonder whether this claim is absolutely correct, for the Hieronymian Calendar for *xiii Kal. Mart.* (AA.SS. nov., vol. 2, pars posterior, 102 f. [Delehaye]) includes the names Donatus, Furtunio (cf. Fortunio), Iulia, Victor, Venustina (cf. Venustus), Cetula (cf. Credula); for *xii Kal. Mart.* (104), Paulus, Marcialis, Fructulus (cf. Fructus); for *ix Kal. Mart.* (107), Victurinus (cf. Victorinus), Mappalicus, Fortunatus (cf. Fortunata). Is it conceivable that there in fact survive in the Calendar, spread over these three days, garbled remnants of the names listed by Lucianus? There they have found a place clustering close to an anniversary date of their most celebrated member, Mappalicus of *Ep.* 10. The names of Mappalicus' companions do not figure in the (sixth century) Carthaginian Calendar; cf. H. Delehaye, *Les origines du culte des martyrs* [2nd ed., Brussels 1933] 380.

21. *ante dies octo per dies quinque medios.* Lucianus seems to

employ an idiomatic use of *medius*; cf. Fronto, van den Hout p. 12.5: *duo menses exacti sunt idibus proximis et dies medii isti aliquot* ("... and since then several days have gone by"). A certain interpretation does not seem possible.

22. *modicum panis accepimus et aquam ad mensuram.* That is to say, they have been given nothing since; they have been returned to their starvation diet (*fame et siti necari*). It sounds like treatment calculated to breed second thoughts—and apostasy. The survivors of this regimen would include the signatories of *Ep.* 23. Lucianus is still alive when Cyprian writes *Ep.* 27; he fades from our sight thereafter.

For the diet, compare the *solo fiscalis* and the *aqua frigida* of *Act. Mont. et Luc.* 6.5.

23. *peto ut sicut hic.* Thus Hartel's text, although he does remark rightly, but unhelpfully, in his *apparatus,* "sicut hic *corruptum.*"

24. *non tantum hae sed et quas scis ad animum nostrum pertinere:* Of course Lucianus has already issued *Ep.* 23 (see n. 12 above)— *pax* for everyone, not just for sisters, who present their case to the bishop. As in *Ep.* 23, Lucianus arrogates to himself hierarchical parlance: "as we have decided" translates *secundum ... nostrum tractatum. Tracto* and its derivatives are favourites of Cyprian's to describe the sacerdotal teaching and decision-making role. Cf. C. Mohrmann, *Études sur le latin des chrétiens* (Rome 1961) 2.70 f.; Watson 271 f. Lucianus is conscious of his part as *minister* and *antistes* of the *floridii* (*Ep.* 21.3.1).

Celerinus is here being granted, in effect, *libelli martyrum* for his sisters.

25. *Saturninus cum comitibus suis, sed et collega meus.* On Saturninus, a confessor from Carthage, see *Ep.* 21.4.2 and n. 36 thereto. Are two of the *comites* named in *Ep.* 21.4.1, viz. Statius and Severianus?

26. *Maris, Collecta et Emerita.* In *Ep.* 21.4.2 greetings are sent by *Macarius cum sororibus suis Cornelia et Emerita.* Do we have here the same family group, with Maris a contraction (or corruption) of Macarius (one ms reads, in fact, *Macarii*)? In that case, Collecta might either be hopelessly corrupt or an alterna-

tive name by which Cornelia was known (cf. Etecusa in *Ep.* 21.3.2 and n. 25 thereto).

A. d'Alès, *La théologie de s. Cyprien* (Paris 1922) 363 n. 1, assumes, without any real warrant, identity with the Novatian-izing Macarius of *Epp.* 51, 53, 54; cf. n. 1 to *Ep.* 21.

27. *sorores Ianuaria, Dativa, Donata.* Here *sorores* appears to have its normal familial meaning (cf. n. 14 to *Ep.* 21). In this group of names Calpurnius and Maria only were specified in *Ep.* 21.4.2 (*fratres tui Calpurnius et Maria et omnes sancti fratres*).

28. *Bassianum et universum clerum.* For a Bassianus who has come from Carthage to Rome, see *Ep.* 8.3.4; if the two are to be identified, that Bassianus in *Ep.* 8 now becomes a Roman cleric who had been visiting Carthage. See further n. 32 to *Ep.* 8.

29. All the texts which I have consulted read *et argentarios et sorores* ("and the bankers and their sisters"). This reads awkwardly and exceptionally in a list where we would expect personal names. *Argentarius* is, as it happens, well attested as such a name and I have translated accordingly (there is a ms variant recording the singular, *Argentarium*). For a Roman Argentarius, see CIL 6.12302: D.M./Argentariae/Optatae/Argentarius/Euhodus et/Optatus . . . , and for further examples from Rome see CIL 6, pars vii (index), fasc. 1, 443. *Argentarius* is cited by I. Kajanto, *The Latin cognomina* (Helsinki 1965) 321, among examples of *cognomina* obtained from occupations (listed 316 ff.), and he provides references to further epigraphic examples of Argentarii and compares *Conductor, Mercator, Negotiator.*

30. *salutant vos sorores meae Ianuaria et Sophia quas vobis commendo.* The more personal turn of phrase, *sorores meae,* along with the expression of special concern from the dying confessor (*quas vobis commendo*) suggest that Ianuaria and Sophia must be Lucianus' own sisters.

LETTER 23

Date and circumstances: Cyprian tells us unequivocally in *Ep.* 27.2.1 that this note was written in response to *Ep.* 15, the letter which he wrote to the martyrs and confessors in an endeavour to control their distribution of certificates of forgiveness and the terms in which they couched them. That appeal, despite the circumspection of its composition, has now hopelessly misfired.

Manifestly Cyprian had not received this document when he wrote *Ep.* 20 (sent to Rome in about the course of July); neither had he received it by the time he replies to Caldonius (*Ep.* 25). *Ep.* 23 goes unmentioned in both these letters but some discussion on such a burning issue as the contents of *Ep.* 23 is demanded by the context of both of these letters. Cyprian is not yet aware of it.

But when he enclosed copies of his *Ep.* 25 both to his own clergy (*Ep.* 26) and to the clergy of Rome (*Ep.* 27), he has, with much heat and indignation, received this declaration. Its chronological place is therefore after *Ep.* 25, but before *Epp.* 26 and 27.

We should also note that *Ep.* 23 precedes *Ep.* 22, which contains (*universi litteras ex compacto universis pacem dimisimus*) a description of this letter. (By the time Cyprian writes *Ep.* 27 he has also received his copies of *Epp.* 21 and 22; see *Ep.* 27.3.2).

For the setting in which this note was composed, see *Ep.* 22.2 (and introductory note and n. 12 to that letter); it is written apparently after Paulus' death *a quaestione* and when orders have been given for the remaining confessors in prison to be deprived of food and water, to the death.

The curt, superior, imperative and, indeed, impertinent tone of this note is outstanding; the reaction to the reproaches of *Ep.* 15 is to adopt an even more supra-hierarchical stance. It is a precious document of the contemporary martyr-mentality, predicated on a powerful conviction in the dignity, status, and prerogatives of the martyrs. It reminds one of the dream of the martyr Perpetua (*Act. Perp.* 13): outside the gates of Paradise the martyrs receive humble obeisance from bishop and presbyter, and before the martyrs' lordly presence the angels can upbraid the clergy for their unseemly quarrels and issue admonishments to go to their unruly laity; the bishop and presbyter appear to be in peril of being shut outside the gates through which the martyrs effortlessly pass. With such a mentality it is understandable that these martyrs-to-be display towards their bishop little concern for personal tact, institutional prudence, and administrative wisdom; but charity towards the lapsed need not be denied them.

1. *universi confessores Cypriano papati s.* On *universi* (emphatically repeated in the body of the letter, *nos universos*), see n. 12 to *Ep.* 22. The writers call themselves with formal correctness in the address *confessors,* but in the letter itself they become generalized into the more emotional and affective category of "martyrs" (*optamus te cum sanctis martyribus pacem habere*); on this see n. 5 below. On the title *papas,* see n. 3 to *Ep.* 8.

The general form of address sets the impertinent tone of the letter. The confessors name themselves first, whereas it was strict epistolary etiquette in writing to a bishop deferentially and respectfully to put his name before yours. See A. A. R. Bastiaensen, *Le cérémonial épistolaire des chrétiens latins* (Nijmegen 1964) 14 ff.

2. *nos universos.* There is a variant reading, *universis* ("to all those whose conduct...."). *Ep.* 22.2.1 makes it clear that this certificate is certainly intended to be of universal application, but insistence on solidarity among the confessors in issuing it is the sentiment we would anticipate finding uppermost. The language of *Epp.* 26.1.1 and 27.2.1 confirms that conclusion: *universorum confessorum litteras; universos eos pacem dedisse.* It would not have been surprising if the original in fact had read, *nos universos universis quibus* ... (cf. *Ep.* 22.2.1: *universi ... universis pacem dimisimus*), but Cyprian does not quote from the letter in such a way as to suggest this formulation.

3. *quibus ad te ratio constiterit quid post commissum egerint.* Cyprian waxes indignant in *Ep.* 27.2 over the *invidia* which this process would rouse for him. There is to be no inquiry into the type of apostasy and its accompanying circumstances (an essen-

tial feature of the ultimate settlement; cf. n. 25 to *Ep.* 15), only into the *opera* and *merita* of the apostate since his fall (cf. n. 24 to *Ep.* 15). Celerinus' double insistence on his fallen sisters' penance and good works (*Ep.* 21.2.2, 4.1) was, therefore, well calculated for a sympathetic reception from Lucianus.

4. *hanc formam per te et aliis episcopis innotescere volumus.* Not only peremptory in message and style, but there is breathtaking grandeur in the vision of the sweeping efficacy which they assume for their resolution. For their decision Lucianus employs a word (*formam*) appropriate for decrees of bishops in council; (cf., e.g., *Ep.* 1.2.2: *contra formam . . . in concilio a sacerdotibus datam:* another touch of Lucianus in his role as *antistes* of the *floridii*). *Forma* is a word with juridical overtones. Cf. A. Beck, *Römisches Recht bei Tertullian und Cyprian. Eine Studie zur frühen Kirchenrechtsgeschichte* (Halle 1930) 97.

5. *optamus te cum sanctis martyribus pacem habere.* By *martyribus* Lucianus will mean not only those who have actually died for their faith (like Paulus, with whose expressed wishes Cyprian's *Ep.* 15 was at variance), but those who are similarly about to die (cf. n. 8 to *Ep.* 22 and, more generally, n. 1 to *Ep.* 15). The use of the epithet *sanctus*, when it also applies to the senders of this letter themselves, is clear measure of their sense of their own worth. On the word consult H. Delehaye in AB 28 (1909) esp. 180 ff.; at 183 he overlooks the testimony of this letter when he remarks: "S. Cyprien . . . qui a souvent l'occasion de parler des martyrs, ne leur donne pas encore le titre de saints; et il en est de même chez ses correspondants. Nous avons vu qu'un siècle après lui, le style officiel de l'église de Rome ne se départait pas encore de cette simplicité." But the fact that this usage here appears to be exceptional to Delehaye's general rule only helps to underscore its message.

6. *praesente de clero et exorcista et lectore Lucianus scripsit.* Can one detect here a somewhat pathetic note? Lucianus appears to write with all the formality of an episcopal missive but his *consilium*, far from consisting of an assembly of sacerdotal colleagues and fellow presbyters, is composed of but two clerics, and they come from the very lowest ranks.

We do not know whether these two clerics were simply

visitors to the confessors or were actually in prison as part of their number; no clerics are apparent in the list of the martyrs in *Ep.* 22.2. Note the order in which they appear: exorcist is superior to lector. So, too, in Cornelius *ap.* Eusebius, *H.E.* 6.43.11, and observe *Lib. Pontif.* 29 (on Pope Gaius, 283–296: *Hic constituit ut ordines omnes in ecclesia sic ascenderetur: si quis episcopus mereretur, ut esset ostiarius, lector, exorcista, sequens* (= acolyte), *subdiaconus, diaconus, presbyter et exinde episcopus ordinaretur.*

Exorcists appear about this period for the first time as a separate clerical grade—in the contemporary letter of Cornelius from Rome (*ap.* Eusebius, *H.E.* 6.43.11), in the letter from Firmilian in Cappadocia (*Ep.* 75.10.4: *unus de exorcistis vir probatus*) referring to events up to 22 years previously, and in Cyprian's own writings (*Ep.* 69.15.2: *quod hodie etiam geritur ut per exorcistas ...*). A special *ordo* was unknown to Hippolytus. Doubtless they were involved in the administration of pre-baptismal exorcism, frequent in the last period of the catechumenate (cf. Hippolytus, *Trad. Apost.* 20); and for baptismal exorcism see Hippolytus, *loc. cit.,* and also *Sent. Episc.* 1, 8, 31, 37. Their duties already include the treatment of demoniacs (cf. *Epp.* 69.15.2 and 75.10.4; cf. *Ad. Demet.* 15; *Ad Donat* 5) and it may well be of the sick as well (cf. *Ep.* 69.15f., and for further evidence on the close connection, commonly assumed, between physical malady and demoniac possession, see Minucius Felix, *Oct.* 27.2, and commentary in ACW 39.316f.).

V. Saxer, *Vie liturgique et quotidienne à Carthage vers le milieu du III*e *siècle* (Vatican 1969) 114; W. H. Frere in H. B. Swete (ed.), *Essays on th Early History of the Church and the Ministry* (London 1918) 305 f.; Brightman in H. B. Swete (ed.), *op. cit.* 341, 389; F. J. Dölger, *Der Exorcismus in altchristlichen Taufritual* (Paderborn 1909) 12 ff., 31 ff.; DACL 5 (1922) 964 ff.; RAC 7 (1969) 1 ff. esp. 67.ff.

The order of reader was already well established as a clerical norm by Tertullian's day; the *lector* was installed by the bishop alone in a ceremony in which he handed him the Book, without the imposition of the hand; cf. Hippolytus, *Trad. Apost.* 11. It is clear from Cyprian that in his view the reader's prime duty was to mount the pulpit and read the Scriptures (cf. *Epp.* 382, 39.4), but by the end of the century the task of reading the Gospel, at least, had been lost to the deacon (and presbyter). At Cirta, early in the following century, the lectors looked after the *codices* in their own homes; cf. *Gesta apud Zenoph.*, CSEL 26.186, 188. The office might be taken up by young men (cf. *Epp.* 38.2.1, 38.5.2) as the first step in their hopes for higher orders (see on *Ep.* 29.1.2); a clear and carrying voice for the tasks of reading and chanting could thus be secured. Though there is wide-spread fourth-century evidence for very young holders of the office (extreme are the five-year-olds of ILCV 1277 A, 1285, and see generally on *lectores infantuli*, J. Quasten, *Musik und Gesang in den Kulten der heidnischen Antike und christlichen Frühzeit* [Münster in Westfalen 1930; repr. 1973] 138 ff.; E. Peterson in *Ephemerides liturgicae* 48 [1934] 437 ff.), not all were by any means so junior (cf., e.g., ILCV 1276 aged 48, 1284 aged 56; at Cirta the readers included a tailor, a *grammaticus* and a *Caesariensis;* cf. *Gesta apud Zenoph.*, CSEL 26.188). For the common use of *pueri* as readers in Greco-Roman cultic liturgies generally, see also Th. Birt, *Die Buchrolle in der Kunst* (Leipzig 1907) 172 ff. with illustrations, to which add the famous scene from the Villa of the Mysteries, A. Maiuri, *Roman Painting* (Lausanne 1953) 51, and detailed picture in A. Stenico, *Roman and Etruscan Painting* (London 1963) 70.

Further discussed by J. G. Davies in JEH 14 (1963) 10 ff.; A. von Harnack in TU 2.5 (1886) 52 ff., esp. 60 ff. on Cyprian's testimony; H. Hess, *The Canons of the Council of Sardica, A.D. 343. A Landmark in the Early Development of Canon Law* (Oxford 1958) 107 f.; A. Quacquarelli, *La retorica antica al bivio* (Rome 1956) 37 ff.; *idem*, in *Convivium Dominicum* (1959) 383 ff.; DACL 8 (1929) 2241 ff.; H. H. Janssen, *Kultur und Sprache . . .* (Nijmegen 1938) 101 ff.; D. Balboni in *Miscellanea liturgica in onore di sua eminenza il Cardinale Giacomo Lercaro* 1 (Vatical City 1966) 444 ff.

LETTER 24

Contents: Caldonius writes for guidance from Cyprian and his fellow presbyters. He has to deal with the case of four exiles who appear to have cancelled any former apostasy on their part by subsequent confession of faith. If any common decision has been reached in Carthage on such an issue, could he be informed.

Date and circumstances: There can be no doubt that this letter and the reply to it (*Ep.* 25) come before both *Ep.* 26, addressed to the Carthaginian clergy, and *Ep.* 27, addressed to the Roman clergy (both letters enclosed copies of *Epp.* 24 and 25). *Epp.* 26 and 27 are Cyprian's next letters to Carthage and to Rome after *Epp.* 19 and 20. Therefore, the letter is to be placed, very approximately, about mid- to late summer 250 A.D.

Bishop Caldonius has been in prison (§ 1.1); he now appears to be released. Perhaps he is, officially, like the Christians he mentions, *extorris,* but he is now capable of managing the urgent affairs of his diocese. Cyprian has circulated widely copies of *Epp.* 15 to 19 to many fellow bishops, but Caldonius was apparently not on the address-list (*Ep.* 25.1.2). He appears, furthermore, to be quite ignorant of Cyprian's being in hiding and of the impossibility of making decisions *ex communi consilio* under those circumstances; and, needless to say, he is innocent of any knowledge of the intense dispute between Cyprian and some of the Carthaginian clergy and martyrs over the issue of granting reconciliation. All this is a salutary reminder of the general havoc and chaos which the persecution has occasioned; when Christians are languishing in prison, dispersed in exile, scattered as refugees, or lying low *in situ,* new of even the most basic facts of the current happenings in the Church of Carthage over the last six months has failed to percolate as far as a fellow African bishop.

The language of the letter is clumsy and impoverished, the ideas are not exactly expressed with precision and the general lay-out of the letter has a distinctly unsophisticated air. This short note confirms the impression which one draws from a study of the *Sententiae Episcoporum* that a gap in formal education existed between Cyprian and many of his episcopal colleagues.

The text presents a number of minor problems. A critical edition is supplied by A. Midoński (1889) 125 f.

1. *Cypriano et compresbyteris Carthagini consistentibus Caldonius s.* Caldonius writes under the clear assumption that Cyprian and his clergy are continuing to enjoy residence and normal relations in Carthage (on *consistentibus*, see n. 1 to *Ep.* 1).

Caldonius was a senior African bishop—he comes third in a list of 42 bishops (*Ep.* 57, 253 A.D.) and in another list of 31 or 32 bishops (*Ep.* 70, 255 A.D.; cf. Augustine, *De bapt.* 5.22.30)—and on the seniority suggested by these lists he is, appropriately, "seasoned and experienced in the Holy Scriptures" (*Ep.* 25.1.1). As he was not present at, or was dead by the time of, the synod of September 256, we do not know precisely his see—estimates have ranged from Numidia (e.g., L. Nelke, *Die Chronologie der Korrespondenz Cyprians* ... [diss Thorn 1902] 38: "wahrscheinlich ein numidischer Bischof"; L. Duquenne, *Chronologie des Lettres de s. Cyprien* [Brussels 1972] 136 n. 4: "son siège, assez éloigné sans doute") to the outskirts of Carthage (e.g., Monceaux, *Histoire* 2.77: "semble avoir dirigé une communauté des environs de Carthage"). That his see was indeed proconsular is highly probable given the company in which he appears in *Ep.* 70. See H. von Soden, *Die Prosopographie des afrikanischen Episkopats zur Zeit Cyprians* (Rome 1909) 256 ff.; E. W. Benson, *Cyprian, His Life, His Times, His Work* (London 1897) 107; J.-L. Maier, *L'épiscopat de l'afrique romaine, vandale et byzantine (Neuchâtel 1973) 272.

Soon Cyprian is to call upon the services of Caldonius as a trusted colleague in his ecclesiastical commission in Carthage (*Epp.* 41, 42) and as an emissary to Rome at the time of the consecration of Cornelius (*Epp.* 44.1.2, 45.1.1, 45.4.2, 48.2.1, 48.4.1), both activities demanding sound and cautious judgment as well as resourcefulness. He can be available in Carthage well before the persecution is over (*Epp.* 41 and 42), whether as refugee or legally released we cannot tell. The indications certainly are that he has been in prison for a time (see n. 5 below), and we might safely assume for him at least one visit to Cyprian's hideaway (cf. the *collegae* there in *Epp.* 38.2.2, 39.1.1).

2. *hi qui posteaquam sacrificaverunt iterato temptati extorres sunt facti.* Caldonius leaves it entirely obscure how those who have sacrificed, and thereby complied with the imperial demands, can be *iterato temptati.* As they were actively repentant (*paenitentiam agentes*) they may well have attracted further official attention (*Christum publice sumus confessi*). See n. 24 to *Ep.* 8 for further explication; and on the penalty of exile, see n. 5 to *Ep.* 10.

3. *possessiones et domos dimittunt et paenitentiam agentes Christum secuntur.* Does Caldonius slip into an allusion to Matt. 19.20 ff., or rather Matt. 19.27 ff./Luke 18.28 ff.? For Cyprian's frequent use of Luke 18.29 f. in contexts of martyrdom, see Fahey 360. Note the confiscations, on which see n. 5 to *Ep.* 10.

4. *Felix qui presbyterium subministrabat sub Decimo.* Estimates have ranged widely as to what this obscure clause might mean. A. Blaise, *Dictionnaire Latin—Français des auterurs chrétiens* (rev. ed. Turnhout 1967) s.v., interprets *subministro* in the unparalleled sense of "administer," "exercise," and concludes that Felix was a presbyter (cf. G. B. de Rossi, *La Roma sotterranea cristiana* [Rome 1864] 1.205: "troviamo menzione d'un prete subordinato ad un altro prete"). Others interpret *subministro* in the unusual sense of "put oneself at the service of" (for which the normal construction is, however, a dependent dative) and conclude, therefore, that Felix was a deacon (e.g., A. d'Alès, *La théologie de s. Cyprien* (Paris, 1922) 315 n. 1; B. Aubé, *L'église et l'état dans la seconde moitié du IIIᵉ siècle (249–284)* [Paris 1886] 96). Others, however, have seen in Felix a layman who served in some capacity the college of presbyters (e.g., G. Bardy in *La vie spirituelle* 60 [1939] 110: "un simple laïque au service de la communauté presbytérale"; A. A. R. Bastiaensen *Le cérémonial épistolaire des chrétiens latins* [Nijmegen 1964] 29: "vraisemblement le conseil de l'évêque et des prêtres"). The latter seems on the whole the most likely interpretation with Decimus figuring perhaps as Caldonius' episcopal predecessor. He may have been,

like the probationers of *Ep.* 29.1.2, *clero proximos,* where *proximus* could carry some of its technical civil service sense of "deputy", "assistant," etc., on which see, e.g., P.R.C. Weaver, *Familia Caesaris,* (Cambridge 1972) 252 ff.). If Felix was in fact a presbyter, observe from the sequel that he was married. On married clerics at this period, see n. 6 to *Ep.* 1.

5. *proximus mihi vinculis (plenius cognovi eundem Felicem).* This must mean that Caldonius has been in prison, though curiously he is never termed "confessor" on any of the dozen occasions on which he is mentioned in the correspondence. Felix was presumably enchained awaiting trial after his earlier apostasy and subsequent arrest.

Caldonius appropriately uses the word *proximus* which would carry special Christian overtones; it was the regular Latin translation for ὁ πλησίον, the biblical "neighbour." See H. Pétré, *Caritas. Étude sur le vocabulaire latin de la charité chrétienne* (Louvain 1948) 141 ff.

6. *fideles extorres facti reliquerunt possessiones quas nunc fiscus tenet.* Does the wording suggest that they took to flight and that their *bona* were sequestrated subsequently? Thus Monceaux, *Histoire* 2.78: "ils s'étaient dérobés par la fuite" and compare *Mart. Tryph.* 4: μόλις ὀλίγοι ἴσχυσαν διαδρᾶναι ... ὧν αἱ ὑποστάσεις ἀνελήφθησαν τῷ ταμείῳ. On the other hand, they are *iterato temptati,* they are made to say *Christum publice sumus confessi;* that sounds like formal arrest and public confession of faith in court. Impressions based on nicety of wording may be, therefore, misleading (especially if there is any allusion to Matt. 19.27 ff./Luke 18.28 ff., cf. n. 3 above). It is Caldonius' intention to convey that all three, Felix, Victoria, and Lucius, are redeeming an initial fall, but he fails to make this perfectly clear.

7. *sub persecutione † eadem.* The reading is far from clear but the uncertainty does not interfere with the general sense (T in fact reads *opere eodem* for Hartel's *eadem* and that renders a reasonable meaning = "in the same way"). Does the way in which Caldonius appears to express himself suggest that the worst of the persecution is now felt to be over?

8. For such coercion, compare the case of Quinta whom the

Alexandrians tried to drag to the shrine and force to offer sacrifice (in 249 A.D., Dionysius of Alexandria *ap.* Eusebius, *H.E.* 6.41.4) and note Cyprian's treatment of the *parvuli* in *De laps.* 9. Eusebius, *Mart. Pal.* 1.4.5, records the case of a Christian discharged after his hands had been put through the motions of sacrifice by force. A further parallel is discussed in E. A. E. Reymond and J. W. B. Burns *Four Martyrdoms from the Pierpont Coptic Dodices* (Oxford 1973) 14 f.

It is clearly intended that Bona's case should appear to be a further instance of a (technical) fall followed by public profession of faith and punishment. I do not, therefore, understand Benson's reconstruction (*op. cit.* in n. 1 above, 78): "Bona was dragged by her husband to the altar, there to justify her reappearance from abroad; but exclaiming, 'The act is not mine but yours' . . . she was exiled again".

9. *universi pacem peterent:* does *universi* suggest that all four are jointly submitting the petition (and are, therefore, sharing exile together)?

10. *si quid ergo ex communi consilio placuerit, scribite mihi.* Caldonius is clearly ignorant of the contents of *Epp.* 15–19 and of Cyprian's personal advice on just this issue in *Ep.* 19.2.3 (and see n. 17 there). Observe the consultative role which the Carthaginian church appears to be expected to play; cf. introductory note to *Ep.* 1.

LETTER 25

Contents: Cyprian reassures Caldonius that his views are right—former apostates who subsequently suffer for their faith have obliterated their fault. He encloses for his informaton copies of five letters he has written on questions concerning the fallen. They have met with approval and agreement from the many bishops to whom they have been sent.

Date and circumstances: On the date see introductory note to *Ep.* 24.

Cyprian does not explain for Caldonius why he and his fellow presbyters have not taken decisions *ex communi consilio.* No doubt the messenger, when he delivered this note, would be expected to provide explication of the circumstances of the correspondence enclosed.

Cyprian's instinct for uniformity of action based on unity of policy is noticeable: for Cyprian, in the catholic faith there ought ideally to be no distinction between visible and invisible church in this world (cf. *Ep.* 68.5.2: *neque enim poterat esse apud nos sensus diversus in quibus unus est spiritus*). No doubt under the circumstances he has gone to much effort to circulate many fellow bishops with copies of his dealings with his Cathaginian church; he has clearly sought their agreement with and endorsement of his arrangements. This is not just drumming up support out of self-protection; Cyprian, as he does so often, perceives his role in the *cathedra* of Carthage as initiator and leader of a united African church. On this practical search for *concordia, consensio, commune consilium* etc., see J.-P. Brisson, *Autonomisme et Christianisme dans l'Afrique romaine de Septime Sévère à l'invasion vandale* (Paris 1958) 49 ff.

1. *exercitatus et in scripturis dominicis peritus.* This stands in sharp contrast with the qualifications of the aberrant Lucianus in *Ep.* 27.1.1: *bene minus dominica lectione fundatus.*—Perhaps there is some allusion to Acts 18.24 (concerning Apollo). This is a possibility omitted by Fahey.

2. *sermonibus suis iustificati quibus se ante damnaverant.* The unusually compressed phraseology is explained by there being an allusion to Matt. 12.37, where Cyprian's text read: *de sermonibus enim tuis iustificaberis et de sermonibus tuis damnaberis (Test.* 3.13). This is an allusion omitted by Fahey.

3. *extorres facti et bonis suis omnibus spoliati.* Cyprian echoes his own words on this precise subject in *Ep.* 19.2.3 (*extorres facti et patria pulsi ac bonis suis omnibus spoliati*), where see n. 15.

4. There is no word here of formal *exomologesis,* etc. Is Cyprian agreeing that Caldonius should now go ahead and formally grant them *pax* and restoration to communion; or does he regard such confessional cases as spontaneously effective, with no further need for any liturgical ceremony of reconciliation?

5. Activities earlier described in, for example, *Epp.* 19.2.1 and 20.2.2. ff., and later in *Ep.* 27.3.1 f.

6. *librum . . . cum epistulis numero quinque.* There is no doubt that the five letters referred to are *Epp.* 15–19, but it remains a moot question whether the expression here implies something else was sent (*liber*) apart from a roll containing copies of the letters (for which *libellus* would be the more usual term). If there was another document, it is strange that it is not further described, and that it has not been sent to the other bishops. An accompanying descriptive summary would be in Cyprian's manner, however (cf. *Ep.* 20).

7. *quae epistulae etiam plurimis collegis nostris missae placuerunt.* Given Cyprian's instinctive rhetroic, it is impossible to guess at the number of recipients this might mean, but it is clear from what follows that circulation was very far from complete even amongst the local proconsular bishops (see n. 1 to *Ep.* 24).

8. *secundum catholicam fidem.* On *catholicus* in Cyprian (where the notion of "whole," "entire", "united" is often as much present as "universal"), see A. Demoustier in *Recherches de science religieuse* 52 (1964) 367 ff.; A. d'Alès, *La théologie de s. Cyprien* (Paris 1922) 154 ff.; H. Dodwell, *Dissertationes Cyprianicae* (Oxford 1684) 7; H. Koch, *Cyprianische Untersuchungen* (Bonn 1926) 102 ff.; H. H. Janssen, *Kultur und Sprache . . .* (Nijmegen 1938) 18 ff.; etc.

LETTER 26

Contents: Cyprian's consistent advice to his clergy has been to wait patiently for the opportunity when they can meet in council together in order to settle the community question of those of their congregation who have lapsed. Many bishops have written reaffirming the wisdom of that counsel of humility and forbearance. And, therefore, they ought to continue with this evangelical policy notwithstanding the letter he has received from all the confessors (it is directed to the other bishops as well). A copy of his correspondence with Caldonius is enclosed.

Date and circumstances: The place of this epistle within the series of Cyprian's correspondence is assured. *Ep.* 23 has now reached him (§1.1, and see introductory note to *Ep.* 23). The letter comes after *Epp.* 24 and 25 (which are enclosed, §3.1), but before *Ep.* 27, for enclosed with that letter was a copy of this present note. We are probably still (like *Epp.* 24 and 25) in mid- to late summer, 250 A.D. (say, August/September). As likely as not, *Ep.* 26 is roughly contemporary with *Ep.* 27, but Cyprian gives in this letter no indication that he has yet received copies of *Epp.* 21 and 22; but he may have had prudential motives in failing to mention those letters.

For it is clear that Cyprian is acting towards his clergy with great caution and forbearance himself. The vehement outburst of heated indignation to which he can freely give vent in *Ep.* 27 (to the Roman clergy) over *Ep.* 23 (and *Ep.* 22) is here carefully kept under restrained control; in his estimation, *Ep.* 23 has only helped to pour oil on the already troubled flames of dissension and disaffection, but in the present letter Cyprian restricts himself to emphasizing, with his politician's instincts, the confessors' stipulation in *Ep.* 23 that each case should be heard before the bishop—and that cannot be done until peace is restored to the Church. With some adroitness he appears to slide over the fact that the confessors request investigation of post-apostasy conduct only; Cyprian assimilates their request to the investigation of individual cases (of actual apostasy) on which he has been insisting all along, in an attempt to bridge the gap between reconciling confessors, impatient lapsed, turbulent clergy—and himself.

Despite these diplomatic efforts, the breach was not successfully bridged. This letter stimulated further (now lost) hostile correspondence, written, provocatively, *ecclesiae nomine* (*Ep.* 33.1.2), in which claim was laid to the peace granted by Paul, (*Ep.* 35.1.2).

1. On the form of address, see n. 1 to *Ep.* 5.
2. Isa. 66.2. See Fahey 215 f.
3. Cyprian is echoing the words of *Ep.* 23. The original's blunt *pacem dedisse* he takes care to soften to *voluerunt . . . ad eos*

pacem a se datam pervenire (cf. *Ep.* 27.3.1: *repraesentari*).

4. *instetur . . . epistulis quas ad vos proximis feceram.* That is, *Epp.* 16 (plus 15 and 17), 18 and 19, all five of which are mentioned in *Ep.* 25.1.2. See also n. 29 to *Ep.* 20.

5. Hartel's text reads *perscripserunt* (some mss have the usual *rescripserunt,* the verb found on the same matter in *Ep.* 25.1.2.), the form suggesting fully considered and reasoned acknowledgements. It is a nicely calculated touch in the art of persuasiveness.

6. *nec ad vos recedendum esse.* Hartel chooses this reading against the variant, *nec ab eo recedendum esse,* which renders entirely satisfactory sense (and which I have translated). Is Hartel's text intended somehow to mean "and that I ought not to yield before pressure from you"? Discussion of the text is in O. Ritschl, *Cyprian von Karthago und die Verfassung der Kirche* (Göttingen 1885) 41 ff.

7. *singulorum causas examinare possimus.* A refrain somewhat more ambiguously phrased in these earlier letters, e.g., *Epp.* 17.1.2 (*examinabuntur singula*), 20.3.1 (*disponere singula*). Cyprian, is, however, perfectly well aware of the ill-will that will now be caused for him by such a process since the declaration of universal reconciliation in *Ep.* 23 (see *Ep.* 27.2.2).

8. *Epp.* 24 and 25.

9. I translate as best I can Hartel's text, *ut dum nobis nec evangelio servire nec secundum universorum confessorum litteras causas suas examinari permittunt* (on *ut dum,* see L. Bayard, *Le latin de saint Cyprien* [Paris 1902] 164; J. Schrijnen and C. Mohrmann, *Studien zur Syntax der Briefe des Cyprians* [Nijmegen 1937] 2.134 ff.). There is manuscript warrant, however, for reading, *ut dum nec nobis nec evangelio [volunt] servire nec . . .*, which certainly renders easier sense ("if they refuse to be obedient to us and to the gospel teachings and won't have . . ."). In any case we have splendidly illuminated Cyprian's ability to emphasize and exploit that one spect of the confessor's letter which fits in with his policy—bishop, gospel, and united confessors being thereby all aligned together, a formidable combination to quell the impetuous lapsed.

LETTER 27

Contents: To the Roman clergy, for their information, Cyprian sends (with appropriately explanatory comment) copies of recent correspondence. Lucianus' activities in issuing certificates of forgiveness in the names of Paulus and Aurelius are outlined; Lucianus' response to the letter Cyprian sent to the martyrs and confessors (urging restraint in such activities) has been to issue, in the name of the united confessors, a universal certificate of forgiveness (copy enclosed). The results of this have been disastrous. Bishops are being attacked by mobs of lapsed demanding for themselves this forgiveness, and in some cases the bishops have succumbed before the pressure. A copy is enclosed of Cyprian's letter to his clergy on these impetuous lapsed, together with his correspondence with Caldonius. Copies are also enclosed of the exchange of letters between Celerinus and Lucianus; in them are revealed the modesty of the one and the laxity as well as the ignorance of the other. Two letters from Rome, one from the clergy, the other from the confessors, have in their firm counsel given welcome strength to Cyprian's campaign against the onslaught. Together both they and he stand, united, as they should be, in their attitude to this question.

Date and circumstances: The place of this letter in the series of the correspondence is clear. It comes after *Ep.* 26 (which is enclosed, §3.2), and it comes after the receipt of *Epp.* 21 and 22 (which are enclosed). But it comes before *Ep.* 29 (which refers to this letter, §1.1) and its enclosures. And no doubt it is contemporaneous with *Ep.* 28 (addressed to the Roman confessors); the replies to both *Epp.* 27 and 28 (that is, *Epp.* 30 and 31) come about the same time, if not together—*Ep.* 32.1.1.

Cyprian has as yet received no reply from Rome to *Ep.* 20. A (now lost) letter has come from the Roman clergy, crossing with that epistle (§4); it is still addressed (like *Ep.* 8) to the Cathaginian clergy, not to Cyprian himself. The response to both *Ep.* 20 and *Ep.* 27 comes together in *Ep.* 30, now addressed to Cyprian personally. This suggests a fairly tight timetable for the exchange of communications. In all probability we are not long after *Ep.* 26 and are still, therefore, as with that letter, in "mid-to late summer, 250 A.D. (say, August/September)." See introductory note to *Ep.* 26 and for further discussion L. Nelke, *Die Chronologie der Korrespondenz Cyprians* ... (diss. Thorn 1902) 41 f.; L. Duquenne, *Chronologie des Lettres de s. Cyprien* ... (Brussels 1972) 138; H. Gülzow, *Cyprian und Novatian* ... (Tübingen 1975) 75 ff.

In tone, the contrast of this letter with Cyprian's contemporary letters to his clergy in Carthage (*Ep.* 26, with its enclosures, and later *Ep.* 29) is sharp and well-defined. They are mollifying and, to some extent, accommodating documents. But here, outside his immediate context, he can allow himself the luxury of voicing the heated indignation he feels and he is free to adopt an open stance of robust inflexibility where Gospel principles are concerned—contrasting with the weakness of some comprovincial bishops found deficient in the courage of their convictions. *Imperite, invidia, impetus, immodestus, ignarus, turbulenti,* etc., are the sorts of word he readily uses here, but they are absent from *Epp.* 26 and 29. As with *Ep.* 20, he does not send (at once) copies of this epistle to his clergy (see *Ep.* 29.1.1)—he merely has occasion to mention a problem that has arisen as a consequence of his wish to despatch a letter (i.e., this letter) to Rome, sent, he says evasively, *urgente causa.* But later, after he has received highly conciliatory and supportive replies from Rome (*Epp.* 30 and 31), he feels in sufficiently secure a position to send his clergy a copy.

Cyprian continues to be anxious that his affairs should be properly presented to Rome. He is still somewhat on the defensive for his reputation, but not so single-mindedly as in *Ep.* 20 (e.g., §3.2: *ut sciretis elaborare circa omnia diligentiam nostram;* §4: *laborantes hic nos et ... totis fidei viribus renitentes*). But now the despatch of so many copies appears to be more in the way of a protective device—he is forestalling variant (and malicious) versions of his activities. And by the open exchange of information and attitudes he is as concerned as before that they should act together in unanimity towards their common problems. In those interests for unity he seems to take diplomatic care at the very end of this letter to provide himself the explanation why (through accident of timing) the last letter from the Roman clergy to Carthage has been directed not to himself but *ad clerum*.

The letter also provides us (§1.1) with a valuable glimpse of the approved circumstances for issuing *libelli pacis*. Mappalicus, before his death, and now a martyr, granted reconciliation to two specific individuals for the most virtuous of motives—*pietas*. Saturninus, in prison after tortures, might properly, under such conditions, have issued certificates of this restricted sort (see further n. 1 to *Ep.* 15).

This letter is apparently sent by the hands of the newly appointed clerics, the lector Saturus and the subdeacon Optatus (see *Epp.* 29 and 35.1.1).

1. *actus noster expositus et disciplinae ac diligentiae quantulae-cumque ratio declarata est.* Cyprian is referring to and deliberately echoing the wording of *Ep.* 20.1.1 There is, for *quantulaecumque*, the variant reading, *quantulacumque*, which would provide the (less satisfactory) sense: "rendered an account—poor as it is—of our zeal."

2. *bene minus dominica lectione fundatus, quaedam conatus est imperite* (Hartel's reading). Cyprian seems to be deliberately offsetting his description of Lucianus here by what he knows the Roman clergy are going to read (in *Ep.* 25.1.1) about that colleague of integrity and faith, Caldonius (§3.2): he is described as *exercitatus et in scripturis dominicis peritus caute omnia et consulte....*

Note the part which the study of the Bible played in Cyprian's view of spiritual formation, as is evidenced in his own spiritual history. On the general question of *lectio divina in* Cyprian, see C. Dumont in *Bible et vie chrétienne* 22 (1958) 23 ff.

3. *iam pridem se auctorem constituens.* See *Ep.* 21.3.1 (and nn. 21 and 24 there), and n. 6 to *Ep.* 23 on Lucianus' leadership. On *iam pridem*, see n. 7 to *Ep.* 1. The phrase, unfortunately, is not of assistance for gauging with any precision the time-scale of Lucianus' activities.

4. *libelli gregatim multis nomine Pauli.* On Paulus, see *Ep.*

22.2.1 f. (and n. 10). Throughout Cyprian eschews describing the man in whose name the offences are largely being committed as a confessor, let alone as a martyr; his death is no *martyrium*, but an indifferent *excessus* (§1.2).

5. *Mappalicus martyr.* On Mappalicus, see *Ep.* 10.4.1 (and n. 20). Cyprian's model in propriety is carefully accorded his martyr's dignity.

6. *matri et sorori suae.* Cyprian is anxious to underline the specificity of Mappalicus' *libelli* (they are made *nominatim*) as opposed to the generality (*gregatim*) of Lucianus' (this contrast is spelt out in *Ep.* 15.4). The words *et sorori* are omitted by a number of mss. We are presumably to place this granting of *pax* by Mappalicus between bouts of the torture which in fact proved in his case to be fatal (cf. *Ep.* 10.4.1)—Mappalicus figured in *Ep.* 22.2.2 among the martyrs listed by Lucianus as supporting Paulus' granting of universal *pax;* now he is carefully shown not to have followed that policy. The cohesion of support for Paulus' policy, stressed by Lucianus, is deliberately undermined.

There is a nice point in citing Mappalicus' *libelli* in favour of a mother and a blood-sister in a letter which encloses a document by Lucianus which grants *libelli* to Christian sisters generally. Cf. *Ep.* 22.2.2: *non tantum hae sed et quas scis ad animum nostrum pertinere.*

7. On Saturninus, see *Ep.* 21.4.2 (and n. 36), and §4 (and n. 28) below. We do not have to conclude from the remarks here that Saturninus was opposed to such certificates, but only that during his period in prison he lacked the special reasons that would induce him to issue any. He figures as another model of proper restraint. It is not incompatible that he might later—if he is identical with the Saturninus of *Ep.* 21.4.2—support Celerinus' request put to the confessor Lucianus, soon to die (as was Mappalicus) for two specific certificates on behalf of Celerinus' two sisters (as Mappalicus issued).

8. The circumstances in which Paulus gave his *mandatum* are described in *Ep.* 22.2.

9. *nesciens Domino magis quam conservo obtemperandum.* Cyprian effectively extracts, by his antithesis, some of the techincal

connotations of *Dominus* ("Master") and *conservus* ("fellow-slave"). For *conservus*, as a by now long-favoured Christian variant of *frater*, see H. Pétré, *Caritas. Étude sur le vocabulaire latin de la charité chrétienne* (Louvain 1948) 161 ff. Is there any allusion to Acts 5.29? On the *dominus-servus* motif in Cyprian generally, see H. Koch, *Cyprianische Untersuchungen* (Bonn 1926) 255, 462.

   10. *Aureli quoque adulescentis tormenta perpessi nomine.* There is a youthful Carthaginian Aurelius who has survived tortures (and other vicissitudes) in *Epp.* 38.1.2 f. and 39.4.2 f. (where see nn.). Though the name is, of course, extremely common at this period, identity is indeed more than highly likely (see also next n.). In that case, by the time of *Epp.* 38 f. Cyprian has successfully drawn the *illustris adulescens* (as he is then prepared to term him) away from the influence of the following of Lucianus, appointed him a lector with special privileges (*Ep.* 39.4.2) and established him as a model in *ecclesiastica disciplina, verecundia, pudor,* and *humilitas* (cf. *Ep.* 38.1.3). He proceeds to make much the same moves with the youthful confessor Celerinus as well.

   11. *quod litteras ille non nosset.* The subjunctive appears to be deliberate—Cyprian is reporting not so much established fact as the reason alleged for Lucianus' writing out certificates in Aurelius' name (on the moods in causal clauses in Cyprian, see J. Schrijnen and C. Mohrmann, *Studien zur Syntax der Briefe des Cyprians* (Nijmegen 1937) 2.99 ff.). The clause is, therefore, not necessarily an obstacle to the identification of this "illiterate" Aurelius with the Aurelius who is soon to be appointed reader in *Ep.* 38.2.

   J. Ferguson in L. Thompson and J. Ferguson (edd.), *Africa in Classical Antiquity* (Ibadan 1969) 185, overlooking the grammatical point, writes of this passage: "It amuses us to hear of an illiterate made a 'reader', but he may well have used the eyes of the mind to better purpose than many use the eyes of the face." He could perhaps have cited for some support of this notion the contemporary work, *Adv. Iudaeos* 10.2 f., which declares that if Jews were to ask any Christian—boy, old woman, widow, rustic—then the Christian would expound the Scriptures to them, illiterate though he be (*sine litteris disserit scripturas eis*).

At first glance P. Oxy. 33.2673 (Feb. 5, 304 A.D.) provides a parallel for an illiterate lector: Aurelius Ammonius, a lector, has his document written (in Greek) for him, "because he is illiterate." But this should only mean that he does not know Greek script—he has a Coptic bible and liturgy (on this interpretation, see H.C. Youtie in HTR 75 [1971] 161 ff.). See also n. 6 to *Ep.* 23, where there is cited evidence, but to be dated to the course of the following century, for undoubtedly illiterate lectors.

12. *Ep.* 15, attached to *Ep.* 20

13. Namely *Ep.* 23. Note the timing—*Ep.* 23 is issued in reaction to the rebukes (phrased with some care though they were) of *Ep.* 15.

14. *in provincia nostra per aliquot civitates.* Cyprian can apparently use elsewhere, *provincia nostra* to describe the area of his episcopal presidency (cf. *Ep.* 48.3.2). But in *Ep.* 48.3.2 *nostra provincia* stands in contrast to the world *trans mare*, whereas here he may very well be meaning simply the (secular) *provincia* of Africa Proconsularis (cf. e.g., *Epp.* 59.16.2, 71.4.1, 73.1.2; in *Ep.* 55.21.1: *in provincia nostra*, could perhaps bear either meaning). Here it seems to mean the immediate area of Africa Proconsularis, about which, under the present circumstances, he is likely to have such information as he now proceeds to give.

On the essentially geographical basis for ecclesiastical provinces at this stage, see Hefele-Leclercq 1.2.1089 f.

15. *sibi repraesentari.* In *Ep.* 26.1.1 Cyprian employs the turn of phrase *ad eos pacem ... pervenire* to express the same notion. Cyprian makes here his own view plain. The martyrs are forcing the bishops into the role of mere executive officers, carrying into effect the orders for peace which the martyrs issue. On Cyprian's (sometimes unusual) use of *repraesento*, see Watson 309; A. d'Alès, *La théologie de s. Cyprien* (Paris 1922) 232 n. 1.

16. *semel.* On this (strong) meaning of the word, cf. n. 4 to *Ep.* 4.

17. That is, *Ep.* 26. The mildness of that letter, with its message of patience and adherence (for the time being) to the *status quo*, becomes remarkable, now that we are given the context in which it was composed.

18. *Epp.* 25 and 26. Cyprian clearly found the hesitant and cautious scrupulousness of Caldonius over these matters sympathetic and congenial.

19. *Epp.* 21 and 22. This is the first mention of this correspondence in Cyprian's own letters. Note the terms of approval for Celerinus (*boni et robusti confessoris*). Cyprian appears to be making moves to prevent any widespread cohesion forming among the confessors centred on Lucianus' party; Celerinus (like Aurelius) is quickly won over to serve Cyprian's cause (*Epp.* 37.1.1 and 39). For the possibility that it may in fact have been Celerinus who sent Cyprian copies of the letters, see introductory note to *Ep.* 21.

20. *veritate ipsa.* This seems intended to mean, literally, something like "by the unadorned truth," "by the source of the truth itself," "by the facts themselves," etc. There is the (easier) variant reading, *veritatem ipsam* ("you will learn the full truth . . .").

21. *quam sit moderatus et cautus et humilitate ac timore sectae nostrae verecundus.* Observe the careful selection of qualities Cyprian wishes to be found in the genuine confessor. On the theme of *timor* in these contexts, see n. 3 to *Ep.* 15. On the word *secta* (for *religio*), cf. Minucius Felix, *Oct.* 4.4: [*non*] *ipsius sectae homo,* and see commentary in ACW 39.179 f.—Cyprian is hinting that Lucianus is forming an alien *secta* or following (he is about to refer to the *aliud evangelium* of Gal. 1.6); the word is not common in Cyprian. It is far from true to say that "he speaks in many places of the Christians as a *secta*" (Q. Howe, Jr., *St. Cyprian and the Christian Experience* [diss. Princeton 1970] 52). But cf. Watson 257; H. Koch, *op. cit.* in n. 9 above, 324 f.; H. H. Janssen, *Kultur und Sprache* . . . (Nijmegen 1938) 113 n. 2.

22. *circa intelligentiam dominicae lectionis . . . minus peritus.* On this, see n. 2 above. Cyprian proceeds to demonstrate this point in the next section (§3.3).

23. *circa invidiam verecundiae nostrae relinquendam facilitate sua immodestus.* A typical piece of richly ambiguous Cyprianic prose. By the word *verecundia* Cyprian verbally, and pointedly, links himself with the *verecundus* confessor, Celerinus (cf. n. 21 above), but he may well wish to *mean* here that the procedure is going to cause him "personal embarrassment" (he has explained

the source of the *invidia* in §2.2). And the *facilitas* ascribed to Lucianus neatly bears, along with the sense of "ease," "ready ability," the moral connotations of "laxity" (cf. *Ep.* 30.3.2: *profana facilitas* = "worldly laxity"). Moreover the expression *verecundia nostra* (in the sense of *ego*) adds a touch of formal chancellery style suitable for a letter addressed to Rome, the phrase further contributing to the refutation of the *insignis persona* charge of *Ep.* 8.1.1. In his previous letter to Rome, in *Ep.* 20.1.2, for parallel motives Cyprian chose to refer to himself as *mediocritas mea.* For such expressions in Cyprian, see Watson 208, 273.

24. Cyprian is alluding, of course, to the conclusion of St. Matthew's gospel, 28.19, a passage which he actually quotes in his accompanying letter to the Roman confessors, *Ep.* 28. He will exploit the verse discussing the Trinitarian baptismal formula in *Ep.* 73.4.1 ff. Cf. Fahey 328 ff. Cyprian never cites any formula used at the *exomologesis,* the penitential ceremony. Cyprian's argument is based on the premise that even the most heinous of sins (and this includes idolatry) are characteristically cancelled by baptism—and that is achieved in the name of the Trinity. It is as if the laxist priests had been claiming that the martyrs did for the apostasy of the lapsed what God did only in baptism for prebaptismal sins, that is, cancel them out without requiring any penance for them. The passage is a good example of Cyprian's taste for a verbal level of argument. (Does there remain any trace of unspoken assumption in this argument that such major delicts, committed after baptism, would normally be "reserved for God"?) For the close connexion in Cyprian's thought between baptism and the remission of sins, see, for example, *Epp.* 69.7.2, 73.7.1f., 73.15.1; *Ad Fort. praef.* 4.

25. *quem Dominus vas electionis suae dixit.* An allusion to Acts 9.15, inserted here to stress the special authority of the quotation he is about to give. See Fahey 414, 608 f.

26. Gal. 1.6 ff. (omitting, in verse 6, *Christi* after *in gratiam*). See Fahey 472.

27. *Opportune vero supervenerunt litterae vestrae quas accepi ad clerum factas.* The purport of this letter (now lost) can be discerned in *Ep.* 30.3.1 ff. Despite its strong-line contents, Cyprian

apparently did not distribute copies of it, though he did distribute copies of the reply to it, *Ep*. 32. Did the form of address (*ad clerum factas*), if nothing else, bear too offensive an affront to himself? Or was there no need—his copy actually came *via* his own clergy, to whom it had already been delivered? *Ep*. 30.3.1 (addressed to Cyprian personally) neatly slides over this point by the use of the second person plural: *superiores nostrae litterae. . . . in quibus vobis sententiam nostram dilucida expositione protulimus. . . .* (elsewhere in that letter Cyprian is addressed in the singular). The way in which the letter is described in *Ep*. 30.3.1 (*dilucida expositione* etc.) suggests that Novatian (who drafted *Ep*. 30) may have been the scribe for this (lost) epistle also. See A. von Harnack in *Theologische Abhandlungen: Carl von Weizsäcker zu seinem siebzigsten Geburtstage* (Freiburg 1892) 13 f.; *idem* in TU 23 (1903) 7; B. Melin, *Studia in Corpus Cyprianeum* (Uppsala 1946) 4; H. J. Vogt, *Coetus sanctorum* (Bonn 1968) 39.

L. Duquenne, *Chronologie des Lettres de s. Cyprien . . .* (Brussels 1972) 120 (somewhat naively) deduces from the fact that the Roman clergy still do not address their letters to Cyprian that not only has *Ep*. 20 not yet reached them, but that *Ep*. 9 has not done so either: "il est à croire que la lettre 9 non plus ne leur est pas encore parvenue, à moins d'imaginer que son contenu n'ait pu suffire à les rassurer sur le point [viz., that Cyprian has not abandoned his flock]." *Ep*. 9 can hardly be considered to have brought to its recipients the complete reassurance that it is here made to bear.

28. *quas beati confessores Moyses, Maximus, Nicostratus et ceteri Saturnino et Aurelio et ceteris miserunt.* Several points can here be made.

The Roman imprisoned confessors enjoy a detailed knowledge of the affairs of the Carthaginian Church, and it has not come from Cyprian (recall the refugee movement glimpsed in *Ep*. 21.2.2, 4.1, and the traffic discerned in *Ep*. 8.2.1). They have picked out as the major addressees of their letter two confessors who have actually undergone *tormenta* (§§1.1, 1.2 above); their dignity is accordingly superior to that of any self-styled leader (such as Lucianus, whose conduct, besides, they manifestly disapprove). There ought to be no clergy of major rank among the imprisoned Carthaginian confessors whom they are addressing; otherwise, by the rules of etiquette, they would have been given epistolary precedence.

The laxity and activities of some of the Carthaginian confessors is well known to them by this time. This letter attacked *inlicitae petitiones,* and those who *in occasione martyrii* wanted to be *praevaricatores evangelii* (*Ep.* 30.4); it provided timely and salutary *morum magisteria* (*Ep.* 28.2.1). It must have been written after the practices, as revealed in *Epp.* 15–17, had become notorious. Again, given the form of description of this letter (e.g., *severitatem evangelicae disciplinae protulerunt*) in §4 of *Ep.* 30 (penned by Novatian) and the high likelihood that Novatian had a hand in drawing up the next letter from the Roman confessors (*Ep.* 31), it is a tempting surmise that Novatian was the *scriptor* for this letter also. See references in previous note.

Saturninus, if he is to be identified with the Saturninus of *Ep.* 21.4.1, may well have gone off to Rome before this letter actually reached him in Carthage; he got to Rome in time to lend his support there to the petition of Celerinus, a letter which Cyprian is now reporting for the first time (§3.2). Did the letter from the confessors in Rome perhaps take a little time to percolate to Cyprian's hiding-place? See further *Ep.* 21 n. 36. (Aurelius, who is at large by *Ep.* 38, may possibly have been released also at the same time as Saturninus).

The Roman confessors are discussed under the following letter, *Ep.* 28.

29. That is, *Ep.* 20; see introductory note to this letter.

Additional Notes

(p. 149 *Ep.* 1 intro.) See now V. Saxer in *Rev. des études aug.* 31 (1977) 56 ff. suggesting a date between September 256 and August 257.

(p. 157 *Ep.* 1 n. 19) For discussion of the word *sportulantium* see Watson 274; L. Bayard, *Le latin de saint Cyprien* (Paris 1902) 181; V. Saxer, *Vie liturgique . . .* (Vatican 1969) 74; H. H. Janssen,

Kultur und Sprache (Nijmegen 1938) 109; X. S. Thaninayagam, *The Carthaginian clergy* . . . (Colombo 1947) 96.

(p. 168 *Ep.* 3 n. 17) See now *Corp. Papyr. Raineri* 5 (1976) no. 11, an actual work-contract between a deacon and his bishop.

(p. 188 *Ep.* 5 n. 16) Dr Diercks now reports to me that MSS Sal NTD in fact all record Victor in the text here.

(p. 204 *Ep.* 8 intro.) A critical edition is supplied by Miodoński (1899) 114 ff. and cf. H. Gülzow, *Cyprian und Novatian* (Tübingen 1975) 25 ff.

(p. 244 *Ep.* 11 n. 33) But see also Prov. 3.12 and Apoc. 3.19 as possible sources.

(p. 244 *Ep.* 11 n. 35) The phrasing is further discussed by S. Deléani, *Christum sequi* (Paris 1979) 98.

(p. 245 *Ep.* 11 n. 48) The word *conversatio* is studied by H.A.M. Hoppenbrouwers in *Conversatio. Une étude sémasiologique* (Nijmegen 1964).

(p. 324 *Ep.* 21 n. 22) But note Ovid *Amores* 1.9.7 *terra requiescit uterque* ("both of them take their rest on the ground"), on the proverbial hardships of the life of soldiers, and lovers.

(p. 336 *Ep.* 22 n. 18) Note that the African text of Lk. 12.58 read *pignerarius* (= ὁ πράκτωρ) *mittet te in custodiam;* see H. von Soden in TU 23 (1909), 237, 328, 480.

(p. 348 *Ep.* 24 n. 4) Felix is further discussed by A. Vilela *op. cit.* 274 f. and R. Gryson, *Les origines du célibat ecclésiastique* (Glembloux 1970) 33 f.

INDEXES

1. OLD AND NEW TESTAMENT

11.54	308	5.3	308	4.2	244
12.25	195	6.10	258	4.18	223
13.14 f.	266	7.9	176		
13.16	257	7.36 ff.	174	*2 Thessalonians*	
14.6	212	8.13	176	3.8	266
14.13 f.	242	9.24 f.	234	3.17	223
14.27	243, 258	10.20 f.	286		
15.12	243	11.27	278, 286	*1 Timothy*	
15.20	257	12.26	293	1.19	295
18.22 f.	167	16.13	211	4.12	169
21.17	211	16.21	223	6.9	214

		2 Corinthians		*2 Timothy*	
Acts		6.16	193, 257	2.4	156
4.32	243	11.23 ff.	266	2.5	209
5.29	358	11.26	266	3.2	169, 241
6	205	11.29	293	4.6 ff.	234
6.1	200	12.2 ff.	266		
6.1 ff.	168	12.2-4	334	*Hebrews*	
7.28	257			12.6	244
9.15	361	*Galatians*			
18.24	350	1.2	189	*1 Peter*	
23.4 f.	167	1.6	360	2.11 f.	256
		1.6 ff.	361	2.21	212
		1.10	180	2.24	244
Romans		4.16	180	4.15 f.	257
2.11	281	5.14 f.	258		
2.24	256	6.11	223	*1 John*	
4.25	244			2.1	245
8.16 f.	195	*Ephesians*		2.6	212
8.18	195	4.22	245	4.4	231
8.35	245	4.27	175		
11.20 f.	257			*Apocalypse*	
12.11	188	*Philippians*		2.5	301
		2.15	256	2.10	249, 266
1 Corinthians				2.23	236
3.16	257	*Colossians*		5.19	325
3.16 f.	193	2.5	308	18.4	307, 308

2. AUTHORS

3. LATIN WORDS

4. GENERAL INDEX

Abthugni, 186
Acacius, 142
acolytes, 67, 202, 206
Acta, 221, 222, 233, 250
actors, 53 f., 161 ff.,
Aemilian, 290
Aemilianus, emperor, 45
Aemilianus, governor, 332
Aemilius, martyr, 39, 145, 335
African Christianity, Jewish origins of, 124
Africanus, martyr, 234
Agape, martyr, 326
Agathonice, martyr, 142
Agrippinus, bishop, 153, 154, 158
Alexander, bishop and martyr, 36, 142
Alexandria, 12, 33 f., 37, 140
Alexius, 108
Amantius, acolyte, 43
Ammon, martyr, 37
Ammonarion, martyr, 37
amnesties, 137
Antichrist, 107, 332
Antioch, 12
Antonianus, bishop, 10
Antoniniani, 23, 25, 133
Antony, 303
Apollonia, martyr, 38
apostates, *see lapsi*
Appius Sabinus, 24, 132
Apronianus, governor, 288
Argentarius, 108, 339
Ariston, martyr, 107
Arrius Antoninus, governor, 318
Asclepiades, 36
Ater, martyr, 37
Attalus, martyr, 209
Aufidius Victorinus, 318
Augendus, ? deacon, 42, 164, 284
Augustine, martyr, 38, 144
Aurelius, lector, 42, 112, 141, 189, 273, 289, 329, 354, 358, 360, 363
Aurelius Ammonius, lector, 359
authenticity, of letters, 71, 223 ff.

Babylas, bishop and martyr, 36, 142
Baebius Marcellinus, aedile, 288
Balbinus, emperor, 4
Baluzius, 306
baptism, 258, 259, 361
baptismal policy, 9

Basilides, lapsed bishop, 132
Bassianus, ? Roman cleric, 70, 108, 218, 306
Bassus, martyr, 107, 336
Besas, martyr, 37
Bible, attitude to, 18, 128, 156, 356
bishops, 54 ff., 83, 90, 93, 145, 146, 149, 150, 155, 158, 160, 161, 164 ff., 171 f., 182, 186, 187, 192, 201, 210, 222, 240, 248, 256, 268, 276, 284, 285, 288, 312, 341, 359
Bona, 109, 349
bribery, 32, 327
burial, christian, 217, 218; *see* cemeteries

Caecilianus, presbyter, 16, 152, 200
Caecilius, 127
Caecilius, bishop, 57, 171, 172
Caesar, 223
Caldonius, bishop, 16, 109, 110, 111, 113, 141, 189, 340, 345 ff., 349, 350, 351, 354, 356, 360
Calpurnius, 106, 108
Candida, 104, 105, 107, 312, 326
Cappadocia, 5
Capsa, 30
Carpus, martyr, 142
Carthage, 12, 13 ff., 123, 124, 125, 187, 315, clergy of, 39–44, 150, 263, 276, 297, 352
Castus, martyr, 39, 145, 335
catechumens, 98, 215, 216, 299
Celerinus, lector and confessor, 26, 34, 42, 103, 104, 106, 113, 114, 129, 141, 189, 197, 237, 272, 289, 312 ff., 330 ff., 342, 354, 357, 358, 360, 363
celibacy, 156
cemeteries, 251, 252; *see* burial, christian
certificates of forgiveness, 27, 90 ff., 98, 99, 112, 270 ff., 280, 287, 296, 309 f., 334 f., 354 ff., 357; *see libelli pacis*
certificates of sacrifice, 27; *see libelli*
Cetula, martyr, 337
charitable programme, 181
Cheltenham List, 8
children, 195
Chione, martyr, 326
Cirta, 186
Claudius Saturninus, 141
clergy, 150; laicisation of, 169; married, 152; payment of, 156, 157, 158; of Carthage, *see* Carthage, clergy of; of Rome, *see* Rome, clergy of

376